Military Inc.

Inside Pakistan's Military Economy

Ayesha Siddiqa

Pluto Press
London • Ann Arbor, MI

First published 2007 by Pluto Press
345 Archway Road, London N6 5AA
and 839 Greene Street, Ann Arbor, MI 48106

www.plutobooks.com

British Library Cataloguing in Publication Data
A catalogue record for this book is available from the British Library

Hardback
ISBN-13 978 0 7453 2546 0
ISBN-10 0 7453 2546 7
Paperback
ISBN-13 978 0 7453 2545 3
ISBN-10 0 7453 2545 9

Library of Congress Cataloging in Publication Data applied for

10 9 8 7 6 5 4 3 2

Designed and produced for Pluto Press by Curran Publishing Services, Norwich
Printed and bound in India

To
the hope in my life, Sohail,
and
the wretched of my land

We shall live to see,
So it is writ,
We shall live to see,
The day that's been promised,
The day that's been ordained;
The day when mountains of oppression,
Will blow away like wisps of cotton;
When the earth will dance
Beneath the feet of the once enslaved;
And heavens'll shake with thunder
Over the heads of tyrants;
And the idols in the House of God
Will be thrown out;
We, the rejects of the earth,
Will be raised to a place of honor.
All crowns'll be tossed in the air,
All thrones'll be smashed.
And God's word will prevail,
He who is both present and absent
He who's beheld and is the beholder.
And truth shall ring in every ear,
Truth which is you and I,
We, the people will rule the earth
Which means you, which means I.

Faiz Ahmed Faiz
America, January 1979

Contents

Acknowledgements

I am grateful to the Woodrow Wilson International Center for Scholars for providing me with funding and the opportunity to spend one year in the United States and research that material that was important for writing this book. I am indebted to Robert Hathaway, Saeed Shafqat and my friend Navnita Chadha-Bahera who took time out of their busy schedule to read some of the chapters and give their valuable comments. Also, a special thanks to Vali Nasr, Ayesha Jalal and Michael Brzoska who gave me new ideas to approach the subject and to look in directions that I had not considered earlier.

The list of people I must thank is long. However, I would especially like to acknowledge the help given by Lt Generals (retd) Syed Mohammad Amjad and Talat Masood, Admiral Fasih Bokhari, Hameed Haroon, Ikram Sehgal, Nazim Haji and Riaz Hashmi, who took the time to give me an insight into the military and Milbus in Pakistan.

I would also like to acknowledge the help rendered by some of my friends in searching for the material. I am indebted to Rabia Saleem, Junaid Ahmed, Rauf and Shehzad for providing valuable support in search of the necessary materials. I must also offer special thanks to my research assistants, Adeel Piracha, Ajaita Shah, Mahrukh Mehmood and James Murath for assiting with the hard work of finding the appropriate material. Also, a special thanks to Murtaza Solangi, whose moral support was essential during my stay in the United States.

Finally, an acknowledgement would be incomplete without mentioning the help and emotional support given by my husband, Sohail Mustafa. He was always there to encourage me to complete my work. I am also grateful to Aziz, Omar and Jamal for making it easy for me to work at home and complete this book. I must also acknowledge the emotional support of my dear friend Saadia Imad who was always there for me.

Last, but not the least, I thank the commissioning editor of Pluto Press, Roger van Zwanenberg. His comments on my initial book outline made me think about what I wanted to write.

Ayesha Siddiqa

Acronyms

ABL	Allied Bank Ltd
ABRI	Angkatan Bersenjata Republic Indonesia (armed forces of the Republic of Indonesia)
ACL	Askari Cement Ltd
ADB	Asian Development Bank
AEB	Askari Education Board
AG	adjutant-general
AMAA	Army Mutual Assistance Association (Turkey)
AWACS	airborne early-warning aircraft system
AWNCP	Army Welfare Nizampur Cement Project (Pakistan)
AWT	Army Welfare Trust (Pakistan)
BICC	Bonn International Center for Conversion
BCCI	Bank of Credit and Commerce International
BF	Bahria Foundation (Pakistan)
CDA	Capital Development Authority/Cholistan Development Authority (Pakistan)
CENTO	Central Treaty Organization
CGS	chief of general staff
CLS	chief of logistics staff – Pakistan Army
CNS	chief of naval staff
CoD	Charter of Democracy (Pakistan)
CPJ	Committee to Protect Journalists (Pakistan)
DCC	Cabinet Committee for Defence (Pakistan)
DHA	Defence Housing Authority (Pakistan)
EBDO	Elective Bodies Disqualification Ordinance (Pakistan)
FF	Fauji Foundation
FFC	Fauji Fertilizer Company Ltd
FJFC	Fauji-Jordan Fertilizer Company
FOTCO	Fauji Oil Terminal and Distribution Company Ltd
FSF	Federal Security Force (Pakistan)
FWO	Frontier Works Organization (Pakistan)
GHQ	General Headquarters
IJI	Islami Jamhoori Ittihad party (Pakistan)
IMF	International Monetary Fund
ISI	Inter-Services Intelligence (Pakistan)
ISPR	Inter-Services Public Relations (Pakistan)
JS HQ	Joint Staffs Headquarters (Pakistan)
JCO	junior commissioned officer
JCSC	Joint Chief of Staffs Committee (Pakistan)
KPT	Karachi Port Trust
MCO	miscellaneous charge order
MGCL	Mari Gas Company Ltd

MI	Military Intelligence
MLC	Department of Military Land and Cantonment (Pakistan)
MMA	Mutahida Majlis-e-Amaal (Pakistan religious party)
MoD	Ministry of Defence
MQM	Muhajir Qaumi Movement (Pakistan)
MRD	Movement for Restoration of Democracy (Pakistan)
MSA	Maritime Security Agency (Pakistan)
NAB	National Accountability Bureau (Pakistan)
NBP	National Bank of Pakistan
NDC	National Defence College (Pakistan)
NGO	non-government organization
NHA	National Highway Authority
NLC	National Logistic Cell (Pakistan)
NoC	no-objection certificate
NPL	non-performing loans
NRB	National Reconstruction Bureau (Pakistan)
NSC	National Security Council (Pakistan)
NWFP	North West Frontier Province (Pakistan)
OYAK	Turkish Armed Forces Mutual Assistance Fund
PAF	Pakistan Air Force
PCCB	Pakistan Cricket Control Board
PIA	Pakistan International Airlines
PIDC	Pakistan Industrial Development Corporation
PIDE	Pakistan Institute of Development Economics
PIU	produce index units (unit of land ownership)
PKI	Partai Komunis Indonesia (Communist Party of Indonesia)
PLA	People's Liberation Army (China)
PMEs	private military enterprises
PML-N	Pakistan Muslim League (Nawaz)
PML-Q	Quaid-e-Azam (Pakistan)
PN	Pakistan Navy
PNA	Pakistan National Alliance
PPP	Pakistan People's Party
PPPP	Pakistan People's Party Parliamentarian Patriot
PR	Pakistan Railways
PSO	Pakistan State Oil
PSO	principal staff officer
QMG	quartermaster-general
RCO	Revival of the Constitution Order (Pakistan)
RMA	Revolution in Military Affairs
SAI	Shaheen Air International Airlines
SCO	Special Communications Organization (Pakistan)
SECP	Securities and Exchange Commission of Pakistan
SF	Shaheen Foundation (Pakistan)
SMS	Securities and Management Services
TFC	term finance certificate
WAPDA	Water and Power Development Authority (Pakistan)

Introduction

The military is one of the vital organs of the state. However, in some countries the military becomes deeply involved in the politics of the state, and dominates all other institutions. Why some militaries become key players in a country's power politics is an issue that has puzzled many. Numerous authors have used various methodologies and paradigms to understand the military's praetorianism. Besides looking at the imbalance between military and civilian institutions, or the character of the society, as causes for spurring the armed forces into politics, the existing literature has also analysed the political economy of the military's influence. Powerful militaries allocate greater resources to the defence budget and force civilian governments to follow suit. However, the defence budget is just one part of the political economy. Commercial or profit-making ventures conducted by the military, with the involvement of armed forces personnel or using the personal economic stakes of members of the defence establishment, constitute a major part of the political economy that has not been analysed systematically. The present study aims at filling this gap. It looks at the political economy of the business activities or the personal economic stakes of military personnel as a driver of the armed forces' political ambitions. This is a peculiar kind of military capital, which is inherently different from the defence budget, and has been termed here *Milbus.*

Milbus refers to military capital that is used for the personal benefit of the military fraternity,[1] especially the officer cadre, but is neither recorded nor part of the defence budget. In this respect, it is a completely independent genre of capital. Its most significant component is entrepreneurial activities that do not fall under the scope of the normal accountability procedures of the state, and are mainly for the gratification of military personnel and their cronies. It is either controlled by the military, or under its implicit or explicit patronage. It is also important to emphasize that in most cases the rewards are limited to the officer cadre rather than being evenly distributed among the rank and file. The top echelons of the armed forces who are the main beneficiaries of Milbus justify the economic dividends as welfare provided to the military for their services rendered to the state.

Since this military capital is hidden from the public, it is also referred to as the military's *internal economy*. A study of Milbus is important because it causes the officer cadre to be interested in enhancing their influence in the state's decision making and politics. Its mechanisms and manifestations vary from country to country. In countries such as the United States, the United Kingdom, France, Israel and South Africa, it operates in partnership with the civilian corporate sector and the government. In other cases such as Iran, Cuba and China, Milbus is manifested through partnership with the dominant ruling party or individual leader, while in Turkey, Indonesia, Pakistan, Myanmar and Thailand the military is the sole driver of Milbus.

1

An inverse partnership exists in these countries between the civilian players and the military because of the armed forces' pervasive control of the state and its politics. This military capital also becomes the major driver for the armed forces' stakes in political control. The direct or indirect involvement of the armed forces in making a profit, which is also made available to military personnel and their cronies, increases the military's institutional interest in controlling the policy-making process and distribution of resources. Therefore, Milbus in Turkey, Indonesia, Myanmar and Pakistan is caused by the military's involvement in politics.

This phenomenon intensifies the interest of the military in remaining in power or in direct/indirect control of governance. This does not nurture the growth of democracy or rule of law, and makes this kind of Milbus the most precarious. The fundamental research question that I believe deserves analysis is whether, when the military echelons indulge in profit making and use the armed forces as a tool for institutional and personal economic influence, they have an interest in withdrawing to the barracks and allowing democratic institutions to flourish. I have sought to find an answer through a case study on Pakistan, which is a militaristic-totalitarian system where an army general is the head of the state, unlike in Turkey and Indonesia.

The case of Pakistan provides an opportunity to understand the issues that emerge from the financial autonomy of a politically powerful military. Pakistan's military today runs a huge commercial empire. Although it is not possible to give a definitive value of the military's internal economy because of the lack of transparency, the estimated worth runs into billions of dollars. Moreover, the military's two business groups – the Fauji Foundation and the Army Welfare Trust – are the largest business conglomerates in the country. Besides these, there are multiple channels through which the military acquires opportunities to monopolize national resources.

The book puts forward three arguments. First, Milbus is military capital that perpetuates the military's political predatory style. The defining feature of such predatory capital is that it is concealed, not recorded as part of the defence budget, and entails unexplained and questionable transfer of resources from the public to the private sector, especially to individuals or groups of people connected with the armed forces. The value of such capital drawn by the military depends on the extent of its penetration into the economy and its influence over the state and society. Consequently, profit is directly proportional to power. Financial autonomy gives the armed forces a sense of power and confidence of being independent of the 'incompetent' civilians. The military, it must be noted, justifies Milbus as a set of activities for the welfare of military personnel. However, the military alone defines the parameters of this welfare. The link between economic and political gains compounds the predatory intensity of such capital.

Second, the military's economic predatoriness increases in totalitarian systems. Motivated by personal gain, the officer cadre of the armed forces seek political and economic relationships which will enable them to increase their economic returns. The armed forces encourage policies and policy-making environments that multiply their economic opportunities.

Totalitarian political systems like Pakistan or Myanmar also have pre-capitalist socioeconomic structures. As these economies are not sufficiently developed, the militaries become direct partners in economic exploitation, while in developed economies the sale of military equipment and services generates profits primarily for the private sector that invests the capital. The military, of course, is one of the secondary beneficiaries of these investments.

The argument that the military are predatory refers to Charles Tilly's concept of the 'racketeer' or 'predator' state which existed in sixteenth and seventeenth-century Europe.[2] The ruling elites in Europe extracted tribute from their citizens in the name of providing security against threats. The rulers maintained large militaries to invade foreign territories in order to increase their power and expand markets for local entrepreneurs. The military was thus central to the system of resource generation, externally and internally. The money for financing foreign invasions was raised by the monarch from the local feudal lords and other concerned parties such as entrepreneurs. According to economic historian Frederic Lane, these individuals paid a 'tribute' as a price for the financial opportunities created by the military's foreign expeditions.[3]

Other commentators like Ashis Nandi also view the state as a criminal enterprise which uses violence against its citizens in the name of national integrity.[4] The common people tolerate the state's authoritarian hand as a price for its maintaining security and cohesion. The price that citizens pay for national security is also a form of 'tribute'. As Lane emphasizes, the state's predatoriness varies with the nature of the regime: a civil or military authoritarian regime is more coercive in doubly extracting resources from its own people. The 'tribute' paid by the citizens for the military services provided by the state increases, especially when the government is controlled by managers who have a monopoly over violence, such as the armed forces.

Lane used the concept of tribute to explain the interaction between the state and society in sixteenth-century Europe, when the French and Venetian empires extracted money from the public (and especially those with significant amounts of capital) to build a military machine which, in turn, was used to conquer and create markets abroad. To restate this in domestic political and economic terms, it means that militaries or states can exact a cost from their citizens for providing security and an environment that facilitates the growth of private enterprise. Milbus is part of the tribute that the military extracts for providing services such as national security which are deemed to be public goods. Since the armed forces ensure territorial security, it is necessary to allow all those measures that are meant for the welfare of military personnel. However, at times militaries convince the citizens to bear additional costs for security on the basis of a conceived or real threat to the state.

Third, the military's economic predatoriness, especially inside its national boundaries, is both a cause and effect of a feudal authoritarian, and non-democratic, political system. In a similar way to other ruling elites such as the feudal landowners and large entrepreneurs, the military exploits resources for the advantage of its personnel. The exploitation of national resources by the elite is a result of the peculiar nature of the pre-capitalist politicoeconomic system. The historian Eric Hobsbawm describes this political economy as one where assets are not only accumulated for deriving capital: rather, they are acquired for accumulating power and influence. Consequently, in a feudal setting land and capital become doubly significant. The acquisition of assets signifies the increase in power of an institution or stakeholder compared with others. The feudal structure thrives on the accumulation and distribution of capital and assets to those in authority, and leads them in turn to compensate their clients in return for their support and greater political power.[5] Hence, the accumulation of capital or assets is not just to gather wealth but to buy additional power.

In the process of seeking benefits, those in power give *carte blanche* to other elite groups to behave predatorily. This nourishes the symbiotic relationship between the armed forces and political power. The patronage of the military as part of the ruling elite becomes necessary for the survival of other weaker players, thus creating a strong patron–client relationship. Hence, any calculation of the net worth of Milbus in a country must include the value of the resources exploited by the military and its cronies.

The nature of military-economic predatory activity, and how it can be seen as 'illegal military capital', are questions we consider later.

DEFINING MILBUS

I base my definition of the term Milbus on a definition in an edited study on the military's cooperative and business activities, *The Military as an Economic Actor: Soldiers in business*, carried out by the Bonn International Center for Conversion (BICC) in 2003:

> economic activities falling under the influence of the armed forces, regardless of whether they are controlled by the defence ministries or the various branches of the armed forces or specific units or individual officers.[6]

The authors describe military economic activities as:

> operations involving all levels of the armed forces. These range from corporations owned by the military as an institution, to welfare foundations belonging to different services, to enterprises run at the unit level and individual soldiers who use their position for private economic gain.[7]

This definition is not, however, entirely appropriate for my purposes here: it is both too narrow and too broad. It includes the defence industry as part of Milbus, but the defence industry is excluded from the definition used for this book, since defence industries are subject to government accountability procedures. BICC's definition is also limited by its exclusion of non-institutional benefits obtained by the individual military personnel, and its failure to focus on their lack of accountability.

I define Milbus as military capital used for the personal benefit of the military fraternity,[8] especially the officer cadre, which is not recorded as part of the defence budget or does not follow the normal accountability procedures of the state, making it an independent genre of capital. It is either controlled by the military or under its implicit or explicit patronage.

There are three essential elements in the new definition: the purpose of the economic activities, the subject of Milbus, and accountability mechanism.

Milbus refers to all activities that transfer resources and opportunities from the public and private sectors to an individual or a group within the military, without following the norms of public accountability and for the purposes of personal gratification. The unaccounted transfer of resources can take many forms:

- state land transferred to military personnel
- resources spent on providing perks and privileges for retired armed forces personnel, such as provision of support staff, membership of exclusive clubs, subsidies on utility bills and travel, and subsidized import of vehicles for personal use by senior officials
- diverting business opportunities to armed forces personnel or the military organization by flouting the norms of the free-market economy
- money lost on training personnel who seek early retirement in order to join the private sector (in the United States, for example, the government incurs the additional cost of then rehiring the same people from the private sector at higher rates).

All these costs are not recorded as part of the normal annual defence budget, despite the fact that the money is spent, or the profits are appropriated, for the benefit of military personnel.

The military organization is central to the concept of Milbus. Therefore, the primary players of Milbus are individual personnel or groups of people who form part of the military fraternity. It must be mentioned that the stakeholders are not limited to serving members of the armed forces (or to the military as an organization). They also include retired personnel and those civilians who depend on military–business associations. The primary beneficiary of this capital is the officer cadre. Because they have greater access to policy makers than lower-level employees, officers are in a better position to generate economic opportunities for themselves, and negotiate perks and privileges with the state and society. The volume of benefits, or the degree of penetration of the military into the economy for the purpose of economic advantages, is proportional to the influence of the armed forces. Greater political power allows the officer cadre to draw greater benefits. This system of benefits is given the misnomer of welfare. However, it must be noted that such welfare is largely supply-driven. The financial burden of the welfare is not defined by the society that bears the cost, but by the recipients – that is, the military.

Finally, one of the key defining features of Milbus is the nature of accountability. Milbus-related activities are not publicized in most countries. In military-authoritarian states in particular, discussion about these operations is off-limits. Any major disclosure or debate is regarded by the armed forces as questioning and challenging their authority. In Turkey, where the parliament cannot question military spending, Milbus is completely out of bounds for civilian players. Consequently, no questions are asked despite the fact that the Armed Forces Mutual Assistance Fund (popularly knows as OYAK) is one of the largest business conglomerates in the country. Similarly in Pakistan, one of the leading military-business conglomerates is the Fauji Foundation (FF). In an inquiry in 2005, the elected parliament was snubbed by the Ministry of Defence (MoD) for inquiring into a controversial business transaction by the FF. The military's welfare foundation was asked to explain to the parliament why it had undersold a sugar mill. The MoD, however, refused to share any details concerning the deal.[9] Factually, resources categorized as Milbus-related generally do not follow the procedures and norms of accountability prescribed for a government institution, or even a military project or programme financed by the public sector. The inability to apply government accountability procedures to Milbus itself increases the possibility and magnitude of corruption.

Purely in terms of the nature of work, Milbus comprises two broad but distinct sets of activities:

- Profit making through the privatization of security. This trend is followed in developed economies. Instead of becoming a direct player in the corporate sector through establishing commercial ventures or acquiring land and other resources, select members of the armed forces offer services such as training or weapons production to generate profit, which is shared with the investors who provide capital for the venture. This approach is highly capitalist in nature, with a clear division between capital and mode of production.
- Military engagement in non-traditional roles such as farming, or running business like hotels, airlines, banks or real estate agencies: all functions that are not related to security. This occurs mainly in developing economies.

What differentiates the two types is not just the volume of financial dividends earned but the extent of penetration of the military in its own society and economy. In the first category, the economic predatoriness is conducted overseas; in the second, it takes place in the country to which the military belongs. The kind of activities a military organization chooses to undertake depends on the nature of civil–military relations and the state of the economy, issues which are explained in greater depth in Chapter 1.

It is important to remember that irrespective of the category or nature of activities, Milbus is predatory in nature. Since this kind of capital involves the transfer of funds from the public to the private sector, as was mentioned earlier, it operates on the principle of limited transparency. Hence, there is an element of illegality about this type of military capital. The underlying illegality is intensified in pre-capitalist politicoeconomic structures. In such systems, which are known for authoritarianism (especially military authoritarianism), the armed forces use their power to monopolize resources. Since a praetorian military inherently suffers from a lack of political legitimacy, it has a greater interest in hiding wealth accumulation and expenditure on privileges for its personnel, which are achieved at a cost to the society. The deliberate concealment is meant to project the military as being more honest and less corrupt than the civilian players. Furthermore, because the economic structures are less developed and streamlined in countries where this activity takes place than in more developed economies, there is a greater element of Milbus operating in the illegal segment of the economy. This type of military capital broadly has an illegal character, and its illegality increases in an underdeveloped political and economic environment.

It is impossible to assess the financial burden of Milbus on a national economy without emphasizing the significance of the military as a fraternity. The military is a disciplined bureaucracy that extends its patronage to its former members more than any other group, association or organization. Thus the most significant group involved in Milbus are retired personnel, especially former officers, who are an essential part of the Milbus economy. The retired officers act as a linchpin for the organization, serving as tools for creating greater opportunities for the military fraternity.

The military's expertise in violence management gives the military profession and the organization a special character. A military is a formally organized group trained in the art and science of war-making. The armed forces as an institution are known for their distinctive organizational ethos, and their members have a strong spirit of camaraderie, which develops during the months and years of working together in an intense environment where people depend on each other for their lives. The allegiance of the retired officers to their organization is relatively greater than could be found in any other organized group, particularly in the civilian sector. Moreover, because retired and serving officers have trained in the same military academies and served in similar command and staff positions, they are part of a well-knit 'old-boys' network whose members tend to support each other even after people have left active duty. Seniority is respected, and interests are mutual, so the retired personnel do not feel out of synch when they move to the civilian sector.

Even when retired military officers enter politics, the connection with the armed forces remains strong. The fact, as mentioned by political scientist Edward Feit, is that generals-turned-politicians retain their links with the military.[10] Military politicians depend on the military institution both directly and indirectly, and thus can be considered as part of its network. Senior military officers-turned-politicians also tend to create their own political parties or provide patronage to political groups. This fact is borne out by several examples in Latin America, Pakistan, Indonesia and Turkey. Political governments recognize the retired military officers as a crucial link with the organization. The former officers are inducted into political parties, given responsible positions in the cabinet, and used to negotiate with the armed forces. This phenomenon is more acute in politically underdeveloped systems. The patronage provided to the former members by the defence establishment is a two-way traffic. The formal military institution provides the necessary help for retired military personnel to grow financially and socially. In return, the retired personnel, especially the officer class, create through political means greater financial and other opportunities to benefit the organization and other members of its network.

Considering the fact that the number of beneficiaries of Milbus is relatively large, and the details of them are mostly hidden or not available, it is difficult to carry out an exact assessment of the financial worth of the military's internal economy. Such a calculation is vital to evaluate the monetary burden that Milbus places on a nation's economy. Ideally, the cost of Milbus should include the net worth of the assets of the military fraternity. However, this level of detailed data cannot possibly be obtained. This inability makes it difficult to conduct a statistical analysis. Given the dearth of complete, transparent and authentic data, the present study will restrict itself to defining and describing Milbus, identifying its areas of activity and highlighting its consequences.

LITERATURE SURVEY

Interestingly, social science research has not systematically looked at the Milbus phenomenon despite the availability of rich anecdotal information (although admittedly this information does not allow for statistical analysis). Perhaps the deficiency of organized data has not encouraged economists to analyse the genre of military capital, and nor does the existing literature on civil–military relations and democracy analyse the link between Milbus and military authoritarianism. Most coverage of the subject comes from those working in the area of security studies or international relations, in a number of countries, but even they have failed to present a cogent and systematic theoretical analysis, although a series of case studies are available, describing the military's business operations or the internal economy in different countries. There are basically three book-length studies – of the United States, Canada and China – along with minor works on Indonesia, Pakistan, post-Soviet Russia and a cluster of Latin American countries.[11]

Caroline Holmqvist and Deborah Avant's studies, which are thematic analyses of the subject, deal with the issue of private security. The two authors view the rise of the private security industry as an expression of the systemic shift in the security sector in the developed world. A number of developed countries such as the United States, Canada, France and the

United Kingdom sell military goods and services to security-deficient states in Africa and states carved out of former Yugoslavia. The military-related goods and services are not sold directly by the states but through private companies. This led to the burgeoning of the private security business, which increased the demand for retired military personnel. Incidentally, the increase in the private security business took place at the time of military downsizing in the West, especially after the end of the Cold War.

Subcontracting the sale of security-related goods and services allowed western governments to downsize without entirely losing their security capacity in terms of human resources. The retired military personnel engaged in the private security business had links with the government and could also be depended upon as a reserve for future deployment if the need ever arose. Moreover, downsizing resulted in a reduction in the state's military expenditure. Some non-western countries such as South Africa have also downsized their defence sector. Holmqvist and Avant evaluate the underlying concept behind private security.

These two theoretical works came later than empirical studies on the private security industry in the United States and Canada, by P. W. Singer and James Davis respectively. Peter Lock, who has tried to problematize Milbus in his paper presented at a conference in Indonesia on 'Soldiers in Business', expressed his discomfort at including writings on private security for the literature survey of this book.[12] Lock's paper looked at the military's commercial activities using the developmental, predatory and state-building paradigm. He was of the view that since private security pertains to the sale of military-related goods and services such as training, providing security for VIPs and strategic installations, and in some cases even fighting wars, these roles are different from the commercial activities usually undertaken by the civilian-private sector. Lock's argument, however, does not take into account the common denominator between the two sets of activities: the military's involvement in both cases is meant to be for the benefit of a select few, and results in costs for the public sector that are usually not included in the defence estimates (see further discussion in Chapter 1).

Other works discuss the sale of non-traditional products by the armed forces. The key study here is the BICC's compilation *The Military as an Economic Actor: Soldiers in business*. As mentioned earlier, the theoretical framework of the BICC study is limited to describing Milbus as a budgetary malaise that happens only in developing or economically troubled states. This is only a partial explanation of Milbus as I define it, a gap that the present study ventures to fill.

In addition, there is a monograph by James Mulvenon about the commercial activities of the Chinese armed forces. Analysing issues of command and control of military-controlled commercial ventures in China and the efficiency of the sector, Mulvenon limited himself to a case study. The book did not evaluate the opportunity costs of Milbus or look profoundly at the theoretical aspects of military capital. The study discusses corruption in the People's Liberation Army (PLA) as the only major ramification of the military's commercialization.

The present study seeks to fill the gaps in the theoretical understanding of Milbus by analysing all types of activities, and providing a link between all those functions carried out by the armed forces that have financial implications for individual members of the forces, the organizations as whole, and the economy at large.

WHAT DRIVES MILBUS?

Militaries engage in civilian profit making for several reasons, ranging from providing a system of welfare or a social security net for retired and serving armed forces personnel, to contributing to national socioeconomic development. Of course, the basic greed of the top echelons of the officer cadre is part of the explanation. Senior generals use their authority to create economic opportunities that will last them post-retirement. However, this kind of military capital cannot simply be explained as an outcome of personal individual greed. The movement from establishing schemes for personal benefits to increasing the power of the organization is neither simple nor linear. In most cases militaries initially sought financial autonomy to meet the organization's needs, especially personnel costs. It is considered vital to provide for the welfare of armed forces personnel whose typical remuneration, all over the world, is less than the private sector norm. Governments feel obligated to provide extra cash or resources for people who guard the frontiers of the state.

Indeed, the search for financial independence is not a new or unique phenomenon. During the Middle Ages, mercenary militaries or their leaders were the 'first real entrepreneurs' to gather resources for fighting wars.[13] The European militaries before the French Revolution lived off the land because the state lacked the strength to subsidize war, and depended on resources exploited by the feudal landowners who formed partnerships with the monarchs.[14] Mercenary militaries were part of the European monarch's coercion-intensive paradigm, which encouraged military force to extract resources for the state. As was previously touched upon by Charles Tilly, countries such as Russia, Sweden and the Ottoman Empire used force to extract taxes from the public so as not to jeopardize their long-term capacity to raise finances for war-making.[15] The method was to assign 'some military officers and civilian officials the rents from crown lands ... so long as they [the officers] remained in royal service'.[16] This happened in other parts of the world as well, with militaries fighting for feudal lords and potentates who also looted and plundered to finance campaigns and meet their financial needs.[17] In more recent times a number of armed forces (for instance, in Indonesia and China) have depended on their internal economies to meet their personnel and operational costs. The internal economy is one of the sources of off-budget financing of defence requirements.

In developing economies, militaries engage in money-making activities with the objective of contributing to national development. Keeping in view the lack of alternative institutions that could undertake development, some

10

armed forces take upon themselves the responsibility to build and sponsor large industries or resource and capital-intensive projects. The Chinese military, for example, initially set up commercial ventures and undertook farming to contribute to self-reliance and national economic development. The PLA's special 'war economy' groups manufactured a large array of products to earn profits. The 'guerrilla industries' donated these profits to war efforts and for financing the welfare plans of army units.[18]

The fact is that most generals view the military's internal economy as an expression of the organization's superior capacity at managing resources, and providing for the overall socioeconomic development of the state. The economic ventures, especially commercial activities, render profits because the armed forces are more disciplined, better organized and less corrupt than the civilian corporate institutions. The military's sense of superiority intensifies in less developed countries which are politically weak and where the civilian institutions do not perform well.

Interestingly, the military's comparative superiority is upheld by a number of western academics. Morris Janowitz, for instance, believes that third world militaries are 'crisis organizations' capable of meeting diverse challenges. Janowitz recognizes the superior capacity of non-western armed forces to deliver results. Samuel P. Huntington, Alfred Stepan and David Mares also subscribe to the view that third world militaries act as socioeconomic modernizers.[19] Manfred Halpern adds to this view through his research on Middle Eastern militaries.[20] The author has labelled such militaries as a case of progressive militarism.

Most of this literature clearly considers the armed forces as products of a specific social milieu. Fragmented or praetorian societies give birth to politically dominant militaries. The present study does not challenge that analysis, as the scope of the study is not a comparative analysis of various institutions of a state, but the study of the impact of the economic interests of the officer cadre in the armed forces, as operationalized through Milbus.

The literature on military corporatism and bureaucratic authoritarianism discusses the strong role of the armed forces, particularly in weak states. The military and development literature written mostly during the 1970s and 1980s endorsed the military's multiple roles in developing states. It could be argued, however, that the acceptance of the military's development and modernization roles belongs to the cold war paradigm, in which the western approach to third world militaries was driven by the logic of the military-strategic partnership between the North and South. Given the political fragmentation of the developing countries, partly as a result of the communist versus capitalist ideological divide, the military appeared as the only credible institution guaranteeing stability and better governance. The armed forces were seen as instruments of domestic stability and as partners that were depended upon for achieving US security objectives, especially regarding communist powers. Various authors have written about the US security agenda of strengthening the military establishments of developing states. Ayesha Jalal and William Robinson, for instance, argue that the US

11

security agenda determined the significance of authoritarian military regimes in Pakistan and Latin America.[21]

The issue, however, is not US interests defining the political agenda of a state. The fact is that territorial or military security is one of the prime products offered by authoritarian or politically underdeveloped states to their citizens. The significance of military security is paramount in 'security' states that are intrinsically insecure. Under the circumstances, the military benefits from its image as a guarantor of national security. This particular role enhances its political influence too. In her study on Myanmar, Mary Callahan discusses the link between the military's role as a provider of security and its sociopolitical influence.[22] In such politically underdeveloped environments the militaries further enhance their reputation as the only credible institution on the basis of their superior knowledge of, and exposure to, modern technology and foreign cultures. Huntington's concept of the 'soldier-reformer',[23] for instance, is based on the perception of third world militaries as carriers of western cultural norms in otherwise underdeveloped societies. It is noteworthy that the military corporatist literature defines modernity in terms of exposure to bureaucratic systems, centralized control, technology and the ability to bring political and economic stability.

The militaries of western countries also engage in Milbus, however. Some of these armed forces are involved in profit making, especially by individual members, to cater for the resource crunch caused by sudden and drastic organizational changes. For example, the drop in the defence budget after the end of the Soviet 'empire' left the military and its personnel in dire straits. The members of the post-Soviet Union Russian armed forces often engaged in illegal money-making ventures to meet financial pressures. On the other hand, defence restructuring in countries such as the United States, France, the United Kingdom and South Africa forced retired officials to form companies which offered military training and equipment for sale to their national and foreign governments.

Whatever the logic for developing hidden and less-accountable means of financial resources, Milbus ultimately enhances the influence of the armed forces in politics, policy making or both. This kind of military capital encourages the officer cadre to perpetuate their organizational influence to reap financial benefits. One of the impacts of the Turkish military's financial autonomy, for instance, is the enhancement of its power. Since the defence establishment is one of the key political and economic players, Turkey's capitalist elite built a partnership with the military to jointly exploit resources. Such a coalition is detrimental to the interests of a restive proletariat. Meanwhile, it gave legitimacy to the military's role as an economic player, especially in the eyes of its fraternity and civilian clients. Milbus, particularly in pre-capitalist socioeconomic and political structures, denotes crony capitalism. The armed forces use their political power and influence to win allies in civil society and generate benefits for the military fraternity, including their civilian cronies. There is further discussion on this issue in later sections.

This military capital is lethal not only because it increases the armed forces' penetration in the economy, but also because of the power it gives the top echelons of the security establishment. The senior generals (both serving and retired) are the primary beneficiaries of the internal economy. The whole economic process of benefits is structured in such a manner that those at top received the bulk. So Milbus cannot be held as benign financial compensation to the guardians of the state's frontiers.

Nonetheless, the military often justifies its intrusion in the economy as part of the overall cost of national security, in which light it is classed as a public good. The cost of Milbus remains excessive in comparison with the services rendered by the armed forces to protect the state and society against external and internal threats. In politically underdeveloped societies in particular, the armed forces project themselves as saviours: protecting the state against corrupt politicians and other exploiters. The building by manipulation of the impression of external and internal threats is central to the structure of the military's economic stakes. The general public is made to believe that the defence budgetary allocation and the 'internal economy' are a small price to pay for guaranteeing security. Threats are often consciously projected to justify spending on the military.

The elite groups in the society have their own reasons to turn a blind eye to the military's economic interests. In military-dominated polities, other dominant groups often turn into cronies of the armed forces to establish a mutually beneficial relationship, as is proved by the Indonesian example. The political leadership and the business sector in Indonesia shared resources with the armed forces, which had established stakes in the economy. The political and military leadership allowed Milbus and encouraged each other's financial stakes to facilitate the perpetuation in power of a certain group. Jakarta never seriously attempted to remove the budgetary lacunae that allowed the armed forces to run their internal economy. Since the Indonesian government could not provide sufficient funds to the military for weapons modernization or to meet personnel costs, Jakarta allowed the armed forces to run commercial ventures through which it could fill the resource gap. Over the ensuing years need was replaced by greed, and the generals built an economic empire in collusion with the top political leaders. Thus, the prominent players had a stake in allowing the military to continue with its profit making.

CONSEQUENCES OF MILBUS

Illegal military capital has a far-reaching impact on the economy, society, politics and military professionalism. To begin with, there are obvious financial costs such as creation of monopolies that cause market distortions. The military fraternity and its civilian clients have an unfair advantage in winning contracts. Second, Milbus often places a burden on the public sector because of the hidden flow of funds from the public to the private sector. Since the military claims that Milbus activities are legitimate private-sector ventures, funds are often diverted from the public to this particular private sector, such as the use of military equipment by military-controlled firms, and the acquisition of state land for distribution to individual members of the military fraternity for profit making. The military establishment, however, refuses to add the cost of its internal economy to the defence budget. Of course, these hidden costs are found primarily in countries where the military has greater political authority.

In other ways too the state wastes resources, as in the money spent on training personnel who leave military service prematurely to get employment in the private sector. Since these trained people resign, the government ends up paying higher amounts for hiring the same services at higher rates from the private sector, so it loses twice over: once on training, and once on rehiring these people. This type of activity takes place in developed countries and those falling into the first type of civil–military relations. The military, of course, is not the driver for privatization of security but a beneficiary. In the United States, for example, there are strong corporate interests that benefit from privatizing security. This movement of military personnel from the public to the private sector is referred to in the literature on private security industry as the 'gold mining' attitude.[24] It has dangerous consequences, in that the corporate sector supports policies that would result in higher profits through the privatization of security services. The senior officers become willing partners of the corporate sector, and this threatens the quality of professionalism in the armed forces. Milbus creates a system of patronage that intensifies in praetorian political systems. In any case, as Ronald Wintrobe argues, military regimes distribute resources more than democracies do in order to win loyalty.[25] Military dictators both punish and reward to win loyalty. Hence, resource distribution is central to coercion.

In socioeconomic terms, Milbus has a profound impact on the relationship between various key political and economic players. One of the consequences is a kleptocratic redistribution of resources. Such a redistributive relationship operates at two levels: within the armed forces, and between the military and its clients. At the first level, economic and other resources are distributed within the military to win loyalty. Higher echelons of the defence management that remain in power or constantly return to power seek additional national resources, and redistribute them to win the appreciation of other significant members of the armed forces. Outside the armed forces, at the second level, the senior military management also distribute resources to win the loyalty of other groups and to divert the attention from the military's financial predatoriness.

In Pakistan, for instance, the government encourages other prominent players from the corporate sector, key political leaders, members of the judiciary and journalists to acquire land or build housing schemes. Consequently, it weakens the criticism of the military's land acquisition, especially by those that have benefited from similar activities. In this respect, as mentioned earlier, Milbus is both a source and beneficiary of crony capitalism. Such redistributive processes encourage both authoritarianism and clientship. The internal economy in fact consolidates the military's hegemonic control over the society through direct and indirect means. While direct means of imposing hegemony involve the military dominating key administrative and political positions in the state and society, indirect methods relate to encouraging the perception that the armed forces have the panacea for all ills of the nation. The indirect control is exercised through strategic partnership with other players.

It is noteworthy that the military builds partnerships both locally and internationally. A glance at the military's commercial ventures in countries such as Pakistan, Turkey and Indonesia bears witness to the fact that international business also builds corporate partnership with military-run businesses. Since the military dominates the state and projects itself as the most credible institution, international players find it convenient to operate through the military-run companies. Senior generals often draw on the military's better image than civilian competitors to attract international business. The effort at positive image building of the defence establishment was obvious in the speech delivered by Pakistan's military president, Pervez Musharraf, at the inauguration of a desalination plant for the Defence Housing Authority (DHA) at Karachi. According to him:

> Then, we have army welfare trust, we have Fauji Foundation. Yes, they are involved in banking ... they're involved in. ... we've got fertilizers ... we are involved even in pharmaceuticals. We are involved in cement plants .... So, what is the problem if these organizations are contributing and are being run properly? We have the best banks. Our cement plants are doing exceptionally well. Our fertilizer plants are doing exceptionally well. So, why is anyone jealous? Why is anyone jealous if the retired military officials or the civilians with them are doing a good job contributing to the economy of Pakistan and doing well?[26]

It is not surprising that the DHA soon found an international partner to invest money in setting up a new housing project in Karachi.

The partnership with international players has a political dimension as well. The military in frontline states (a strategic connotation) offer their services to major geopolitical players. The United States has often become a patron of military regimes, with the aim of achieving its geopolitical objectives in return for political and economic support to military-run governments.

Clientship is one of the obvious consequences of Milbus. Numerous domestic players see the efficacy of partnering with the armed forces to gain political and economic dividends. Such partnership strengthens the armed forces. The added power increases the military's appetite for power and its economic predatoriness. This means that the military's political clout is not just based on its own strength but also on the financial and political power of its collaborators or clients. Hence:

> Political power + economic power (military fraternity x cronies) = military's political capital

According to this equation, members of the military and their cronies benefit from the military's authority. So while there might be friction amongst
the key political and/or economic players over leadership or domination of
the state, there might be little problem regarding the use of military force as
a tool for bolstering political authority for whoever holds the reigns of the
government.

The elite groups have an obsession with their own interests to the
degree that they completely fail to take into account the long-term implications of gorging on national resources. They utterly disregard any concern
for the 'have-nots' and overlook the negative consequences, such as the
overall depletion of resources. This behaviour creates a predatory environment. Such an environment is defined as a condition where the ruling elite
(both civilian and military) are driven by short-term gains at the cost of
ignoring long-term benefits. In such conditions, there are no long-term
ideological loyalties, and the prominent players engage in compromise and
adjustment based on a brutal and singular pursuit of their own interests
without any short or long-term reckoning. This singular pursuit of power is
detrimental to institution building and to minimizing the military's role in
politics and policy making.

It must be noted that predatory behaviour, a feature of Milbus, generates friction and tension in the state and society. On the one hand, it
increases social and economic insecurity, and on the other, it creates friction between the forces controlling the state, such as the ruling oligarchy,
and the rest of the society, especially the dispossessed fraction. The implications are more drastic in post-colonial or restructured states where,
according to Vali Nasr, state–society relations are fluid or unstructured. In
such environments, politically powerful forces like the military, political
parties, religious forces and large business interests try to shape the state
according to a peculiar 'blueprint' that suits their personal interests. Forcing the society to take a certain direction or do the bidding of the powerful could push the common people, or a select group of people, in
opposite and competing directions.[27] Any form of predatoriness hence
represents the interventionist tendency of the elite groups (of which the
military is one), and contributes to aggravated relations between the state
and society.

Indonesia and Turkey are key examples of political and economic
predatoriness creating a rift between the state and society, and within the
society as well. Because the redistribution is highly elitist it deepens the
chasm between the ruling elite and the masses. Lesley McCulloch's report
on the violence in Aceh, Indonesia shows how political and economic
predatoriness distorts domestic ties. The paper provides interesting details
of the military's extortion in Aceh. The armed forces and the police are
engaged in human rights abuses and forcible appropriation of land for
commercial purposes.[28]

It seems clear that the armed forces do not think about these consequences. In developing states in particular, where Milbus is found in the
most perverse form, armed forces consider their internal economy to be

16

a naturally earned privilege. Since the armed forces protect the state, the society is liable to provide for the benefits of individual members of the armed forces. Such logic is given to legitimize the military's commercial interests, which are acquired through the use of political power and influence. The organization's political clout is also instrumental in keeping a lid on its business interests. For instance, the Turkish military does not allow people to question the defence budget or the military's business outlays. Peter Lock, who has looked at the theoretical aspects of Milbus, says:

> It is for example conceivable that the military elite anticipates a profound crisis of the state and seeks its own productive resources aiming at autonomy and institutional stability in the midst of the turmoil shattering the civil society. The adoption of such a strategy presupposes an elitist self-image of the military.[29]

Such a self-image unfortunately has a high political cost. Milbus creates vested interests that do not encourage the building of democratic norms and institutions. Militaries that develop deep economic interests or have a pervasive presence in the economy shrink from giving up political control. In fact, the tendency is to establish the organization's hegemony in the state and society. The military's hegemonic control is noticeable in the cases of Pakistan, Indonesia and Turkey.

From the professional standpoint, the armed forces' exposure to money-making takes its toll on professionalism. The example of China is a case in point. The protection given to businesses in the form of immunity from civilian monitoring and prosecution resulted in corruption.[30] James Mulvenon also mentions corruption as one of the implications of the Chinese military's commercial ventures and the PLA's involvement in non-military activities.[31] Thus, more than providing for the welfare of the soldiers, Milbus activities cater for the personal ambitions of the military's top elite. In any case, the organization's higher management uses its position of being part of the ruling elite for profit making.

Obviously, the inequitable distribution of resources in the armed forces creates problems for the organization and undermines professionalism. Since the distribution of economic opportunities depends on the benevolence of the higher echelons, junior and mid-ranking officers tend to earn favours from the senior officers. As will be seen from the case study of Pakistan, this tends to cloud the judgement of personnel who hope to secure advantages and post-retirement benefits. This happens in other countries as well, such as China. However, Beijing tried to solve the problem of the lack of a professional ethos in the PLA by emphasizing greater professionalism. The Revolution in Military Affairs (RMA) introduced in the PLA, especially in the 1990s, aimed at cutting down the non-military roles of the armed forces, by measures such as forcing the military to disinvest in the services industries sector.[31] The Chinese armed forces still have a role in the defence production sector.

MILBUS AND PAKISTAN

Pakistan's political future has been the subject of enormous concern and scholarly debate since the events of 11 September 2000. Many of the questions centre around the future of the Pakistani state. Can democracy ever be strengthened in Pakistan, given the multiple challenges it faces? Does the regime of General Pervez Musharraf wish to restore sustainable democracy, as it claims? What means can be found to insulate Pakistan's democratic institutions and political structures from future military intervention? Traditionally, studies on Pakistan's democracy, civil–military relations or politics have addressed these questions by analysing the comparative strengths and weaknesses of the political forces and the military. Since 9/11, US policy makers' generous statements endorsing Musharraf's apparent efforts to strengthen democracy were just one example of a mindset that views non-western militaries as relatively more capable than civilian institutions.

The fragility of Pakistan's political system, however, cannot be understood without probing into the military's political stakes. The fundamental question here is whether the Army will ever withdraw from power. Why would Pakistan's armed forces, or for that matter any military that has developed deep economic stakes, transfer real power to the political class? The country is representative of states where politically powerful militaries exercise control of the state and society through establishing their hegemony. This is done through penetrating the state, the society and the economy. The penetration into the society and economy establishes the defence establishment's hegemonic control of the state. Financial autonomy, economic penetration and political power are interrelated and are part of a vicious cycle.

Today the Pakistan military's internal economy is extensive, and has turned the armed forces into one of the dominant economic players. The most noticeable and popular component of Milbus relates to the business ventures of the four welfare foundations: the Fauji Foundation (FF), Army Welfare Trust (AWT), Shaheen Foundation (SF) and Bahria Foundation (BF). These foundations are subsidiaries of the defence establishment, employing both military and civilian personnel. The businesses are very diverse in nature, ranging from smaller-scale ventures such as bakeries, farms, schools and private security firms to corporate enterprises such as commercial banks, insurance companies, radio and television channels, fertilizer, cement and cereal manufacturing plants, and insurance businesses.

This, however, is not the end of the story. At the institutional level, the military is also involved directly through its small and medium-sized enterprises. This is one of the least transparent segments, which makes it difficult to exactly calculate the net worth of the military's internal economy. Operations vary from toll collecting on highways (motorways) to gas stations, shopping malls and to other similar ventures.

Finally, there are a variety of benefits provided to retired personnel in the form of urban and rural land, or employment and business openings.

The grant of state land is a case of diverting the country's resources to individuals for profit. The business openings, on the other hand, show how certain individuals make money through using an organization's influence. The connection of these military entrepreneurs with the armed forces opens more doors for them than for private-sector rivals. The individual favours also reveal a kleptocratic redistribution which has a financial and opportunity cost. This kind of economic empire cannot be established, and money-making opportunities would not be available, without the political and organizational power of the armed forces.

The beginning of Milbus in Pakistan coincided with the military moving into the political front. Although some of the activities, such as granting land to individual officers and soldiers, were inherited from the pre-independence colonial army, the post-1954 growth of the military's internal economy was unprecedented. The indigenous breed of military officers that took over the higher command of the three services of the armed forces around 1951 aimed at consolidating political power through increasing their influence in decision making and establishing the organization's financial autonomy. The need to bring affluence to individual personnel was done through Milbus, which became a process of granting perks and privileges. This enhanced the organization's ability to manipulate the national resources at a systematic level, and greatly increased the financial and economic power of both the institution and its personnel. The latter was done through establishing business ventures controlled by the armed forces. The rather rapid promotions of junior officers to take command of the military in India and Pakistan had an impact on the overall quality of the military organizations. In Pakistan there was an added factor of lax political control of the organization, which nurtured political ambitions among the top echelons of the army. The Indian political leadership, on the other hand, took measures to establish the dominance of the political class and the civil bureaucracy.[33]

In consequence, the Pakistan Army pushed itself into direct control of governance through sidelining the weak political class. Martial law was first imposed in 1958. Since then, the military has strengthened its position as a dominant player in power politics. Over the 59 years of the state's history, the army has experienced direct power four times, and learnt to negotiate authority when not directly in control of the government. Pakistan's political history exhibits a cyclic trend of seven to ten years of civilian rule interrupted by almost a decade of military rule. As a result, the political and civil society institutions remain weak.

This powerful position also allowed the military to harvest an advantageous position in politics. The organization morphed into a dominant 'class' exerting considerable influence on society, politics and the economy. The military have their own norms, corporate culture, ethos, rules of business, established economic interests and financial autonomy, and exercise strict control over entry into the organization. While armed forces personnel can seek appointments in civil bureaucracy, no member of any civilian institution can imagine getting a position in the armed forces. These restrictions are due to the professional character of the military, and the fact that the military jealously guards entry into the organization.

After 1977, the armed forces made a concerted effort to establish themselves as an independent professional and social class that had the power to act in its own interest, like any other dominant class in the country. The army, which is the largest service and the most politically influential, forced the civilian regime in 1985 to pass a controversial amendment to the constitution, which empowered the president to dismiss the parliament. This legal mechanism was a security valve to enable the military to dispense with regimes that questioned its authority or were not trusted by it. Subsequently, the military regime of Pervez Musharraf formed the National Security Council (NSC) in 2004, and this transformed the status of the military from being an instrument of policy to a awesomely powerful organization that could protect its interests as an equal member of the ruling elite.

The idea of setting up the NSC had been broached consistently since 1977. Modelled on the Turkish and Chilean NSCs, the newly founded council elevated the armed forces' position from merely a tool of policy making to an equal partner in civil and political society. One of the key arguments of this book is that the economic stakes of the military elite, and their financial autonomy, played a vital role in persuading them to push for an independent status for the organization. The independent economic power not only enhanced the sense of confidence of senior military officers, it also gave them a sense of superiority. Thus, political and economic independence is a lethal combination in an army known for its 'Bonapartist' tendencies.

The issue of the linkage between the internal economy of the armed forces and its prominent position in politics in Pakistan remains understudied and largely unresearched. This is true for most countries where the military has a prominent economic role. Such lack of attention does not necessarily signify a lack of interest. There are four explanations for the absence of consistent research. First, commentators on Pakistan's economy, politics and civil–military relations traditionally considered the defence budget as the primary form of military capital. It must be noted that there is, in any case, very little analysis available of the defence economy in Pakistan. Given the general lack of transparency in this particular area, economists or political scientists have rarely analysed the political economy of national security. Historian Ayesha Jalal has looked at the political economy of the military, but she confined herself to the defence budget.[34] More recently, Hassan-Askari Rizvi has discussed Milbus without providing much detail.[35] The omission, however, is primarily because of the absence of data.

Second, Milbus grew surreptitiously. Formally established in 1953–4, the military's internal economy did not grow as rapidly or noticeably as the defence budget. It was after the third martial law in 1977 that the military started to work more consistently on expanding its economic interests. This coincided with the efforts to establish the military as an independent entity parallel to all other political and civil society players. Contrary to claims from the armed forces that the NSC is necessary to strengthen democracy, the underlying concept is to establish the military's position as an independent entity that can present and support its interests like other members of the ruling elite. Moreover, as the defence establishment gained experience of governance and political control, it expanded its economic interests as well. Each military regime gave greater advantages to its personnel than its military predecessor, and became more accommodative of the personal interests of its officer cadre. Each military leader, for his own survival (and legitimacy), has to reward the senior echelons of the military to ensure their allegiance and establish unity of command in the forces. The progression of providing more and better-quality benefits to military personnel is only natural, especially because one of the arguments of the military rulers is that the civilian leadership wants to weaken and destroy the armed forces. Hence, the privileges are meant to mitigate any concerns, if there are any, about the weakening of the military institution. Gaining greater financial autonomy is a symbol of the organization's power.

The third explanation for the lack of research pertains to the obscurity of military capital. Since Milbus aims primarily at providing benefits to individuals, especially senior personnel, the armed forces tend to be highly protective of the relevant data. Like the Turkish armed forces, Pakistan's military is extremely protective of its interests and does not encourage any serious debate on the defence budget or Milbus. Non-military people are barred from accessing information related to Milbus because of the peculiar legal provisions that protect Milbus-related information from exposure. The four foundations are registered under laws that categorize them as private-sector entities which cannot be examined by government auditors. Such legal provisions hamper the government and the Auditor-General's Department from taking any action if and when they find an irregularity in accounts or observe an unauthorized flow of the funds.

The fact is that over the 58 years of the country's history, there has been little pressure from the political leadership or the civil society on the military not to expand its economic interests. It is only recently that some members of the political opposition, such as Senator Farhatullah Babur and Sherry Rehman, have begun to question the military's economic empire. The political leadership did not view Milbus as threatening, or ignored Milbus so as not to displease the generals excessively. The commonly accepted logic is that since Milbus is central to the military's interests it would be unwise to take on the organization. Furthermore, economic incentives were deliberately given to the armed forces to please the generals and buy their sympathy so that they would not disturb the regime(s). This behaviour did not take account of the fact that greater financial autonomy strengthened the military politically, organizationally and psychologically.

The military has been strengthened politically in comparison with other domestic players because of its financial autonomy. As the military can engage in profit-making ventures, which is not its primary role, it grows confident in raising resources independently for which it would normally look to the government and the private sector. The popular perception in military circles is that the various business projects are more efficiently administrated than most public-sector industries, businesses run by civil bureaucrats and even the private sector. Such a notion, however, is unfounded. This book reveals the inefficiency of the military-controlled commercial operations through empirical evidence. There are high financial and opportunity costs in building and sustaining the military's influence in power politics, and these burden the national resources.

Referring to the earlier discussion regarding the Pakistani political leadership's negligence of understanding the link between the military's political and economic ambitions, this book argues that the politicians did not proactively discourage the armed forces from establishing their political influence. The military is seen primarily as a political arbitrator that is called upon to negotiate between competing political interests or factions. The political leadership's main problem with the military is not related to the organization's influence or political involvement, but to its dominance of the state. Given the authoritarian behaviour of the ruling elite, there is little reservation in using the military's organizational power to further the interests of some members of the ruling elite at the cost of others.

Both popularly elected prime ministers like Zulfiqar Ali Bhutto, Mian Nawaz Sharif and Benazir Bhutto, and internationally trained technocrat premiers like Moeen Qureshi and Shaukat Aziz, shirked from questioning the perception that a powerful military has a right to snatch a comparatively larger share of resources. These politicians are among many who have never seriously challenged the concept of the use of military force in politics. The question that arises here is, why has no civilian institution ever forcefully challenged the military or its role in governance? There are two explanations for this tacit cooperation. First, there is a symbiotic relationship between military force and political power. The members of other elite groups in the country accommodate the military's interests for mutual benefit. This is a case of collective over-plundering, a concept that can be explained better through Mancur Olson's theoretical framework of kleptocratic distribution of resources.[36]

According to Olson's concept of roving and stationary bandits, roving bandits enforce a higher cost on the settled community (town or village) they pillage. By engaging in collective over-plundering, the roving bandits impose a negative externality on the society, resulting in a depletion of resources. This ultimately reduces the dividends for the bandits as well. The stationary bandits, on the other hand, are rational, since they settle down in a community and agree to willingly protect the society against roving bandits in return for economic gains. The entire paradigm is based on the negotiation of mutual interests. Applied to Pakistan's case, this means that the politicians or other dominant classes view military power as a tool to extract benefits while denying the same to other citizens. This behaviour is reflective of the feudal tendencies of the society, or the ruling elite. The Pakistani military is no exception. Incidentally, it also shares this feudal attitude. Its feudal-authoritarian attitude is prominent despite the claims that the military is a modern institution following newer sociopolitical trends.

Second, there is a mutual dependency between the military and other elite groups The military regimes have been the source of power for most political leaders and some important members of the corporate sector. The country's history shows how a number of politicians or entrepreneurs were produced and propelled into prominence by the military.

Hence, the dominant classes including the military are bound in a predatory partnership that has serious consequences. Most obviously, it undermines the interests of the common Pakistani citizen. For instance, land distribution tends to favour the elite at the cost of the landless peasants. Similarly, the distribution of other essential resources also favours the 'haves' rather than the 'have nots'. The plight of the fishermen in Sindh at the hands of paramilitary forces, and the landless peasants in Okara after 2001, indicate the usurpation of resources by the military. In both cases the military (including the paramilitary) literally fought against the segments of the community involved in order to control resources. Such events indeed create an imbalance in society.

In spite of the collective over-plundering, the non-military elite has never seriously challenged the military's advantages or influence. With their eyes on getting into power, the majority of politicians in particular never question the perception of a dominant threat that the military present in justifying their presence. The external threat from India is used to justify greater investment in defence rather than socioeconomic development, so there is an absence of an active protest against the military's infiltration into the society and economy. Over the years, national security has developed into a dogma almost on a par with religious ideology. People from civil society such as journalists, politicians and human rights activists who are not convinced of the justness of the military's political and economic domination are often coerced into submission. In consequence there is barely any institutional protest against the armed forces' primacy.

The political silence is a cost itself. The absence of serious challenge strengthens the military's power, which in turn further weakens civilian institutions. With weak institutions the state and society become more fragmented, which is an unhealthy condition for socioeconomic development. Moreover, it establishes an environment of patronage and cronyism that does not bode well for the future of democracy in Pakistan. Much the same is the case in Indonesia, Turkey and other states where militaries are encouraged to build huge financial empires.

Despite its promises and claims to restore democracy, Pakistan's military government, installed in October 1999, is not different from the previous military regimes in terms of not allowing civilian institutions to strengthen. Besides other factors, the military's internal economy is a key motive behind the regime's disinclination to bring about a major change. Having reaped the dividends of political control, Musharraf and his generals will only introduce 'guided democracy' in which their interests remain unchallenged. A strong political system also means greater transparency and accountability, which is unacceptable to the military and the elite.

Does this make sustainable democracy in Pakistan a tall order? Not necessarily, but the recipe for strengthening democracy may be a strong domestic movement backed by external pressure. The various examples from Latin America provide some insight into how the military's influence can be reduced. The Chilean, Honduran and the Nicaraguan militaries also had large economic empires, but they were pushed back into their barracks. The changes in the Latin and South American political systems, however, are attributable to a combination of domestic struggle supported by exogenous pressure from the United States and the international community. It seems clear that the internal political environment drew the attention of the United States to the need to support dissident groups in Latin and South American countries, in order to bring change in a region considered vital to American interests. The threat of communism played a major role in convincing Washington to facilitate a rearrangement of relationships amongst the players in its neighbourhood. Hence, the military in Chile, for instance, had to agree to downgrade the power of the NSC and withdraw numerous political and economic perks. Similarly, in Pakistan's case the recipe is to encourage a strong mass-based political movement that aims at ending authoritarian rule, including that of the armed forces. The potential role of external players in supporting the domestic political forces will be invaluable.

OUTLINE OF THE BOOK

This study is both exploratory and analytical. It presents some new data regarding Pakistan military's internal economy to explain the behaviour of Milbus. The unavailability of data was initially a serious issue. Except for an article-length study conducted in 2000 (the first exploratory research), and a series of articles published in a few Pakistani and US newspapers, there is very little that was out in the open.[37] Given the sensitivity of the topic, there is also a risk involved in conducting this research. It must be reiterated that the military jealously guard their secrets, especially those pertaining to their key interests. The defence budget and the hidden economy are two key areas central to the power and political interests of the armed forces. General Musharraf's regime's subtle management of the media has kept journalists away from probing into the military's economic interests. The government uses both rewards and coercion as tools to manage the media. Incidentally, some information was made available as a result of the questions and answers sought by the parliamentary opposition after 2002.

As a result of this, it was not possible to produce a perfect data set regarding the actual size of the military's internal economy. Therefore, the study uses a qualitative rather than a quantitative framework. Its fundamental strength is in outlining the structure of the military's internal economy by defining the areas that must be included in any research on Milbus. It also presents a rough assessment of the financial worth of this hidden military capital and its impact on the overall economy.

I have used both secondary and primary sources for the book. During the course of research I also found that one of the reasons for the media and civil society's inability to highlight the military's economic empire is that there had never even been a consistent effort to extrapolate the data that is available, such as the annual financial reports of some of the companies. Out of the 96 projects run by the four Pakistani foundations I have mentioned, only nine are listed with the Securities and Exchange Commission of Pakistan (SECP). I have used the reports of these military companies as part of my secondary data along with newspaper reports.

The primary data comprises over 100 interviews with individuals including businessmen, politicians, retired military personnel, and political and defence analysts. Some critical data was provided by sources whose identity cannot be disclosed. I was able to piece together some of the historical facts about Milbus from interviews with former and serving managers of the foundations. Although their revelations were understandably selective, it was possible to get a sense of how they thought about the military's involvement in politics and the economy. It is not surprising that most of the former military officers completely denied their organization's involvement in business.

It must be mentioned that defining Milbus has not been an easy task. Extensive literature on military corporatism, bureaucratic authoritarianism and civil–military relations has to be examined to be able to define the concept of Milbus. An analysis of the internal economy would not have been be possible without coining a definition that explained this segment of the military's economy. A new definition will hopefully help those suffering from the impact of Milbus to debate the problem with their governments. That the lack of a clear definition impeded the political opposition from forcefully stating their case against Milbus in Pakistan was obvious during a parliamentary debate in 2005. Despite the consistent efforts of opposition members to pin down the army for its involvement in commercial corporate activities, a strong case could not be made because no one could properly define the boundaries of the military's hidden economy. Moreover, these parliamentarians could not present a strong case regarding the opportunity costs of Milbus. The definitional and theoretical portions of this book are therefore intended as a contribution to the existing literature on the military's power in the political economy.

The book has 10 chapters. **Chapter 1**, 'Milbus: a theoretical concept', defines and explains the linkage between Milbus and civil–military relations. The basic argument is that Milbus is a phenomenon prevalent in most militaries. The extent of the military's penetration into economy and society is however, directly proportional to its political power and its relationship with other societal and political players. The manner in which a military operates depends on the nature of civil–military relations and the strength of the political institutions of the state.

This chapter outlines six distinct categories of civil–military relations. In all these types, the power of the military to develop and protect its stakes varies with the strength of the state. The first two types of civil–military relations are found in states where the political forces are relatively strong. This is followed by three distinct classifications of states known for the strength of their military rather than their political forces. Finally, there is a type of military that benefits from the failure of the state. Found mostly in Africa, such militaries partner with warlords to loot and plunder the state's assets.

Chapter 2 is the beginning of the case study of Pakistan. Since the political power of the military determines the extent of its economic predatoriness, this chapter is an effort to understand the development of the Pakistan Army's power and its praetorian character. Entitled 'The Pakistan military: the development of praetorianism, 1947–77', the chapter discusses the gradual strengthening of the armed forces. Besides commenting on the political growth of the armed forces, this chapter includes an explanation of the mandate of the military, its ethnic composition and its organizational structure.

Pakistan's military is the most powerful institution in the country. This relatively superior capacity can be attributed to the organization's role as the saviour of the state. Such a role was launched soon after the country's independence in 1947. The first war with India set the political course of the country. Allowing the military to initiate a major operation without sufficient civilian control propelled the army into significance. Henceforth, external threat was used as the *raison d'être* of the armed forces and the source of their power. In fact, external threat was defined to include internal security matters as well. Unchecked by any other institution, the military defined the national interest.

The civilian elite of the country also had a role to play in propelling the military to significance. The organization was primarily seen as a political force multiplier for the civil bureaucracy, who did not realize that the military would gain wings of its own. The first martial law of 1958 had aimed at establishing the rule of the civil bureaucracy. Instead, power was hijacked by the ambitious army leadership. There were a number of factors that strengthened the armed forces, the most important being the relationship between the military and the three dominant classes identified by Hamza Alavi.

This chapter also argues that the armed forces essentially had the character of a military ruler. They did not intend to leave politics. Therefore General Ayub Khan, the first martial law administrator, used the Muslim League and the basic democracy system to establish permanent control. The takeover of General Yahya Khan from General Ayub was not a second military takeover, but a counter-coup that indicated a change in the army and the state's command at the top. The army continued into politics until 1971–2, when it was pushed back as a result of its failure in a war with India.

Chapter 3, 'Evolution of the military class, 1977–2005', continues the debate about the enhancement of the military's political power. It also highlights how the growth of the financial interests of the officer cadre of the armed forces enhanced the financial autonomy of the military fraternity, and provided it with the clout to become independent of all other players.

26

Democracy was restored in 1972, but the army ensured that power was transferred to Zulfiqar Ali Bhutto, who was closer to the military establishment than his rival, Sheikh Mujeeb-u-Rehman from East Pakistan. Bhutto represented the landed-feudal class, which is part of the ruling elite of the country.

However, the military could not completely control the political system. The 1970s was a decade of populist politics in Pakistan, which brought relative empowerment to the masses. Given the interests of the class he represented and his own power ambitions, Bhutto failed to institutionalize the people's power or strengthen democratic institutions. Instead, as is argued in Chapter 3, the elected prime minister rebuilt the armed forces. Consequently, the army marched right back into the corridors of power in 1977.

From this point the army's top leadership struggled to strengthen the military's economic interests and find new ways of institutionalizing the organization's power. General Zia ul Haq, the third chief martial law administrator, initiated the debate on establishing the NSC, an institution that would give the armed forces a permanent role in governance. Although General Zia did not succeed in establishing the NSC, he managed to introduce constitutional provisions such as Article 58(2)(b) which empowered the president to dismiss an elected government. This provision was used often during the 1990s to sack political regimes.

The plan for creating the NSC finally succeeded in 2004 during the reign of the fourth military ruler, General Pervez Musharraf. Although the NSC was not established during Zia's regime, the military gained prominence and could not be pushed back even after the military dictator's death in a mysterious plane crash in 1988. In fact, the politicians contributed to the strengthening of the military's economic interests. The armed forces were provided with greater opportunities for economic exploitation. These economic interests combined with the armed forces' political ambitions played a major role in pushing them to institutionalize their power.

Chapter 4, 'The structure of Milbus', outlines the organizational configuration of the Pakistan military's economic empire. It explains the command and control structures, and the various methods used to exploit economic resources. The military's economic empire operates at three distinct levels: through the direct involvement of the organization, economic exploitation through its subsidiary companies, and by granting advantages to individual members of the military fraternity. This pattern is similar to Indonesia's, where the top political leadership preys on the economy along with the military institution.

Chapter 5, 'Milbus: the formative years, 1954–77', discusses the growth of Milbus in the years from 1954–77. From the mid-1950s, the armed forces expanded their stakes in all three segments of the economy: agriculture, manufacturing and service industry. These 23 years have been divided into two phases: 1954–69 and 1969–77. These periods roughly overlapped with the political changes in the country. The first 16 years were the formative years during which the armed forces gradually established their foothold in politics and the economy. The second set of six years reflects the civilian interlude in the form of democratic rule of Zulfiqar Ali Bhutto. This is the only time when Milbus did not grow rapidly, because of the political leader's plans to check the autonomy of the armed forces. However, Bhutto failed in curbing the military's political or financial autonomy because of his dependence on military force to attain personal political objectives.

Chapter 6, 'Expansion of Milbus, 1977–2005', is about the growth of Milbus from 1977 to 2005. These are the years when the military's internal economy grew phenomenally. After the imposition of the third period of martial law in 1977, the military undertook various projects to support its economic interests, including setting up new institutions such as the SF and BF to further institutionalize its economic exploitation. The military's economic role got a further boost during the ten years of unstable democracy. From 1988–99, the political governments gave added economic advantages to the armed forces in return for their support. During this period, the military entered uncharted territories such as the finance and banking sector. The last period saw the expansion and consolidation of the military's economic interests. Coinciding with the fourth military takeover in 1999, these years witnessed much greater penetration of the defence establishment into society.

Chapter 7, 'The new land barons', discusses the armed forces' urban and rural land acquisitions. Pakistan suffers from the problem of inequitable distribution of resources, especially land. There are a few people with large land holdings, while the 30 million landless peasants struggle for survival and remain in search of land. However the dominant classes, including the military, have not looked to equalize the situation, but have focused on satisfying their own appetites for land.

The British tradition of granting land to the military for certain purposes has been exploited for the benefit of the senior echelons of the officer cadre. The feudal attitude of the state and its military is demonstrated by the pattern of land distribution and monopolization of vital resources such as water. Although ordinary soldiers are awarded land as well as officers, they do not get access to water to develop the agricultural land. This facility is restricted to the senior officers. Such elitist distribution of resources puts the senior officers in the same class as the big civilian feudal landowners. The distribution of urban land also reveals the power of the ruling elite. Instead of solving the problem of the lack of housing, successive governments have opted to award prime urban land to the officer cadre of the armed forces and other elite groups.

Pakistan's military, however, do not see their economic advantages as exploitation. The various perks and privileges are justified as welfare activities. **Chapter 8**, 'Providing for the men: military welfare', considers the argument of the armed forces. The welfare programmes for serving and retired personnel are carried out mainly to make military service attractive for able-bodied citizens. This welfare is driven by its own politics and dimensions. At one level, distribution of welfare funds is driven by the relative influence of the potential beneficiaries. The senior officers tend to get a larger chunk of benefits than the ranks. At another level, there is inequitable distribution of resources because of the skewed recruitment policy, which shows a bias against smaller provinces and certain ethnic minorities. This imbalance contributes to the existing ethnic tensions in the country.

Chapter 9, 'The cost of Milbus', analyses the financial cost of the military's internal economy. The data presented in this chapter question the military's assertions about the financial efficiency of its commercial ventures. Some of the military's larger business ventures and subsidiaries have required a financial bail-out, burdening the government. Despite the military's claims that these businesses operate in the private sector, the various companies use government resources. This behaviour creates market distortions, increasing the financial and opportunity costs of Milbus. The military's internal economy also compromises professionalism in the armed forces.

Chapter 10, 'Milbus and the future of Pakistan', looks at the cost of the military's economy on its professionalism and the politics of the state. The conclusion, based on the evidence in the earlier chapters, is that Milbus is both politically and socially expensive. Politically, it nurtures the military's power ambitions. A military with such deep-rooted vested interests cannot be removed from a dominating position until there are significant changes in the country or in the international geopolitical environment which force the armed forces to secede political control.

Socially, it reduces the society's acceptability of the military as an arbitrator and increases the alienation of the underprivileged, the dispossessed and the have-nots. Milbus represents the institutionalization of economic exploitation, and this has an impact on the military's character. This kind of economy transforms the military into a predatory institution which uses power for the economic advantages of the armed forces, especially the military elite. Already depressed by the greed of other dominant classes, common people even lose hope in the military's ability to deliver justice as an arbitrator. The resultant alienation could push the society towards other, often extreme, ideologies. It is important to find out whether the increase in religious conservatism in Pakistan, Turkey and Indonesia, the three counties falling into the parent–guardian category of civil–military relations, is just a coincidence or a result of the changes in the character of the armed forces.

1 Milbus: a theoretical concept

The concept of Milbus was defined at length in the introduction, as a 'tribute' drawn primarily by the officer cadre. As was explained, this portion of the military economy involves the unexplained and undocumented transfer of financial and other resources from the public and private sectors to individuals, through the use of the military's influence. Milbus as a phenomenon exists in many countries. However, the size of the 'tribute' and the consequent level of the military fraternity's penetration into the economy are directly proportional to the military's control of politics and governance, and the nature of civil–military relations in a particular country.

This chapter identifies six distinct types of civil–military relations, each dependent on the political strength of the state. The theoretical model presented here revolves around the concept of a politically strong state that is known for its stable pluralist tendencies. The military fraternity's ability to penetrate the state and society or establish its hegemony is determined by the strength of the political system. A weak polity is a sure sign of a weakened state, and therefore greater intrusion of the armed forces at all levels of the economy, political and societal system. The various civil–military relations models presented are relevant for understanding the intensity and scope of the military's economic exploitation. Although all militaries vie for resources, their exploitation will increase according to the extent of their political influence.

CIVIL–MILITARY RELATIONS FRAMEWORK

The state is an important subject in political science literature, and there are numerous prisms through which analysts have looked at it. The most important dimensions are its structure, functions and the capacity to perform its roles. From a structural standpoint, a state is described as:

> an organization that includes an executive, legislature, bureaucracy, courts, police, military, and in some cases schools and public corporations. A state is not monolithic, although some are more cohesive than others.[1]

Like a human body, a state is composed of a set of organs meant to perform certain functions. The link between a state's structural components and its functions is defined as:

> a complex apparatus of centralized and institutionalized power that concentrates violence, establishes property rights, and regulates

society within a given territory while being formally recognized as a state by international forums.[2]

Similarly, Charles Tilly has given a list of seven core functions that states perform:

- state making
- war making
- protection
- extraction
- adjudication
- distribution
- production.[3]

The 'statist' literature focuses in particular on the state's capacity to deliver. In its relationship with the society or people at large, the state is perceived as a 'supra' entity that exercises dominance over other competing institutions such as the family, community, tribe and the market.[4] Hence, the state's strength is gauged by its capacity to deliver certain services to the society. Conversely, the state's capacity is also determined by its control over the society.

The relative strength of the various institutions and their relationships have an impact on the capacity of the state, and this is what makes the state relatively strong or weak. In this study, the state's capacity is determined not only by its capability to perform these functions, but also by the relationships between the various players. States that allow multiple players to negotiate their share of political influence and national resources are considered stronger than those where political debate is limited or arrested through the military's influence. In other words, the framework does not treat the state as a monolith that decides issues with a 'singular' mind, but as a set of relationships that determine the allocation of resources according to their relative power.[5]

In fact, the relative power of the multiple players, their relationship with each other, and their ability to freely negotiate their interests are key features of the politically strong state identified in the theoretical framework presented in this chapter. The relative political power that various players have to compete for resources ultimately shapes the allocative process. The competition also generates tension amongst the various competitors, because of the strife and uncertainty that is characteristic of the struggle accompanying the allocation of resources.[6]

In a nutshell, the state's capacity is determined by the nature of interaction between the various stakeholders, and the plurality of the political process determines the direction of the allocative process, and the peculiar objective of the state. The purpose of a state is essentially that of an arbiter providing direction to the relationships between the players. Therefore, there are four basic dimensions in the study of the state: (a) the nature and competing interests of stakeholders, which (b) affects the structure of the state, which (c) in turn determines the capacity of the state, and (d) defines its role. This order could be reversed, creating a cyclical rather than a four-tiered structure. To structure this in reverse, a state's role could conversely have an impact on its capacity, influence its structure and affect the links between the stakeholders.

This basically means that the strength of a state, or what distinguishes a strong state from a weak one, is not just its capacity to complete certain tasks, but its ability to regulate relationships that can help it achieve the set of specified objectives.[7] The state thus moves beyond Tilly's conception of a supra-entity that exercises dominance over other competing institutions such as the family, community, tribe and the market.[8]

It is equally important to look at the power game that is played to control the state. Competition between the various actors and their interests lies at the heart of the state–society relationship. It is this competition that shapes politics.[9] Although there is no perfect formula for all players to get the share they deserve or desire, it is vital to have a political environment that allows the possibility of competition. A pluralist political system provides greater opportunity for the state to co-opt people rather than coerce them to support the official policy perspective. Moreover, the pluralist political structure strengthens the larger civil society to negotiate its rights with the state. Some authors see a state's stability in the context of its ability to dominate civil society.[10] However, in this study, state stability and control, which was the focus of a number of authors on Latin America like Guillermo O'Donnell and Juan Linz,[11] is not the key determinant of the strong state. Rather, it is the state's ability to allow multiple actors to play, and provide a relatively level playing field for the purpose, that ensures the development of a state–society relationship based more on consent than coercion. It must be remembered that states use both coercion and consent to fulfil their functions.

Therefore, the present framework is centred around political pluralism as a primary feature of state–society relations and for evaluating the strength of the state. Established and institutionalized democracy is viewed as a basic method of expression of pluralism and for accommodating multiple interests. Furthermore, electoral democracy as an established norm is the basic minimum prerequisite. These preconditions automatically exclude democracies in transition and states where the military manipulates politics from the back seat from being seen as strong states. Electoral democracy is primarily viewed as a tool or an indicator of a political culture that supports pluralism. It must also be noted that pluralism and democracy are not used in a normative sense. These concepts are essential for an environment where multiple actors can negotiate and renegotiate both political and economic space. The environment is geared not to allow the military or any other player to permanently suppress any 'competitive claimants'.[12]

Nor does pluralism undermine sensitivity to the quality of power relationships in a state, since the model takes social cleavages into account. While the framework recognizes the primacy of the state as an instrument of policy and for delivering certain goods to civil society, such as security and development, it does not support turning the state into an instrument of class domination or the supremacy of a particular group. In short, the framework of defining a strong state makes use of the state-corporatist concept of 'enforced limited pluralism'[13] or 'inclusionary' corporate autonomy.[14] This allows for a strong state from a functional standpoint as well as admitting multiple players or power centres.

Political pluralism as expressed by democratic political rule is essential for two reasons. First, politically, it serves as a security valve against a military takeover of the state and society, or the domination of a strong group or clique. Since the military is a country's primary organized institution trained in the management of violence,[15] it has greater capacity to exercise coercion, and the organizational capacity to dominate civilian institutions.[16] Having the capacity to coerce people, the armed forces have a natural edge over other players to dominate the state and society, especially in a non-democratic environment. The military are key players in policy making in all parts of the world. The national security agenda makes it imperative for the political society and policy makers to bestow a special status on the armed forces and their personnel. However, if unchecked the military can dominate all other stakeholders through their sheer organizational strength and power. In fact, the military can become the state itself, as will be shown in the case study of Pakistan. A strong state, on the other hand, is known for treating its armed forces as one of many players, and as an instrument of policy that can be used both internally and externally.

A democratically strong state is at the core of this theoretical model. As we move away from this fulcrum, the strength of the state gradually diminishes, and the weakening political structures may be dominated by political parties, individuals, military regimes or warlords. The peculiar nature of civil–military relations eventually determines the extent to which a military will exploit national resources.

A TYPOLOGY OF CIVIL–MILITARY RELATIONS

There are six identifiable typologies of civil–military relations:

- civil–military partnership
- authoritarian-political-bureaucratic partnership
- ruler military domination
- arbitrator military domination
- parent-guardian military domination
- warlord domination.

Since the relative power of the political system establishes the strength of the state, which in turn determines the military's capacity to penetrate the political, social and economic realm, each typology is distinguished by the political and economic system, nature of the civil society, and the level of military's penetration into the polity, society and economy (see Table 1.1).

In the first type, the military is subservient to civilian authorities. This is due to the strength of the civil institutions and civil society. The system is known for its free market economy, which allows the military to gain advantages through partnership with the dominant political and economic players rather than to operate independently. The armed forces are distinguished by their professionalism, which includes subservience to the civilian authorities.

The military of the second category is similar in terms of its dependence on civilian authorities. However, the armed forces draw their power

Table 1.1 Civil-military relations: the six typologies

	Civil–military partnership	Authoritarian political party–military partnership
Political system	Democracy	Party control
Civil society	Assertive	Controlled
Control of military	Civil government	Political party
Control of military: historical perspective	Civil	Political party
Military character	Professional	Professional
Military key role	External threat	External threat
Secondary roles	PK, ND, ACA	PK, ND, ACA
Political legitimacy	Nil	Nil
Military's political influence	Subordinate	Subordinate
Military's political intervention	Nil	Nil
Military rule	Nil	Nil
Military's control of state and society	Nil	Nil
Economic system	Free market capitalism	Controlled economy
Military in economy	Subordinate	Subordinate

Key: PK: Peacekeeping, ND: Assistance in natural disasters, ACA: Assistance to civilian authorities in domestic emergencies, PC: Political control, PF: Policing functions from the dominant political party, individual leader/s, or the ruling dispensation. Despite the fact that the economy is not structured on a free-market principle, the military does not operate on its own but benefits from its association with the party/leader. The armed forces are primarily professional except that they have a relatively greater role in internal security and governance.

The next three categories show different forms of military domination. This is because of the praetorian nature of the societies and the historical significance of the armed forces in power politics. The secondary roles of

Ruler military	Arbitrator military	Parent-guardian military	Warlord type
Military rule	Military/civil authoritarianism	Military's constitutional control	Warlord/group leaders
Weak	Fragmented	Fragmented	Weak
Military	Military	Military	Warlords
Military	Military	Military	Military/civil
Neo-professional	Neo-professional	Neo-professional	Non-professional
Internal threat	Internal threat	Internal threat	Self-protection
PK, ND, ACA, PC, PF	PK, ND, ACA, PC, PF	PK, ND, ACA, PC, PF	ND, PC, PF
Alternative institution	Political arbitrator	Permanent arbitrator	Plunderer
Primary	Dominant	Primary	Partner
Yes	Yes	Yes	Yes
Yes	Periodic	Permanent	Partner
Complete	Dominant	Military hegemony	Partner of the war lord
Pre-capitalist	Pre-capitalist	Pre-capitalist	Anarchic
Dominant	Dominant	Dominant	Dominant

such militaries include policing functions and political control. The key difference between the three types is in what has been defined here as the military's stated political legitimacy.

The term 'legitimacy' does not refer to civil society's acceptance of the military's role, but to the mechanism through which the military justifies its political influence. So while the ruler-type military presents itself as an alternative institution that has to control the state, the arbitrator type rationalizes its dominant role as a political and social arbitrator that steps into governance to correct the imbalance created by the political leadership. The parent-guardian type, on the other hand, uses constitutional mechanisms to consolidate its presence as a permanent arbitrator. The permanent role of an arbitrator is meant to secure the state from any internal or external threats posed by outside enemies or domestic actors who might weaken the state through their indiscretion. The warlord type, which is the final category, presents an extreme case of an anarchic society, where the military loots and plunders in partnership with dominant civilian players.

A strong political system or political party control will force the military to take a subservient role. In such cases the role of the armed forces will be defined by the civilian leadership and primarily limited to external security. The role is significant because it determines the level of the military's penetration into the state and society. Internal security roles tend to increase the military's involvement in state and societal affairs. The armed forces' overall penetration, on the other hand, influences the political capacity of the state. In a nutshell, the typologies summarize all the possible interactions between a state and society and its armed forces. (See Table 1.2 for an overview of the comparative types.)

THE CIVIL–MILITARY PARTNERSHIP TYPE

This type is found mostly in stable democracies known for a strong and vibrant civil society and sturdy civilian institutions. The political environment is known for firm civilian control of the armed forces. Historically, the militaries are subservient to the civilian government and are considered as one of the many players vying for their share of resources. The militaries customarily do not challenge civilian authority because of their sense of professionalism and restricted scope to do so. Hence, the armed forces are professional in the true Huntingtonian sense: a strong corporate culture and submission to civilian authorities. This kind of professionalism is inherently different from the 'new professionalism' of praetorian militaries in Latin America, South-East Asia and other regions.

The primary role of militaries in this category is fighting external threats. The armed forces get involved in internal security duties as well, but that is mainly at the behest of the civilian authorities or under their firm political guidance. The military's sense of professionalism and restriction to an external security role can be attributed to the strong civil society and democratic institutions such as the media, judiciary, human rights organizations, election commissions, political parties and government audit institutions. The media

Table 1.2 Types of civil–military relations

		Civil society		
		Partner	**Dominant**	**Hegemonic**
M I L I T A R Y	Civil–military partnership	USA, France, UK, South Africa, India, Brazil, Israel		
	Political party–authoritarian military partnership	China, Iran, Cuba, Sri Lanka		
	Ruler military		Chile, Haiti, Burma, Argentina	
	Arbitrator military		Pakistan (pre-1977), Turkey (pre-1961), Indonesia, Thailand, Vietnam, Cambodia, Bangladesh	
	Parent-guardian military			Pakistan (post-1977), Turkey (post-1961), Indonesia (post-1966)
	Warlord		Nigeria, Ethiopia, Sierra Leone, Angola, Somalia, Sudan	

in particular are quite strong, which makes it imperative for the armed forces to operate in their well-defined area of operations.

Broadly speaking, the political system in the countries that fall in this category can be termed as state-corporatist in structure, in which interests are represented 'through vertical functional organization of officially sanctioned forms of association'.[17] The state is capable of imposing its will on society as well as allowing for negotiation between multiple stakeholders for control. Consequently, political agendas emerge through a consensus between the players, with each one being able to negotiate its share without fear of the military's domination. This, however, does not necessarily suggest an ideal form of democracy. In fact, there is a variation in the quality of democracy. As well as the United Kingdom, the United States, Germany and France, states such as India, South Africa and Brazil fall in this category.

These other states have a different political history, culture and traditions, and the evolution of the state and society has not followed the same trajectory as in the western countries. India, for instance, is termed as a political culture bordering on praetorianism.[18] Bitter periods of political repression, such as during Indira Gandhi's government in the 1970s, reflect its latent authoritarian tendencies. However, despite this bad patch and the existing authoritarian nature of Indian politics, the military in India has been kept under firm civilian control. The armed forces are viewed essentially as an instrument of policy. Such a character of civil–military relations was deliberately built into the political design of the Indian state, and its civilian leadership has jealously guarded its control of the armed forces. India's first prime minister, Jawaharlal Nehru, ensured the military's subservience to the political leadership and the civilian bureaucracy through encouraging a particular kind of a defence-administrative culture.[19] Over the years, the military adapted to the civilian domination of the state and defence policy making, and never ventured to challenge the supremacy of the civilian leadership.

Similarly, South Africa has a democratic culture distinguished by control of the armed forces. Although the country is known for its history of apartheid, a liberal political culture and professionalism in the armed forces were created through reforms of the security sector. The restructuring was meant to introduce a culture where the military would not dominate the political discourse and governance.

These countries have over the years moved towards a civil–military partnership in politico-military terms and/or in the economic sphere. In the first instance, the military has become more than just an instrument of policy, and has gained greater significance in the country's politics and policy making because of the evolution in its role. The greater role in countering internal threats has resulted in a partnership between the civil and military in a number of countries such as the United States, France, the United Kingdom, Israel and India.

The Israeli military's role in fighting the Arab *intifada* brought substantive changes in civil–military relations, making the armed forces much more significant for the state than in the past.[20] The new role also means that the military cannot be overruled in the same fashion as was envisaged by earlier Israeli leaders such as David Ben-Gurion. Similarly, the change in the nature of threat after 9/11 altered the relationship between the military and the civilian authorities in the United States. The changed role meant an increase in the defence establishment's role in governance. The CIA, FBI and other agencies play powerful roles and often deal with more than internal security. From a planning perspective, a closer link between the home, foreign and defence departments, which often happens with a rise in internal threat resulting in a greater internal security role for the armed forces, almost always leads to a stronger civil–military partnership. The military becomes a more important member of the policy-making power coalition.

In the United States, the changing of the state's role – the public sector was downsized after the end of the cold war – transformed the role of the armed forces as well. The relative strengthening of the armed forces led to a greater involvement of serving and retired military personnel in decision making. The US-Israeli civil–military relations model, which is also found in other countries in this category, is not confrontational but brokers a partnership approach. This does not mean that the military is not controlled by the civilian authorities or is involved in politics. However, the greater role in internal security increases the military's influence in decision making and governance.

The civil–military partnership has in fact both a politico-military and an economic dimension. While a closer linkage between the civilian decision makers and military authorities is established through changes in the military's role which lead it to focus more on internal security, a partnership is formulated in developed economies for reasons of profit making as well. This economy also falls into the category of Milbus. The private military enterprises (PMEs) and private security businesses in the United States, the United Kingdom, France and South Africa are some of the examples of economic benefits accruing to the civilian-corporate sector and the military from a partnership. Established mainly during the 1990s, the PME businesses employed retired military personnel for security duties in countries like Bosnia, Rwanda, Croatia, Somalia, Sierra Leone and Iraq.

This type of partnership allowed the military organizations in these countries to use the PMEs for furthering geopolitical interests, much more conveniently than by acting directly. In most cases, the private security contractors can undertake tasks that governments or militaries would not risk for political or other reasons. The organizational and human resource capacity of the military fraternity, made available after 'rightsizing' (or downsizing) of the security sector, was viewed as a potential that could be employed effectively rather than wasted. Numerous PMEs such as Halliburton, MPRI, Kellogg, Brown & Root and DynCorps benefited from the ongoing Iraq war The war created opportunities for a variety of stakeholders from the private sector, political society and the armed forces. The private sector benefits were clearly financial. The PMEs did not have to invest resources in training people, since retired military personnel brought priceless training with them.

The politicians reaped both political and financial dividends. Most of the top hundred companies benefiting from defence contracts had also contributed to the election campaigns of top lawmakers, especially members of the US House and Senate Defense Appropriations Subcommittees.[21] The civil–military collaboration provided lucrative post-retirement job opportunities for military personnel. The 'beltway' jobs (jobs outside

Washington, DC, and in various areas of activity) in the United States have led to 'double-dipping', or in some cases 'triple-dipping', by security personnel. These terms refer to military personnel having two to three sources of income other than the pension they get after retirement.

The existing literature has not analysed the real cost of this three-way collaboration. There are definite financial costs for the government, in terms of resources wasted on training personnel who leave the military and join the PMEs. Moreover, the PMEs carry out tasks at a higher price. Government accountants would argue that privatization of security has long-term financial and diplomatic advantages, as it actually reduces the cost of maintenance and also saves regimes from political embarrassment at the return of body bags. However, this leads to an increased lack of transparency and risk of corruption. There is the threat of potential profiteers pursuing policies that benefit them in the long run.

There were numerous references to questionable decision making during the Iraq war. For instance, out of the US$4.3 billion worth of contracts won by Halliburton during 2003, only half were based on competitive bidding.[22] According to a 2004 Department of Defense (DoD) report, 'these were not cases of dollars themselves being routed to the wrong company, but rather of the Pentagon misreporting of where the money went in its procurement database'.[23] Another report highlighted the fact that a private contractor, MPRI, wrote the Pentagon rules for contractors on the battlefield and performed intelligence work in the battlefield. MPRI's ability to undertake such tasks raises serious concerns about the standards of management, and the impact of this collaboration on the overall integrity of the government and the defence establishment.[24]

The PME business creates an incentive for a more militaristic perspective to policy making, particularly in the upper echelons of the armed forces where the bulk of the economic dividends are concentrated. A militarily aggressive policy, either domestically or geopolitically, will increase the significance of the armed forces, and increase the state's dependence on the institution. The officer cadre in a capitalist economy, unlike in a pre-capitalist politico-economic structure, vies for greater share in capital formation rather than in accumulating assets. This does not make this kind of Milbus benign. If it is not controlled and monitored properly, this type of Milbus can impact the functioning of the state and the future of democratic institutions. Those benefiting from a partnership would, for instance, propagate a more authoritarian political structure where questionable decisions cannot be challenged by civil society. The threat to democratic and civil society institutions posed by this kind of Milbus is comparable to the threat from the military-industrial complex in the United States that President Dwight D. Eisenhower warned his nation against in 1961. In his famous farewell speech to the nation, the US President warned his people against the 'unwarranted influence' of this burgeoning sector.[25]

In this typology, it is the existence of democratic norms that stops the military's influence from penetrating all segments of the economy, polity and society.

THE AUTHORITARIAN-POLITICAL-MILITARY PARTNERSHIP TYPE

This type is found mostly in communist states or countries with authoritarian political party control. Power is concentrated in a single party, or in an individual or group of people who dominate the political system. Some of the representative cases in this category are China, North Korea, Cuba, Syria, Egypt, Iraq, Russia, Sri Lanka and post-Islamic revolution Iran. Contrary to Amos Perlmutter's classification of Cuba as a military regime of the army-party type, Cuba has been bracketed here with Syria, Iraq and Egypt as cases of a political-party–military partnership.[26] This is because the military in Cuba is subservient to Fidel Castro and his family.

As in a civil–military partnership, the second type represents a military that is basically an instrument of policy used by the key political party or individual leader controlling the state. This is not to suggest that the political structure is similar to the one found in democratic states. The political system is less pluralist, and the civil society is restricted and dominated by the ruling political dispensation. In this type, the military plays a crucial and a far more significant role to enforce the policies of the top leadership. However, the political legitimacy rests primarily with the political party or a charismatic leader. Individual rulers, such as Cuba's Fidel Castro or Egypt's Gamal Abdel Nasser, benefit from keeping the military to play second fiddle to them. Nasser, for instance, created alternative civilian institutions to counter the military, which he otherwise depended upon to ensure his political survival.[27] Conscious of the organizational power of the armed forces, the political parties or individual leaders do not risk giving the military greater authority.

The political party is a forum for societal consensus. The strength of the political system lies in the power of the political party or the ruling civilian elite, which does not permit the armed forces to take control. In this respect, the political party or ruling dispensation substitutes for the strong civil society that is found in the first category. The military or paramilitary forces are used as instruments to back the sociopolitical agenda of the ruling party and ensure the stability of the state. In most cases, the military's significance in policy making is recognized primarily in its role in state formation or securing the integrity of the country.

The political–military partnership is based on the symbiotic relationship between the centralized political party and the armed forces. The latter draws strength from the party as well as giving strength to it. This is because, as in China's case (between 1920 and 1980), the revolutionary military that spread out in the regions, operating at a regional level, provided support to the Communist Party. In doing so, however, the armed forces also consolidated their political position in the regions.[28] The Communist Party and the military supported each other and vied for a greater share in a cooperative framework. The military, in a Communist Party system, is viewed as: 'Janus-faced. It is the guarantor of the civilian party regime and protector of party hegemony.'[29] This makes a case for cooperation rather than confrontation.

41

The militaries in this category are trained to be professional. The professionalism includes subordination to the civilian authorities. However, it must be noted that most countries in this category have revolutionary-turned-professional armed forces. The one exception is Sri Lanka, where a ceremonial military evolved into an agent of state coercion, exhibiting the praetorian tendencies of the ruling ethnic group, the Sinhalese. Over the years, the Sri Lankan military was responsible for killing thousands of Sinhalese and Tamils. It butchered 60,000 youths in the insurrection in the island's south in 1977 alone.[30]

Such militaries are generally known for greater involvement in internal security. There is a thin line between the military, paramilitary forces and the police force. Therefore, the militaries of this category act as a tool of coercion for the ruling party. It must be reiterated that the coercion is carried out at the behest of the ruling party/leader. So, while the military has a lot of influence, as in China, Sri Lanka, Syria and Iraq, the armed forces remain subordinate to the political leaders or parties. Governance in particular remains the forte of the political party or individual leadership. Civil society institutions are relatively weak, except for the key political party or group. The political party/leader acts not only as a forum, but also as a controller of all political discourse.

From a Milbus perspective, these militaries have a deep penetration into the economy. The defence establishment's logic for establishing an internal economy is not to accumulate assets but to generate capital for personal and organizational benefit, in partnership with the ruling party. One of the reasons for the military's involvement in the economy directly relates to the origins of the organization. As a result of its involvement in state/nation building, such militaries are expected to play a larger role in governance than the earlier category. The organization's role in socioeconomic development allows it a role in the economy. This is certainly true of countries such as China, Syria, Cuba and Iran. The armed forces are used systematically to help the ruling party govern the state. This includes participating in running the economy.

The military is often engaged in profit making to bridge the financial resource gap in the defence sector. In these states the governments do not have the capacity to provide for the armed forces, or face a shortage of funds to foot the total bill for the defence sector, so the secondary role of the armed forces is significant. As an instrument of the political party, the military also undertakes development work, contributing to the state's resources. The party remains central to political and economic exploitation. The power of the political party presents the possibility of divesting the military of its internal economic mechanisms, as is evident from the Chinese case. In 1998, Beijing removed financial stakes held by its armed forces in order to professionalize a 'people's army'.[31] The official order, however, did not automatically lead to a complete divestiture. The top echelon of the officer cadre was reluctant to close shop because of its personal financial interests. Thus, as pointed out by Frank O. Mora, the Chinese PLA continued to have an influence on the economy despite the emphasis on

42

reorganization.[32] The development of a symbiotic relationship between the military and the leadership at the top of the political party structure presented the military with the opportunity to negotiate concessions for itself, and dissuade the political leadership from punishing the armed forces for 'shirking'.[33]

The party leadership may also be unwilling to demand a professional cleansing of the armed forces because the political and military leadership have shared interests. Being direct beneficiaries of the economic redistribution, senior commanders of the armed forces are reluctant to enforce a complete turnaround. The reluctance to contain the military's activities, as suggested by James Mulvenon, is a deliberate design. The Chinese armed forces were taken out of the service sector but not stopped from playing a role in manufacturing industry.[34]

An authoritarian political system is geared to redistribute resources among its own members and its allies.[35] In Iran's case, kleptocratic redistribution became sharper after the Islamic revolution as a result of the involvement of vital political players such as the former president, Hashmi Rafsanjani. This influential leader provided patronage to the Hezbollah militia to exploit resources and feed religious charities (*bonyads*).[36] Equally noticeable is the joint exploitation of national resources by the dictator Fidel Castro's family and the armed forces in Cuba.[37] The Iranian Hezbollah, Cuban Army, and even the Chinese PLA represent instruments of power, coercion and extraction. There is a symbiotic relationship between authoritarian regimes and auxiliary agencies like the military or paramilitary, which is often used for political suppression, securing continuity of the regime and extracting resources.[38]

Some militaries act independently of the political party structure in looting resources. However, these are instances of individual rather than institutional involvement, such as in post-1991 Russia. The restructuring of the Soviet Union and lack of sufficient funds led desperate soldiers to engage in looting and plunder. The financial autonomy of the defence establishment can be minimized through an increase in financing and oversight.

THE RULER MILITARY TYPE

A ruler military refers to the type that considers itself as an alternative to civilian institutions and installs itself in direct power permanently. The defence establishment views itself as key to the security and integrity of the state, state building and socioeconomic development. This self-acquired role allows the armed forces to impose totalitarian control on the state and launch themselves into politics without any promise of a return to democracy. However, because of its totalitarian nature this type of military is normally challenged by civil society, especially when the armed forces engage in systematic and prolonged human rights violations.

The primary difference between this and the other two typologies of military domination is the control of politics. Politically, it is different from the other two types because this type of military tends to acquire long-term and direct political control. The prolonged direct rule exhausts any element of moral legitimacy that the military has, resulting in resistance from civil society. The military's civilian partners can be among those who tend to rebel. The resultant political chaos results in greater human rights violations, and this further increases the chasm between the military and the wider society. This is where this type differs from the other two military types. The arbitrator, for instance, does not remain in direct control for long. The parent-guardian creates constitutional provisions for indirect political control. In this respect, the ruler type is totalitarian in character (see Table 1.3).

The typology of military rule draws upon Perlmutter's classification of praetorian militaries into rulers and arbitrators. A ruler military has a propensity to remain in power. The nature of civil–military relations is inherently different from the other two types of military rule because the armed forces in this category are averse to transferring power to the civilian leadership, and fully acquire control of the state and governance. This model includes Latin American states during the 1970s and the 1980s such as Chile, Argentina, Ecuador, Nicaragua, Peru and Haiti, and others that experienced prolonged military rule. The list also includes modern-day Myanmar, where the military continues to be in direct control.

One of the main reasons for prolonged direct rule is the weak nature of civil society. However, since the ruler type lacks political legitimacy, it can be pushed out of politics and governance through a combination of external and internal pressure. The return of democracy to Chile, Argentina and other Latin American countries is a case in point. The years of military coercion in the form of human rights violations drew reactions from the civil society, which managed to organize itself with financial, moral and political support from outside.

The ruler military is not professional or trained to deal with external threats. Despite tension at the borders and ongoing military conflicts, there is no major external threat to the survival of the state. The militaries relish in large budgetary allocations and enjoy significance because of their role as guarantors of national security. However, the emphasis on internal threat allows for a greater emphasis on internal security and the military's link with domestic politics. The internal security role also exposes the military more to political stakeholders, and makes the institution sensitive to political ills.

The literature on bureaucratic authoritarianism in Latin America sheds ample light on the rise of militaries to power. The ruler militaries are inherently revolutionary armed forces that lack a professional ethos in terms of their organizational capabilities and subjecting themselves to civilian control. Huntingtonian professionalism is not the ethos of these defence establishments. Such militaries gravitate toward politics as a result of the lack of a political consensus and unity in these countries. The lack of an elite consensus keeps the militaries in power. The military sees itself as an alternative institution capable of modernizing the society and forcing it to conform through coercion. In most of these postcolonial states there are few

Table 1.3 The three military types

		Civil society		
		Totalitarian	**Partner***	**Hegemonic****
M I L I T A R Y	Ruler type	Myanmar, Chile, Nicaragua, Haiti, Argentina, Peru, Sierra Leone		
	Arbitrator type		Pakistan (until 1977), Turkey (until 1961), Indonesia (until 1966), Bangladesh	
	Parent-guardian type			Pakistan (post -1977), Turkey (post-1961), Indonesia (post-1966).

*   In this type, the military does not exercise direct control permanently. In fact, it controls through building partnerships with civilian players.

**   Hegemonic relates to subtle but complete control of the society, politics and the economy. These militaries establish pervasive control of the state and the society through political as well as constitutional and legal measures.

people or groups of people who have an exposure to the foreign/western concept of modernity.

Military rule takes three forms: personal, oligarchic and corporatist.[39] These subgroups signify various degrees of civil–military relations. They also indicate the extent to which the military leadership relies on partners among civilian bureaucrats, technocrats or the political leadership for governance. The civilian partners, however, remain subservient to and dependent on the armed forces. In addition, these three categories are critical in understanding the nature of kleptocratic distribution in states ruled by a ruler-type military.

The first subtype includes Idi Amin's Uganda, General Somoza's Nicaragua and Francois Duvalier's Haiti. The political system is dominated by the dictator/despot who distributes restrictively among his sycophants.[40] This style of rule, however, creates dissension within the military. Nevertheless, the military acts as a key player in power sharing. The organization's support is crucial for the dictator, who uses coercion within the defence establishment as well as the society to expand his political support base.

Peru, Chile, Ecuador and Myanmar fall into the second subgroup, the oligarchic type. The ruling class relies on the support of an otherwise autonomous military institution. The dependence is also structural, with greater use of the military institution for governance and for political partnership. The ruler-oligarchic type tends not to go into a partnership with a political party. The group of officers consider themselves capable of governing without civil-political stakeholders, whom the military replaces.[41] In a post-colonial paradigm, the military views itself as an alternative institution with the capacity to build and modernize the state. In doing so, however, it alienates other players; so it becomes like the colonial state itself, which, according to political analyst Kalevi J. Holsti, did not hold the intention of building a state.[42]

Finally, the corporatist design refers to the institutional involvement of the military in politics and governance. It is also marked by an inverted military–civil partnership: the military acts as a principal rather than an agent of civilian leaders. The civil and political societies are transformed into an instrument of modernization directed by the armed forces. Quintessential states following this pattern are Brazil and Argentina. While the military becomes the patron and remains the locus, it inducts other institutions and partners in policy making and modernizing the state. For instance, the technocrats are included in the power alliance to manage the state through a highly centralized control system which curbs political growth.[43] The highly bureaucratic-authoritarian system builds a tactical relationship with other players. The idea is to get 'technical' support for governance and the implementation of policies.[44]

As mentioned earlier, the distribution of resources under the ruler military type is highly kleptocratic. The key beneficiaries are the military and its cronies. In fact, there is greater rank-and-file military involvement in the exploitation of resources. Since the military considers itself as the primary institution for state building, the security and integrity of the state, and societal modernization, it dominates resource distribution. However, this has high costs as well. The ruler military type creates conditions that are best explained using Mancur Olson's roving bandit metaphor.[45] This refers to authoritarianism creating socioeconomic anarchy. Roving banditry, as opposed to stationary banditry, increases transaction costs and reduces the productivity of an economy. Although all military-authoritarian rules have high cost, the ruler type is most expensive because of the damage it does to politics and civil society. The anarchy is not only caused by kleptocratic distribution (this kind of redistributive system can be found in the other two military types as well), but is also a manifestation of the violence and socio-political chaos caused by the armed forces. Myanmar, for instance, is one of the obvious cases of a military generating a high cost for the economy, the politics and society.

Economically, Myanmar suffered because of the direct involvement of military officers in looting, illegal possession of private property and opium smuggling. Minimizing or curbing such activities becomes an arduous task mainly because, as Mary Callahan puts it:

> States that pursue coercion-intensive, military solutions to internal security and political crisis will likely see their military take on a range of functions – law enforcement, economic regulation, tax collection, census taking, magazine publishing, political party registration, food aid distribution, and so on – that have little to do with traditional defence responsibilities.[46]

Such unfortunate conditions create economic anarchy and transform the socio-political and socioeconomic environment into an unfriendly atmosphere for the general public. In Myanmar's case, the military's totalitarian behaviour even forced capable people into exile.

Some of the larger economic costs of kleptocratic redistribution come from the creation of unhealthy monopolies. Personalized and oligarchic rules in particular tend to breed monopolies. The ruler military tends to distribute resources to the armed forces and its cronies. The number of beneficiaries increases with the subtype. The corporate model, for instance, redistributes comparatively more because of its alignment with other groups. Brazil is a key example of the distribution of resources to the military and a group of technocrats and businessmen who were put in charge of economic planning.[47]

Contrary to the view that militaries in developing states are modernizers,[48] the benefits of the military's involvement in politics and the economy are much lower than the costs. Studying the impact of military rule in Latin America, Jerry Weaver goes a long way to challenge the notion that military rule benefits the middle class.[49]

THE ARBITRATOR MILITARY TYPE

This military type, which is derived from Perlmutter's classification, is known for acquiring direct political control periodically but shirks from prolonging its rule. Hence, this type has a propensity to return to barracks soon after it appears to have solved the problem it came to fix by taking control of the government. The arbitrator type has a proclivity to act as a back-seat driver. It tends to remain in the back seat until it is forced by circumstances to intervene directly. The decision to intervene, however, is based on the organization's own assessment of the situation.

Arbitrator militaries view themselves essentially as a balancer of power between the various competing political forces. They draw the moral legitimacy to intervene from their self-acquired role of providing stability and bringing progress to the nation. Suspicious of the capacity of political players to protect the state, internally and externally, such militaries acquire a watchdog role to stop the corruption of civilian actors.[50] In doing so, they also create the logic for their periodic intervention.

The military's role as an arbitrator is also a result of the peculiar nature of the society. In a praetorian society, where politics is 'formless' and ridden with factionalism, the military get an opportunity to step in occasionally as a substitute for social forces that do not exist.[51] Some examples in this category are Indonesia (pre-1966), Pakistan (pre-1977), Turkey (pre-1961), South Korea, Thailand, Cambodia, Vietnam and Bangladesh.

Why does the military not prolong its rule? Is the temporary intervention an indicator of the strength of the civil society? In some cases like Bangladesh the military is kept out of prolonged direct rule because of the relative strength of the society. The civil society's ability to agitate vociferously against a totalitarian dispensation forced the Bangladeshi military out from governance and direct rule. However, such societies are not strong enough to reduce the armed forces' role as an arbitrator. The society is considerably fragmented, and this is detrimental to the strengthening of pluralism in the state.

Perlmutter provides a host of explanations for the military not prolonging its direct rule. The military might remain in the back seat because of:

- acceptance of the existing social order
- willingness to return to the barracks
- the military's lack of an independent political organization
- the concept of a time limit for army rule
- the military's character as a pressure group
- a low level of national consciousness
- fear of civilian retribution
- concern for professionalism.[52]

The author's third point regarding the military's lack of an independent political organization is very important. Since the military is trained to be a professional force to deal with external threats, it does not have the political legitimacy to continue in power. The realization of its lack of political legitimacy keeps the military in the background, although in an influential position. So despite the moral legitimacy to intervene periodically, the military cannot continue in power for long. The civil society is fragmented but not sufficiently weak to allow for prolonged totalitarian control by the armed forces. The inability of the armed forces to prolong its rule as a result of resistance from the civil society is clear from the case of Bangladesh.

In some cases, such as pre-1961 Turkey and pre-1977 Pakistan, the defence establishments were not fully prepared to introduce long-term direct rule or build alternative mechanisms such as constitutional arrangements for perpetuating their influence. The military's political intervention in Pakistan, for instance, started with General Ayub Khan (1958–69), who was followed by General Yahya Khan (1969–71). The Ayub Khan regime in particular depended on the civilian bureaucracy because it did not have sufficient experience in ruling the country. Moreover, after they lost the war with India it was impossible for the armed forces not to transfer power to the elected civilian leadership. The subsequent regimes of General Zia ul

Haq (1977–88) and General Pervez Musharraf (1999 to date) were more prepared to seek extraordinary arrangements to prolong the military's participation in governance.

As mentioned earlier, the arbitrator military is different from the rule type because of its greater sense of professionalism. The tendency is to keep the rank and file out of politics and economic management. There are, however, two types of militaries that fall in this category. One is represented by the Indonesian military, and has greater rank and file involvement in governance and economic management. The other, exemplified by Turkey, Pakistan and Bangladesh, seeks political partnership for enhancing its influence. In the second case in particular, the armed forces use internal and external threats as the main reason for perpetuating their role in governance. In Kemalist Turkey, Ataturk legitimized the military's role in governance as a defender and protector of the constitution and the national integrity from the threat from outside, as well as the hazard of corrupt civilian rule. Hence, the military was also the guarantor of good governance and honest civilian rule.[53]

In most cases in this category, 'professionalism' refers to a new professionalism in which the role of the armed forces extends beyond fighting wars. This means a greater role in internal security and governance.[54] Thus, the armed forces in all these countries are involved with issues of political instability, meeting challenges to national ideology, or countering various sources of internal and external violence. The military regards itself as the guardian and guarantor of national security, extending beyond the simple definition of territorial security.

According to Perlmutter's definition, this type of military seeks civilian partners to whom it hands over power from time to time. The military merely projects itself as an arbitrator. This means returning to barracks as soon as the problem is solved. The officer cadre claims to aim to transfer power to an 'acceptable' civilian regime at the earliest opportunity to give semblance of democracy, but the military always operates as a 'behind-the-scenes' pressure group which establishes partnerships with political parties and other groups or associations.[55] This is another case of an inverted principal–agent relationship in which the military is generally in the driving seat. The military seeks out partners among civilians such as bureaucrats, technocrats, businessmen and religious and ethnic groups, so both parties can perpetuate the existing power relationship to their mutual benefit.

The military seeks civilian partners for both political and economic benefit. Indonesia is a typical example of an arbitrator military. The civilian and military leadership have an almost equal share in Milbus. Starting with Sukarno, and under Suharto and all subsequent political leaders, the military was granted a share in exploiting the national resources. The armed forces were in fact partners with the civilian leaders from the beginning of the Indonesian state, as a result of the military's role in fighting the Dutch forces during the War of Independence in 1945–9.[56] The tension between the revolutionary political set-up, the Partai Komunis Indonesia (PKI), and the armed forces of the Republic of Indonesia,

Angkatan Bersenjata Republic Indonesia (ABRI), compounded with the problem of weak democratic institutions, resulted in the military's repeated political intervention. The political anarchy established the military's non-military role, which was officially endorsed through three fundamental documents: the 1945 Constitution, the *Pancasila* (the state ideology), and the *Sapta Marga*, the code of honour of the ABRI which requires the army to defend the *Pancasila*.[57] Such legal provisions enhanced the military's role in politics and the economy.

The military's involvement in socioeconomic and political governance has a high cost, however, especially in terms of its professionalism. The expansion of the military's role in the economy deepens its influence in politics. As a result the armed forces begin to face problems in the performance of their core function of territorial security. The challenges the military faces as a result of the fusion of external and internal security roles were sharpened in the case of Indonesia, where the military predominantly played an internal security function.

The fundamental question is whether a political system that engenders the military's financial autonomy can strengthen the civil society to reduce the military's influence. Will an arbitrator military that has built economic interests remain an arbitrator for ever, taking over the reigns of government only at times of perceived crisis? The military's role can only be limited to arbitration in cases such as Bangladesh, where the government has systematically encouraged the armed forces to look at other options for their financial survival. One of the reasons for the Bangladeshi military's abstinence from taking over direct control lies in the source of the armed forces' financial autonomy. Dhaka's military depends on UN peacekeeping missions to earn financial benefits, and as a result it has remained out of power since 1990–1. The Bangladeshi armed forces depend on their good relations with the civilian government to seek greater opportunities of involvement in the peacekeeping missions. The Bangladeshi military's commercial ventures are also dependent on the earnings from the peacekeeping missions. Over the years, Dhaka's armed forces have built stakes in the hotel industry, in textile and jute manufacturing, and in education. Bangladeshi civil society is, perhaps naively, not alarmed by such developments. The political analysts see the commercial ventures as a tradition passed on by the pre-1971 Pakistan army. Furthermore, it is believed that the military would not risk losing its profit-making opportunities through the UN missions.[58] There is very little thought given to the possibility that the military might not be offered opportunities by the United Nations, in which case it might be forced to look at other options to gain financial advantage.

Despite their involvement in the UN peacekeeping missions, the militaries of Pakistan, Turkey and Indonesia engage in profit-making ventures. Their economic exploitation is a result of their political power. These three militaries have in fact been politically powerful since the early days of independence of their states, as a result of their involvement in politics. The financial autonomy of these armed forces is dependent on their political autonomy, and their political influence is likely to grow undeterred, or at least not be minimized, unless their authority is seriously challenged both internally and externally.

In analysing military intervention Perlmutter did not look at the armed forces' influence on the political economy, especially the financial interests of the officer cadre. Once a military is allowed to 'shirk', it tends to expand its role in politics and the economy. The term 'shirk' is drawn from Peter Feaver's work on civil–military relations in the United States, and refers to the military's refusal to obey the commands of civilian policy makers.[59] Weak political forces, unable to play the strong principal, find it increasingly difficult to avoid conceding greater political and economic space to the armed forces. The Pakistani, Turkish and Indonesian militaries, for example, gradually built political power to support their economic interests. Each successive military dictator learns from his predecessors how to maximize political influence to gain greater economic dividends. The militaries then find constitutional ways of perpetuating their control of the state and society. It is for this reason that these three cases have been put into a separate category, which is discussed in the next subsection.

THE PARENT-GUARDIAN MILITARY TYPE

As mentioned earlier, the three countries that qualify for this category are Pakistan, Turkey and Indonesia. These armed forces are known for institutionalizing their political power through constitutional/legal provisions. Such changes are brought about through the help of civilian partners that are dependent on the military for their survival. So while the rank and file is kept out of governance, a select group of top and middle-ranking officers continues to control the state in partnership with the other members of the larger military fraternity (see the Introduction for definition of this term).

The civilian partners play a crucial role in endorsing the political role of the armed forces. This can be done through simple parliamentary approval, as in the case of Indonesia, or through constitutional changes such as the establishment of a National Security Council (NSC), as in Turkey and Pakistan. It is important to note that the three cases in this category are of arbitrator militaries turned into the parent-guardian type. The key argument is that because of their growing economic interests, the armed forces tend to institutionalize their political power to secure their dominant position as part of the ruling elite. With constitutional/legal changes endorsing their extra-military role, the armed forces no longer remain just an instrument of policy, but become an equal partner, sharing power and national resources with other members of the ruling elite. In fact, the ruling elite tends to draw its power and influence from its partnership with the military.

The shift from one type to the other indicates a change in the thinking of the military regarding its placement in the political power hierarchy of a state. (This type of change, as mentioned earlier, is not documented or analysed by Perlumutter in his several works on civil–military relations.)

Henceforth, the military institutes itself as a permanent element in the country's power politics and governance. The institutionalizing of the military's power is considered necessary to protect the corporate interests of the armed forces, and is an indicator of the officer cadre's suspicion of the political players. Since the civil society and political actors cannot be trusted to protect the integrity of the state or ensure that the military's interests are safeguarded, it is vital for the defence establishment to create a permanent place for itself in politics, which transcends all political dispensations.

The civil society has to be made aware of the looming presence of its 'protector' in hindering any indiscretions. Militaries in this role are intellectually sharp in analysing the environment and formulating survival strategies accordingly. Since they do not intend to relinquish control of the state, such militaries hide their intentions by partnering with civilian players who are usually kept in the forefront. The civilian–military relationship is a patron–client type, which also serves the purpose of weakening any strong agitation against the military. The military's civilian clients thwart any move towards consolidated agitation against the military's domination. The adaptability of the organization is almost chameleon-like.

In Indonesia's case, a permanent institutionalized role was endorsed by the Provisional People's Congress, which recognized the dual function of security and political control of the armed forces in 1966. According to the official statement:

> The non-military function of the Indonesian Republican Armed Forces' members, as citizens and Pancasiliast revolutionaries to devote themselves in every field to fulfil 'the message of the people's suffering' and for the sake of the Revolution's resilience, must be acknowledged and continuance guaranteed.[60]

The military's political role was added to its security function as part of the concept of *dwifungsi*, or dual roles. The civilian partners, namely President Suharto and his cabal, who had ridden to power on the shoulders of the military, allowed the armed forces to dominate the civil bureaucracy as well as acquire control of the economy.[61]

The Turkish military, on the other hand, institutionalized its role through establishing the NSC, an organ of power numerically tilted in favour of the armed forces. Its composition – six officers and five civilians – gave a clear advantage to the armed forces, which had already penetrated the political system and had members in the civil bureaucracy and the parliament. (The issue, however, is not of numerical strength. The military members of the NSC in Pakistan are fewer in number – four military, nine civil – but have greater power, which can be attributed to the military's traditional control of power politics.) The Turkish military also possesses a huge presence in the society and the economy. Public surveys have been supportive of the armed forces, which is attributable to their popularity as well as their powers of coercion. For instance, it is illegal to criticize the military in Turkey or to discuss its budgetary or off-budgetary allocation.[62]

Similarly, Pakistan's military started to seek an independent institutionalized presence in politics after 1977. The regime of General Muhammad Zia ul Haq (1977–88) initiated the idea of a NSC, and one was finally established in April 2004 by General Pervez Musharraf (1999 to date). Unlike the first military regime of Generals Ayub and Yahya Khan (1958–71), the Zia government understood the significance of institutionalizing the military's role in politics and governance, and found a recipe for achieving this objective. One of the lessons that the military dictator Zia learnt from the past was the need to protect the military's interests. Despite rebuilding the military after an embarrassing defeat in a war with India, the civilian regime of Zulfiqar Ali Bhutto had relegated the armed forces to a subordinate position. The problem of the reduction of the military's power could only be tackled through institutionalizing the military's role in governance.

Having evolved from an arbitrator type, the parent-guardian military contains some of the characteristics of the former type, such as building partnership with technocrats, civil bureaucrats, businessmen and selected political players. These civilian partners render support to the military establishment, and in turn depend on it for their political survival and economic benefits. A military-sponsored system of patronage is one of the features of the armed forces' institutional-political power. An institution such as the NSC indicates the military's permanent position in the country's power politics. A realization of this power forces some civilian players to support the military, and vice versa.

The transformation of the military from an arbiter to a parent-guardian is a gradual process, which is attributable to the prolongation of a combination of the military's political and economic interests. The military justifies the institutionalizing of its power as a prerequisite for strengthening democracy. The inclusion of senior generals in decision making at the highest level of the government is meant to serve as a firewall against any irresponsible behaviour by the civilian leadership. In fact, the civilians (civil bureaucracy, political leadership or the indigenous bourgeoisie) misread the military's withdrawal to the barracks as the organization's willingness to transfer power. The civilians also misjudge the military's appetite for power, because they do not understand the connection between the armed forces' financial and political autonomy. It is generally believed that if they offer the military economic advantages, it an be bribed into a compliant partnership in which the generals allow a particular political dispensation to rule. It is often not realized that it is hazardous to bribe soldiers with greater economic, political and social advantages, exposing them to the vulnerabilities of the political leadership, as has happened in Pakistan's case. Exposed to the failings of the political class, 'soldiers' tend to become insecure about their benefits, leisure and income, all of which they associate with the survival of the state; hence the need for the military's intervention.[63] This perpetuates the military's interest in institutionalizing its control of the state and decision making.

The parent-guardian military is central to the process of redistribution of national resources. When the military is one of the dominant economic players, it tends to distribute resources among the members of its own fraternity. The military aims at institutionalizing both its political and economic control. The expansion of economic interests is undertaken through a complex network that binds together serving and retired military as well as certain civilians who benefit directly from the military-business complex. For instance, the Turkish military interventions of the 1960s and the 1980s were aimed at strengthening the oligarchic position of a coterie of senior generals, who had forged an alliance with the business elite as well.[64]

So an assessment of Milbus must include the value of the military's economic interests and those of its civilian partners. The parent-guardian type of military encourages crony capitalism. The behaviour of the corporate sector is influenced by the presence of the military, because the major civilian-corporate players depend on the armed forces' patronage for their survival and growth. The economic partners rarely confront the military on its share or extra-legal concessions, mainly because (as was reported in Turkey's case) of fear, or concern for rewards that the military could deny or ensure to them through its powerful position.[65]

The redistribution mechanism has a direct bearing on the structure of Milbus. The military's internal economy is operated through the organization, its subsidiaries and individual members. These are not different levels but three interconnected strands which support each other. The influence of the institution is used to build channels of opportunity for its members to explore and monopolize resources. This is different from establishing monopolies, as ruler militaries often tend to do.[66] Although Milbus could result in creating monopolies in some areas, the tendency is to monopolize resources along with other partners. Under a parent-guardian type of structure, individual members and subsidiary organizations play as crucial a role as the institution itself. Individuals work as drivers of the internal economy. While they benefit from the organization's influence, the individuals also work as a source for creating opportunities for the organization. Thus, an assessment of the net value of Milbus needs to include benefits distributed at all three levels: institutional, subsidiaries and individuals.

The net value of the internal economy is better hidden in this typology than in the two previous categories, mainly because of the limited involvement of the rank and file in economic ventures. The military institution acts as a patron that provides opportunities and financial capital to its members. The dividends of Milbus are highly concentrated at the top. Although some benefits are distributed to the soldiers, the bulk of the dividends are creamed off by the officer cadre. The peculiar structure of power and resource distribution can be found in all the three countries listed in this category.

The combined political and economic influence of the armed forces has a huge socio-political and economic cost. However, the military's influence cannot be reduced because of the fragmentation of civil society, especially the weak political parties. A major change can only be made possible through mass mobilization combined with pressure from outside the country.

THE WARLORD TYPE

Finally, the warlord type refers to a political system where the nation-state is on the verge of disintegration or has failed. The collapse of the state gives rise to the power of individual leaders or groups that use military force for political and economic exploitation. A number of African states like Ethiopia, Zaire, Mozambique, Liberia, Sierra Leone, Somalia and Rwanda, and Afghanistan are representative of this typology.

Such states represent a breakdown of centralized political control and are unable to deliver services to their people. Thus, the standards of service delivery and governance are extremely poor. The political system is highly clientist, in which the political, ethnic or group leaders offer patronage to groups of people, as in the feudal system prevalent in sixteenth and seventeenth-century Europe. Prominent political leaders depend on ethnic and clan politics for winning popularity and controlling national resources.[67] The warlords provide patronage to the group of people who submit to their authority. In a conflict between warlords, as happened in Ethiopia and Afghanistan, the warring parties try to deny basic services such as food and shelter to the rival warlord and the population aligned with him.

The warlord's power is dependent on military force, which might be either local or bought in from outside. The use of private military contractors hired from the West by some African warlords is an example of dependence on externally acquired military force.

The inability to reach an elite consensus makes warlordism a preferred method of exploitation. Sierra Leone is cited as an example of the deliberate destruction of the state by its leaders, who later turned themselves into warlords.[68] In such cases the power of the warlord determines the extent of the exploitation of resources. The warlords are driven by ethnic or religious rivalry, and aim at both capturing resources for themselves and their clients, and denying them to the rival group/s. There is, in fact, no concept of a unitary consolidated state interest. In cases such as Afghanistan, Ethiopia and Sierra Leone, the state is in fact unable to raise funds for its civil and military bureaucracy. Under these circumstances, the warlord plays a key role in projecting military power and using his military force to generate resources for those under his patronage.

The lack of resources does not allow the emergence of professional militaries, for the state to ensure the military's allegiance, or for military professionalism. The underpaid military is tempted to engage in looting resources personally or forming smaller associations to do so. Ruling regimes often hire gunpower from outside, as well for their own protection against rival groups or to exploit natural resources such as diamond and gold mines. Regimes tend to develop a dependency on foreign state and non-state allies, resulting in the 'crowding out' of state institutions.[69] The military and ex-combatants are tools for exploiting economic resources, as are hired armed men from other countries. The might of the warlord rests on mustering the military strength to create a monopoly over plunder in a specific area. The tools and forces of war are an essential component of the fragmented exploitation of resources. Militaries are instrumental in assisting the warlords in robbing the state of its resources. At times armed forces could take direct control, but instead they engage in a joint plundering of the state in partnership with a political leader who has the charisma and power to muster public support and following.

The militaries are ragtag, revolutionary and non-professional. These are combatants on the loose or under the command of a warlord, who engage in looting for survival.

While the warlord-type militaries and their personnel plunder the state for their gains, other armed forces use institutional methods to get a greater share of national resources. The militaries all over the world are one of the many institutions of a state vying for influence and a share of national resources. While some militaries are instruments of the state or the ruling dispensation, others dominate the state to a degree where the organization becomes synonymous with the state. Such differences in a country's political and military structure must be analysed to understand the fundamental nature of political and economic exploitation.

What the armed forces get in terms of national resources is directly proportional to the political influence they exercise. The civil–military relations in a particular state are therefore central to the larger issue of understanding the depth of a military's internal economy. The greater the defence establishment's influence, the lesser the transparency of its resources and the more ability it has to exploit resources compared with other players. It is important to understand the connection between civil–military relations and Milbus, or the link between the military's political influence and its ability to exploit resources for the personal gratification of the officer cadre.

The fundamental argument presented in this chapter is that despite the fact that all militaries tend to engage in profit-making ventures, the nature of the economic exploitation is related to the nature of the political system and environment. In states where the military is subservient to the political players, whether these are the civilian authority at large, a political party or an influential leader, the exploitation inside the state and the military's penetration into the society and economy is comparatively less deep and controllable. A pluralist political system tends to treat the armed forces as one of the important institutions vying for political control or share of resources. Moreover, in such a system the military is primarily an instrument of policy, used strategically by other dominant actors to draw political and economic dividends.

The pluralist tone of the political system, however, begins to fade in systems where the military become influential. Furthermore, as militaries establish political influence, they tend to penetrate the economy in a much more intense manner. The militaries then transform themselves into patrons responsible for, or playing a dominant role in, the distribution of resources. Although in the three military domination models of politics the armed forces take over governance or political control to ensure national integrity, their economic activities are not altruistic. The economic role is part is an outgrowth of their political influence. In fact, the picture of the military's political power is incomplete without an analysis of its ability to exploit resources. The generals tend to use the logic for the dominant role of the military as a guardian of the state to draw benefits for its members. Thus, there is an economic logic for the continued political power of the defence establishment.

The civilian authorities or political players tend to give less credence to the military's internal economy, as will be observed later through the case study on Pakistan, The financial stakes of the officer cadre are, at best, considered critical to the interests of the generals, but are not seen as something linked with the military's political ambitions. It is true that the military does not necessarily have to acquire power to allow the officer cadre profit-making opportunities. However, the prolongation of the military's power, or the deepening of its influence in decision making and governance, is bound to expose the officer cadre to the economic benefits of perpetuating its political influence. Therefore, the more the military's influence in politics, the greater are the economic advantages that accrue to the senior officers, and these in turn increase their interest in perpetuating the military's influence and political control.

The six civil–military relations typologies are also representative of different levels of economic exploitation by the armed forces. The first two types refer to cases where the military is used by other dominant players to gain economic advantages. In such cases, the military is instrumental in economic exploitation, but as a secondary player and not as a primary actor. In the later types, however, the military is a primary beneficiary. Furthermore, the armed forces play the role of a patron, providing political and economic benefits to their civilian clients or partners.

It has been argued that the military's financial and political autonomy are interconnected. While the organization's political influence may vary according to the nature of the political system, the military's financial autonomy plays a critical role in enhancing its desire to influence politics and policy making. From the standpoint of Milbus, it is important to understand the relationship between the political and financial autonomy of the armed forces. It must be understood that even in pluralist political environments the military will lobby for a greater share of resources by influencing policy making. Since the military is one of the key players vying for a greater share, it is bound to lobby for greater opportunities, as has happened in the United States, Israel and other more politically developed states.

In less pluralist political settings such as Pakistan, the case of which will be discussed at length in this study, the military's financial autonomy will increase an interest in strengthening and institutionalizing the organization's dominant position in power politics. The institutionalizing of the military's power does not bode well for the future of democracy in a country. Unless there are significant external or internal pressures that force the military to surrender its power, the military will continue to dominate the state.

2 The Pakistan military: the development of praetorianism, 1947–77

The story of Milbus in a certain state is primarily about its military's penetration of the national economy, which is directly proportional to the organization's political influence. As was argued in the previous chapter, the power of the defence establishment intensifies with the organization's financial autonomy, and especially its capacity to exploit national resources.

This chapter examines the history of the Pakistan military's political influence from 1947 to 1977. The historical background focuses on how the military gradually acquired political ambitions and grew in power. This period was marked by the gradual build-up of the army's political clout, which is fundamentally different from the ensuing years during which the military developed into an independent class. I argue that during these 30 years Pakistan's military showed the tendencies of a ruler-type military, which aims to control the state and its governance, especially after it took over the reins of government in 1958.

Although democracy was seemingly restored in 1962, the action and policies of the first military dictator, General Ayub Khan, proved to weaken civilian institutions. He imposed the army's hegemony through his personal control of the state and its politics. Ayub Khan's personal rule was interrupted in 1969 with General Yahya Khan's takeover. This change did not indicate any break in army rule: rather it was a coup within a coup. The actual change, though temporary, came in 1972 after democracy was restored in the wake of the army defeat in a war against India. The loss of the eastern wing and the surrender of 90,000 soldiers was a major shock which forced the military to the background for a few years, at least until the second military takeover in 1977.

One of the reasons for the prolonged military control relates to the weakness of the political parties. The impotency of the political leadership and the civil bureaucracy can be attributed to their attitude and composition. As a part of the dominant classes in the country, the civil bureaucracy and the political elite have always viewed the armed forces as an essential tool for furthering their political objectives. This use and abuse of the military created a unique political niche for it. The acceptance of the military as a political arbiter, compounded with its prominent role as the guardian of the country's security, sovereignty and ideology, added to its significance compared with other domestic players.

The analysis draws upon Hamza Alavi's thesis about Pakistan as an 'overdeveloped state' in which the military remains central to the interests and politics of the dominant classes. Alavi, a prominent political scientist following the Marxian school of thought, wrote about the sociopolitical dominance of the ruling classes and the power of the state's civil and military bureaucracy compared with the political parties. The combination of factors such as the military's dominance and the weakness of political forces nurtured praetorianism in the country.

Amos Perlmutter, an expert on civil–military relations, defines a modern praetorian state as one that 'favors the development of military as the core group and encourages the growth of its expectations as a ruling class ... constitutional changes are effected and sustained by the military, which plays a dominant role in all political institutions.'[1]

THE MILITARY INSTITUTION

The Pakistan military is the most politically influential institution in the country. Some view it as the largest political party. However, the military's constitutional mandate as laid down in Article 245 of the 1973 Constitution is limited to securing the frontiers against external threat, and assisting in national emergencies or natural disasters on the request of civilian authorities. The role given to the armed forces in this particular constitution was similar to the one laid down in the earlier constitutions of 1956 and 1962.

The military in Pakistan is a voluntary service comprising 650,000 personnel. The army is the largest service, with 550,000 personnel, and politically the most potent as well. This is followed by the Pakistan Air Force (PAF) with 45,000 personnel and the Pakistan Navy (PN) with a 25,000 workforce.

The bulk of the military personnel come from the province of Punjab. The organization is known for its ethnic homogeneity. Approximately 75 per cent of the army is drawn from three districts of Punjab, the area known as the 'Salt Range.'[2] Another 20 per cent are from three to four districts in the North West Frontier Province (NWFP). The other two provinces, Baluchistan and Sindh, together have about a 5 per cent share of personnel. The number of ethnic Baluch, which is not more than a couple of hundred, is even less than the number of ethnic Sindhis in the armed forces. This ethnic composition plays a major role in the country's politics, since it dovetails into the tense relationship between various ethnic communities and centre–province relations.

The military's homogeneity contributes to its corporate ethos, and provides the essential bonding, especially among the officers, that gives the organization the appearance of a monolithic force. The military's recruitment pattern follows the British tradition of procuring personnel from certain key areas. The British military, as Tan Tai Yong argues, created the myth of the 'martial race' with reference to the Punjabis, as part of their drive to restructure the armed forces. After the mutiny of Bengal Army in 1857, the pattern of recruitment brought greater number of Punjabis into military service.[3] The Punjabis were more willing to fight for the British in return for material rewards and greater employment opportunities. The recruiting manuals 'closely identified ... these "martial races" ... down to

59

the relevant sub-castes and places from which they were to be found'.[4] As a result, the percentage of Punjabis in the military rose from 32.7 per cent in 1858 to 53.7 per cent in 1910.[5]

Mustafa Kamal Pasha, author of *Colonial Political Economy*, asserts that the basic idea behind selective recruitment:

> rested on the premise that groups that had shown a warrior instinct during the Mughal period were worthy candidates. But a full-blown theory of the 'martial races' was still in a nascent form in the period before 1857. It was only after the events of 1857 that the British began to exclude certain groups from the colonial army on a systematic basis.[6]

The myth of Punjabis and Pathans from NWFP as the 'martial races' was propagated even after the country's independence in 1947, and served the purpose of retaining the ethnic composition and inherently elitist fabric of the armed forces. Moreover, the British bias against recruitment of Bengalis, Sindhis and Baluch was maintained. The continuation of the recruitment pattern also fed into the tension between the centre and the smaller provinces, particularly Baluchistan. As a result, Baluch leaders view the armed forces 'not as a national military, but a Punjabi force with a mercenary and exploitative character'.[7]

The Pakistan military's ethnic homogeneity also reflects its elitist ethos, and according to the academic Eric Nordlinger, there is a peculiar social imbalance in the dominance of the military by West Pakistanis, especially Punjabis.[8] The author referred to Pakistan's example to counter the argument made by Morris Janowitz that militaries in developing societies are more committed to social change than the civilian members of the ruling elite.[9] Nordlinger's argument is that the reforms initiated by military regimes do not necessarily indicate a willingness to threaten the interests of the ruling classes. The high-ranking officers of the armed forces pursue and protect the interests of the upper-middle class. Therefore, the military's recruitment from the lower-middle class does not translate into a preference for the interest of this class.[10]

The sociopolitical dynamics of Pakistan's military demonstrate that the military uses its political influence for the social mobility of its own personnel. Since the mid-1950s, the military's recruitment in Pakistan changed from the upper-middle class to the lower-middle class. However, this did not necessarily result in any social revolution inside the forces. The military's echelons pursue policies to acquire opportunities and assets that facilitate capital formation, which enhances the position of military officers and brings them onto a par with other members of the ruling elite. Moreover, the senior officers pursue social elitism within the services. A military source talked about the presence of elitism in the army, which gives the sons of senior generals or those having access to senior officers better career opportunities than others.[11] A social bifurcation is also encouraged in the officer cadre: it disallows free mixing between the families of senior, mid-ranking and junior officers. During discussion with a psychologist working for the PN it was found that most of the psychological problems referred to her related to the social pressures created by the intense social stratification within the services. For instance, the senior officers discouraged their children from associating with those of the junior officers.[12]

The social stratification also has another dimension: the difference in the significance of the three services of the armed forces. The organizational structure of Pakistan's military reflects the continental nature of the country: the army has greater numbers of personnel and more overall institutional power than the other two services. The PAF and PN are much smaller than the army, and their significance in national security plans depends on the extent to which the army's leadership see the smaller services contributing to the larger service's war-fighting plans.

The three main services are hierarchically organized, and the principal staff officers and area commanders (all three-star) are extremely influential in internal management and overall decision making. However, the chiefs of the services (four-star) are the ultimate authority. The army chief, as head of the largest service, is considered most powerful. The service's intelligence unit (Military Intelligence, MI) has greater strategic power than its counterparts in the PAF and PN. The term 'strategic' refers to MI's ability to gather intelligence about politicians or other civil society actors. Even the working of Inter-Services Intelligence (ISI) are for all practical purposes controlled by the army chief, despite its being an inter-services agency whose head is answerable only to the prime minister. The control of intelligence agencies bolsters the power of the army chief.

The head of the army enjoys even more power than the chairman of the Joint Chief of Staffs Committee (JCSC), an organization raised in 1976–7 for joint planning and control of the armed forces. Supposedly, the chairman of the JCSC has greater significance because of his mandate for joint planning. However, the military organizational restructuring carried out in 1976 did not give the Joint Staffs Headquarters (JS HQ) any control of the personnel and operational planning of the three services.[13] As a result, the three service chiefs operate more like the pre-1976 commanders-in-chiefs of their services, with complete operational authority.

The JCSC serves as a forum for joint discussion among the senior personnel of the three services, and as a 'post office' to communicate decisions regarding allocation of resources or other administrative matters.[14] The army, however, seems to have monopolized this institution as well. The chairman of the JCSC is no longer appointed on a rotational basis but is drawn from the army, excluding the PAF and the PN. However, over the years the sense of power enjoyed by the army has permeated the other services and lower ranks as well. While the officer cadre is conscious of the military's role as guardian of the country's sovereignty and a force that keeps the country together, the junior officers and the ranks have increasingly become conscious of the political impregnability of the armed forces. The organization considers itself the sole judge of national interests. Civilians are frowned upon as incompetent, insincere, corrupt and driven by greed.

The military is hierarchically organized, with maximum authority vested in the service chiefs. This power of the chiefs echoes the organization's traditions and norms prior to the 1970s, when the title 'commander-in-chief' for each service was replaced with the term 'chief of staff' The defence restructuring implemented by Zulfiqar Ali Bhutto after 1973 aimed at reducing the influence of the army chief and bringing the military under greater control of the civilian government. These objectives were to be achieved through strengthening the Ministry of Defence (MoD). Henceforth, the three services were to be placed under the administrative control of the MoD, which was headed by a minister answerable to the Cabinet Committee for Defence (DCC) of the parliament. However, this provision remains true only in letter and not in deed.

According to the former army chief, General Jahangir Karamat, 'the organization does not like or permit sub-cultures. It frowns at outspokenness and lack of discipline. You have to accept this when you join. It rewards you if you stay in line.'[15] Therefore, the army stringently protects its hierarchically organized institutional structure for discipline and to maintain its internal organizational power.

THE MILITARY'S PRIMARY ROLE

The military attained its central role in the post-colonial state of Pakistan by being its protector. The centrality of the armed forces as the guardian of the state was intrinsic, and compensated for the deep sense of insecurity that infested the state after its birth in 1947. The prominence of external threat during the early years was crucial in defining the parameters of the future state–society relationship. As in Argentina, where the military-controlled state defined the boundaries of the state–society linkage through propagating the national security paradigm,[16] Pakistan's military intervened to protect the state, which had created as a homeland for the Muslims of the Indian Subcontinent. Hence, protecting this state from external and internal threat was essential. Achieving material development and modernization, and ensuring territorial cohesion, were paramount, and so these were defining parameters used for negotiating the relationships between the various players. Stephen P. Cohen's analysis succinctly defines the Pakistan Army's multidimensional role: 'There are armies that guard their nation's borders, there are those that are concerned with protecting their own position in society, and there are those that defend a cause or an idea. The Pakistan Army does all three.'[17]

The military acquired these multiple roles soon after the country's independence in 1947, as a result of the first war with India. The country's policy-making elite tends to define threats to national security mainly in terms of the perceived peril from New Delhi. India's hegemonic policies and belligerent attitude are considered to be the greatest threat to the survival of the state. Over the past 50 years and more, the dominant school of thought that has influenced policy making believes that the Indian leadership has never been comfortable with an independent homeland for the Muslims, and would not lose any opportunity to destroy or invade Pakistan. Policy makers are equally uncomfortable with India's urge to gain regional or global prominence. Any reference to India acquiring a prominent role, especially as a result of its comparatively greater military capacity, is seen as a potential threat and as inherently antithetical to Pakistan's security interests.

This first war with the neighbouring state in 1947–8 established the primacy of the national security agenda. From then onwards, military security was given maximum priority, resulting in the government allocating about 70 per cent of the estimated budget in the first year for defence.[18] This budgetary allocation symbolized the prioritization of the state and national agenda. According to Hussain Haqqani, a research fellow at the Carnegie Endowment for International Peace, after the first war, '"Islamic Pakistan" was defining itself through the prism of resistance to "Hindu India."'[19]

The Indian threat had an immediate effect in making the military more prominent than all other domestic players. This development was accompanied by lax control of the management of the armed forces by the civilian leadership. In fact, the founding father was unable to take firm control of the armed forces during the early days. Mohammad Ali Jinnah could not even enforce his decision to deploy troops in Kashmir. General Gracey, the Pakistan Army's commander-in-chief, expressed a reluctance to obey Jinnah during the 1947–8 war for which he was not admonished. However, a prominent Pakistani historian, Ayesha Jalal, claims that the military did not resist its orders, but Jinnah was convinced to change his earlier decision to deploy troops in Kashmir by General Auchinleck, the joint commander-in-chief for India and Pakistan.[20] In contrast, Cohen holds the founding father responsible for lax control over the army by leaving ultimate strategic military decision making to General Gracey.[21] In any case, the war opened a Pandora's box by defining Pakistan as a state that viewed its existence from the perspective of its hostile relations with India. Brig. (ret.) A. R. Siddiqui is of the view that 'the use of tribals that had gone into Kashmir to take control of the Kashmir valley led to the war, thus sealing the fate of Kashmir and turning Pakistan into a military-dominated state'.[22]

Since this first military conflict, Pakistan has fought two-and-a-half further wars with India over the unsettled dispute about Kashmir. The military establishment and the policy-making elite view the issue as critical for Pakistan's security. In the words of Pakistan's president and army chief, General Pervez Musharraf, 'Kashmir runs in our [Pakistanis'] blood.'[23] However, the issue is part of a larger perception of India as being inherently hostile to Pakistan. Military leaders such as Musharraf believe that the end of the Kashmir dispute might not necessarily result in a complete easing of the tension with India, so despite the post-2004 peace overtures with India, there is no fundamental change in the military's thinking regarding a possibility of friendship with the traditional foe.

Perhaps more importantly, the military also tends to see internal security issues and domestic political crises as extensions of the larger external threat. The rise in ethnic and sectarian violence in the country is a development that can be attributed to the covert and nefarious activities of India's intelligence

63

agencies. There is a popular notion that unless they were provoked and funded by external actors, especially New Delhi, the various ethnic and sectarian groups would not be able to cause violence in the country. This perspective is challenged by Hussain Haqqani and Hassan Abbas, who explain the rise in ethnic and religious violence as a result of the military's policies. Religious extremists, and the religious and ethnic parties in general, are allowed to play a greater role in support of the defence establishment's national security objectives.[24] The military allowed the religious parties to produce the necessary personnel for deployment on any front where help was needed.

The discussion of national security as determining the army's utility for the state also serves as a reminder of the primacy of the military's corporate interests, which play a significant role in the formulation of state policies. Just like in India, little attention is paid to erroneous policy making and bad governance, which is directly responsible for domestic unrest and sociopolitical fragmentation. Since the military has acquired the role of the guardian of the country's sovereignty and overall security, the organization tends to view domestic political crises from the perspective of the external threat.

Similarly, the military looks at internal crises such as the problems in Baluchistan, Sindh (during the 1980s), or in the tribal areas bordering on Afghanistan, as the results of India's hobnobbing with the miscreants in Pakistan. Security against India, it must be reiterated, is the *raison d'être* of the armed forces. Hence, the military leadership and the overall Pakistani establishment consider it essential to strengthen the military, and view a possible reaction primarily from a classical realist perspective. All forms of interaction with Pakistan's larger neighbour, including cultural links and trade and commerce, are seen from the standpoint of national security.

THE MILITARY'S SECONDARY ROLE

Besides fighting wars, Pakistan's armed forces are involved in multiple activities within the borders of the country, ranging from building roads, catching electricity thieves, running commercial ventures and weeding out corruption to running the state. The military considers itself as an alternative institution capable of contributing to socioeconomic and political development. In fact, such a role is now seen as part of the primary role of providing military security.

A certain school of thought on Pakistan's armed forces, whose writings are categorized here as 'propagandist' literature, extols the military's contribution to national development. Authors such as General Fazal Muqeem Khan, General Ayub Khan, Raymond Moore, Brian Cloughly and Pervaiz Cheema view the military as a nation-builder. In fact, the expansion of the military's influence in politics and governance is seen as a manifestation of its ability to perform as a nation-builder. It is claimed that the military is sucked into governance and politics because it is the most modern and capable institution.[25] Its role in politics, however, is acquired grudgingly because of the incompetence of the political leadership. The military, according to Muqeem Khan, essentially, is a reluctant intruder that:

64

is above politics and parties. The performance of its officers and *jawans* and the basis of its traditions spring from their readiness to serve the state and the nation in the best way they can do ... it [the army] has acquired a unique spirit and sense of purpose and has proved itself Pakistan's greatest stabilizing force.[26]

The military's organizational discipline versus the inefficacy of political institutions is one of the major justifications for the army's political intervention.[27] The military's positive role in non-western countries is a favourite theme of a number of other prominent western academics, such as Samuel P. Huntington. According to his standpoint, such militaries are generally better placed to undertake nation-building than the ill-groomed politicians. Cheema goes even further in subscribing to the military's perception that the lack of literacy causes weakness of democracy. The author does not, however, explain why the absence of high literacy levels has not weakened political institutions in India, which has much the same history as Pakistan.

This propagandist literature naturally accepts the army's role as a neutral political arbitrator which has a desire to protect the state against internal or external threats. Therefore, authors such as Cloughly are dismissive of all Pakistani prime ministers from Zulfiqar Ali Bhutto (1971–7) to Mohammad Khan Junejo (1983–5). Cloughly does not show any patience to assess the causes for the dismissal of some of the political regimes, or the varied tones of the country's politics.[28] Under these circumstances, the army is an umpire between competing political forces, as well as between the common people and 'corrupt' political regimes. Such a view is shared by the military's officer cadre as well. Military personnel mock civilians for their inability to perform functions meant to be carried out by civilian institutions, which the political governments then invite the armed forces to carry out, such as weeding out ghost schools[29] and cleaning up water channels. However, such secondary roles are performed by militaries all over the world without their considering themselves superior to civilians.

THE MILITARY IN POLITICS AND GOVERNANCE

Not everyone endorses this view, however. Some analysts of Pakistan's politics do not believe that the military's role in politics and governance is a natural extension of its greater organizational capacity, or the result of the weakness of the country's political leadership. A second category of works, defined here as the 'counter-plottist' literature, examines the military's multiple roles critically.[30] Authors such as Ayesha Jalal, Saeed Shafqat, Hussain Haqqani and Hassan Abbas find the army to be extremely manipulative. The general essence of their argument is that the military deliberately acquired its multiple roles and weakened the state and its political system for its own interests.

Jalal, for instance, looks at the military's political influence as a corollary

65

of its alignment with foreign powers such as the United Kingdom and the United States. These two states were drawn towards the Pakistan Army because of their larger strategic objectives. The alignment was mutually beneficial for these powers and Pakistan's military, which eagerly and independently sought a strategic linkage with them in order to outmanoeuvre its domestic competitors. The military's political influence is a direct result of its *rentier* character. This means that the military sought material and general support and approval from its strategic allies in return for fulfilling their security objectives. The silence of external powers regarding military takeovers, and the foreign aid received by military governments for weapons modernization, strengthened both the civil and military bureaucracy in contrast to political institutions. Jalal believes that the foreign assistance helped alleviate the weakness of the bureaucracy which the military suffered from in 1947.[31]

Saeed Shafqat also subscribes to Jalal's views.[32] He is of the notion that the tacit support from Washington ultimately translated into the military's political strength. The support was primarily in the shape of military-strategic alignment and weapons transfer, which bolstered the image of the armed forces compared with civil society and civilian institutions. The urge for weapons acquisition developed Islamabad's dependency on the United States. The military weapons transfers and cooperation in the security sector are the key aspects of the bilateral linkage. The acquisition of quality weapons from Washington significantly strengthened the military to stand up to the perceived threat of a Indian military onslaught. Relations with China fall in the same category.

The relations with the United States, in particular, are extremely important politically. Many in Pakistan believe that the armed forces conspire with the United States to gain strength compared with civilian institutions and other domestic players. However a former US diplomat, Dennis Kux, does not subscribe to the counter-plottist theory, and sees the help provided to military regimes as an accident of history, or an evidence of the better capacity of army regimes in Pakistan.[33] However, the fact remains that successive US administrations have closely cooperated with military regimes in Pakistan and other countries without any qualms, with the aim of fulfilling US strategic objectives. The US academic Stephen Cohen is of the view that interaction with the United States exposes the military to better training and modern technological concepts, which is then touted as an example of the armed forces' greater capacity to bring about sociocultural and economic modernization, and control the state effectively through better training and technology.[34]

The accounts of the propagandists and counter-plottists explain one aspect of the dynamics of Pakistan's politics, related to the military's strength, but do not give the whole picture. Undoubtedly the military has acquired a far greater role for itself in the running of the state. However, the power of the 'men on horseback' has to be explained in relation to the power of other domestic players. Moreover, an analysis is needed of why the civil society did not fight back against the military, as it did in Bangladesh, to get the armed forces out of politics. Apart from the populist movement in the country during the end of the 1960s, there are hardly any signs of civil society making a concerted effort to push the army back to the barracks.

It is imperative to expose the concept of weakness of political institutions. Were the political forces inherently weak, or made weak? Pakistani political scientists Saeed Shafqat[35] and Mohammad Waseem hold the civil bureaucracy responsible for the relative weakness of civilian institutions and the increase in the military's influence. The military rode into prominence on the shoulders of the civil bureaucracy. The first military coup in 1958 was a result of a political alignment between the civil and military bureaucracy. In any case, before the coup the real power lay with the executive, which was identified with the higher bureaucracy.[36] The coup itself was a consequence of the battle between political forces and the civil bureaucracy. In the post-colonial state of Pakistan, the executive or the bureaucracy can be understood as 'a group of bearers of office authority [that] … reduces the political parties to the role of mere brokers, who manipulate public relations in their favor and thus function as a legitimacy factor'.[37] The power equation between the executive and the legislative during the early days of the country's independence was inherited from the British. The colonial power controlled India through strengthening the state bureaucracy.[38] This pattern persisted in the ensuing years, and the civil-military bureaucracy developed an interest in controlling the state and its politics.

The weakness of the political forces is a sign of fragmentation and factionalism among civil society and the political class.[39] The deep divisions between the political leadership indicate a structural flaw in the segmented character of Pakistani society, which will be explained further.[40] According to political analyst Edward Feit, such societies approach a praetorian syndrome characterized by (in Banfield's term) 'amoral familism'.[41] This concept refers to a system in which each group focuses on maximizing its own interests and forms temporary coalitions to further its interests. Such an approach is antithetical to institution building. Given the problem of the absence of a neutral political arbiter compounded with the issue of self-interests, the major societal groups begin to view the military as a political referee which could negotiate between the various political forces and help the ruling parties in furthering their interests.[42]

Such collusion between various power groups in Pakistan is explained by Hamza Alavi, who describes the weakness of Pakistan's political institutions as the crisis of an overdeveloped state. This is perhaps the most relevant explanation. The term 'overdeveloped' refers to the relative institutional strength of the state bureaucracy compared with political institutions, which resulted in a never-ending political crisis in the country. In his Marxian context, the author describes the post-colonial state as an 'overdeveloped' structure operating on the principle of peripheral capitalism, a concept that recognizes the plurality of economically dominant groups whose rival interests and competing demands are mediated by the state, which is composed of a strong civil-military bureaucracy and weaker political institutions.[43] Thus, the ultimate arbiter role can only be played by the stronger civil-military bureaucracy and not by democratic institutions.

The state, Alavi argues, plays a central role, acting in the interests of other groups, which the author refers to as the three dominant classes: the landed-feudal class, the indigenous bourgeoisie and the metropolitan bourgeoisie. These three groups constitute the ruling power bloc that competes in the framework of peripheral capitalism.[44] While some form of capitalist mode of production and economic redistribution introduces itself in the form of post-colonial capital, the pre-capitalist system remains preserved.[45] The military's stakes are intertwined with those of these three groups, making it imperative for the military and the other groups to protect each other's interests. Thus, the military's relevance for the country's politics is a result of the symbiotic relationship between military force and political power, especially of the ruling elite. The dependence of the dominant classes on the military does not allow the civilian institutions to penetrate the military as much as the military infiltrates civilian institutions.

According to Alavi's theoretical formulation, the political flaws of prominent leaders such as Zulfiqar Ali Bhutto, for example, are not personality traits but are caused by structural behaviour determined by the norms of peripheral capitalism.[46] Despite the reference to socialist ideology, Bhutto could not afford to keep his politically left-leaning partners. This, as Alavi points out, was a result of the 'pull' of his class interests rather than just a simple personality quirk.[47] Therefore, the inaptitude of the political leaders in dealing with the military, which appears to be more like political naiveté or sheer innocence in Haqqani's work, is actually a structural problem.[48]

The relationship between the military and the three classes gains significance for all these players because of the importance of the bureaucracy in this 'overdeveloped' state. The bureaucracy is trained to protect the state from external as well as internal threats. According to Alavi, 'the [civil and military] bureaucrats were brought up on the myth of "guardianship," the idea that it was their mission to defend the interests of the people as against the supposed partnership of and personal ambitions of "professional" politicians.'[49] Thus, the military's role in the state was not restricted to coercion, but also involved the legitimation of regimes, a task the organization could perform because of its authority and standing in the state and society.[50] Over the course of time, the military began to benefit from the state, acquiring various concessions in the form of land and lucrative positions.[51]

Alavi's theory explicates the cooperation and conflict that could be observed between the various players, including the armed forces. Seen from the author's peripheral capitalism paradigm, the tension between the three dominant classes and their bid to control the armed forces at different times is understandable. Influenced by personal power interests and conscious of the centrality of the bureaucracy to the state apparatus, the political players attempt to control the military institution and tools of violence through various means. The creation of new legal control mechanisms, buying off senior officers, changing the army chief, and establishing alternative auxiliary paramilitary organizations were, and remain, some of the many ways to exercise control over the armed forces.

Therefore, the primary explanation for the skewed civil–military relations lies in the peculiar political structure of the state and the relationship between the dominant classes. The military did not accidentally gain power but was led to it, albeit inadvertently, through the relationship of the dominant classes with force. The desire of the dominant classes to use the military as a tool for power projection erodes the neutrality of the state and its bureaucracy, making the military a player in political contestation. Moreover, since the civilian leadership uses the military for its own power objectives, the politicians or other significant civilian players fail to impose strict norms for a principal–agent relationship in which the military is subservient to the civilian state from the onset.

The dependence of the ruling elite on the military, which gradually strengthened the armed forces, is analysed in the next subsections.

INITIATION TO POWER, 1947–58

As was mentioned earlier, the military gained prominence in the state apparatus soon after the country's birth, as a result of the first war with India. After the death of the founding father, Jinnah, in 1948, Pakistani politics was riddled with the problem of factionalism. The political contest took place on three fronts:

- amongst the various political groups for the control of the state
- between the civil and military bureaucracy and the political class
- between the military and other dominant civilian actors.

The political leadership used authoritarian tactics and a divide and rule policy to establish their political strength. For instance, Liaquat Ali Khan, the country's first prime minister, manipulated politicians in the Punjab in his interest. However, when confronted with the situation of losing control of the largest province to a prominent leader of the Muslim League in the Punjab, Mumtaz Daultana, Liaquat Ali Khan connived with the governor-general to dissolve the assembly and bring the province under the direct control of the central government. This situation continued for two years, until the elections in March 1951.[52]

The friction between various factions, the urban and rural elements within the main political party – the Muslim League – and the tension between the centre and the federating units made it difficult for the country to acquire a constitution. The first constitution was promulgated in 1956, nine years after the country's creation. The factionalism inside the political parties also divided party politics along regional lines.[53] While the Awami League concentrated its efforts in East Pakistan, the Muslim League dominated the politics in the western wing of the country. Such political factionalism led to frequent dismissal of governments. From 1947 to 1958 Pakistan had seven prime ministers and eight cabinets.[54] Furthermore, the extravagant and viceregal behaviour of the political elite set it apart from the common people. The issue was not just the use of colonial practices by the political leadership, such as keeping military secretaries and *aides de camp*, but their inaccessibility to the general public.[55] This behaviour undermined the image of the politicians.

Other domestic forces, such as the civil bureaucracy, viewed the political chaos as advantageous to their wresting control of the state. The civil bureaucracy was as powerful as in India. The main difference, however, between the two civil bureaucracies was in their approach to military power and political control. While the Indian civil bureaucracy recognized and accepted the dominance of the politicians, and established control over the armed forces through strengthening the institution of the Ministry of Defence (MoD), Pakistan's civil bureaucracy chose to partner with the military to further its dominance over the political leadership. The civil bureaucracy – represented by a bureaucrat-turned-politician, Ghulam Mohammad, the governor-general during the early 1950s – viewed the military as a junior partner capable of keeping the raucous politicians at bay. The governor-general's trust lay more in the army generals than the civilian prime ministers.

Ghulam Mohammad asked General Ayub Khan to take over the government, replacing Prime Minister Bogra with whom the governor-general had had a falling-out in 1954.[56] Ghulam Mohammad's successor as governor-general, Iskandar Mirza, who was also a former bureaucrat, equally relied on the army. A close friend of Ayub Khan's, Mirza increasingly involved the military in the functioning of the state.[57] According to Lt.-General (rtd) Chishti, the civilian government's decision not to retire Ayub Khan in 1954 but to give him a role in the cabinet weakened the political regime.[58] Such favours to the army chief smacked of a conspiratorial partnership between Ayub Khan and the governor-general, which was vital for the latter's survival and that of the civil bureaucracy-dominated state.

Saeed Shafqat claims that the Ayub–Mirza alliance was the civil bureaucracy's bid to forge a superordinate–subordinate relationship with the armed forces.[59] The office of the governor-general was abolished after the introduction of the first constitution in 1956, in which Mirza insisted on becoming a powerful president. To ensure his army friend's allegiance, Mirza twice gave Ayub Khan an extension as commander-in-chief, first in 1954 and later in 1958.[60] These personal concessions, however, would prove exceedingly costly to the civilian leadership. In 1958, the military could no longer be treated as a junior partner and the superordinate–subordinate relationship was reversed. Although Mirza imposed martial law on 7 October 1958, Ayub finally decided to bring the military to the forefront through a counter-coup on 27 October 1958.

The bickering for greater power and authority benefited the senior military leadership. It must be noted that the army's earlier leadership rose to prominence by chance. Neither Ayub Khan nor General Yahya (the second commander-in-chief) was selected to the top rank for his impeccable career

70

record. While Ayub Khan made it to the top by sheer luck, Yahya Khan was deliberately propped up as Ayub Khan's faithful ally in the Army.[61] Later commanders questioned the ascendancy of both these senior commanders, and doubted their professional competence.[62] These men were opportunists set to enhance their personal power. Some of these officers began to draw personal economic benefits as well, such as acquiring large chunks of evacuee property previously owned by civilians (and abandoned by Hindu migrants) in the military cantonments.[63] Here, the military circumvented the state's right to claim possession of these properties.

To make itself more relevant for the state, the military strengthened itself institutionally through enhancing its control over defence and foreign policy making. The political leadership was far too fragmented to establish control over the military and issues of national security. The senior generals, especially Ayub Khan, who was the first army chief, insisted that defence matters were the military's forte. According to Hamida Khuhro's biographical account of her father, Mohammad Ayub Khuhro, who was a Muslim League leader in Sindh, Ayub Khan was adamant about monopolizing all matters pertaining to the armed forces. For instance, the general was not happy with the prime minister, Sir Feroz Khan Noon's decision to authorize the civilian minister of industries and supplies to procure military equipment. Ayub Khan also wanted the prime minister to endorse his third extension as the army chief.[64] The political conflict between the political and military leadership finally ended in the first takeover by the army in 1958.

It was necessary for the military to establish domination over defence and foreign policy issues because the defence budget was a major share of the national expenditure, and swallowed about 68 per cent of the central government's revenues.[65] Development expenditure and centre–province relations were held hostage to the perceived Indian threat. The central government had to control the provinces to exercise control over the distribution of resources and provide for a stronger military institution.

The armed forces also found other ways of strengthening their institution, such as building an alignment with the United States. To assuage their fear of their larger neighbour, India, the civil and military leadership sought links with greater military powers. Starting from the early days after independence with Jinnah,[66] leaders sought the United States as a 'patron of choice' that could provide the military with the necessary technology and diplomatic support to keep India at bay.[67] Reportedly, the army's commander-in-chief, Ayub Khan, visited the United States on his own initiative and without prior approval from the cabinet to seek military and economic assistance.[68] Later, Ayub Khan's decision to join the Central Treaty Organization (CENTO) benefited the army tremendously. Washington, on the other hand, found Pakistan's army a willing partner in pursuing US military-strategic objectives regarding the Communist Soviet Union. The financial and military aid received from the United States improved personnel training and technology in the armed forces. The technological and larger military cooperation, according to Cohen, impacted on the armed forces' organizational structure and identity.[69] A better organizational capacity improved their leadership confidence with other players, and gave the military an image of being a more efficient organization. This approach reveals the western bias of equating technological prowess with modernization.

It is noteworthy that the political leadership did not try to create an alternative national agenda besides military security. Therefore, since the creation of the country, it has projected the image of an insecure homeland state for Muslims which can only be protected through greater military security. This approach grew more popular in the ensuing years, resulting in the further strengthening of the armed forces.

THE RISE TO POWER, 1958–71

The years from 1958 to 1971 saw a crucial transformation in civil–military relations, during which the army established itself as the key political force. During this period the military appeared more of a ruler type which aimed at taking control of the state permanently. The army initially ruled directly through imposing martial law. This status was changed when Ayub Khan introduced the second constitution in 1962, and imposed his personal rule on the country, first as army chief, and later as field marshal. A third change took place in 1969 when Ayub Khan was replaced by the army chief Yahya Khan, who ruled until the army was compelled to withdraw from politics after the humiliating defeat in 1971–2.

Contrary to the existing studies that consider the Ayub Khan and Yahya Khan military rules as two separate regimes, it is argued here that Pakistan's military had become a ruler type, which had had ambitions to control the state for a long period. The Ayub Khan and Yahya Khan governments were not two different regimes but one continuous military rule in which the only change was in the topmost leadership. The reintroduction of democracy in 1962 was similar to the Indonesian concept of 'guided democracy', according to which the military would gently teach the people how to democratize. Perhaps this is the reason that the Pakistani political analyst Pervez Cheema asserts that all army chiefs have tried to strengthen elected governments,[70] which means that they supported democracy. However, Ayub's supposedly democratic rule and his replacement by Yahya Khan indicated the military's intention of remaining in power. Under Ayub, the military had acquired political and financial autonomy which gave it the confidence to retain its hold over the state.

The military's ascendancy to power, as mentioned earlier, was a result of a coalition between the civil and the military bureaucracy. In bringing the military to power, the civil bureaucracy had misread the tenacity and intent of the armed forces. President Iskandar Mirza had brought in the army in October 1958 to restructure the political scene in his favour. Some declassified UK documents reveal that the diplomatic services were apprehensive of Mirza's possible use of the army to get rid of 'undesirable elements' in case the election results were not favourable. The suspicion was that 'the President himself may take a hand in the provocation of violence in order to clear the way for the intervention of the army and the postponement of elections'.[71] However, Mirza could not dictate his terms to the army, and ended up transferring power to the GHQ. It did not take long for Ayub Khan to assume direct control of the political situation rather than remaining a puppet in the hands of his friend, President Mirza.

The Pakistan Army under Ayub Khan sought an equal relationship with the civil bureaucracy, to stabilize the political situation and manage the country more efficiently than the distraught politicians. Lacking knowledge of the functioning of government, the military did not push the civil bureaucracy out of prominent positions in the government. Instead, the army GHQ partnered with the civil bureaucracy for running the affairs of the state. So the initial coercion of the civil bureaucracy by the military administration did not necessarily minimize the significance of civilian bureaucrats. The generals needed the support of the bureaucracy to establish firm control over the state and minimize the legitimacy of the political class. As in Turkey, the Pakistan Army's officers distrusted the politicians and were keen to manage the country themselves.

Therefore, under Ayub Khan, the army embarked upon the process of restructuring politics to produce, through a gradual and a guided process, a legitimate regime acceptable to the civil-military bureaucracy.[72] The guided process included the coercion of some politicians and parties, and the induction or co-option of others, as well as the creation of new political institutions and processes that could produce a highly sanitized version of politics acceptable to the GHQ as a system which would not hinder the organization's power interests. The introduction of the Elective Bodies Disqualification Ordinance (EBDO) in 1959 was meant to coerce the political class. Although this law was claimed as a punitive measure against any public office-bearer for misconduct in office,[73] it was used to ban and marginalize key political parties and leaders.

Ayub Khan's rule can be divided into two periods: the first with a military face, from 1958 to 1962, and the second involving civilianization of military rule (from 1962 to 1969), aimed at creating a highly centralized presidential system and generating client relationships.[74] To support the argument that the post-1962 Ayub Khan rule was a continuation of the army in power, Edward Feit aptly says that:

> if a man was a career officer immediately before taking power, if his associations subsequently were still military, if his style remained military, and if all indications were that his heart was still with the army, his government is still a military government even when his commission is laid aside …. Soldiers who act in politics through the force of the army will thus continue to be considered as soldiers, even when, to outward appearances at least, they have left the ranks, unless there is overwhelming evidence of a change of view. The use of the army as a vehicle to power is thus a major qualification.[75]

The military government instituted various measures to bring the political and civil societies under its firm control, through manipulating and exploiting other classes, or by using pure coercion. The control over the media and labour unions further diminished the possibility of strengthening democratic institutions. The Basic Democracies system launched in October 1959, with the stated objective of strengthening democracy at the grass-roots level, marginalized the power of the representative government by heavily peppering the system with civil bureaucrats. This system of guided democracy comprised elected and non-elected representatives, with a local administration acting as the eyes, ears and stick for the central government, enabling it to maintain sufficient authority over the politicians. Similarly, the shift from a parliamentary to presidential system through a new constitution in 1962 was based on a system of indirect elections that conformed to the principle of guided democracy. Intriguingly, this concept was being tried out by another general-turned-politician elsewhere: President Sukarno of Indonesia. The Indonesian president abandoned the system of parliamentary democracy in 1957, and replaced it with 'guided democracy' in which the polity and economy would develop under his tutelage and that of his cabal.[76]

The presidential elections held in 1965 enforced a presidential system of government that was dominated by an army general, Ayub Khan, who also became the indirectly elected president. The change of the political system from parliamentary democracy to presidential form was meant to legitimize military control through giving it the face of an elected regime. The most senior military leadership engaged with the civil bureaucracy and sought new political partners to strengthen their hold on the state. Contrary to his earlier policy of coercing the civil bureaucrats, Ayub Khan opted for a compromise with the civil bureaucracy, by not curtailing the power of the central superior service officers (popularly referred to as the CSP class).[77] Moreover, the links between the civil and military bureaucracy were bolstered through initiating the process of inducting military officers into the civil service.

The regime also enhanced the scope of the military's corporate interests by presenting great incentives such as awarding land to officers and *jawans* (soldiers), and providing them with jobs in military-run industries.[78] While there were direct benefits for Ayub Khan and his family, the economic incentives were created to establish the military's financial independence from the government, and other institutions perceived as inferior to the armed forces.

Ayub Khan's takeover was not hugely resisted, because of the weakness of the political forces to muster support amongst the masses and to start popular political agitation. Except for the movement for the partition of India, Pakistan's politics had a highly elitist nature. The lack of resistance against the military's dominance, as this study tries to establish, was largely because the ruling elite tried to partner the military to pursue their political and economic interests. In fact, the civil-military bureaucracy played a key role in giving birth to the indigenous bourgeoisie or the business-industrialist class, which formed part of the dominant elite identified by Hamza Alavi. The transformation of the trader-merchant class into the business-industrial class through institutions such as the Pakistan Industrial Development Corporation (PIDC) resulted in national economic uplift as well as creating new partners for the bureaucracy.

During the 1960s, the famous 22 families who owned about 68 per cent of Pakistan's industries and 87 per cent of its banking and insurance assets were sympathetic to their source of power, the army.[79] The landed-feudal class that traditionally dominated politics also developed links with the bureaucracy and the industrial class. It is a false perception that Ayub Khan's land reforms diluted the power of the feudal landowners or were meant to bring in social reforms. The land reforms merely squeezed major landowners by forcing them to undertake some readjustments. The alterations in the landownership ceiling, which was scaled down from an infinite number to a restriction on individual land ownership of 36,000 produce index units (PIUs), forced the big landlords to transfer land to other members of their family or clan. Thus, the political power structure barely lost its feudal character.

The ruling military did not show any signs of wanting to disturb the interests of the ruling elite. One of the reasons for this leniency was that the military itself was also involved in the exploitation of the state's land resources. Ayub Khan and the senior military generals had acquired agricultural land in Sindh and other provinces. Land reforms were therefore used as a coercive tool to win the support of landowners. India, it must be remembered, had legally abolished feudalism in the earlier days after partition, allowing ownership of a maximum of 10 acres per family. In any case, the socialist agenda of Nehru did not suit the continuity of the institutional symbols of feudalism. Pakistan's leadership, on the other hand, did not offer any substantive sociopolitical national goal.

The three dominant classes in Pakistan – the landed-feudal, the indigenous bourgeoisie and the metropolitan bourgeoisie – found common ground with the military, and acted to serve their joint interests during the Ayub-Yahya military regime. The various economic policies instituted under Ayub Khan, such as the 'bonus voucher' scheme and the devaluation of the currency, benefited industrialists and landowners; the mechanization of agriculture primarily benefited larger landowners at the cost of the small landholders and poor sharecroppers, and the authoritarian economic modernization strengthened the civil bureaucracy as it managed the process.[80] The military itself started to establish its interests in the agricultural and industrial sectors as well as in the civil bureaucracy. None of the ruling classes showed any interest in eliminating peripheral capitalism or changing the feudal nature of politics, nor did they stop using the military as an instrument of personal power. While the politicians were annoyed with Ayub Khan's manipulation of power to become the president and change the political system from parliamentary democracy to a presidential form of government in 1962, no efforts were made to improve the understanding of what had led to this, or to prevent politicians from using military or authoritarian tactics as part of the political discourse.

The mistake that the politicians continue to make is not to recognize the fact that they were equally as responsible as the army for bringing the military party into politics. The ultimate effort is to control the armed forces or enter into an equal relationship, with the objective of taking complete control of the defence establishment at some opportune time. Zulfiqar Ali Bhutto broke ranks with Ayub Khan in 1966, despite the fact that his career had been shaped and he mentored by the military dictator, and created the country's first popular party, the Pakistan People's Party (PPP). Bhutto's populist politics utilized mass protest as a tool to exhibit his force. Using popular slogans like *roti, kapra* and *makaan* (bread, clothing and shelter), the PPP tuned into the discontent of the growing number of working-class people disenchanted with the elitist politics and policies of the Ayub regime. Meanwhile, resistance grew in the eastern wing of the country, where people were discontented with the policies of the military regime as well as with the dominance of the western wing. The Bengali leader, Sheikh Mujeeb Rehman, protested against the Punjabi domination and demanded greater political autonomy. The military government, however, chose to react through the use of force rather than with conciliatory measures.[81]

The political unrest in the country was the military's first brush with populist politics. In addition to the sociopolitical instability caused by street agitation, the picture challenged Ayub's image as a leader in control of the nation's destiny. The worsening conditions convinced the army of the need for a change of face. However, they did not visualize immediately handing over power to a civilian leader. The replacement of Ayub Khan with Yahya Khan was the army's response to the political conditions, and a bid to safeguard the institution's relatively superior image. The economic and political crisis created by Ayub Khan's policies challenged the military's image as an apolitical and neutral institution.

Ayub's replacement in 1969 did not bring about any change in policy or a reduction in the army's pursuit of its institutional self-interests. Yahya Khan brought in more of his uniformed colleagues to run the show. The new general failed to even review his coercive political management and machinations. Yahya held elections in 1970 with the hope of bringing in a civilian regime that would be acceptable to the GHQ. According to Haqqani, the army would have preferred to see a coalition of Muslim League and religious parties in power.[82] However, the elections did not produce this result. The two parties that came to the fore were the Awami National Party in East Pakistan and the Pakistan People's Party in the western wing, led by the popular political agitator Sheikh Mujeeb-u-Rehman and Zulfiqar Ali Bhutto respectively. The results of these elections showed the clear political divide between the two wings, which expressed the ethnic tension between East and West Pakistan.

The Awami League bagged 288 of 300 seats in the East Pakistan legislature, and 167 of 300 seats in the National Assembly (the total number of seats for East Pakistan in the National Assembly was 169). This gave it a clear majority to form the government at the centre. Its closest rival was Bhutto's PPP, which secured a total of 85 seats in Punjab and Sindh. (The number of seats in West Pakistan was Punjab 85, Sindh 28, NWFP 19,

76

Baluchistan 5 and Tribal 7, making 144 in total).[83] However, as was explained by a prominent political commentator on Pakistan, Lawrence Ziring, 'the Bengalis were not only distant from the Pakistan "heartland," they were also somewhat far removed from the urgencies that influenced the leaders and people of West Pakistan.'[84]

RETURNING TO DEMOCRACY, 1971–7

The 1970 election results were not honoured by the military regime or the political elite of the western wing. Their attitude and the hostile reaction of Bengali leaders led to a stalemate which intensified further into a political crisis. These seven years heralded a transformation in the political environment, but one which was based on tragedy resulting from the political intolerance and short-sightedness of the leadership.

Despite the majority won by Rehman's Awami League in the elections, the West Pakistani establishment, which included the military and other dominant classes, was uncomfortable with the idea of transferring power to the Bengalis, whom they considered ethnically inferior. In his book about the 1971 debacle, an army officer-turned-intellectual, Sadiq Salik, quoted another Pakistan Army officer as saying, 'Don't worry ... we will not allow these black bastards to rule over us.'[85] Such derogatory remarks expressed the ethnic bias and exclusivity of the army, the majority of the Punjabi population and the West Pakistani leadership. The army leadership had to make a difficult choice between Rehman and Bhutto, which resulted in delaying the transfer of power to either of the two leaders after announcement of the election results.

Eager to get into power, Bhutto played upon the military's attitudinal bias against the Bengali leadership. The PPP leader's defiant attitude caused the postponement of the National Assembly which was to be held in Dhaka in March 1971.[86] He threatened all politicians with dire consequences if they attended the session. This was an insult for the Bengali people and their leadership, who had since independence experienced unequal and insulting treatment by the West Pakistani elite.

Bhutto's stance intensified the political crisis, and led to a political stalemate between the two wings. The Pakistani establishment clearly made the situation in Pakistan look like an uncomfortable internal situation that threatened the country's integrity. Islamabad saw the unrest in East Pakistan as part of a larger Indian conspiracy to undo Pakistan. The army launched a military operation, 'Searchlight', against the Bengali resistance on 15 March 1971 in which the army cracked down on all dissent in the eastern wing.[87] Human rights atrocities in the eastern wing increased to such an extent that these became noticeable to the foreign diplomats stationed in Dhaka and elsewhere in the region. The various US government departments/agencies in Washington warned the Nixon administration of the selective genocide and killing of Awami League supporters, Hindus and university students.[88] The famous 'Blood Telegram' sent by the US Consul-General in Dhaka, Archer Blood, strongly dissented from the policies of the

US government of supporting a military regime that indulged in serious human rights atrocities.[89]

The Army GHQ in Rawalpindi depended on US support to secure its position domestically. Ayub Khan had laboured to forge a military-strategic alignment with the United States to allow the institutional strengthening of the armed forces. Pakistan received major military assistance from the United States during the period from 1958 to 1971. The alignment was built around US interests in fighting the Communist Soviet Union. Washington was not enthusiastic about disturbing the alignment, nor did it wish to see the power equation change in favour of India, which had refused to align with it. Thus, when confronted with the issue of supporting India or Pakistan during the 1971 crisis, Washington did not want the military regime in Pakistan to be put under excessive pressure. President Nixon communicated to all concerned in the US administration, 'To All Hands: Don't squeeze Yahya at this time.'[90] This move to crack down on all dissent in the eastern wing was justified by Pakistan's ambassador to the United States, Agha Hilaly. According to the envoy, a 'great tragedy had befallen Pakistan and the army had to kill people in order to keep the country together'.[91] Thousands of Bengalis were killed and women raped, and this added to the general mayhem and ruckus. This ultimately lead to the breaking-up of the country.

The PPP leader seemed to ignore these atrocities when he defended Pakistan after an Indian attack on the eastern wing later in the year. Bhutto's impassioned speech to the UN Security Council on 15 December 1971, in which he lambasted India and the rest of the world, tore up his notes, and stormed out of the meeting declaring that 'I will not be party to legalizing aggression',[92] won him accolades as a nationalist leader and sympathy from the armed forces. Earlier, in November 1971, Bhutto had been sent by General Yahya as the government's envoy to China to seek Beijing's help in the war against India.[93]

On 16 December 1971 Pakistan's military commander in East Pakistan surrendered to Indian forces, and a new state of Bangladesh was carved out of Pakistan. This led to a crisis of legitimacy which made it imperative for the army to withdraw from politics. Thus, as Saeed Shafqat states, it was not Bhutto's election victory but the tragic conditions caused by the defeat in war, that facilitated the transfer of power from the army to him.[94] The army was left only with the option of partnering with Bhutto, who, according to Haqqani, was seen as reasonably sympathetic to the military's pro-Islam and anti-India agenda.[95] These two issues were central to the military's conception of its role. Besides, Bhutto had supporters inside the army as a result of his interaction with it during his tenure as Ayub Khan's foreign minister. In the absence of a constitution – the 1962 constitution had been abrogated by Yahya – Bhutto assumed power in December 1971 as the president and chief martial law administrator.

Bhutto's entry to the corridors of power did not bring about a qualitative difference in the country's political environment, despite the fact that he offered a relatively revolutionary agenda. His slogan of Islamic socialism, followed by his policy of nationalizing industries and strategic sectors such as education, was seemingly aimed at empowering the masses and curbing the clout of the industrial and business elite in the country. Bhutto's mass populism did encourage a shift towards the psychological political empowerment of the masses. However, he was unable to sustain the change despite having ridden to power on the shoulders of popular slogans. The sociopolitical environment remained authoritarian. Bhutto's arrival did not herald a change in the predominantly feudal tone of the country's political structure.

Bhutto's rule, it must be reiterated, is one of the examples of coalition building between the military and the landed-feudal class. Sir Morrice James, the British high commissioner to Pakistan in the mid-1960s, aptly described Bhutto as 'a Lucifer, a flawed angel'.[96] Indeed, Bhutto was a democrat and an authoritarian at the same time. The inherent contradictions in Bhutto's personality were mirrored in his politics. He was a truly charismatic leader who failed to strengthen democracy, empower the masses or reduce the significance of the armed forces.

Like a Machiavellian prince, Bhutto tried to maximize power through adopting a dual approach of propagating populist measures and coercing other players. The land reforms and nationalization of private business and industry aimed at cutting down the power of other classes and Bhutto's own feudal class rather than transferring the control of land and other resources from the ruling elite to the masses. In fact, his land reforms were as meaningless as those of Ayub Khan, because they were aimed at pressurizing his political opponents rather than bringing about any substantive change.

Bhutto destroyed his chance for strengthening civilian institutions when he mistreated the sociopolitical ideologues in his party, cracked down on his critics, and sacked the Marxist elements within the PPP. Towards the end of his regime, he had almost completely revised his political agenda by giving a greater number of party tickets to the landed gentry for the 1977 elections than the 1970 elections.[97] Shafqat attempts to defend Bhutto's policies rather feebly by suggesting that the intent behind the leader's authoritarianism was the search for stability, while others describe his errors as emerging from the flawed structure of the state and the influence of Ayub Khan's earlier policies.[98] It was inevitable that Bhutto would make these errors because of the larger systemic problems.[99] He was, after all, a member of the ruling class, and ultimately a hostage of his class and its interests. Given the pre-capitalist structure of the political economy, the landed-feudal and other dominant classes would not have benefited from a metamorphosis of the sociopolitical and socioeconomic environment that empowered the masses or strengthened democratic institutions. The PPP leader eventually struck deals with the civil-military bureaucracy to keep firm control over power. While he strengthened the civil bureaucracy by turning bureaucrats into managers of public-sector industries and businesses, he pursued policies that equally bolstered the military's significance.

From the standpoint of Bhutto's relationship with the military, he made the blunder of miscalculating the resilience of the armed forces in thwarting the strategic changes he had brought about in their management. Initially, he seemed to have taken a major step forward in changing the command and control structure of the organization. For example he created the Joint Chiefs of Staff Committee which was made responsible for joint planning, strengthened the MoD by bringing the three services under the MoD's administrative control, granted the prime minister the position of the supreme commander of the armed forces, replaced the designation of commander-in-chief by that of chief of staff, and made all the service chiefs equal in stature. Furthermore, the 1973 Constitution promulgated during Bhutto's rule declared the abrogation of the constitution to be an act of treason punishable by death.

Bhutto attempted to control Milbus by stopping the growth of the military's commercial ventures, which curtailed its financial autonomy. However, these measures were reduced to nothing by the lack of change in the overall tenor of policy making. He erred by viewing the military as a junior power that could be controlled and utilized for promoting his interests, and so he allowed the army to regroup. The military capitalized on Bhutto's dependence on military force for building his personal political power. It emerged from the ashes of 1971 sufficiently strengthened to prepare for another takeover in 1977.

Bhutto basically made the mistake of not restructuring the priorities of the state and failing to alter the nature of his own politics. In the first instance, his security and foreign policies remained geared to the classical-realist paradigm. This paradigm naturally strengthens the significance of the military. He shared the military's hawkishness on India and national security. He made every effort to fulfil the armed forces' weapons modernization plans despite the fact that the country was socially and financially recuperating from the effects of its war with India. He was also responsible for starting the nuclear weapons programme, a capability he considered necessary to counter India's hegemonic designs, even if it meant 'eating grass'.[100]

There were two reasons for his military-strategic realism. First, Bhutto was well versed in the discourse of state power. He valued power, and as a man with a larger vision, he could appreciate military prowess. Second, the strengthening of the military was aimed at giving confidence to the generals regarding Bhutto's political leanings. He did not want the generals to have an impression of him as a populist leader determined on bringing socialism, or changes that would jeopardize the interests of the ruling class.

Despite these measures, Bhutto eventually failed in discouraging the military from taking over power. This was because of the particular nature of his politics. He made the classic mistake of letting the military look into his political affairs and note his weaknesses in dealings with his political opponents. Available accounts on Bhutto's interaction with the military, such as the memoirs of General Gul Hassan Khan, show his inclination to politicize the army for personal objectives such as strengthening his position in relation to his opponents. The general mentions how he discouraged Bhutto from trying to politicize the army.[101]

In his instinct for survival, Bhutto tried to partner with the military by giving them a role in administration, imposing martial law in major cities such as Karachi, Lahore and Hyderabad to curb the political unrest and mass demonstrations. The army was asked to fire at the demonstrators. This was tantamount to politicizing the army. However, senior officers felt that the regime's policies would divide the army from within, and refused to support Bhutto's excesses. Reportedly, three army brigadiers resigned because their troops refused to engage in killing the anti-Bhutto demonstrators.[102] It is clear that Bhutto had failed to convince the military that the opposition movement represented a conspiracy against the state. The incident of the brigadiers' resignation worried senior generals: they felt that the politicization of the military was damaging its organizational norms and ethos.

The prime minister had got into the habit of discussing the political situation with the top generals. In addition, as General Gul points out:

> his recognized link with the Army was the Chief of Staff, but every Tom, Dick, and Harry who was a corps commander, and at times even PSOs, were commanded to attend these [Bhutto's] deliberations. This was a fatal blunder on Bhutto's part: he was, for his own ends, politicizing the Army and, worse still, unconsciously furnishing the generals with an opportunity to witness the insecurity that had gripped him.[103]

In addition, the tenor of Bhutto's policies was determined by his dependence on military force and an authoritarian ethos. This was demonstrated by his handling of a political crisis in Baluchistan. He tried to solve the friction between the centre and this small province, which had escalated to an insurgency, by deploying the army and by establishing (in May 1973) a paramilitary force, the Federal Security Force (FSF) as a tool for coercion. He placed the FSF under his direct control. The military operation in Baluchistan in 1973 led to the killing of about 6,000 Baluch.

This was also an expression of the PPP leadership's failure to institutionalize party democracy. The creation of the FSF, which operated like Bhutto's private *Savak*, signalled to other political leaders the significance of military force in the political discourse. However, the FSF also deepened the fears of the generals regarding Bhutto's intention to minimize the importance of the military. The establishment of an auxiliary force would ultimately reduce his reliance on the army.[104]

Ultimately the army moved once again to regain control of the state. The elected prime minister had failed to develop a strategic civil–military partnership with the armed forces and harness the power of the generals completely to the advantage of the civilian players. The fact is that Bhutto's over-assertive instincts made coercive force relevant for the country's politics. This attitude made him redundant in the eyes of senior generals, who regained the confidence to march into the corridors of political power in 1977.

The army struck hard at the roots of populist politics by assassinating Bhutto. The prime minister was arrested, tried for murder and hung in 1979. The Machiavellian prince had turned into the tragic character of Christopher Marlow's *Dr Faustus*, who had sold his soul to the devil for power and become a victim of his own intellect. Ironically, the military killed the leader who was responsible for rebuilding the institution. Abdul Hafeez Pirzada, one of the prominent cabinet members of the Bhutto government, claimed that the military had always conspired against Bhutto and was, in fact, using him to build back up the position of the army from the onset.[105]

Bhutto's loss of power and later his death at the hands of the military regime was an end of an era, which had represented the peak of populism, in more than one way. First, the military coup had put a sudden end to civilian rule. Second, the takeover by the army had overthrown the first popularly elected parliament. Third, the years to come heralded a change in the fundamental character of the armed forces. As will be discussed in the next chapter, the military underwent a gradual transformation from a ruler type to a parent-guardian type in the ensuing years. Furthermore, it became much more adept in using ingenious methods of political bargaining.

The period from 1971 to 1977 represents a lost opportunity in more than one way. The six years of civilian rule saw the gradual shift of the state from what appeared initially as the regime's ability for radical political thinking to a greater conservatism. To placate his power sources, Bhutto granted greater concessions to the religious right. The political government's tilt towards religious ideology naturally strengthened the military's case for protecting an ideological state from internal and external threats. More importantly, the cry of help to the military by the ruling PPP or the opposition parties basically inflated the army's power perception of itself, and failed to recognize the superordinate status of the civilian government. In this crucial period the military clearly recognized that the structural flaws of the political system would enable it to dominate the state.

However, Bhutto alone cannot be held responsible for strengthening the armed forces. The structural lacunae in the country's political system, which led to the military's significance compared with civilian institutions, date back to the early days after the country's birth in 1947. The significance of the national security paradigm determined the organization's importance for the state. Successive governments failed to promote a social development agenda, and instead gave greater importance to the national security paradigm for the sake of personal political legitimacy. The authoritarian nature of politics compelled the civilian leadership to partner with the military, and to propel the armed forces to greater significance than all other institutions of the state. In addition, the lax control by a weak political leadership provided the generals with the confidence to assert that the military was a core group responsible for the security and functioning of the state. Hence, the seeds of praetorianism were sown from the onset.

3 Evolution of the military class, 1977–2005

The military staged a comeback to politics in 1977 with the intention of institutionalizing its control of the state and relationship with civil society. The populist movement towards the end of the 1960s had seriously threatened the supremacy of the military and its control of the state. The civil society was not weak to the degree that the military could impose its rule permanently. Although the three dominant classes, which Alavi discusses and which have been mentioned in the previous chapter, were authoritarian and used force for their advantage, these classes would not allow the military to play a role beyond that of an arbiter.

The political crisis made the military conscious of street power and the resilience of the political players. Bhutto's years in politics had made the generals aware of the possibility of outside intrusion in their organization, which to their minds had to be protected against all meddling. Hence, the defence establishment could not completely rely on the civilian players as dependable junior partners that would continue to accept the military's domination endlessly. The generals would have to coerce the civil society into sufficient submission, or negotiate with members of the three dominant classes.

The period under study in this section can be divided into three phases: 1977–88, 1988–99 and 1999–2005. During the first ten years the military engaged in coercion and human rights violations. However, this technique challenged its legitimacy as an arbiter. From then onwards, the military changed its approach and negotiated a partnership with select members of the dominant classes through the use of subtle coercion and bribery. While coercion took place during the last phase as well, the last seven years are more noticeable for the consolidation of the military's power.

The GHQ sought legal and constitutional provisions to establish its position in the power equation. The legal framework allowed the armed forces a permanent place in power politics as an equal member that was not dependent on the civilian authorities for the protection of its core interests. This is what was referred to in Chapter 1 as the parent-guardian military type. Under this arrangement, the armed forces no longer remained an instrument of policy but acted as an equal partner in decision making. Furthermore, they could determine the security and internal stability of the state without constantly remaining in the political forefront. The military fraternity had developed sufficient economic stakes to not want a permanent exit from power. These interests, in fact, demanded that the class protect them through legal institutional mechanisms, even at the cost of democratic norms and practices.

It is clear that the process of institutionalization, as has been argued in here, could not have taken place without a commonality of interests with the dominant classes. Owing to the pre-capitalist or authoritarian character of the country's sociopolitical system, the military was bound to enhance its power and authority unabated.

THE COERCIVE MILITARY, 1977–88

The second phase of army rule in the country was known for its oppression and human rights violations. General Muhammad Zia ul Haq, the army chief, took over the reins of government by overthrowing a popular prime minister, Zulfiqar Ali Bhutto, who had been accused of excesses against his political rivals and rigging the 1977 elections. The religious right and the opposition parties took to the streets in protest at Bhutto's actions, and asked the army to intervene. The political opposition tactfully mixed ideology with mass politics to obtain the desired result.

The urban poor proved to be the political capital used by the opposition to get a favourable result. The Pakistan National Alliance (PNA), dominated by the religious parties, motivated the urban poor, the proletariat and the orthodox segments of society, including those in the armed forces, by its call for the imposition of *Nizam-e-Mustafa* (the system of Sharia law). The movement had the desired effect because 'it [the call for Sharia law] started adversely affecting the soldiers, who, by tradition, were religious-minded. Some of the military commanders expressed apprehensions that a prolonged exposure of troops to public agitation might erode their military discipline.'[1] Further encouragement was provided by some politicians opposed to Bhutto, who wanted the military to intervene.

But the opposition movement did not completely erode Bhutto's mass appeal. By 1977, Bhutto's PPP had the status of a secular national party that reached out to most parts of the country. Zia ul Haq basically used four options to neutralize the popularity of the PPP.

The first methodology involved coercion of civil society institutions. The regime's coercive measures included:

- killing an elected prime minister through a sham legal trial
- imposing media censorship
- suspending fundamental rights granted by the constitution that Bhutto had introduced in 1973
- banning labour and student unions
- cracking down on all public protest.

Bhutto was rearrested in September 1977 on a charge of the murder of one of his political opponents, Ahmed Raza Kasuri. The Supreme Court was arm-twisted into giving him the death sentence, and the deposed prime minister was hanged by the army in April 1979.[2] The death of Bhutto was a signal to the public regarding the regime's zero tolerance to opposition: it indicated its absolute control over all national matters. The killing of the elected prime minister was one of the draconian measures that altered the relationship between the military and the political leadership for ever.

Although he had strengthened the armed forces, an act that should have made him a hero in the eyes of the military, Bhutto was ultimately punished for breaking the most sacrosanct norm by dishonouring the army chief, who is considered as the ultimate authority in the military circles. He had publicly humiliated Zia. According to the US ambassador, Hummel, Zia had little choice but to hang the prime minister, because, as the ambassador suggested, 'if I had been in Zia's shoes I would not have wanted a live Bhutto in some prison from which he could escape at any time or be sprung'.[3]

Not satisfied with the prime minister's assassination, the military regime undertook other coercive measures to wipe out any speck of populism in the country, acting against both political leaders and their vote bank. Meetings of all senior political leaders were monitored by the intelligence agencies, through bugging devices or human intelligence. Reportedly, major political leaders of the PNA and the Movement for Restoration of Democracy (MRD), which was a coalition of political parties opposed to military rule, were 'wired to the intelligence agencies'.[4] The Zia regime also banned all major sources of public protest, including the student and labour unions. According to a prominent Pakistani journalist, Mushahid Hussain, who later under Musharraf's regime morphed into the military's client, Zia followed the Turkish model for banning student unions. The military dictator actually visited Turkey in 1984 with a bunch of education sector administrators to learn how Ankara had dealt with politically orchestrated campus violence.[5] The regime also followed the Turkish model in dealing with labour unions. The PPP and its support base, consisting mostly of the urban and rural poor, primarily the proletariat, had to be marginalized and forced into submission to make way for the interests of the military and other classes. The media was dealt with even more harshly. The military government amended Section 499 of the Pakistan Penal Code with the objective of prosecuting newspaper editors for publishing stories against the interest of the regime.[6] Zia's rule was exceptionally bad for its treatment of the media. For instance in 1978, for the first time in the country's history journalists were whipped under sentences passed by military courts.[7]

Second, the GHQ co-opted the religious right and used religious ideology to muster support among the general public. The alliance with the religious parties and propagation of Islamic culture were meant to establish the military's hegemony over the civil society.[8] The creation of the office of 'nazim-e-salaat' (controller of prayers), and the introduction of Sharia law and Islamic banking in the mid-1980s were some of the tools used to fight the secular image of Bhutto's party. These measures gave the military dictator a symbolic legitimacy.[9] The state propaganda also condemned Bhutto for his drinking. Thus, it claimed the army had taken control of governance to clean the state of the debauched leadership that had been taking the society away from its Islamic norms.

Pushing the society towards social conservatism required the military to cosy up to the religious right and the socially and politically conservative elements. It must be noted that the Pakistan of the 1960s and the 1970s was

85

socially comparatively liberal. The relationship between the armed forces and the religious right eventually converged as a result of the war in Afghanistan. The religious parties were encouraged to open *madrassas* (informal religious schools) and recruit common people to fight in Afghanistan against the invading Soviet forces. A relationship also developed with the urban-based trader-merchant class, which was socially conservative.[10]

The linkage between the military and the religious right also brought sociopolitical legitimacy to the military. Like the Turkish armed forces, Pakistan's military entered into 'a collusive arrangement with the integrated economic elite' to perpetuate:

> a super-strong executive in the tradition of Ottoman monarchic office and ... favor quasi-fascist groups [religious groups] [that] ensured that no liberalizing challenge could emerge with sufficient power to threaten their [military and other groups] role as self-appointed and sole guardians of the 'organic' nation.[11]

However, the partnership with the religious parties had a sociological cost for the military, as it stimulated a religious ethos in the armed forces. Zia introduced religious education into military training, and instructed all commanders to ensure that prayers were offered by the officers and soldiers.[12]

Third, the Zia regime created a new set of parties and politicians to neutralize the PPP's popularity. This was necessary to downplay Bhutto's fame amongst the working class and other dispossessed people, and to undermine populism in the country. The PPP hallmark was that it had brought in a new age of mass politics to the country.[13] Therefore, Zia sought alternative political constituencies and a new breed of politicians who were loyal to the military establishment through introducing the 'local bodies system'. This approach demonstrates the military's greater capacity than any other institution of the state to penetrate civil society and the country's politics. Instead of strengthening democracy, the local bodies system 'undermined the PPP's national appeal' through 'localization of politics'.[14]

The local body elections were held on a non-party basis which undercut the significance of the political party system and created an apolitical cadre of political representatives at the grass-roots level. Moreover, the local body representatives were empowered over the traditional political party system, by giving them development funds which were used in cooperation with the district administration. The basic idea was to create a new system of political patronage controlled from the top, rather through the involvement of the existing political parties. The local body elections minimized the significance of the PPP and other political parties.

The national elections were held on a non-party basis in 1985. Contrary to the government's claim that elections held on a non-party basis would produce a new or better set of political leaders, most of the seats in these elections were bagged by members of landed-feudal class, tribal chiefs and influential religious officials with feudal backgrounds.[15] The absence of any substantive change in the quality of political representatives was intentional. The elections were meant to wean the candidates, most of whom were from the ruling elite, away from their parties and towards the military-dominated establishment. Since their political survival depended on the military, these politicians were keen to become clients of the establishment rather than the political parties.

These non-party elections threw up a weak civilian regime. Zia handpicked a prime minister, Mohammad Khan Junejo. The toothless parliament was coerced into passing the controversial Eighth Amendment to the 1973 Constitution. Passed in 1985, it allowed the president instead of the prime minister to become the supreme commander of the armed forces and to have the power to sack the parliament. The parliament was also coaxed, blackmailed and coerced into agreeing to indemnify all acts of omission or commission by Zia and his cabal of generals after the 1977 coup.[16] The coercive capacity of the military worked very well on these parliamentarians, who had major personal stakes which they could not afford to compromise for the sake of democracy. The military general-president did not allow the elected representatives to change the course of policies.

A rift was created between Zia and Junejo when the prime minister ordered an inquiry into an explosion at a military ammunition depot at Ojhri near Rawalpindi in April 1988, in which hundreds of innocent people died. There was also civil–military disagreement on the Afghan policy. Zia showed who was in control, and sacked the Junejo government in early 1988 on charges of corruption.

The army under Zia skilfully used the intelligence agencies to manipulate the political parties. The Inter-Services Intelligence (ISI) gained strength throughout the 1980s because of its close involvement in the Afghan war, and was also involved in forming the alliance of opposition parties, the Islami Jamhoori Ittihad (IJI), and the Muhajir Qaumi Movement (MQM) to counter Bhutto's PPP.[17] The regime's adroit use of religious ideology and ethnic identities was also meant to perpetuate political factionalism, which had always strengthened the army's control over politics. Sociopolitical fragmentation would naturally result in strengthening the myth of the military as a national saviour.[18] The MQM and the IJI were meant to counter Bhutto's persistent popularity in his home province, Sindh, and other parts of the country. The MQM has been accused of perpetrating violence in the urban centres of Sindh.[19]

Fourth, the military dictator reached out to other classes as well to create greater acceptability for his regime. His coalition built linkages with big business, which shared Zia's hatred for Bhutto and his unpopular nationalization policies. In any case, the strengthening of big entrepreneurs was essential for the military's external and internal war efforts. From the perspective of Islamabad's external policy, the alliance with big business helped muster resources for the military's modernization. Agha Hassan Abidi of the Bank of Credit and Commerce International (BCCI) bankrolled the procurement of military equipment during this period.[20] Another businessman, Seth Abid, was reputed to have helped Islamabad acquire components for the nuclear programme. Of course, the cooperation was reciprocated. These two entrepreneurs and many others were allowed to draw their pound of flesh in return for their cooperation with the military-dominated state. Zia began to undo the PPP's controversial nationalization policy, and strengthen the business and industrial elite.

Domestically, the military regime also strengthened important entre-preneurs to neutralize Bhutto's support base, which included the labour and student unions. An alliance with the trader-merchant class or big busi-ness was also sought to create alternatives to Bhutto's PPP. The rise of Nawaz Sharif, who became Pakistan's premier twice during the 1990s, is a case in point. The resurrection of the Sharif family's Ittefaq group of busi-nesses and industries is one of many cases of the army's co-option of the industrial-business and trader-merchant groups. Sharif, the eldest son of one of the prime owners of the Sharif family businesses, Mian Mohammad Sharif, ascended to significance in Punjab's politics and later in national politics in the same fashion as Zulfiqar Ali Bhutto had risen to significance under Ayub Khan. He was used to minimize the influence of the landed-feudal class, which tended to be aligned with the PPP. All military regimes create clients who act as the civilian face of the regime and legitimize the military's control, and are nourished by the defence establishment as a replacement for the times when the bulk of the military has to withdraw to the barracks.

The military's ultimate objective, however, continued to be to find more dependable methods to legitimize its political power and role, such as revis-ing the legal and constitutional framework. The Zia regime also used extra-constitutional methods, such as holding a referendum in December 1984 to seek public support for his continuation in power. Zia used Islam as a shield in seeking public support in this presidential referendum. The referendum question was phrased to suggest that if people supported Islam, they also automatically supported Zia's continuation in the presidential office for the next five years. Like Ayub Khan, Zia sought legitimacy for the continuation of his and the army's power through a popular mandate.

Again, the way in which the army sought a permanent role through the head of the service was similar to the events of the 1960s. Zia became pres-ident without removing his uniform, which showed his need to maintain his connection with the armed forces, his main power base. The president certainly did not intend to give up power, but his rule ended with his death in a mysterious plane crash on 17 August 1988. Although the results of an inquiry into the accident were not made public, there is no evidence to suggest that the crash was deliberately caused, perhaps as a result of an upheaval in the higher echelons of the army. In any case, the army is known for its tradition of not visibly protesting against the authority of its chief.

Zia clearly had personal religious inclinations, but he also had political reasons for collaborating with religious parties. He used them for civilianiz-ing the military rule,[21] and for amassing political power: for instance, by using religion as a pretext to dissolve the system of parliamentary democracy.

Reportedly, he believed he could have used the Sharia law to declare a slightly modernized system of caliphate, which would have meant the rule of an individual rather than a group of elected representatives.

Despite these machinations, the military regime was still unable to ride the political tiger without creating legal and constitutional ways of securing the defence establishment's interests and its permanent role in the polity. Clearly, the GHQ was not satisfied with its role as an arbiter. Although the client politicians and other co-opted civil society actors provided an alternative to the PPP, the fact was that the civilian players formed an alternative source of power, which ultimately had greater legitimacy than the armed forces. The army was not certain about the extent to which it could depend on the civilian players to secure its interests.

The safeguards for the armed forces were instituted in the form of the Eighth Amendment to the 1973 Constitution. This empowered the president to sack a government, become the supreme commander of the armed forces, and appoint the heads of the three services and the chairman of the JCSC. Article 58(2)(b), which empowered the president to dismiss a government, was the most controversial provision, but it was effective in protecting the military's interests. According to this amendment:

> The President shall dissolve the National Assembly if so advised by the Prime Minister and the National Assembly shall, unless sooner dissolved, stand dissolved at the expiration of forty-eight hours after the Prime Minister has so advised, (2) Notwithstanding anything contained in clause (2) of article 48, the President may also dissolve the National Assembly at his discretion, where, in his opinion ... a situation has arisen in which the Government of the Federation cannot be carried on in accordance with the provisions of the constitution and an appeal to the electorate is necessary.[22]

Over the ensuing years, the law has been invoked five times to remove successive elected administrations on charges of corruption. However, this has never been done on the advice of the prime minister. The elected premier represented the alternative power centre, which had to be kept in check through empowering the president. Zia shrewdly manipulated the parliament of his hand-picked prime minister, Mohammad Khan Junejo, to pass this controversial amendment which ensured the permanent weakening of democratic institutions. Such legal provisions no longer required the armed forces to stage a coup to come to the political forefront. The senior generals could simply prevail upon the president, if the office-bearer was not a military official, to remove an elected government. Four governments were removed during the 1990s despite the fact that the army chief was no longer in the seat of power.

The further strengthening of the military's role was carried out through the introduction of the 'Revival of the Constitution Order' (RCO) that created the National Security Council (NCS). Similar to its Turkish counterpart, the Pakistani NSC was envisaged to have an advisory role in recommending declarations of a state of emergency, security affairs and other matters of national importance. Although Zia eventually did not establish the NSC, the issue shadowed future governments until the matter was finally settled with the NSC's creation in 2004. The military's officer cadre was determined to play the role of a parent-guardian protecting the state from the civilian leadership, at the cost of the growth of democratic institutions. The period from 1977–88 was therefore marked by the military maintaining its role in politics without keeping its rank and file in the forefront of state functioning.

Zia did not vociferously pursue the issue of the NSC for two possible reasons. First, dropping the issue was a *quid pro quo* for the National Assembly agreeing to the other controversial amendment to the 1973 Constitution that empowered the president to dissolve the parliament. This legal provision had already made him powerful enough to take care of the interests of the armed forces. Second, he probably could not have aimed for such a complete maximization of the power of the armed forces when the international environment, which had been favourable earlier, had begun to swing the other way. With the signing of the Geneva Accords in April 1988, which facilitated the withdrawal of Soviet troops from Afghanistan, Pakistan's significance as a front-line state diminished. As a result, its military did not remain vital to US interests.

The United States' urgent move to bail out of Afghanistan without a prolonged security commitment in the region initiated a dialogue between Washington and the civilian regime in Pakistan. The Junejo government keenly cooperated with the United States to facilitate the withdrawal of the Soviet troops from Afghanistan. Islamabad's signing of the Geneva Accords did not endear the Pakistani prime minister to his military. He had violated the sacrosanct principle of interfering in matters considered vital by the military. In effect, the signing of the Geneva Accords by the civilian government improved relations between the political government and the United States, which in turn bolstered Junejo's confidence. The United States for the first time in many years gave precedence to the civilian players in Pakistani government over the military it had comfortably shared a bed with since the early 1980s. It was in Washington's interest to disengage after the withdrawal of the Soviet troops.

Such developments tied Zia's hands in forcing the option of the NSC on the civilian government. It must be mentioned that Zia ardently opposed the Geneva Accords on the basis that they did not accommodate Islamabad's strategic concerns regarding Afghanistan's future. Thus, Zia saw the US–Pakistan military alignment slowly wither away before his death in 1988.

During the 1980s the relationship with the United States had provided a tremendous source of strength to the ruling military. The Reagan administration offered Pakistan two aid packages of US$3.2 billion (Rs.185.6 billion) and US$4.2 billion (Rs.243.6 billion). Islamabad was also provided with state-of-the-art F-16 fighter aircraft, and there was also talk of giving Pakistan the extremely high-tech airborne early-warning aircraft system

(AWACS). Although this technology was not provided, the overall military technological and financial cooperation improved the Pakistan military's standing in the region and at home.

Considering the cooperation between the two countries during most of the 1980s, the popular myth of Pakistan being run with the help of 'America, Army and Allah' deepened considerably. This relationship was established primarily after Ronald Reagan's election victory in 1980 augmented the military's image as a national saviour and Pakistan's primary institution. The Soviet invasion of Afghanistan in December 1979 suddenly made Zia, who had earlier been a pariah, into a favourite of the United States and the western world. Before the early 1980s, bilateral relations between the two countries were at their lowest ebb because of various contentious issues between the two states. It was Moscow's invasion of Afghanistan that saved the day for Pakistan's military dictator.

To return to Pakistan's domestic politics, democracy was restored in 1988 as a result of the general elections held that year which brought the PPP back to power. However, the presence of the controversial Article 58(2)(b) created an abiding tension between the military and the political class long after Zia's death.

A THORNY PARTNERSHIP, 1988–99

The elections held in November 1988 ushered in a period of unstable democracy that has become known for a quick succession of governments. During these ten years Pakistan saw eight prime ministers, including four caretaker prime ministers, one of whom was brought in from the World Bank to mind the country for a period of three months.[23] The military, as the ultimate arbiter, tweaked the political system every two years, especially when it saw the civilian regime challenging the defence establishment's authority, or it perceived a substantive threat to the polity.

For instance, the army was accused of forcing the dismissal of Benazir Bhutto's and Nawaz Sharif's first governments for challenging the military's authority. Benazir Bhutto was quite helpless against the army's conspiracy to overthrow her government in 1990. Her government was removed in a coup-like manner.[24] She got into trouble with the military over issues important to its interests, such as the appointment of the corps commanders and the chairman of the JCSC. Benazir Bhutto also replaced the head of the ISI, Lt. General Hameed Gul, with a general of her choice, Major-General Shamsul Rehman Kallu. This did not make her popular with the army, and hence the organization retaliated.[25] Reportedly, the higher echelons of the army, who were extremely unhappy with her attempts to curb their power by interfering in internal matters, used the ISI to remove her from power. The army chief, General Aslam Beg, and the head of the ISI, Lt. General Asad Durrani, obtained a slush fund of approximately Rs 60 million (US$1.03 million) from a private bank, and used this to execute the plan for Bhutto's removal.[26] The money was given to the ISI to destabilize the civilian government.

Later on, the army played the role of an arbiter in resolving the crisis between the president and the prime minister. The army's involvement led to the removal of Bhutto's successor, Nawaz Sharif. They first persuaded the president, Ishaq Khan, to force Prime Minister Sharif to resign. However, the Supreme Court declared the president's removal of Sharif to be illegal and unconstitutional, and this led to a political crisis.[27] The army chief acted as an umpire and forced both Ishaq Khan and Sharif to resign. This was a face-saving solution that was manipulated by the GHQ to solve the crisis.

Intriguingly, the politicians did not seem to have learnt any lessons from the earlier decades, or even from the manner of Zulfiqar Ali Bhutto's ousting, and continued to lean on the military. Each regime considered itself smarter than its predecessors, and seemed to believe it could lure the army to support it by offering the generals greater economic incentives and opportunities. During these ten years, the military was called on time and again to tip the balance against the regime without any concern for the country's political future. According to Lt.-General (rtd) Talat Masood, politicians constantly requested the army to intervene on their behalf against their opponents. Such behaviour encourages the armed forces to play a role in politics.[28] Did the politicians not have any political acumen? Did Benazir Bhutto and Nawaz Sharif, the two key politicians, not think about the value of mutually agreeing a political code of conduct that would keep the military at bay? Why did the political leadership indulge in providing political and economic sweeteners to the military? Two explanations have been suggested.

The first argument, which is more popular than the second with the military, views the political crises as a consequence of incompetent handling of the situation by politicians. It holds the political and civil society responsible for all the ills the country has suffered, and continues to suffer from. Even the most junior officers of the armed forces believe that the army is obliged to intervene because of the inept handling and greed of the politicians. Such a notion is upheld by the military's civilian clients as well. For instance, Mushahid Hussain, who was information minister during Sharif's second tenure and later crossed over to join ranks with Pervez Musharraf, is of the view that:

> the politicians on both sides of the divide have again demonstrated their inability to rise beyond partisan considerations. Only when they are told to 'behave' by the men in 'khaki' do they 'fall in line' and it would have been better for their own image that such moves for reconciliation should have been initiated of their own accord rather than being pushed from above.[29]

Although it could be argued that Hussain's statement indicates his political metamorphosis after 1999, when he was intimidated by the Musharraf government into abandoning Sharif, his argument is considered an adequate commentary on the quality of the country's politicians. The

92

military bureaucrats are of the view that politicians are inherently inept because of their lack of grooming in governance and managing the state. The former head of Musharraf's National Reconstruction Bureau (NRB), Lt.-General (rtd) Tanveer Naqvi, elaborates this point:

> During my association with NRB, I met as many people and institutions as possible to learn from best practices, including the German Foundation. They told me that these foundations, belonging to political parties, have institutionalised training and education of Parliament and Parliamentarians. Every German member of Parliament goes through a training course. I come back to that probably the cause of it all is the fact that those who want to be and ought to be in control are not necessarily equipped to be in control, and therefore they are unable to assert themselves morally and intellectually to acquire control. The more we invest into that [training of MPs] in direct proportion will be our pace for civilian supremacy and oversight of Armed Forces.[30]

Naqvi's views are representative of the military officers' belief in their own intellectual superiority, and the civilians' perceived inferiority. The director-general of Inter-Services Public Relations (ISPR) in the early days of Musharraf regime, Maj.-General Rashid Qureshi, for instance, is of the view that the average military officer is better qualified and more intelligent than an average civil bureaucrat, and definitely more effective than a politician.[31]

Given the inability of politicians to discipline the armed forces, military officers have come to believe that their organizational training and discipline make them more capable of running the affairs of the state. This notion is also accepted by the civilian beneficiaries of the military regime. For instance, one of the female parliamentarians nominated to the National Assembly on special seats for women (created by changes brought in by Musharraf), Donya Aziz, expressed her reservations about the politicians' ability to reduce the military's political influence. She was of the view that the military is far more organized and better disciplined than the politicians, who often lack sincerity of purpose.[32] Others, such as the prominent Karachi-based entrepreneur Razzak Tabba, attributed the politicians' comparative inability to their lack of education.[33]

However, this argument is highly questionable. There is no evidence to substantiate the claim. After all other countries, including neighbouring India, with which Pakistan has a common history, have survived political authoritarianism and turmoil without allowing their military to step into the politicians' shoes. Despite the fact that the Indian Army is involved in internal conflict, often in a coercive mode, and the military leadership complains about the civilian authority, the country's political and military leadership ensure that the military is subservient to civilian control. Pakistan's armed forces officers believe this difference is due to the greater sincerity and forthrightness of Indian politicians.[34] However, the Indian military officers also take responsibility for upholding democratic principles. For instance, the

Indian Army chief, General Sam Manekshaw, refused to assist the prime minister, Indira Gandhi, during the imposition of a state of emergency in the country during the early 1970s.

Another example from India relates to the issue of army chiefs granting greater power to the army deployed in Kashmir. The senior commanders rejected a suggestion by an army officer that this be done out of a concern to keep the armed forces apolitical.[35]

Interestingly, the military pursued the idea of political training. The Musharraf regime started national security workshops at the National Defence College (NDC) for politicians, journalists, civil servants and businessmen, and seriously considered opening a 'political school' for women parliamentarians.[36] These people were lectured about various issues of strategic importance in a sanitized military environment, which was intended to persuade them of the grandeur of the military life. Those selected for the workshops included parliamentarians, of whom 90 per cent were not even familiar with parliamentary procedures, according to a member of the Pakistan Muslim League (Q-group), Asiya Azeem.[37] This proposal deliberately ignored the fact that the military was not above board either, and bore its share of responsibility for the intellectual underdevelopment of the politicians. In any case, the political parties operate in an authoritarian fashion, and the top leaders, who are clients of the military, do not allow democratic discussion. Moreover, training cannot solve the problem of the structural flaw created by the authoritarian nature of politics. According to Justice Majida Rizvi, the military's role cannot be curtailed, because 'when the vested interests of the elite become common then how can you check the military's role expansion?'[38]

An alternative view voiced by a US security expert, Dr Ashley Tellis, explains Pakistan's political crisis as a representation of the politicians' inability to differentiate between micro and macro rationality. While micro rationality pertains to the narrow interests of individual leaders, the macro picture concerns the long-term vision of politics in the country, the region and the world. In short, the Pakistani politician, being a rational egoist like his/her counterparts in the rest of the world, thinks in terms of personal interests. However, unlike in some other countries, Pakistan's politicians tend not to think beyond very short-term interests.

This, Tellis adds, is a result of the continued military rule. Over the years, the country's political leadership has lost its ability to imagine a long-term future or think in terms of macro rationality.[39] This means that the politicians do not strategize about pushing the military back by harnessing their own authoritarian tendencies. Tellis's argument tends to see Pakistan's politics from a linear perspective. Given the military's propensity to conspire against civilian authority, the politicians are not able to think long-term or stabilize the political situation. This was apparent in the overthrowing of Benazir Bhutto and Nawaz Sharif, as was mentioned above. Sharif, who was a product of General Zia ul Haq, was initially brought to power with the army's help to replace Benazir Bhutto in 1990.[40] His removal in 1993 was a result of differences with the army chief over the government's support for the US military initiative against the Iraqi invasion of Kuwait. Sharif and the army also became estranged because of disagreements over the military operation in Sindh against the ethnic party MQM, which was the ruling party's political partner.[41] Clearly, the army's decisions prevailed on most issues and the leaders were sacked for disagreeing with the GHQ. Therefore, political analysts such as Zia-u-Din believe that political governments have little space to manoeuvre.[42]

Benazir Bhutto returned to power in 1993, only to be dismissed again in 1996. The lacklustre economic performance of the country over the first couple of years of her government, compounded by her poor reputation as a head of government and her inability to prevent her spouse from indulging in corruption, did not earn her accolades.[43] She was removed despite the fact that she had opted not to confront the military over their core interests, and had supported them on other matters the GHQ considered important, such as the Kashmir issue.[44] Haqqani is of the view that her dismissal was more a result of the efforts of the religious-conservative forces, and the military's realization that she was unable to get continued US support. Washington and Islamabad had divergent views on Afghanistan and nuclear proliferation.[45] The Brown Amendment to the US Constitution, which allowed Washington to transfer some weapons and military spare parts to Islamabad, was passed during her tenure, but the quality of bilateral relations remained poor.

Bhutto's removals in 1990 and again in 1996 are symptomatic of the 'divide and rule' game played by the GHQ. Even while Bhutto was the premier, her power in the centre and in her home province of Sindh was diluted by the army's use of Nawaz Sharif's Muslim League. Bhutto similarly counterbalanced her political opponent by providing an alternative prime ministerial candidate when the army was not happy with Sharif.

The military's intelligence apparatus played a key role in encouraging the divisions between the political actors.[46] The intelligence agencies gained strength through their enhanced role in regional and global geopolitics, and through greater involvement at home. Political horse-trading was rife during these ten years, as part of the manipulative mechanisms used by the ISI and other intelligence outfits, and resulted in an increase in political and economic corruption. However, political governments were always dismissed on charges of financial mismanagement. For the military, corruption served as a security valve to be turned on and off as a means to regulate the political system. The military basically replaced one set of corrupt politicians with another in order to sustain its own power base.

CONSOLIDATION OF POWER, 1999–2005

The most recent period has seen the end of this period of civilian power, and the return of the military to the saddle. These years have also witnessed the defence establishment consolidating its power through additional legal and constitutional provisions, and curbing the attempts of the civilian authorities to establish their dominance.

Having returned to power in 1997, Sharif lost it in 1999 because of his open confrontation with the army chief, Musharraf, whom he had removed from office. He was subsequently accused of risking the lives of more than 200 passengers of a Pakistan International Airlines (PIA) flight from Sri Lanka, including the army chief, by not permitting it to land on Pakistani soil. Sharif was nervous about allowing Musharraf to return to Pakistan soon after he had replaced him as the chief of the largest armed service. However, his plan backfired and some important corps commanders staged a coup on behalf of Musharraf. Sharif's dismissal brought the military directly back into the seat of power.

There had been a fierce battle for supremacy between the military and the civilian authorities in the last days of Sharif's government. The prime minister had gained confidence through getting a two-thirds majority in the 1996 elections, and this had helped him to remove Article 58(2)(b) from the 1973 Constitution. He also became confident of his ability to reduce the army's power after he forced Musharraf's predecessor, General Jahangir Karamat, to resign (replacing him with Musharraf). Sharif was unhappy about a statement Karamat had made regarding the need for a NSC which would give a permanent role to the armed forces in political decision making. Although Sharif later claimed that he appointed Musharraf because he thought unfair the military's policy of considering only the top three or four officers for appointment as service chief,[47] the fact was that he was sure of Musharraf's loyalty, as was claimed by other senior commanders at the time.[48]

Nawaz Sharif opted to give Musharraf, as army chief, dual charge of the army and the JCSC. (In April 2000 Admiral Fasih Bokhari, who was the naval chief and the commander in line through seniority for appointment as chairman of the JCSC, resigned as a result.) However, Sharif obviously miscalculated his own ability to manipulate the military. He also erred in gauging the tenacity of the military institution in defending its political autonomy. By 1999 it was in the process of morphing into an independent class (see more discussion on this in the next section). When Musharraf proved beyond his control, Sharif replaced him with General Zia-u-Din Butt. Although Butt was a senior general, he was not from the fighting forces, and because of this his appointment undermined the army's normal appointment process.

One of the causes of the rift between Sharif and Musharraf (and the reasons for the army's support of him) was that the army chief appeared to have thwarted the prime minister's efforts at negotiating peace with the traditional arch-rival, India, without bringing the military on board. The government arranged a welcome ceremony at the border for the Indian prime minister, Atal Bihari Vajpai, who had come to sign the famous Lahore Declaration. In this both countries agreed to start a composite dialogue to ensure the resolution of all outstanding disputes, and expand contacts in other areas such as trade and tourism. Musharraf expressed his resentment of the peace process by refusing to attend the welcome ceremony.

Further embarrassment was caused to the political government in Islamabad when conflict surfaced after Vajpai's visit to Pakistan. In 1999 a restricted group of senior army generals launched a military operation against India at Musharraf's behest, which later came to be known as the Kargil Crisis. There is still no definitive and acceptable explanation from the Pakistani side of why Musharraf embarked on a war path at a time when peace was being negotiated via the Lahore Declaration, but it is undoubtedly true that the Kargil Crisis demonstrated the underlying tension between the civilian and military authorities in the country.

Bokhari, the former naval chief, believes that Musharraf decided to remove Sharif because of the threat that the prime minister would institute an inquiry into the Kargil issue.[49] This would clearly have undermined the power of the army chief. The military moved to assume direct control on 12 October 1999. Obviously, this gave it greater power to implement regulations (such as a replacement for Article 58(2)(b)) to remove the civilian leaders of central and provincial governments. The corps commanders' bid to protect Musharraf was not just about defending an individual, it was a matter of upholding the perceived sanctity of the institution. Sharif could not be allowed to replace the seniormost general, who was from the fighting forces, with another general who was not.

However, Bokhari's account of Sharif's removal is only part of the explanation and not the whole. The government's talks with India are part of the larger picture regarding the competing powers of the political forces and the military. Three interconnected issues basically indicated the relative strengthening of the political forces under Sharif: the forced resignation of the two service chiefs, the reversal of the controversial constitutional amendment, and the peace talks at almost the same time. This progressive strengthening of the civilian prime minister suggested that he might eventually have acquired the confidence to publicly question the army chief's judgment regarding the Kargil operation. An inquiry into this controversial military action would have been unprecedented in Pakistan's history. Moreover, it would have symbolized the final victory of the civilian forces over the military.

The army would not allow its authority to be questioned. The resignation of Karamat, in particular, had created consternation amongst the officer cadre, who saw the move as an insult to the armed forces. Similarly, the peace talks with India, particularly the agreement to hold a composite dialogue that would include the Kashmir dispute but not focus on the issue, seemed to challenge the military's *raison d'être*. Removing Sharif was therefore also an expression of the military restoring its monopoly over critical foreign and defence policy issues.

Interestingly, in 2004 the Musharraf government started a composite dialogue with New Delhi. However, the difference between the Sharif and the Musharraf peace initiatives lay in the fact that the army chief was able to persuade the armed forces that the peace overtures were part of his strategy to secure the country's larger interests. The country needed economic and political stability, and this was what he was trying to bring about through the peace talks. Also, the dialogue with India was presented as a new method to ensure the resolution of the Kashmir dispute. The army, as the guarantor of the country's sovereignty and national honour, was presented as the best judge and moderator of the peace overtures.

On a separate note, it must be pointed out that sceptics question the credibility of Musharraf's peace overtures. They argue that he started the dialogue out of consideration for the wider political environment, which did not support conflict on the Indian Subcontinent, and to improve the country's economic conditions.[50] The dialogue has led to no substantive change in Islamabad's overall policy towards India. It continues to peg new initiatives, such as trade and greater people-to-people contact between the two countries, on the resolution of the Kashmir issue. So while the army does not want an escalation of tension or the eruption of a war with India, it does not intend to let go of the issue when this would reduce the military's significance and alter its image as the nation's guardian, especially when there is no indication from India that it is willing to resolve the issue by agreeing to any minor or major territorial changes. Even if the dispute is resolved, the development might not necessarily result in a substantive improvement in relations. The bilateral mistrust is far too deep to allow for friendly relations between the two neighbours.

Unlike his predecessors, Musharraf did not declare himself as chief martial law administrator: he took the more neutral title of chief executive. However, the imposition of military rule in 1999 was indeed a coup. The style of it shows the military's acumen in adapting itself and its tactics to internal and external environmental trends. Instead of making itself unpopular through a crudely overt method of declaring martial law, the army high command chose to penetrate the political system and the society in a more subtle manner. The regime was also far more tactful in intimidating the media than the Zia government: it clearly wanted to avoid acquiring the reputation of its military predecessor. Under Musharraf the media is considered to be freer than even during the previous civilian government. However, in spite of this the regime is known for expressing displeasure about news reports that create a negative image for it, and journalists are targeted selectively, resulting in the harassment and disappearance of approximately 48 journalists to date under his rule.[51] Seven journalists were killed after being involved in reporting domestic conflict in the NWFP and Baluchistan in 2006. According to investigations conducted by the Committee to Protect Journalists (CPJ), the bullets found near the bodies were identified as types frequently used by the intelligence agencies.[52]

While building its relatively positive image, the military embarked upon rebuilding the political system through creating alternative constituencies and seeking out a new set of politicians who would do the GHQ's bidding. This process used techniques such as the 'localization of politics' which was carried out by the previous military regimes. The Musharraf regime renamed it devolution of democracy. As a result, local governments were elected both directly and indirectly in the country's 96 districts, 307 tehsils and 30 city town councils, and 6,022 union councils.

The local government elections, held on a non-party basis, brought to the fore new faces in politics. This does not necessarily denote a break from the control of the dominant classes, as these new representatives owe their allegiance to the central government, especially the Musharraf regime that created them, rather than political parties. Under the devolution of democracy plan, the locally elected members are responsible for making and implementing development plans, in which they are assisted by the local administration. The members of the national assembly and the senate, who were elected soon afterwards in 2002, do not have any role to play in the local governments elected at the grass-roots level. According to Mohammad Waseem, such localization of politics is 'a sure recipe for unbridled centralism'.[53] Devoid of any party affiliation, these politicians enhanced the government's administrative control of politics. The local government representatives certainly came in handy during the May 2002 presidential referendum, held before the general election the same year, as these people ensured that the ballot boxes returned full and the votes were in Musharraf's favour. However, the manner of filling the ballot boxes was questionable. Like Zia's, Musharraf's referendum question did not leave a lot of options for the common people. The question was:

> For the survival of the local government system, establishment of democracy, continuity of reforms, end to sectarianism and extremism, and to fulfil the vision of Quaid-e-Azam, would you like to elect President General Pervez Musharraf as president of Pakistan for five years?'[54]

Musharraf had promised to establish good governance in the country, but the fact that the public turnout was limited demonstrated the people's lack of confidence in the army-controlled political system. One source cites a mere 15 per cent turnout.[55] The opposition parties claimed the turnout to be a mere 5 per cent.[56] However the government claimed it was 70 per cent, of which 98 per cent voted in the president's favour.[57] Clearly Musharraf did not intend to leave power or transfer authority completely to the politicians.

The general elections at the end of 2002 followed this referendum, and were an example of the military establishment's mastery of pre-poll rigging. They did not merely manipulate the election-day process, they controlled the lead-up to the elections. They barred the top leaders of the two main political parties, the PPP and the Pakistan Muslim League – Nawaz (PML-N, Nawaz Sharif's party) from returning to Pakistan to contest the elections, and also launched a massive media campaign against Benazir Bhutto and Sharif.[58] In addition, some election observers are of the view that certain key members of the newly formed alliance of the religious parties, the MMA, were supported by the government to contest the elections. If they won seats it would neutralize the PPP and PML-N, which were both considered as arch-rivals of Musharraf.[59] The support included the withdrawal of lawsuits against MMA candidates.

Although Musharraf did not contest these elections, he did not want Benazir Bhutto and Nawaz Sharif or their parties to get a popular mandate. Hence, supporting the MMA and the MQM (the party supported in Sindh) was a strategy to undermine the position of these two leaders in the general elections. The military regime also coerced politicians through the creation of organizations such as the National Accountability Bureau (NAB). This organization, established under the National Accountability Ordinance of 1999, had the mandate of punishing, arresting and disqualifying those found guilty of corruption from holding public office or contesting elections.[60] Subsequently, the NAB was used to harass politicians into compliance. It was accused of creating the 'king's party,' a name given to the PML-Q (Quaid-e-Azam), by clearing its members of charges of corruption. Meanwhile, the NAB coerced opposition members through instituting cases against them or through seeking their disqualification by the national accountability courts.[61] Among the prominent members of the opposition who were victimized through the accountability ordinance was a prominent member of the PPP, Yusuf Raza Gillani, who was accused of misusing official cars and telephone facilities.[62]

Despite these manipulations, the government could only get a split mandate, and had to indulge in further manipulation through forcing a split in Bhutto's PPP. Fearful of losing perks or being involved in court cases or victimized by NAB, 20 members of the PPP defected to form a group called the Pakistan People's Party Parliamentarian Patriot (PPPP), before joining ranks with the PML-Q, which enabled the PML-Q to get the majority required to form a government. The conversion of the PPP members is an extraordinary example of the GHQ's political manoeuvring. This was the first instance of defection from the ranks of the PPP.

Neither the parliament nor the government were free operators. The elected members were not allowed sufficient room to manoeuvre by the executive, represented by the army-president. The tension in the king's party and its strategic affairs were managed through tight central control by the president. Like any civilian authoritarian leader or feudal lord, Musharraf played a direct hand in settling differences between the PML-Q leaders and their allies such as the MQM. Instead of strengthening democratic institutions, as Musharraf claimed, he encouraged clientelism, in which the politicians of the ruling party, especially the top political leaders, became his clients.

Yet again, the army managed to create a new set of clients who offered all their support to the army-chief-turned-president. On several occasions the two top leaders of the PML-Q, Chaudhry Shujaat Hussain and Pervaiz Elahi, talked about their intention not to collaborate with Benazir Bhutto,[63] who was immensely disliked by Musharraf, and their willingness to re-elect Musharraf as the president.[64] Musharraf intended to get an extension as president beyond 2007. His power was necessary to guarantee the army's dominance, but this could only be achieved through manipulating the political parties.

It was Musharraf's position as the army chief that gave him the capacity to manipulate politicians. Clearly, the political system was hijacked by the army-president, who had to be constantly reminded of the fact that his power would not be challenged by the PML-Q. Consequently, the PML-Q's internal decision making reflected its authoritarian character, of which some of its members complained.[65] Some members also accused the government and party of using them to rubber-stamp decisions.[66] The internal divisions resulted in a frequent change of prime ministers. From 1999 to 2005 the country saw three prime ministers, including one caretaker premier. The prime ministers were changed through internal political coups in the king's party without the president dismissing the parliament. The continuation of the parliament was projected as a sign of stability and strengthening of democracy. The army had turned Pakistan into a bureaucratic-authoritarian state in which the president was a military man and the prime minister an international banker brought in from Citibank in the United States to ensure economic and political stability as best suited the ruling coalition. The parliament and ruling party politics were subservient to the executive. Such conditions give credence to Waseem's argument that:

> [the] Parliament in Pakistan is a subordinate legislature. Here, the executive is, without exception, a pre-eminent player on the national scene. It initiates decisions in party forums, which are translated into law through the legislative procedure, and are then rigidly defined, implemented and controlled by the bureaucracy. Given the domination of extra-parliamentary forces over the power structure of Pakistan, parliamentary institutions are often considered by political players as necessary accoutrements of a modern ruling structure. In other words, these institutions legitimize the existing political order. Even if real power resides outside the legislature, the power holders need to win legal and moral authority. Not surprisingly, each of the four military governments tried to fill the gap of legitimacy by holding elections in 1962, 1970, 1985 and 2002.[67]

Obviously, these circumstances did not leave a lot of options for the politicians. However, the military's coercion provinces only part of the explanation for the politicians' behaviour. The question that arises is why the politicians succumbed to the military's coercion without mobilizing the party cadres or the general public.

The fact is that there is a growing disenchantment among the general public with the behaviour of the political class. The sudden absence of populist politics in Pakistan can only be explained through understanding the structural flaw in the country's sociopolitical system: that is, the pre-capitalist or authoritarian nature of the political system, in which the ruling elite use force to attain their objectives. Since the dominant classes are focused on maximizing their power, the politicians are easily co-opted by the military rather than playing the political game through fair means. According to this explanation, which is one of the main arguments put forward in this chapter, the politicians cooperate with the military because of their commonality of interests, and because their main problem is not with the military's use of force to fulfil its political objectives, but with its control of their authority. Indeed, this is the essence of the system of clientelism in which politicians or other prominent members of the ruling elite, such as big landowners and businessmen, support the military in return for personal favours or the military's support.

Musharraf sought public support for his political clients by personally lobbying for the PML-Q candidates before the elections scheduled to be held in 2007. For instance, during a public gathering in Chakwal – a district in Punjab – the president requested the people to vote for his candidates and stressed the importance of supporting his political system, as it would strengthen democracy in the country. He tried to further strengthen the case for his political partners by conducting a negative campaign against the opposition parties. He called upon the public's sense of nationalism by categorizing the opposition leaders as anti-army, an attitude that could not be allowed in the national interest. His emphasis was that 'a strong army guarantees a stable Pakistan. Therefore, the army must grow strong and we will make it stronger.'[68]

Musharraf's leadership did not eliminate authoritarianism and bring about a change in the country's politics. The new parliament was, in fact, like 'old wine in a new bottle'. The members of the king's party used their influence to flout rules and misuse their authority. For instance, the federal law minister's son beat up a fellow passenger on a PIA flight in the presence of his father, for the sin of questioning whether airport security had checked him before he boarded the flight.[69] The minister did not apologize and he continued with this behaviour. Later, he beat up a waiter in a five-star hotel in the capital city.[70] Interestingly, the PML-Q leadership did not seriously admonish the law minister.[71] In fact, the PML-Q's behaviour was similar to that of the PML-N, which was ousted on charges of corruption and political high-handedness. Like the PML-N members who stormed and attacked the Supreme Court in 1997, PML-Q activists ransacked the Peshawar Press Club to prevent party dissidents from holding a press conference. Reportedly, dozens of journalists sustained injuries.[72]

Besides engaging in authoritarian behaviour, the PML-Q leadership benefited financially by supporting Musharraf. The economic exploitation by politicians aligned with Musharraf was ignored by the president, since they legitimized his rule by giving him support.

This type of behaviour signifies the semi-authoritarian nature of the country's sociopolitics. Here, the concept of 'semi-authoritarianism' is borrowed from Michael Mann's seminal work, *Sources of Social Power*. The author uses the term to explain conditions in Imperial Germany, Austria-Hungary and Japan, as an amalgamation of the old-regime or monarchical rule and an authoritarian political party system. While this means the introduction of universal male suffrage, the political system does not recognize the rights of the masses or serve the interests of the people.[73]

To apply this argument to Pakistan, the political parties operate within the framework of their own interests, and particularly the interests of their leaders. Under these circumstances, the politicians find it beneficial to partner with the military to gain benefits. In fact, throughout the country's history the political players have conceded power to the armed forces with the intention of maximizing their own interests. Consequently, the defence forces have been transformed into something resembling the military of Bismarck's Germany: autonomous, and not controlled by the state and society. There is an inherent dichotomy between the civilian players' perception of civil–military relations and their own control of politics, and the political reality. A semi-authoritarian system can only enhance the power of the military. The symbiotic relationship between the dominant classes and the force represented by the military institution is too strong to break the civilian players' dependency on the armed forces.

Stephen P. Cohen also mentions an elite partnership in his latest book, *The Idea of Pakistan*. He is of the view that the country is basically controlled by a small but 'culturally and socially intertwined elite', comprising about 500 people who form part of the establishment. Belonging to different subgroups, these people are known for their loyalty to the 'core principles' of a central state.[74] These key principles include safeguarding the interests of the dominant classes.

The continuous role of the military as an arbiter is both a cause and effect of the lopsided behaviour of the dominant classes, especially the political leadership. The very fact that the prominent politicians continue to use the military as a political balancer of power, and refuse to negotiate their power or power interests through democratic means, allows the armed forces to play a dominant role. It is important to note that the prominent politicians such as Bhutto, Sharif and others prefer to use the military as an umpire rather than concede space to each other. Each of these leaders has been known for fermenting trouble and unleashing reprisals against the other, through targeting their party faithful or close relatives, and attacking each other's personal interests. While Bhutto unleashed a vendetta against Sharif by floating rumours about his corruption and instituting court cases, the latter paid in the same coin. Bhutto's husband, Asif Zardari, was kept in prison under corruption charges for most of Sharif's two tenures as prime minister. Instead of strengthening the democratic process inside her PPP, Bhutto is known for an authoritarian control of her party and politics, a behaviour that won her unfavourable comments from the national press. Najam Sethi, a prominent journalist, berated Bhutto as an 'arrogant, reckless, capricious and corrupt ruler who surrounded herself with sycophants, lackeys and flunkeys and squandered away a second opportunity to serve the people of Pakistan'.[75]

At this point it is appropriate to mention Bhutto's guilty participation in the political crisis between President Ishaq Khan and Prime Minister Sharif. Smelling the tension between the president and the prime minister, she turned the heat up by threatening to march on the capital, Islamabad. Allegedly sensing the rising political tension, the army chief, Waheed Kakar, jumped into the fray. While assuring the concerned players of his reluctance to interfere directly, he convinced Sharif to resign. The prime minister agreed to a conditional surrender combined with Ishaq Khan's resignation. Kakar finally intervened indirectly and sent both Sharif and Khan home.[76]

Sharif's behaviour was no different. The leader's party goons attacked the Supreme Court during a hearing on a case against the government. Reports indicate the involvement of senior party members including the Punjab chief minister and prime minister's brother, Shahbaz Sharif.[77] The experience was traumatizing for the highest court of law, for which it was the first experience of blatant coercion. The courts had been manipulated in the past, and were known for cowering before military governments, but this was the first time that force had been used in a brutal and obvious manner.

Nawaz Sharif also passed a new accountability law in May 1997 to target political opponents. This was in addition to the anti-terrorism act passed in August of the same year, authorizing law enforcement agencies to conduct searches and arrest suspects without warrants. Other self-strengthening measures included the 14th Amendment to the 1973 Constitution to curb dissent inside the party. The party leader was given the power to throw out a member from both the party and parliament for floor-crossing.[78] More than curbing corruption, this measure aimed at boosting the party leader's capacity at arm-twisting.

From the perspective that sees political instability as a cause of the military's domination, the power of the GHQ (as has been discussed at length earlier) established a pattern of instability in which the army co-opted members of the political class to enhance its hold over the country's polity. In fact, the military's continued interference in politics established 'amoral familism',[79] a behaviour in which various political actors partnered with the military, though temporarily, to maximize their interests against those of their competitors. This behaviour, including that described earlier, can be termed as elite predatoriness, in which the dominant classes are driven by their short-term objectives without taking into consideration the long-term costs of their actions. The military is repeatedly sucked into politics by the political leadership to balance one political player against the other, but without taking into consideration the negative implications of involving the armed forces in managing the state. The preoccupation of the dominant classes with their short-term gains, in contrast to a macro rationality (for both military and civilian actors), transforms the character of the state. Not only does such behaviour weaken the democracy, the state and the political system turns predatory. The institutionalizing of military power thus adds to the state's predatory character. This particular transformation of the state weakens the prospects of political pluralism. The resultant conditions are counter to the interests of the common people.

It is noteworthy that the political elite are not the only force partnering with the military for short-term gains. Other actors, such as members of the corporate sector and the media in Pakistan, also cohabit with the armed forces to gain certain advantages. Interestingly, the military in Turkey, where the political conditions are almost synonymous with Pakistan's, also thrashed out a partnership with the corporate sector. The socioeconomic and sociopolitical order after the military takeover in Turkey in 1980 reflected a Faustian bargain between the new capitalists and the military. The emergent capitalist class accepted the military's influence because it was convinced of, or was willing to accept, the military as the only credible force that could fill the organizational space vacated by the collapse of the civil service and elected officialdom. A partnership with the armed forces was seen as the only guarantee of a sound future.[80]

In Pakistan's case, traditionally the big entrepreneurs have benefited from a coalition with the military. It is worth remembering that the entrepreneurial class owes its existence to the Ayub and Zia regimes. While Ayub helped the establishment of big business, Zia was responsible for empowering the big business houses through reversing Zulfiqar Ali Bhutto's nationalization policy. Subsequently, some of the large business houses entered into a coalition with the civilian governments, and later with the Musharraf regime, to benefit from the state's capacity to reward them. The liberalization policy that resulted in the privatization of public-sector financial and industrial units benefited a number of businesses, including the military-controlled companies. The military regime favoured its cronies as much as the civilian governments, and so exacerbated the problem of crony capitalism, a problem that is deeply rooted in the country's political system.

According to a Pakistani columnist, Shakir Hussain, 'The cardinal rule of business everywhere is, "survival of the fittest", while in Pakistan it is, survival of the fattest, and most connected.'[81] Connections are crucial in monopolizing resources along with other members of the ruling classes. One of the manifestations of monopolization of resources was the generous loans granted to big entrepreneurs and feudal landlords. Since the banking sector is regulated by the state, successive governments have facilitated the granting of huge loans to their cronies, or turned a blind eye to loan defaulters. The long list of major financial loan defaulters first compiled by the caretaker government of Prime Minister Moeen Qureshi in 1993 was an example of how the politicians and big business used political influence to their advantage. It named people who owed the state amounts over Rs.1 million (c.US$17,250).

The civilian prime ministers also squandered state resources. For instance, both Bhutto and Sharif awarded land worth US$166.6 million (Rs.9.7 billion) to friends and cronies.[82] In August 1993 Qureshi promulgated an ordinance creating a committee to overlook the distribution of state land, which had until then been subject to the discretion of the head of the government. According to the caretaker prime minister, he was appalled at the discretionary power he inherited to sign off state land to whomever he wanted. The ordinance was never presented by Qureshi's successor, Benazir Bhutto, to the parliament for extension.[83] Her lack of action demonstrated the fact that there were no takers for such a law. Both the civilian and military leadership were beneficiaries of arbitrary norms of land distribution, or other advantages provided by the state.

Shahid-ur-Rehman's book *Who Owns Pakistan?* is an eye-opener in bringing to light details of how various business groups benefited from the privatization policy. In most cases it reports, huge public-sector companies were sold to large private entrepreneurs without transferring their financial liabilities. The buyers were only handed the assets and the business.[84] The author is of the opinion that 'Privatization in Pakistan is the classical example of corrupt politicians and ever-corrupt bureaucrats working in concert to turn a lemon into an orange.'[85] The financial mismanagement is not restricted to civilian players: the military business complex drew its own benefits, as is fully explained elsewhere in this book. In fact the Army Welfare Trust, a subsidiary of the army, was one of the major loan defaulters.

This looting and pillage of national resources by the ruling elite did not stop despite the claims made by successive military regimes that they were cleaning up the political and economic systems and establishing good governance. Pakistan's history bears witness to the fact that despite their being in control of the state for long years, the country's armed forces did not manage to bring about substantive and structural change. In fact, Feit believes that during the military's rule 'few elite interests are actually threatened for the sake of the [social and political] balance'.[86] The military has a tendency to feed itself and the interests of other key groups, whose cooperation is sought for the purpose of political legitimacy. Despite its image as an umpire, the military suffers from a lack of legitimacy in the long term. The generals attempt to plug this hole through bolstering the interests of other groups and creating new players.

EVOLVING INTO A MILITARY CLASS

One of the main arguments presented in this chapter is that the military evolved into an independent class that ensured its share in the state and its decision making through creating institutional processes. This development was first ensured by establishing the military's hegemony over the state and its political system. Like Ayub Khan and the Zia regimes, the Musharraf regime also embarked upon sustaining military rule through appointing the army chief as the country's president. That control was ensured through the presidential referendum that has already been discussed. Musharraf also took two specific measures to institutionalize the military's control of politics: first, the restoration of Article 58(2)(b), and second, establishment of the NSC.

The process of institutionalizing power indicates a fundamental change in the character of the armed forces. While acknowledging the relative resilience of the political forces in contesting for their share of power, the military also ensured that it became an equal partner in decision making to guarantee the stability of the central state. Since the experience of the Ayub, Yahya and Zia regimes had taught the generals that they could not completely suppress the civilian forces, and that the international environment would not allow a complete battering of democratic forces either, the GHQ tried to find other ways to become a partner in state power. The army had to set up political 'fire breaks' such as the restoration of the controversial clause that would allow the president to dismiss the parliament, and setting up an institutional mechanism to keep the political players in check. The military no longer remained an arbiter that would return to barracks after restoring some level of stability to the political system. It had by this time turned into the parent-guardian type, which ensured its control of the state and society through institutional methods such as the NSC.

The NSC Act passed in April 2004 gave the military a permanent role in decision making and governance. The creation of this special council was also the culmination of the armed forces' almost 44 years of struggle to establish themselves as a prime domestic player. The act established the NSC as a consultative body headed by the president, with the role of deliberating on strategic issues ranging from national security and sovereignty to crisis management. Besides four military officers (the chairman of the JCSC, and the chiefs of the army, air force and navy staff), the NSC comprises eight civilians: the president, the prime minister, the chairman of the Senate, the speaker of the National Assembly, the leader of the opposition in the National Assembly, and the chief ministers of all four provinces.[87] The creation of the NSC morphed the armed forces into a class and a parent-guardian type that was unwilling to leave the functioning of the state to the civilians. The permanent presence of the four most senior military personnel ensured the continued protection of the defence forces' interests, and participation in moulding the socioeconomic and political future of the state.

The PML-Q's media advisor, Mushahid Hussain, claims that the new organization was not meant to challenge existing democratic organizations. This is because of its consultative character. In his view, the Turkish model that Pakistan seems to have followed does not indicate an enhancement of the power of the armed forces.[88] However, a closer look at the Turkish model of the NSC shows how the military's power was gradually enhanced. The amendment in the 1961 Turkish Constitution carried out in 1982 institutionalized the NSC as the highest non-elected decision-making body of the state. In Turkey, one of the spin-offs of the institutionalizing of military power was an increase in military officers' political and economic strength.[89] In any case, it is almost impossible to restrict a praetorian military in an elite-dominated society to a limited role and treat its recommendations merely as advice that can be ignored. To involve the armed forces' in any form of decision making, or give them a formal role in administration at even a basic level, is inviting the trouble of reducing the civilian capacity to monitor or punish the military for shirking from its role as an agent. As in Pakistan, the Turkish military used its political power to draw economic dividends.

The basic idea of the NSC revolved around the Turkish model of government.[90] With the creation of the NSC, the armed forces did not remain politically neutral. However, the political leadership, especially those partnering with the military, showed a lack of sensitivity to the potential threat of conferring a formal political role on the armed forces. Even the coalition of religious parties, the MMA, which had initially resisted the idea, ultimately caved in and accepted the NSC. In any case, the religious parties were opposed to General-President Pervez Musharraf wearing the two hats of head of state and head of the army at the same time, rather than to the general concept of military participation in politics. The religious right did not have a major issue with accepting the army's permanent role in politics. The MMA dropped its opposition to the NSC concept after Musharraf promised to give up the office of the army chief by December 2004. The president later reneged on this commitment. Musharraf's views were that he could not shed his responsibilities as army chief because of the global and domestic geopolitical environment. Pakistan's role in the war against terrorism, and the threat posed by terrorism, made it imperative for him to consolidate his political and organizational strength.

Contrary to Musharraf's claim that the NSC was necessary to strengthen democracy and to stop the irresponsible behaviour of politicians, it was formed to protect the military's interests and to enhance the organization's position as the guardian of the state. By 2004/05, the military had established political and economic interests which had to be safeguarded by institutionalizing its power. Like other dominant classes in the country, the armed forces were instituted as a separate entity with a firm control over entry into the organization. The military is a separate class that cuts across all other classes. Its members belong to the landed-feudal class, and the indigenous and metropolitan bourgeoisie. However, there are no hard and fast rules that bar those from other social classes from entering the military. In fact, over the years the lower-income groups have also managed to join the armed forces, and gained social mobility as a result. The institution provides its members with sufficient financial opportunities to improve their lot. However, entry into this class is tacitly restricted to certain ethnic groups, and depends on predetermined and tightly controlled organizational standards and mechanisms. While vertical mobility within the military class is determined by prescribed bureaucratic-organizational norms, the members of this class enjoy the most horizontal mobility. Over the years, the military class has been able to penetrate all other classes and groups because of its political influence, a privilege prohibited to other classes. Members of the military fraternity have become feudal landlords as well as businesspeople. Hence, money or other resources are not the criteria for membership.

In addition, the organization has established norms which cannot be challenged from outside the organization. The high regard for the hierarchical organizational system, the primacy of the chief of the service, especially the army chief, the distribution of national resources among members of the military fraternity, and the protection of all serving and retired members of the armed forces, are some of the norms that are strictly upheld by the organization. In fact, the other classes and the general public are forced to respect these norms.

Over the years, the military has penetrated the state, society and economy, in ways that are both physical and intellectual. Intellectual penetration refers to the military's ability to market its image as the only disciplined organization, with superior capabilities to the civilian institutions. Although the notion of the military's superiority is not popular in Baluchistan and Sindh, this is certainly the perception in the largest province, the Punjab. Furthermore, in most public-sector educational institutions there is an almost unquestioned acceptance of the classical realist paradigm for understanding strategic issues or international relations. This is primarily the result of the state's ability to market military power as the key option for its security as a state. The military fraternity is the main beneficiary of this image, which is necessary to protect the interests of the armed forces and its civilian allies.

The political stakes of the armed forces are intertwined with their economic interests. The organization has craftily established its stakes in the economy, which must be protected through political control. The intellectual and physical hegemony of the military actually serves the purpose of guarding these economic interests. Given the image of the military as a key protector of the state's sovereignty, the economic stakes of the organization are rarely challenged. Even the religious parties, which seem to be questioning Musharraf's control of the state, hardly have any reservations about the military's economic interests. The leader of Jamaat-i-Islami, Qazi Hussain Ahmed, when asked about the corporate ventures of the armed forces, saw these activities as a contribution to national socioeconomic development.[91] Maulana Fazl-u-Rehman, leader of another religious party, Jamiat-ul-Ulema, was a little more critical of the military's economic interests, and confessed that politicians had slipped up in not checking the defence establishment's financial autonomy.[92] However, he was not forceful in his condemnation of Milbus, nor did he offer any concrete plan to discourage the growth of the military's internal economy.

The views of Qazi Hussain Ahmed quoted earlier show his inability, and that of many other political leaders, to understand the link between the military's political stakes and its economic interests. This negligence can be attributed to the ideological partnership between the religious right and the armed forces. However, the other political parties can equally be accused of ignoring the intricate linkage between the military's political power and its economic strength. After all, it took the PPP and the PML-N quite a few years to understand the linkage. Benazir Bhutto and Nawaz Sharif, who were both responsible for strengthening the military's economic interests, finally recognized the negative consequences of encouraging the military's internal economy. In issuing a jointly agreed Charter of Democracy (CoD) in May 2006, both leaders agreed to reduce the economic power of the armed forces.

The military's internal economy (or Milbus) is a serious issue because it indicates the organization's financial autonomy, and this in turn bolsters the military's political influence. The fact that the military fraternity can raise resources and generate profit independently reduces its psychological dependence on civilian governments and institutions. The military's internal economy has evolved over the 59 years of the country's history. Its economic empire was initially established in 1954, a date that also represents its initiation into political power. Its major expansion (as will be demonstrated in the following chapters) took place after the second military takeover in 1977, after which it grew unimpeded as a result of the systematic and institutional growth of military influence in politics, economy and society.

The military's commercial stakes grew in new spheres of business, including the finance and banking sectors and many other areas. These changes increased the military's share of private-sector assets and made the organization into one of the dominant economic players in the country. The economic operations began to be conducted more vociferously at three levels:

- through direct organizational involvement
- through subsidiaries
- through individual members of the fraternity.

The financial rewards and opportunities for expansion were also clearly distributed amongst the military's cronies from other dominant classes. The Pakistan military's economic empire grew like Turkey's. It is noteworthy that officers of the Turkish armed forces are typically given executive positions in large corporations on their retirement from active service. An Army Mutual Assistance Association (AMAA) was also established in 1961 to provide financial benefits to retired officers. However, the dividends increased after General Sunay's election to the presidency in 1966.[93]

In both the Turkish and Pakistani cases, the power of the military's corporate interests led to greater stakes in political control, and vice versa. In Pakistan's case the growth of the military's economic empire was proportional to the increase in the organization's political power. The most noticeable increase in the size of the military's internal economy, and the organization's penetration into society and the economy, obviously took place during the 1990s and after, when the GHQ sought legal and constitutional arrangements to institutionalize its role in decision making and the country's power politics. By the start of the twenty-first century the military fraternity had penetrated all levels of the society and economy. Members of the military fraternity (both serving and retired personnel) were found in all major institutions, including parliament and the civil bureaucracy. There were over 1,000 serving and retired officers working at various middle and senior management levels. Moreover, a number of retired personnel were made heads of major public-sector universities and inducted into think tanks.

The Musharraf regime is known for providing greater opportunities to the military fraternity through inducting serving and retired members of the armed forces into significant public-sector positions. There has also been an increase in the military's involvement in urban and rural real estate, and this can be considered as one of the primary sources of economic activity in the country, especially after 9/11. It is even more important that the GHQ has become extremely protective of its commercial interests. The retired members of the armed forces and the defence establishment joined hands in discouraging any criticism of their economic stakes. The protection of the military's position as a dominant economic actor is a corollary of the organization's evolution into an independent class that protects its interests zealously. The military fraternity is a separate group that has the political clout to establish its stakes in the control of the state and its resources. Moreover, it has institutionalized its power and risen from being a tool of policy implementation to an independent actor and a shareholder in power, along with the other dominant classes.

As has been discussed in this chapter, the redistribution of resources and opportunities was not limited to the military, but included the military's clients as well. The political players in Pakistan, and other dominant classes or groups such as the civil bureaucracy and the entrepreneurial class, are bound in partnership with the military fraternity. Although the cooperation is for mutual benefit of all the concerned players, it particularly strengthens the hands of the military. This is detrimental to the strengthening of democracy in the country. The political players, in particular, are forced out of power at the behest of the military any time the organization feels threatened by them. Unfortunately, the political leadership continues to negotiate with the senior generals, and as a result is enveloped in the GHQ's divide and rule policy.

It is not realized, however, that the civil–military relations imbalance is a structural problem caused by a lack of understanding of the intricate relationship between the military's economic and political interests. Furthermore, as it has been argued in this section of the book, it was not so much the lack of realization that has prevented politicians from understanding the dynamics of military power, but the flaw in the character of the sociopolitical system and the particular nature and interplay of the dominant classes. Since the country's sociopolitical system is predominantly authoritarian and has a pre-capitalist structure, the ruling classes are not averse to using military force to further their personal political and economic interests. The elite therefore continue to strengthen the armed forces, and contributed to the evolution of the military fraternity into a class.

4 The structure of Milbus

The military in Pakistan is a formidable political player with greater influence than any other actor. The organization's political control, which was discussed in the two previous chapters, is also a manifestation of its financial autonomy. Over the years, the military has built an economic empire that strengthens it institutionally. Pakistan's Milbus has a highly complex structure, which will be explained in this chapter.

THE ECONOMIC EMPIRE

Pakistan military's internal economy has a fairly decentralized structure, operating at three levels and in three segments of the economy: agriculture, manufacturing and the service sector (see Table 4.1).

Although the critics of the military's economic role focus their attention on its four subsidiaries – the Fauji Foundation (FF), Army Welfare Trust (AWT), Shaheen Foundation (SF) and Bahria Foundation (BF) – the economic empire extends beyond these four organizations, as is obvious from Table 4.1. Because of the lack of transparency, a large part of the military's internal economy remains invisible. The hidden portion comprises commercial ventures carried out directly by different segments of the military organization, and economic benefits provided to individual members of the military fraternity. A glance at Figure 4.1 will show that Pakistan's Milbus is a complex network in which various channels generate economic opportunities.

As the main controlling authority for the defence establishment is the Ministry of Defence (MoD), it is at the apex of the economic network. The MoD controls the four main planks of Milbus: the service headquarters, the Department of Military Land and Cantonment (MLC), the FF and the Rangers (a paramilitary force). The MLC is responsible for acquiring land for further allocation to the service headquarters, which is then distributed

Table 4.1 The Pakistan military's control of the economy

	Institution	Subsidiaries	Individual
Agriculture	✔	✔	✔
Manufacturing	✔	✔	✔
Service sector	✔	✔	✔

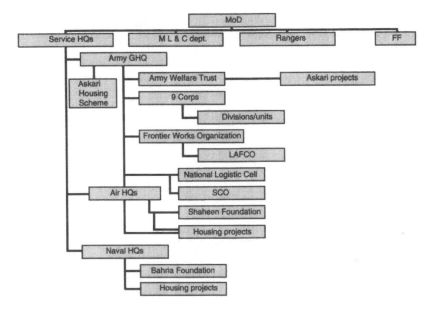

Figure 4.1 Milbus: the structure

among individual members. The MLC also controls the FF. The chairman of the FF is the secretary of defence. The MLC also comes under the MoD.

The economic network broadens further at the level of the service headquarters. The three services have independent welfare foundations, which are directly controlled by the senior officers of these services. In addition, the nine corps of the army, subdivided into divisions and units, run independent ventures, identified in this study as military cooperatives. Then there are institutions such as the National Logistic Cell (NLC), the Frontier Works Organization (FWO) and the Special Communications Organization (SCO), which are controlled by the army. The Pakistan Rangers, which is a paramilitary organization, comes under the administrative control of the MoD as well.

Placing the MoD at the top of the organizational chart does not, however, mean that the economic initiatives are centrally planned. It simply indicates the administrative position of the MoD in the overall system of defence administration in the country. Each of the three services plans independently. In fact, the MoD is used as a forum to negotiate economic opportunities and the monopolization of resources. For instance, it is used to obtain ownership of provincial or federal government land and sanction its distribution between the three services, which then allocate it to their personnel. The various government departments such as the MoD or the MLC are an administrative mechanism for economic exploitation.

The operations of Pakistan's Milbus represent a cross between the Indonesian and the Turkish models. It is similar to the Indonesian Milbus in the multiple levels of the military's internal economy. Indonesia's armed forces, *Angkatan Bersenjata Republik Indonesia* (ABRI), conduct commercial ventures through a number of welfare foundations. They also run cooperatives which are operated directly by the organizations through the rank and file involvement of their personnel. In Pakistan's case, the cooperatives started to grow mainly after the 1980s as a result of the general financial empowerment of senior military commanders. While the Pakistan military's cooperatives draw on the military's public-sector resources including labour, they have not necessitated the establishment of a separate cadre of officials specializing in economic and political management. This is one of the key differences from the Indonesian system. Another difference concerns the financial or administrative linkage with the civilian public-sector institutions. Unlike in Indonesia, the Pakistan military's internal economy is an independent entity.

The similarities with the Turkish model involve the management of resources and administration of commercial ventures. In order to avoid the involvement of serving personnel in direct business activities, the military mainly uses its influence and resources to provide welfare funds for investment. The four welfare foundations are controlled by the service headquarters and run by retired military personnel. The profits are distributed between the shareholders, who again are retired military personnel.

The inter-services rivalry within the armed forces is reflected even in the structure of the internal economy. Unlike the Turkish military foundation, OYAK, which represents the interests of all services, Pakistan's Milbus is known for the independence of the three armed forces. The three services have separate welfare foundations and housing schemes. On the surface there does not seem to be competition between the three services, because of their difference in size. However, all three have engaged in an unbridled expansion of their commercial and other economic operations.

The military's economic empire operates at three distinct levels:

- direct involvement of the organization
- subsidiaries
- individuals.

The next sections explain the structure and operations at each of the three tiers.

LEVEL 1: THE ORGANIZATION

At this level the military is directly involved in profit-making activities. The commercial operations comprise two distinct segments: first, major public-sector organizations controlled by the army, and second, the co-operatives. The three major public sector organizations are the NLC, the FWO and the SCO.

The National Logistic Cell (NLC)

Created in August 1978 by the quartermaster-general (QMG) of the army, the NLC is the largest goods transportation company in the country. It has one of the largest public-sector transport fleets in Asia, of 1,689 vehicles. The company also engages in the construction of roads, bridges and wheat storage facilities. Although it is presented as an attached department of the Ministry of Planning and Development, the basic control of the organization is with the army (see Figure 4.2).

In terms of strategic management the organization is part of a civilian organization, the Ministry of Planning and Development, as mentioned above. The NLC board is headed by a chairman who was the federal minister for planning and development. This was subsequently changed to the minister for finance. The members of the board comprise the federal ministers for communication, railways, and food and agriculture, the deputy chairman of the Planning Commission, the federal secretaries for planning and development, finance, communication and railways, and the Pakistan Army's QMG, who is also the secretary of the board. The ground operations, however, are managed by the army. The NLC is staffed by serving army officers. The four main divisions highlighted in Figure 4.2 are headed by serving officers with the rank of brigadier.

The NLC is staffed by about 7,279 people of whom 2,549 are serving personnel. The rest are retired officers and civilians. The civilians mainly work in administrative and clerical positions. The organization is managed through a national logistics board headed by a chairman who is a federal minister. However, the operational control of the organization is with the

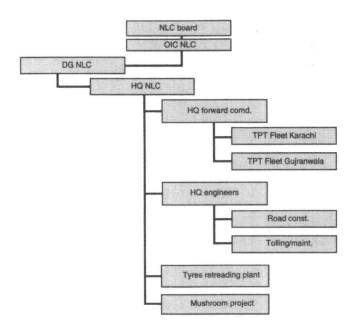

Figure 4.2 Structure of the National Logistic Cell

115

army's QMG. The estimated net worth of the NLC in 2000–1 was Rs.3,964.652 million (US$68.356 million).

The company was established in 1978 to deal with a specific crisis of major bottlenecks at the only operational seaport at Karachi. The QMG, Maj.-General Saeed Qadir, was instructed by General Zia ul Haq to launch operation 'Survival', aimed at creating an independent cell to be placed under the Ministry of Communication, which at that time was being run by Qadir. Its mandate involved the establishment of an infrastructure to transport goods from Karachi port, and building roads and other facilities for wheat storage.[1] Hence, the NLC is one of the prime examples of a 'replacement' institution. This concept involves the military filling a gap or replacing an inefficient civilian institution through creating a parallel structure which is under the control of the armed forces. According to Qadir, he was given a broad mandate from the onset, which included not only transportation but also constructing and repairing the roads network that was considered necessary for transporting goods from one part of the country to another.[2] The organization was also involved in providing support to the Afghan operation during the 1980s.

Frontier Works Organization (FWO)

The FWO was established in 1966 to construct the 805 km Karakoram Highway.[3] It remains the largest contractor in the country for constructing roads and collecting tolls. The company is staffed by the army's corps of engineers, which was put together to construct the road link between Pakistan and China. Although it is staffed by army personnel, the organization was initially put under the control of the Ministry of Communication. However, it was later brought under the administrative control of the MoD.

Even after the completion of the Karakoram Highway the organization was not disbanded. It was seen as a reserve force that could be utilized during a future conflict or cater for any unforeseen emergency, but in fact it is engaged in commercial ventures. Currently, all the government's major road construction projects are undertaken by the FWO. In addition, the organization manages toll collection on all major and minor road networks in the country, a job that was once given to private contractors. Since the mid-1990s, the FWO has grown as one of the primary contractors for public-sector road construction. After 1999, the FWO established another sub-organization, LAFCO, which is a joint undertaking with other private-sector contractors.

Special Communication Organization (SCO)

The SCO was originally established in 1976 to handle a project to establish a telecommunications network in Azad Jammu Kashmir and northern areas.[4] It is an army establishment jointly controlled by the signals directorate of the service and the Ministry of Information Technology. The organization was revitalized towards the end of the 1990s and given the task of expanding the telecommunications network in the areas mentioned.

The cooperatives

The ventures referred to here as cooperatives are small and medium-sized profit-making activities carried out by the various military commands. The businesses are diverse in nature, and vary from bakeries and cinemas to gas stations and commercial plazas and markets. This category also includes money-making activities such as imposing tolls on national highways and selling sand along the seashore, and contracts for fishing in the coastal areas.

The control of these profit-making ventures is fairly decentralized. They can be run by army units, divisions or the corps headquarters, and use lower-ranking personnel as free labour. The sizes of the ventures also vary, from small operations like bakeries and poultry farms, to large ones such as gas stations and highway toll collection organizations. In 2004 the Ministry of Defence provided a partial list of about 50 such commercial projects, which allegedly made about Rs.134 million (US$2.3 million) in the financial year 2003/04.[5] However, there was no detail available regarding the legal position of these projects or the way they were being managed.

LEVEL 2: THE SUBSIDIARIES

The most transparent segment of Milbus is the military's four subsidiaries, the FF, AWT, SF and BF. Although senior generals ignore or refute any suggestion that these subsidiaries represent the military's involvement in commercial ventures, their claim is not supported by the structure of command and control of these organizations. All subsidiaries are controlled at the top by senior generals or members of the MoD. Furthermore, as can be seen from Figure 4.3, the foundations have the status of subsidiaries of their respective parent services. This sign for one of the colleges of Bahria Foundation in Bahawalpur claims it to be a subsidiary of the Pakistan Navy.

The four foundations run about 100 independent projects, which include heavy manufacturing industries such as cement, fertilizer and cereal production. In addition, some of the foundations are involved in the insurance business, information technology, banking and education. In recognition of the fact that the armed forces have a better reputation than a number of civilian institutions, the link with the parent services is advertised to attract business. This is certainly true in the real estate business, where the value of property tends to appreciate in areas controlled by the armed forces or their subsidiaries. The military organization is central to the Milbus network, as is obvious from Figure 4.4. The influence of the defence establishment plays a key role in obtaining public-sector business contracts and securing industrial or financial inputs at subsidized rates. These concessions put the foundations ahead of their private-sector competitors.

Figure 4.3 The sign of Bahria Foundation College, Bahawalpur, marks it as a subsidiary of the Pakistan Navy

It must be reiterated that the welfare foundations flaunt their connection with the armed forces. This is obvious from the fact that the four foundations use the insignia of their parent services. The issue of the use of insignias was in fact challenged in the Supreme Court in a public interest case by a lawyer, Wahab-ul-Khairi, in 1990.[6] In Khairi's view, the foundations were in contravention of the Companies Ordinance of 1984 and the Trade Mark Act of 1940, which forbid any private venture or party to use the name of the state or the armed forces or the founder of the country. He pleaded with the court to ban all the commercial activities of the military, because in his view such tasks diverted the armed forces from their core activity of defending the country's frontiers. The case he brought concerned a specific allegation of corruption in a commercial operation involving the navy's BF. The BF not only blatantly denied the charges, but also denied using any of its links with the navy for commercial benefits. Despite the fact that the case was dismissed on technical grounds, it did raise the issue of how these foundations exploit their deep connection with the armed services for profit maximization.

Regarding the link between the foundations and the services, there are numerous cases in which the businesses have unlawfully used the military's resources. The fact that the higher management of the three services and the foundations is the same makes the transfer of resources possible.

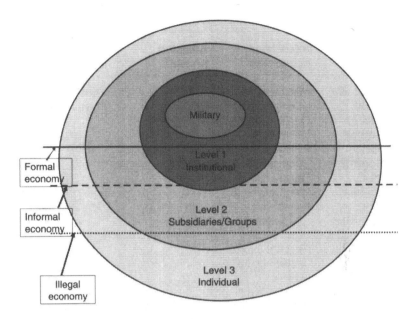

Figure 4.4 The military's institutional linkage with Milbus

The Fauji Foundation (FF)

The Fauji Foundation (*fauji* means soldier) was established in 1954 under the Charitable Endowments Act 1890, for the welfare of ex-servicemen. It was the first organization of its kind in Pakistan, meant to cater for the welfare of military personnel from all the three services. As in the Turkish model, the military sought initial funding for this institution: the Rs.18 million (US $300,000) capital investment was money provided by the Royal British military in 1947 as Pakistan's share of the post-War Services Reconstruction Fund for reinvestment purposes. The fund was established by the British to provide financial help and welfare benefits for British war veterans.[7]

The money was used to set up some industrial units in the western wing of the country. Today the FF is one of the largest business conglomerates in the country (see Table 4.2).[8]

The FF is also a major taxpayer in the country.[9] However, until the beginning of the 1970s it was exempt from paying taxes.[10]

The FF started its industrial operations in both wings of the country. The industrial operations were primarily in consumer-oriented, non-tradable commodities like rice, flour, jute and textiles. In 1982 it had assets with an estimated worth of Rs.2,060 million (US$35.52 million), in the shape of 29 industrial units.[11] Currently its declared assets amount to Rs.9.8 billion (US$169 million), with a total of 25 independent projects. Out of the total number, about 18 are completely controlled by the FF, while the remaining seven are

Table 4.2 List of Fauji Foundation projects

Fully owned projects	Associated companies	Affiliated projects	Investment Board
Foundation Gas Fauji Corn Complex Fauji Security Services Fauji Sugar Mills Overseas Employment Services Fauji Foundation Experimental & Seed Multiplication Farm	Mari Gas Company Ltd Fauji Cement Company Ltd Fauji Fertilizer Company Ltd Fauji Fertilizer Bin Qasim Ltd Foundation Securities (PVT) Ltd Fauji Kabirwala Power Company Ltd Fauji Oil Terminal & Distribution Company Ltd	Foundation University	Pakistan Maroc Phosphere, S. A

listed as subsidiaries, with shareholdings by other parties as well.[12] Most of the heavy manufacturing industrial projects are categorized as subsidiaries, which means that these are shareholding ventures. The fully owned projects mainly comprise agri-based ventures such as farms, the motorway project and educational institutions. Out of the total of 25 projects, only the fertilizer and cement factories are listed on the stock exchange.

Employing about 6,000–7,000 retired military personnel, the foundation is run by a governing board that is predominantly controlled by the army. One of the features of the organization is the domination by the largest service, the army, despite the fact that it was meant to be a tri-service organization. About 80–90 per cent of jobs are taken by army personnel, with remainder being divided between the air force and the navy. All the managing directors of the company have been senior retired army officers.

At a glance, the organizational structure gives the impression of a highly centralized structure (see Figure 4.5).

The strategic control of the organization is in the hands of the MoD and the military establishment. The Committee of Administration is the apex body that gives overall direction. The chairman of this committee is the secretary of defence. The members comprise the chief of general staff (CGS), the QMG, the adjutant-general (AG), the chief of logistics staff – Pakistan Army (CLS), the deputy chief of naval staff (training and personnel) – Pakistan Navy, and the deputy chief of air staff (administration) – PAF. The secretary of the Central Board of Directors acts as the secretary of the

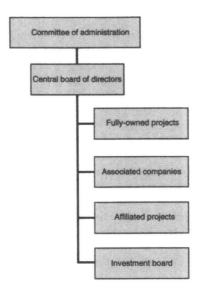

Figure 4.5 Organizational chart of the Fauji Foundation

committee. The operational planning and running of the foundation is the responsibility of the Central Board of Directors. The chairman of the board is the secretary for defence, and the vice-chairman is the managing director of the FF, who is a retired army lt.-general. All the members of the board are from the FF, with roles such as directors of finance, planning & development, industries, systems evaluation & development, human resource & administration, welfare (education), welfare (health), corporate advisor, and secretary to the board. The Board of Directors carries out the overall plans which are presented to the Committee of Administration for approval. A report of the performance of the FF is also presented to the Committee of Administration.

From an operational perspective, the FF is decentralized like its three sister organizations. It has four major divisions: fully owned projects, associated companies, affiliated projects and the Investment Board. The first division comprises all those projects that are totally financed by the FF. The other two divisions have major funding from the FF but have administrative independence. The last category covers the FF's international partnership. This is a joint undertaking between the Fauji Group (represented by the FF, the Fauji Fertilizer Cooperation and Fauji Foundation Bin Qasim Ltd) and Office Cherifien des Phosphates, Morocco with 50:50 equity (between the Pakistani and Moroccan owners), for the production of 375,000 metric tonnes of phosphoric acid per annum. The project is scheduled to start operations by mid-2007.[13]

The decentralized structure is necessary for two reasons. First, the FF cannot have total control over projects that are not fully funded by it.

Second, because some of the associated companies are headed by senior officers equivalent in rank to the MD of the FF, it would be difficult to have central control. For example, the managing director of the FF and the director industrial (popularly known as heading Fauji Fertilizer) are both retired lt.-generals.[14] This does not mean that there is no consultation between the two. However, smooth running calls for lax control and independence for the fertilizer group. A senior general would be far more comfortable exercising independent control of his unit. On the other hand, the previous experience of these senior officers as colleagues helps business communication. The basic philosophy here is that old associations help in developing the understanding and confidence in an individual that in turn is necessary to obtain better results for an organization. This concept was explained by the managing director of the FF, Lt.-General (rtd) Mohammad Amjad, in the context of why General Musharraf preferred to appoint military personnel to head public-sector corporations.[15]

The FF claims to provide for the welfare of 8.5 million beneficiaries, who comprise ex-services staff and their dependants.[16]

Army Welfare Trust (AWT)

The AWT is the army's welfare foundation, established in 1971 to create greater employment and profit-making opportunities for the largest service. The army felt that the welfare needs of its personnel were not being met by the FF. Some tend to link this creation of a new organization with the dire economic straits that the military was in after the US arms embargo of the 1960s.[17] The army was facing a resource crunch between the two wars of 1965 and 1971.

As is obvious from Figure 4.6, the AWT is controlled by the army GHQ. The managing director (MD) of the Committee of Administration, which is the apex body, is also the MD of the AWT. The office bearer is the AG of the army. However, because of the AG's busy schedule, he appoints an acting MD. The members of the committee include the CGS, QMG, CLS and the MD of the AWT. The acting MD does not, however, participate in the meetings of the committee as a full member. The committee supervises the work of the Board of Directors, which is also chaired by the AG. The vice chairman is the MD of the AWT, who works with the help of seven directors.

The trust was opened with an initial endowment of Rs.700,000 (US$12,100) under the Societies Registration Act 1860, with the specific purpose of generating funds for 'orphans, widows of martyrs, disabled soldiers, and providing for the rehabilitation of ex-servicemen'. Currently the AWT runs 41 independent projects, of which it has shareholdings in about 13 are while the rest are completely owned (see Table 4.3).

Of these projects, only the five in the financial sector (such as the bank, leasing and insurance companies) are listed with the stock exchange. The group boasts of having total assets worth Rs.50 billion (US$862.1 million). It provides employment to about 5,000 ex-services staff.

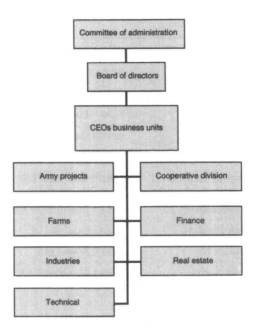

Figure 4.6 Organizational chart of the Army Welfare Trust

The AWT was raised with a totally different method of providing for welfare. Unlike the FF, which created projects for welfare, the AWT aimed at generating profit for distribution among its shareholders. This was done through investing welfare funds in industrial and other profit-making ventures. The money is borrowed from the benevolent fund account maintained in the GHQ. This account, in turn, is formed by compulsory deductions from the pay of army personnel for welfare purposes. The AWT was also set apart from the FF because it did not pay taxes on its industrial and other projects until 1993, because of its identity as a welfare institution. Taxes at concessionary rates were, however, levied in 1992–3. Interestingly, there was no uniform tax rate applied on the organizations. The AWT and FF pay tax at roughly 20 per cent on their profits, while the SF and BF are charged a higher rate of 30 per cent. Sources attribute this to the greater political influence of the army.[18]

Shaheen Foundation (SF)

The Pakistan Air Force followed the larger service in opening its own welfare foundation in 1977, again under the Charitable Endowments Act 1890, with seed money of Rs.5 million (US$86,000). Like the AWT, the SF is controlled by the PAF (see Figure 4.7).

At the top is the Committee of Administration headed by the chief of the air staff. While the vice-chairman is the deputy chief of air staff

Table 4.3 List of AWT projects

Askari Stud Farms (two farms)*	Army Welfare Shops (four shops)
Askari Farms (Two farms)	Army Welfare Commercial Project
Askari Welfare Rice Mill	Askari Commercial Bank
Askari Welfare Sugar Mill	Askari Leasing Ltd
Askari Fish Farm	Askari General Insurance Company
Askari Cement (two plants)	Askari Welfare Saving Scheme
Askari Welfare Pharmaceutical Project	Askari Associate Ltd
Magnesite Refineries Limited	Askari Information Service
Army Welfare Shoe Project	Askari Guards Ltd
Army Welfare Woollen Mill	Askari Power Ltd
Army Welfare Hosiery Unit	Askari Commercial Enterprises
Travel agencies (three different agencies)	Askari Aviation
AWT Commercial Plazas (three buildings)	Askari Housing Scheme (at six different locations)

* These farms cover 16,000 acres of government land for which it receives no revenue

(operations), its members include the deputy chiefs of air staff (administration), (personnel), (training) and (engineering), the director-general of the Air Force Strategic Command, the inspector-general of the PAF, and the MD of the SF. The committee supervises the work of the Board of Directors, which is headed by the MD of the SF, who is a retired air vice marshal. The board, which makes and implements business plans, comprises the deputy MD, director admin, human resource and welfare, director finance, and executive director Shaheen Projects (which are listed in Table 4.4). Other than the MD and the deputy MD, the members are civilians.

The idea was to create greater opportunities for welfare, especially when the top management was not happy with its meagre share in the tri-service FF. The PAF's share in welfare and rehabilitation opportunities and the management of the FF is not more than 5 per cent. Currently, the SF employs about 200 retired personnel, the bulk of whom were technicians/airmen rather than officers. Commensurate with the service's comparative size and influence, the SF is not a large organization. It runs about 14 independent projects, none of which are listed on the stock exchange (see Table 4.4).

The SF claims to have a worth of more than Rs.2 billion (US$34.4 million),[19] with an estimated annual turnover of Rs.600 million (US$10.3

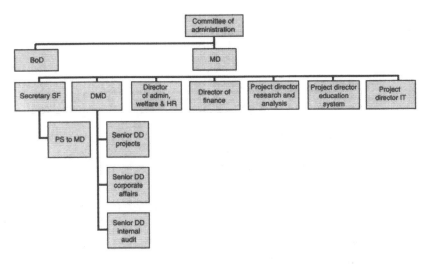

Figure 4.7 Organizational chart of the Shaheen Foundation

million).[20] Its project sizes are relatively small, with the biggest being the airline, and the real estate that it owns in three major cities. Most of its expansion took place during the 1990s. The projects depend primarily on the resources of the air force and the service's ability to generate business for the SF. Most of the projects, as is obvious from Table 4.4, are related to the airline industry, cargo, or otherwise depend on orders from the PAF. There are, however, rare cases like insurance where there is no commonality or shared experience. Assessing the SF is highly problematic because of the lack of transparency. None of its companies are listed with the stock exchange and data is not available through any other source.

Bahria Foundation (BF)

Not to be left behind in the race, the navy established its own welfare foundation in January 1982. Registered under the Charitable Endowments Act 1890, the BF was opened using the service's own welfare funds, which amounted to Rs.3 million (US$52,000). Like its sister foundations, the BF is controlled by an armed force, in this case the navy (see Figure 4.8).

Table 4.4 List of SF projects

Shaheen Air International[21]	Shaheen Complex (two projects)
Shaheen Air Cargo	Shaheen Pay TV
Shaheen Airport services	FM-100 (radio channel)
Shaheen Aerotraders	Shaheen Systems (information technology)
Shaheen Insurance	Shaheen Knitwear
Shaheen Travel (three projects)	

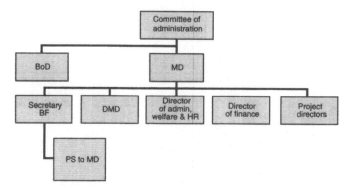

Figure 4.8 Organizational chart of the Bahria Foundation

Although very little is known about the administrative structure of the BF, sources indicate that the organization's structure is similar to SF. The BF runs 19 projects (see Table 4.5), none of which are listed with the stock exchange.

Its estimated value is around Rs.4 billion (US$69 million). Getting official assessment of its worth was difficult because of a resistance by its employees and naval personnel to discussing their business ventures. This resistance is partly because of the controversy regarding some of the projects, especially the housing schemes. Most of the BF's relatively capital-intensive projects, like Bahria Paints and the real estate development programmes, are shareholdings. These projects have raised a lot of questions because of the involvement of controversial characters and news of financial mismanagement.

LEVEL 3: THE MEMBERS

Any discussion of Milbus would be incomplete without mention of one of its integral components, which is also the most difficult to quantify. The benefits provided to individual personnel are part of the internal economy because significant benefits are provided to serving and retired members of the armed forces as part of the military's system of patronage. Individual members of the military fraternity, especially retired officers, receive financial dividends because of the strong client–patron relationship, in which the military organization is central to the distribution of rewards or profit-making opportunities. In such cases the economic or political exploitation is not necessarily institutional, but individuals can use their connection with the regime or the powerful institutions to create personal wealth. Therefore, the informal monopolization of resources by individuals has been included in the discussion on Milbus.

This informal pattern of exploitation is also visible in other countries, such as Cuba, China and Syria.[22] According to political analyst Frank O. Mora, senior military officers use their positions in a non-democratic system

Table 4.5 List of BF projects

Falah Trading Agency	Bahria University
Bahria Construction	Bahria Shipping
Bahria Travel & Recruiting Agency	Bahria Coastal Services
Bahria Paints	Bahria Security & System Services
Bahria Deep Sea Fishing	Bahria Catering & Decoration Services
Bahria Complexes	Bahria Farming
Bahria Town & Housing Schemes	Bahria Holding
(three projects)	Bahria Harbor Services
Bahria Dredging	Bahria Ship Breaking
Bahria Bakery	Bahria Diving & Salvage International

to generate benefits for themselves.[23] The evidence from Pakistan suggests that this linkage is more than cursory because it tends to use structured institutional support to gain personal benefits. It is, as mentioned earlier, extremely difficult to put a value to this segment of the economy. Nevertheless, the picture of Milbus would be incomplete without mentioning this category, which is related to the benefits provided to personnel.

The advantages can be divided into two, the visible and the non-visible. The core visible perk is the urban and rural real estate provided to retired and serving officers and officials of the armed forces (see Chapter 7 for a detailed discussion). While it is comparatively easy to put a value to the land, it is more difficult to quantify the subsidies provided to the senior officers for developing the land and building the various housing schemes. The land is acquired by individuals through laws and rules made at the institutional level for the greater benefit of individuals.

Other benefits include jobs, especially after retirement. The Musharraf regime, for instance, has provided about 4,000–5,000 jobs to military officers and officials in various departments and ministries of the government. The employment for serving and retired military personnel is not generated through a process of open and fair competition, but it is part of the preferential treatment given to members of the military fraternity. These jobs are therefore not filled by open competition, nor do they attract the best minds available in the public sector. The pay and perks of these jobs have a financial cost to the state, which needs to be included in the discussion on Milbus.

The invisible benefits are the business or other opportunities obtained by retired personnel using the influence of their parent organization, the defence services. Retired personnel tend to use their contacts in the armed forces to enter the weapons procurement business as defence contractors. This is nothing unusual. However, the more ambitious senior officers can enter into other ventures as well, and use their contacts in the military or the government to obtain advantages. One of the key examples in Pakistan is private ventures like the Varan Transport Company. Owned by the daughter of the former head of the main intelligence agency, ISI, Lt.-General (rtd)

Hameed Gul, the company is a clear example of how a military-oriented patronage system benefits its clients. Varan was given preferential access to bus routes between the twin cities of Islamabad and Rawalpindi, and as is discussed in Chapter 6, the company's management and drivers behaved with impunity.

Since the debate started in Pakistan regarding the military's involvement in the economy, there has appeared to be a lack of clarity over constitutes Milbus. Most of the debate revolves around the four welfare foundations, which do operate a large array of commercial activities. However, there is a lot that is visible to the common people, but not documented as part of Milbus. Under the circumstances, I believed it important to identify the structure of this economy and describe each of its essential components.

The military's internal economy comprises three distinct levels, as has been discussed in this chapter. While the subsidiaries of the welfare foundations are the easiest to quantify, the value of the other two levels needs serious quantification and systematic calculation. The purpose of this section of the book was to provide a qualitative framework that basically described each segment of the military economy.

5 Milbus: the formative years, 1954–77

Milbus in Pakistan dates back to 1954, when the first welfare foundation was established. The senior generals of the army had sufficient political and administrative autonomy to take the decision to invest welfare funds in starting commercial ventures. The beginning of these activities also marked the military's intention to carve out a greater niche for itself than protection of the frontiers of the state. The numerous industries that were set up in both wings of the country added to the military's credibility of being able to contribute towards the nation's socioeconomic development. In this respect, the large industrial projects were highly symbolic. Not only a sign of the military's contribution to national development, these factories signified the organization's power. Unlike the development sector, the armed forces had the resources to establish large industrial and business projects, and this enabled it to transform its activities from individual industrial and business projects to the Milbus empire. In the ensuing years the economic empire grew slowly but steadily.

During the period under study Milbus grew most significantly in the years from 1954 to 1969, when the military's influence in government was growing, or when it gained direct control of the government. The growth of the military's internal economy, however, stagnated during the years of extreme political crisis (1969–72), and remained depressed under the rule of the civilian leader, Zulfiqar Ali Bhutto. This can be attributed to the relative strength of the civilian government. Moreover, these years also represent a time when the military had not started evolving into a parent-guardian type and an independent social class.

This chapter examines the growth of the military's internal economy during these formative years.

SETTING UP THE ECONOMIC EMPIRE, 1954–69

The military established its first welfare foundation in 1954, with funds received from the British as part of Pakistan's share of the Post War Services Reconstruction Fund, which had been established in 1942. However, unlike in India where the funds were distributed amongst those who had fought during the Second World War, Pakistan's military generals opted to use the funds to establish large industrial projects. This is perhaps because the Indian military was forced to comply with tougher mechanisms of accountability and subservience to political governments than its counterpart across the border. The literature on Pakistan's military does not provide any explanation of the defence establishment's motivation to go into business except for the welfare of its personnel.[1]

This can be termed the institutional self-interest paradigm, in which economic activities are pursued for the betterment of the institution and its members. The military's perks are justified as part of the welfare that becomes necessary to alleviate the material concerns of armed forces personnel, in comparison with other groups or institutions. The military personnel interviewed for this book justified the perks sought by the military by comparing these with the benefits enjoyed by civil servants, especially those serving in administrative posts in districts. Given the fact that the military considers itself as a primary institution of the state, they believed the perks of the officers should match those of the civil servants.[2]

There are two other possible reasons for the development of the military's internal economy, which have not previously appeared in the available literature on Pakistan. The first is based on a combination of the paradigms of the military as strategic national saviour and organ of national development. Considering the military's ability to determine its own direction and to contribute to national development, the organization takes upon itself the responsibility of contributing to the authoritarian economic modernization of the nation-state.[3] The military's commercial activities benefit from the economic development model that is important for the survival of the state which the armed forces are meant to guard. Here, the emphasis is on the superior capacity of the defence establishment to achieve progress that others cannot undertake so well.

I deduced this perception of the military's greater capacity from my discussions with various military personnel. According to the head of the Armed Forces Services Board, Brig. (rtd) Zahid Zaman, 'military officers have greater analytical capacity than civil servants'.[4] In comparing the military with the civil bureaucracy, he was trying to establish the military's intellectual and moral superiority over another relatively strong institution. Others do not restrict themselves to domestic comparisons. In the eyes of Lt.-General (rtd) Amjad and Maj.-General (rtd) Jamsheed Ayaz, the armed forces can conduct business or politics because of their expertise in managing men and materials during service. The two officers emphasized the military's superiority at managing commercial or political responsibilities by comparing Pakistani generals with international political leaders from military backgrounds, such as President Dwight D. Eisenhower, General Colin Powell and President Ronald Reagan.[5]

The second explanation relates to Locke's anarchic paradigm, in which economic activities are driven by the greed of individual personnel. The greed is linked with the organization's power and authority. Powerful generals conveniently use the system to satisfy their personal greed and ambitions. Pakistan's Milbus case often reflects an overlapping of institutional self-interest and the anarchic paradigm, where senior generals use their institutional authority and military mechanisms for personal predatory appropriation.

The underlying concept behind starting the first foundation was to create an autonomous system of welfare for armed forces personnel. This was a case of institutional self-interest. Nonetheless, the development also served the purpose of creating the image of the military as a strategic national saviour that contributed to national development through setting up major industries.

The Fauji Foundation (FF) invested in various industrial units in areas with high consumer demand, such as tobacco, sugar and textile production. In the western wing of the country, investments were made in the acquisition or establishment of the Khyber Tobacco Company in Mardan, a cereal manufacturing factory at Dhamial near Rawalpindi, a sugar mill at Tando Mohammad Khan in Sindh, and a textile factory at Jehlum. In the eastern wing it acquired or established East Pakistan Lamps and East Pakistan Electrical Industries (both at Dhaka), a rice mill at Rangpur, a flour mill at Chittagong and a jute mill near Dhaka. It also had financial stakes in Fauji Ceramics and West Pakistan Lamps Ltd which were later liquidated.[6]

The FF was one of many West Pakistani investors in East Pakistan, a situation that invoked the ire of the country's Bengali population. The people of the eastern wing accused the government of representing the interests of west Pakistani capital and its establishment. The common people's anger was mainly directed against the establishment, especially the military which was predominantly Punjabi and Pathan. In the case of the FF, the profits from its business ventures were repatriated to the western wing for reinvestment in welfare projects in areas where the military came from. This contributed to the inequitable distribution of resources.

There are no records available regarding the performance of these companies, or details of returns on investment, except for a commentary by Raymond Moore, according to whom these factories were well managed and were profit-making units. However, the financial viability of at least some of the units was debatable. For instance, the textile mill had to be closed down despite its tax breaks and the frequent injection of capital to upgrade its hardware and for other kinds of expansion.[7] The military managed to seek financial help from the government for its ventures. Despite this evidence, the military insists that the foundations are not part of the public sector.

There is no evidence of any serious objection raised by the civil society or the political leadership to the military's economic build-up. There are three possible explanations for the apparent complacency of the civil society. First, the dominant elite did not object to the military's expansion of its organizational interests because these were embedded in the larger stakes of the ruling elite, which dominated the state and its polity. According to Alavi, the post-colonial state of Pakistan mediated:

> between the competing interests for the three propertied classes, namely the metropolitan bourgeoisie, the indigenous bourgeoisie and the landed classes, while at the same time acting on behalf of them all to preserve the social order in which their interests are embedded, namely the institution of private property and the capitalist mode as the dominant mode of production.[8]

131

The state's bureaucracy, especially the military, was in any case responsible for bolstering the economic power of the dominant classes and building the major entrepreneurs in the country. The army chief who later became the president in 1958, General Ayub Khan, had also created the domestic private sector. The government's financial and institutional assistance was instrumental in building up the large industrial and business houses in the country. The Pakistan Industrial Development Corporation (PIDC) and other institutional mechanisms were used to provide financial loans and other incentives to potential entrepreneurs.[9]

Ayub Khan, who had taken control of the reins of the government, was keen on economic growth and establishing import-substitution industries. Developing military industries was part of the authoritarian economic development paradigm he used for the socioeconomic development of the state, which benefited both the military and civilian private sectors. As military dictator he was instrumental in building the famous 22 families, who owned about 68 per cent of the industries and 87 per cent of the banking and insurance assets. As a result they were sympathetic to their source of power, the army.[10] The private entrepreneurs and other dominant classes, who were clients of the military, hardly objected to tax breaks given to the FF-operated businesses, because the private industrial sector also received incentives during this period.

Second, the private entrepreneurs did not complain because the military presented its industrial and business projects as a contribution to national socioeconomic development. The FF, like the private entrepreneurs, was a beneficiary of the state-sponsored authoritarian economic modernization. It must also be noted that during the formative phase of the economic empire, there were fewer cases of senior generals engaging in predatory appropriation. Like the armed forces of Kemalist Turkey, Pakistan's military considered itself responsible for nation-building and the security of the state. The country's economic security was part of the military's larger role of ensuring the security and integrity of the state. In this respect, Pakistan's military was no different from others such as the Turkish armed forces, which intervened to check an economic slowdown and bring about economic progress. An expert on Turkey, Tim Jacoby, believes that the military elite consider economic progress important because of their dependence on national resources for purchasing weapons and strengthening the armed forces.[11] The military's business-industrial complex, in fact, indicates the will of the defence force's echelons to spearhead the drive for economic development. In Pakistan, the political and economic changes were part of the great 'revolution' that Ayub Khan claimed to have introduced through acquiring power in 1958.[12] The military business complex was part of the drive towards fulfilling his economic development agenda, which focused on establishing import-substitution industries.

It is also worth mentioning that the decade of the 1960s saw the military's rise to power and significance in other countries as well, such as Turkey and Indonesia, which also represent the parent-guardian type. The Indonesian military under Suharto was making headway in the business sector. This work was undertaken in collusion with Suharto and his cabal, and with the use of serving military personnel. Turkey, on the other hand, followed Pakistan's model in investing the military's pension funds in developing its industrial-business empire. Ankara imposed a 10 per cent levy on the basic salary of every military personnel to raise funds for investment.[13] In these three cases, the militaries aimed at bringing about national economic growth and affluence for its personnel. More importantly, as it appears from Turkey's case, the military-industrial or business complex was meant to 'promote the private sector and to place itself [the military] closer to the emerging bourgeoisie'.[14]

Third, the civil society, particularly the political leadership, did not have the capacity to stop the armed forces from enhancing their institutional autonomy. The military bureaucracy in the country was relatively stronger than the political leadership and the rest of the civil society. The military was part of the larger bureaucratic institution of the colonial state of Pakistan, which had acquired relatively greater maturity than the political institutions. This maturity, which led to greater autonomy from the bureaucratic machinery, was inherited from the days of British rule.[15] The politicians, on the other hand, were engulfed in the domestic political crises that led to rapid changes in government. As part of its praetorian character the military highlighted the weakness of the political leadership and presented the civilian institutions as corrupt, inept and redundant.[16] The political leadership certainly did not have the capacity to stop the military bureaucracy from gaining further autonomy through developing 'an independent material base in the society'[17] in the form of its commercial projects.

The period from 1954 to 1969 is crucial in terms of enhancement of the military's political ambitions. The military took over the state and projected itself as the primary definer of national interests, at the forefront of undertaking the political and socioeconomic development of the state. The most senior army general and the country's first military dictator had imposed indirect army rule through bringing about constitutional changes. The new constitutional framework introduced a presidential form of government led by General Ayub. The military dictator sought political legitimacy through projecting the organization's contribution to the nation's development.

Using the paradigm of the military as a strategic national saviour, it took upon itself the responsibility for infrastructure development, such as constructing the 805 km long Karakoram Highway connecting Pakistan with China. The Frontier Works Organization (FWO) was established in 1966 for the purpose of building this road. The organization was retained beyond the completion of its initial objective and later developed into the primary road construction giant in the country. Senior generals, such as Lt.-General (rtd) Asad Durrani, justify the continued presence of the FWO by claiming that a strategic contribution like the Karakoram Highway could not have been possible without it. He was of the view that 'where would we [Pakistan] have been if FWO wasn't there?'[18] The organization's website also touts the construction of the highway as an example of the military's superior capacity.[19]

Given the military's perception of itself as a superior entity, Ayub Khan brought serving and retired members of the organization into the government. He also inducted military personnel in the civil service to help him with governing departments and the country at large. Since the armed forces personnel were considered the most reliable and above board, they were trusted more with managing the government departments and the country. Senior military officers were therefore appointed to senior posts in public-sector corporations and other departments.[20]

The induction of military personnel into the government was more than just a matter of bringing the right people to the management of the state. The top management of the armed forces was also concerned about building and strengthening the corporate ethos. The institutional fabric of the armed forces appeared to be under threat during the 1950s. The army high command was jolted by a failed coup attempt, popularly known as the 'Rawalpindi Conspiracy', involving 53 officers and a number of civilians. In March 1951, a group of military officers and some prominent civilians with a leftist orientation, such as the famous Urdu poet Faiz Ahmed Faiz, were accused of planning a coup to overthrow the civilian government and establish a military council, which would hold elections for the legislature and resolve the Kashmir issue through the use of force.[21]

Although the attempt failed and a trial was held in which the officers were ultimately pardoned, the incident pointed to the need for building a stronger organizational ethos, or a 'social contract', between the military's high command and other members of the organization. The junior and mid-ranking officers were assured of rights over national resources, or were taken care of during and after service in return for their duty to the nation and loyalty to senior officers. Such a contract would work as the additional glue that bound the officers together. The system of welfare in which the personal needs of the officer cadre and the soldiers were catered for in return for their allegiance to the senior management, especially the commander-in-chief (later the chief of staff), was one of the important factors in transforming the military into a fraternity.

The military operated on the principle of taking care of its members from the 'cradle to the grave', seeing to their needs even after retirement. The organization's welfare needs were effectively catered for by the senior generals. Indeed, as commander-in-chief of the army, Ayub Khan had lamented the physical conditions of the armed forces personnel.[22] These were ameliorated through establishing organizations such as the FF. The basic purpose of the FF was therefore to provide for the welfare of war veterans and their dependants in an institutional manner. The profits earned through the five businesses initially established under the umbrella of the FF were to provide funds for setting up hospitals and schools, or to provide grants to those in need. This welfare structure would become an essential component of the 'corporate' character of the armed forces. Military personnel are proud of the way in which the institution takes care of its men.

Under this strategy, other personal benefits were provided as well, such as the grant of agricultural land to military personnel. Although agricultural land was also awarded in Punjab, it is the land grant in Sindh started under Ayub Khan that is remembered as the hallmark of the land redistribution policy. This is because after 1947 the most significant amount of land reclaimed for agriculture (through building reservoirs and canals) was in Sindh. The military was given 10 per cent of the approximately 9 million acres of land reclaimed through the construction of the Kotri, Guddu and Ghulam Mohammad dams in Sindh. The government also gave land to some senior civil bureaucrats, who were the military regime's partners.

According to Hassan-Askari Rizvi's study, approximately 300,000 acres were given to military officers in Sindh during Ayub's rule.[23] However, another report indicates the total allocation in Sindh to be over 1 million acres, most of which was given during Ayub's regime.[24] In addition, there were compensation schemes for those personnel who had lost their land as a result of waterlogging. They were given replacement land in the interior of Sindh.[25] The practice of giving land to the military was justified as a continuation of an age-old British tradition to allocate reclaimed land to loyal military personnel.

Most of the economic dividends were institutional, as is obvious from the earlier discussion,. However, as the army increased its control of the state there was a commensurate increase in the benefits that senior generals mustered for themselves and their families. Ayub Khan, for instance, became notorious for providing favours and advantages to his son, Gohar Ayub, who had started in business and acquired substantial industrial holdings after resigning his commission from the army.[26] The son's financial stakes brought disrepute to the father. Such personal advantages depended on the influence of the military both politically and institutionally. This was a case of senior officers using the organization's influence for predatory economic advantage.

THE ERA OF RESTRAINT, 1969-77

The growth of the military's internal economy started to slow down after the end of Ayub Khan's rule in 1969. There was no substantial increase in the military's business-industrial complex during the three years of General Yahya Khan's rule. The slowing down of Milbus was not because of any change in the mindset of the armed force's high command regarding perks and privileges for the military fraternity. In fact, like Ayub, Yahya Khan brought in more of his uniformed colleagues to run the show. The change was rather a result of the acute political crisis that engulfed the country.

The second welfare foundation, the Army Welfare Trust (AWT), was established on 27 October 1971, about two months before the war with India. This was purely an army organization controlled by the GHQ, established with the purpose of providing for the welfare of retired army personnel and their dependants (see organizational details in Chapter 4). It was considered imperative to build a second organization dedicated entirely to the army as it was claimed the FF could not cater for the welfare needs of the army.[27] This logic is questionable given the fact that the FF was already dominated by the army. The AWT was structured in a different way from the FF. Unlike the tri-service welfare foundation, the newly established AWT had greater financial dependence on its parent service. The GHQ provided investment to the AWT for its business projects, the returns of which were to be given to retired army personnel and their dependants. Moreover, the army high command could also ask for financial help from the AWT, supposedly for its other welfare projects as and when required (see details in Chapter 8).

No other enterprise other than the AWT was established at this time. As mentioned earlier, the lack of activity was a result of the domestic political conditions. Yahya Khan had overthrown Ayub Khan's semi-military government. Although most of the existing literature on Pakistan's politics categorizes the political change as a coup, the change is more correctly described as a successful counter-coup, in which the army's high command decided to sack a senior army general. Yahya Khan, as the new army chief, had greater power over the officer cadre than Ayub Khan, who had moved himself up the organizational ladder by self-promotion to the rank of a field marshal, a move that distanced him from the actual control of the service. In any case, his economic policies, which had brought temporary economic relief to the country, had become diluted during the political crisis.

Ayub Khan's policies had resulted in concentration of wealth in the hands of a few, a policy criticized by many including the internationally acclaimed Pakistani development economist, Dr Mehboobul Haq, who has written about the financial and political domination of 22 families in the country during Ayub's era. Such a concentration of wealth increased frustration among the common people. In addition, Ayub's political system of basic democracies added to the aggravation of the small landholders, peasants, the working class and other groups who did not view the regime or its political methodology as catering to the needs of poor people.[28] The government's most favoured 'basic democracies' system strengthened the bureaucratic state instead of empowering the people, and the new constitution introduced in 1962, which marginalized non-state-sponsored political parties and groups further eroded people's confidence in the government. Furthermore, legal provisions such as the Universities Ordinance and the Press and Publications Ordinance drove a wedge between the regime and the affected communities such as students and journalists. In consequence there were mass protests in both wings of the country against the military's political and social coercion. In the western wing the public frustration was channelled by Bhutto in gathering support for his semi-socialist agenda and for his new political party, the Pakistan's People's Party (PPP), which was formed in September 1967.

The problem in the eastern wing, however, was much more acute. The inequitable distribution of resources was more pronounced in East Pakistan, where the general public were inherently hostile to the idea of their subordination to the Punjabi-dominated establishment in the western wing of the country.

Furthermore, the ethnic differences between the two wings were embedded in the politics of the state. Over the years, the differences culminated in the formulation of a six-point agenda by the Awami National Party of the eastern wing, demanding greater autonomy for the federating units. Ayub Khan's government not only resisted these demands but implicated and later imprisoned the Bengali leader, Mujibur Rehman, in December 1967 in the famous 'Agartala Conspiracy'. He was accused of conspiring with the Indian government for the creation of an independent state. Although the government could not finally prove the charges and the case was based on flimsy evidence,[29] it deepened the divide between the government and the Bengali leadership and populace.

It was in these circumstances that Yahya Khan took charge of the country in 1969. However, there was no substantive change in Islamabad's policies regarding East Pakistan, which resulted in further estrangement between the two wings. It was the war with India that proved to be the last nail in the coffin of an united Pakistan.

The end of the war in December 1971 brought about domestic political change in Pakistan, which had an impact on the growth of Milbus. Zulfiqar Ali Bhutto, who became the first popularly elected prime minister, did not encourage the military's political or financial autonomy. He tried to dilute the financial autonomy of the armed forces through challenging the military's authority to distribute certain perks and privileges. For instance, he took away some of the land that had been given to military personnel as part of his land reforms exercise.[30] Moreover, he did not encourage the opening of other welfare foundations, and the third one was not established until after Bhutto's fall in July 1977.

Bhutto viewed the armed forces primarily as a policy instrument, and therefore he used them for carrying out developmental work, such as developing a communications network in Azad Jammu, Kashmir and the northern areas. The creation of the Special Communications Organization (SCO) in 1976 basically aimed at using the military's development potential rather than giving the organization extra authority. Bhutto clearly had no desire to make the military autonomous or to support any activities that enhanced its independence from civilian institutions, or indeed from himself. However, Bhutto failed to put life into his plans to curtail the power of the armed forces. Like Dr Faustus, he was divided between two urges: to bring about a new sociopolitical system that would empower the masses and democratic institutions, and to acquire absolute power for himself. He ultimately gave in to the latter desire, which inadvertently led him to strengthen the political power of the armed forces. As a consequence the military removed him from power in 1977 and assassinated him in 1979. Ultimately, Bhutto's flawed politics and the GHQ's interests brought the military back to power.

The end of Bhutto was the end of an era of restraint of the military's political and financial autonomy. The years discussed in this chapter represent an initial phase of the military tasting direct power for the first time, but they also represent more than that. Like the ruler-type militaries of Latin America, Pakistan's armed forces viewed themselves as the primary institution responsible for the integrity of the state and its socio-economic development. This particular understanding was also reflected in the nature of their economic exploitation. Most of the industrial projects were undertaken as a contribution to national development and the welfare of military personnel.

However, certain other activities such as the exploitation of land resources were driven by the military's perception of itself as an autonomous strategic national saviour with the right to appropriate any amount of national resources for the betterment of its members. Pakistan's Milbus belied the self-righteous streak of the military's senior management. Land and other resources or foreign aid could be utilized for the betterment of military personnel since they were more responsible than any other political or civil society player. This was also the period when the economic predatoriness of senior officers of the armed forces began, and this trend increased in the ensuing years.

6 Expansion of Milbus, 1977–2005

One of the lessons that the generals learnt from civilian rule, especially the years under Bhutto, was that the army could not leave national governance in its entirety to politicians. Even though Bhutto had failed to strengthen democracy and establish the dominance of civilian institutions, he had posed challenges to the military's authority and autonomy. Consequently, Zia ul Haq's regime sought to re-establish both the dominance and the autonomy of the armed forces. During the years under study, the senior generals acquired the political power that allowed them to engage in predatory financial acquisition. The economic power, in turn, is what deepened their appetite for political power. The growth of Milbus during the period under study marks the GHQ's efforts to re-establish the military's financial autonomy, and also shows how senior generals used their greater power to manipulate resources for their personal advantage. Milbus emerged as a parallel economy that transformed the armed forces into a dominant economic actor.

The enhancement of the military's financial autonomy was not a coincidence. It was an outcome of the army's efforts during this period to carve out a permanent role for the organization in managing the state. The various legal and constitutional provisions introduced during ten years of Zia ul Haq's rule and consolidated by the Musharraf regime transformed the military from a tool for policy implementation to an equal partner in policy making. The political governments had their own ulterior motives in turning a blind eye to the defence force's growing economic power. The political autonomy, combined with the economic independence that was sought through enhancing the military's capacity for financial exploitation, turned the military fraternity into an independent class. This chapter analyses the growth of Milbus and its contribution to strengthening the senior echelons of the military, and bolstering their intention to remain powerful.

RE-ESTABLISHING FINANCIAL AUTONOMY, 1977–88

These ten years cover the period of Zia ul Haq's rule, which ended in August 1988 with his death in a mysterious plane crash. The military dictator brought the army back to power. The military's expansion in the economic sphere was a corollary of the organization's political control.

This was the period when a number of new provisions were introduced to expand the military's share in the economy. These included steps to benefit both the military organizationally and individual officers. During these years there was major infrastructural and sectoral expansion of Milbus. While the various welfare foundations started new industrial projects, they also expanded into new areas of business activity: what is referred to here as sectoral expansion. The growth of the military's economic interests coincided with the organization's return to power. The dominance of the state provided the GHQ with an opportunity to exploit resources and enhance the military's financial autonomy.

The link between political control and economic exploitation by the military can be observed in other places as well, such as Turkey and Central America. An expert on the political economy of military business in Central America, Kevin Casas Zamora, believes that the growth of the military's commercial activities in this region was 'a consequence of the region's long-standing tradition of military dominance over the body politic'.[1] Commenting on Turkish politics, William Hale observed that when they assumed power in 1960 and 1980, the armed forces seized the opportunity to secure increased salaries and fringe benefits for the officer corps. However, he ruled out any suggestion that the military's political intervention was caused by the organization's financial stakes. According to Hale, 'the historical record indicates that corporate interests [commercial stakes] have almost certainly been less important than other political and social concerns'.[2] However, Hale's analysis did not take into account the linkage between the Turkish military's financial autonomy and its political power.

The financial and political autonomy of the armed forces are interrelated in a vicious circle, as will be demonstrated in this chapter. While political power is a prerequisite for the military's exploitation of national resources, the armed forces' financial autonomy deepens its interest in retaining control of the state. This observation can be applied to Pakistan, where political power determined the intensification of the corporate interests of the officer cadre, as demonstrated in their financial perks and privileges.

Pakistan's military disagrees with this analysis. Most of the 40 senior Pakistani military officers interviewed for the present study, some of whom had served or were serving in responsible civilian positions in the Musharraf regime, denied that economic interests had caused the military to intervene, or had any link with its political power. They believed that the armed forces took control of the state to save it from irresponsible politicians, and that the economic activities were not at all linked to the organization's political strength. There were, in fact, no politics behind the commercial ventures, which were purely to provide for the welfare of military personnel and add to the economic well-being of the nation.

For example, the governor of the Punjab, Lt.-General (rtd) Khaled Maqbool's response to a question about the politics of the military's economy was, 'have we [the military] deprived anyone of economic resources? Why should there be any objection to these commercial ventures when all that the military is doing is adding to the overall advantage of the country?'[3] Interestingly, the 'institutional memory' of the armed forces that Admiral Saeed Mohammad Khan[4] talked about does not include any analysis of the larger impact of the military's internal economy. The admiral's mention of 'institutional memory' refers to the professional norms and ethos of the armed forces and its internal cohesion.

There are dissenting views about the benign nature of Milbus, and not

all military officers agree that the commercial vent
serve the purpose of welfare. Col. (rtd) Bakhtiar K'
the Defence Housing Authority (DHA) clubs in '
the notion that the commercial ventures provid
He was of the view that the military's internal (
of senior generals, and the soldiers barely got any...
fact that 'all policies made at the GHQ are not good for ⌐
commercial ventures basically represent the greed of senior offic...

Under Zia, Milbus, which had taken a back seat under Bhutto, star...
expanding again with greater vigour. The economic activities were
commensurate with the army coming back to power in full force. Zia
sought legitimacy by partnering with the religious elite, the landed-feudal
class and the business elite. He reversed Bhutto's policy of nationalization
of key sectors such as business, industry and education. The privatization
policy was meant to strengthen private entrepreneurs and overall economic
conditions in the country. The military regime's attitude to politics and civil
society was like that of any bureaucratic-authoritarian regime, which aban-
dons democratic norms and principles to 'promote an authoritarian political system that will (it is believed) facilitate more effective performance by
the role-incumbents'.[6]

The military was one of the beneficiaries of Zia's drive for economic
growth. He took measures to establish the military's financial autonomy,
and made himself popular among his main constituency, the armed forces,
by empowering the senior commanders. He was conscious of the importance of keeping his generals happy and satisfied. He allowed his corps
commanders to operate secret 'regimental' funds. These were special secret
funds at the disposal of commanders, who had complete control over the
flow of resources from and to this special budget.

The regimental fund is like a black hole, where resources are sucked in
with little accountability. The funds drew upon two sources of input: transfer from the defence budget to be used for classified projects, and money
earned through opening smaller ventures, which are categorized in this study
as cooperatives. There is no accountability for these funds, nor are there
proper checks and balances to ensure that they are used for operational
purposes or welfare needs, and not for the personal benefit of the commander
or other senior officers. Sources talked about senior commanders using these
funds for renovating their accommodation, and on projects meant for the
comfort of their own families rather than betterment of the soldiers.

The individual powers of the senior commanders were further
dispersed at the divisional and unit level. The divisional and unit
commanders were also allowed to start small business ventures and retain
funds under the budgetary heading of welfare. The cooperatives were part
of the larger policy of giving financial autonomy to the armed forces. The
sacking of Prime Minister Mohammad Khan Junejo's regime in early 1988
was partly because of Zia's discomfort with the political leader questioning
the perks of senior officers. Although he was a premier hand-picked by the
military dictator, Junejo had publicly announced his intention to put

...ls in smaller and locally made Suzuki cars rather than the imported ...they normally used. In addition, his order to hold an inquiry into the ...hri' camp disaster invoked the wrath of Zia, who sacked his government ...n charges of corruption.

The dismissal of Junejo's government and that of subsequent regimes indicates a dichotomy in the military's approach to corruption. According to the editor of the English-language newspaper *Daily Times*, Najam Sethi, 'the military bends the rules and make their own rules so that no one can call it corruption. When politicians do the same it is called corruption.'[7] In the case of the management of regimental funds, the senior generals do not consider that they are mishandled.

The special financial power of individual commanders could not be questioned by the government's prescribed mechanism of accountability. The army's top leadership has repeatedly defended its 'right' not to be questioned by parliament or the public regarding its working or how it spends its funds. In fact, officers get extremely annoyed at any suggestion that the armed forces lack accountability: they consider them to be 'cleaner' than the public or private sector. The military not only considers itself above board, it also attaches high value to its own standards. For instance, the head of the Institute of Regional Studies, Maj.-General (rtd) Jamsheed Ayaz Khan, is of the view that the military's system of accountability is foolproof.[8] The general's claim is not supported by some senior members of the government's primary audit agency, the Department of the Auditor-General of Pakistan. According to one officer of the department, 'the regimental funds are not auditable and the method of "feeding" these funds is very shady'.[9]

As was mentioned earlier, the Zia regime was interested in empowering the military institution, and as a result it engaged in promoting within the military institution the sense of being an independent class with an unique political capacity, which was therefore justified in gaining greater perks and privileges. Lt.-General (rtd) Faiz Ali Chishti categorized the commercial ventures, and the system of perks and privileges, as a case of 'favouritism and nepotism'.[10] Efforts were made to develop infrastructures primarily for the benefit of the military fraternity, such as a separate schooling system for the children of armed forces personnel. In 1977, the GHQ decided to develop its own schools inside army cantonments.[11] The idea was to provide a better-quality education for the children of military personnel.

The army's schools are part of the elite system of education in the country, which can be found in the civilian sector as well. According to Tariq Rahman, these educational institutions use English as the language of instruction, and provide a chance for social mobility that ordinary government-run schools do not.[12] Pakistan's educational system is designed as an 'elite' versus a 'non-elite' system. Being part of the elite group with ample political muscle, the army could buy quality education for itself. A good schooling and college system also fed into the army's requirement for personnel. A number of officers' children trained at these elite schools would eventually join the service.

Entry to the army-run schools was restricted to children of army officers.

Although there was no legal bar on the entry of the children of junior commissioned officers (JCOs) and non-commissioned officers (NCOs) to these schools, it is mainly the children of senior officers who attend them. In some cases, the social class differentiation between the officer corps and the soldiers is prominent. For instance, the Pakistan Navy (PN) has different schools for the children of sailors. This internal social differentiation inadvertently apes the stratification found in other classes as well. However, the educational facilities are presented by military officers as an example of what their spokesman, Maj.-General Shaukat Sultan, described as the military's capacity to run institutions and systems more efficiently.[13]

The argument about the military's greater efficiency was also used for establishing other organizations, such as the National Logistics Cell (NLC). This organization was created in 1978 to deal with a cargo-handling crisis at Pakistan's only seaport, in Karachi. According to a letter issued by the office of the chief martial law administrator (that is, Zia ul Haq), there was a threat of a crisis because of a shortage in the supply of essential goods. The scare was that inefficient management at the seaport had increased the time taken to dock and unload cargo and other ships to such a degree that there could be a serious shortage of wheat in the country. The poor management at the Karachi port cost the government US$14.3 million in demurrage to foreign shippers.[14]

The response of Lt.-General (rtd) Saeed Qadir, who was then the quartermaster-general (QMG), was to establish an independent set-up that could be run through the army with the minimum of involvement of civilians – which, it was argued, would minimize corruption and inefficiencies. The NLC is now involved in multiple activities such as transportation and the construction of roads and bridges. The management claim to have improved conditions tremendously at the Karachi port. This assertion is borne out by the data given in Table 6.1.

NLC's higher share of cargo transport shows the role that the organization played in the transportation of goods. However, others contest the NLC's claims. In fact, officers of the Railways Department complained about the

Table 6.1 Comparative capacity for cargo transport, 1995–2000

Year	NLC (tons)	% of total cargo	Private transport (tons)	% of total cargo	Railways (tons)	% of total cargo
1995–6	711,770	52.86	407,053	30.23	227,688	16.91
1996–7	819,210	52.52	460,901	29.55	279,451	17.92
1997–8	666,559	64.00	472,387	34.00	72,289	2.00
1998–9	511,667	33.00	911,946	59.00	123,629	8.00
1999–2000	215,766	20.00	839,952	77.00	39,839	3.00

Source: NLC HQs Report.

NLC hijacking their business.[15] They were of the view that the military's transport company used its influence to secure a major chunk of the transport business. It is apparent from Table 6.1 that the railways' share did reduce dramatically after 1997–8. The military regime built and strengthened its own organization instead of revitalizing the Pakistan Railways, which had, until the creation of the military transport company, been the main cargo transporter in the country. The creation of the NLC was not a case of privatizing cargo transport but of shifting work from one public-sector institution to another, and hence creating a duplication of efforts.

The company also built wheat storage centres, a task that was part of its original mandate. Its stated profit from 1990–1 to 1999–2000 was approximately Rs.954.9 million (US$16.46 million).[16] One former army chief, Mirza Aslam Beg, claimed that these profits are evidence of the NLC's efficiency. The general was of the view that the NLC and the FWO are not part of the military, but because they are manned by military personnel and do not have a civilian character, they are far more productive than private-sector organizations.[17] However, the NLC's supposed profitability is not necessarily a result of greater efficiency: it is linked with its ability to capitalize on its association with the army to get government contracts and to push out its private-sector competitors. The NLC enjoys greater advantage in securing contracts than any other private or public-sector transport company. Its connection with the army has cushioned it from overall competition in the market. For instance, the land provided for its sites in various parts of the country is state land, a facility that gives it a major advantage over private-sector organizations. NLC vehicles also do not face the checks and controls that an ordinary transportation company is likely to encounter at the hands of customs, police and other authorities. The private-sector transporters have to carry the cost of corruption by these officials, and the NLC does not.

Under Zia, the defence forces also began to expand their financial power for the benefit of their members, especially the senior echelons. It must be reiterated that the military's economic empire underwent a vertical and horizontal expansion commensurate with its political power. This expansion manifested itself in three forms. First, the regime granted greater benefits to individual members of the fraternity, rewarding them with rural and urban land. Second, as mentioned earlier, numerous cooperative ventures were started to establish the military's financial independence. Third, the subsidiaries were allowed to expand their business operations at the risk of penetrating most segments of the economy and the society. The establishment of two other welfare foundations, one by the Pakistan Air Force (PAF) (the Shaheen Foundation, SF) and the other by the PN (the Bahria Foundation, BF) represented part of the horizontal expansion.

The SF was created in 1977.[18] It was established on the same principles as the AWT: that is, using pension funds for investment in business and industrial projects. Apparently, the PAF's high command wanted to create greater welfare opportunities for its members. The service had a small share of the welfare resources and jobs in the FF, and its 5 per cent share in FF projects was not considered sufficient to accommodate ex-PAF personnel or provide

144

welfare facilities. However, the expansion replicated the inter-services rivalry that could be observed in the distribution of the defence budget between the three services, and in arms procurement (see Figure 6.1).

The PAF's example was soon followed by the PN, which lost no time in establishing the BF in January 1982.[19] There was no justification for the navy's independent set-up other than inter-services competition. There had not been any major personnel layoffs after 1971 war to precipitate this development. The service's personnel were limited in number in any case: it was the least significant of the three armed services in the national military-strategic plans. The country's defence plans do consider a potential naval blockade of the main seaport at Karachi, as happened during the 1971 war, but the plans remain oriented towards fighting a land battle rather than a long-drawn-out skirmish where sea power would make a difference.[20]

The former naval chief, Admiral Tariq Kamal Khan, claimed he opposed the idea of establishing the foundation, and wanted to close it down during his tenure as the service chief (1983–6) because the senior officers of the PN spent about 40 per cent of their time during meetings of the principal staff officers (PSOs) on discussing the foundation. However, he could not do so because of 'the hue and cry raised at such a suggestion'.[21] The senior commanders obviously did not want to surrender an opportunity for economic empowerment.

The BF used the same management concept as the AWT and the SF. It used welfare resources for investment in business and industrial projects, rather than opening hospitals, schools and the like. Like those of the other foundations, BF's ventures were run by retired military personnel. This

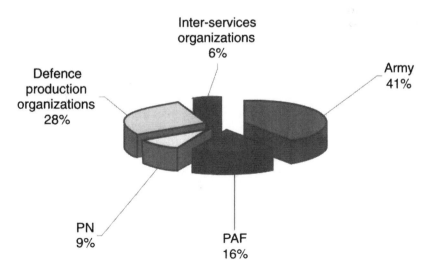

Figure 6.1 Division of the defence budget
Source: Siddiqa-Agha (2001, p. 83).

peculiar staff induction principle did not make these institutions private-sector operations, as is claimed by most armed forces personnel. In most cases appointments to the welfare foundations were made when officers reached the tail end of their careers in the military, making the jobs an extension of their careers rather than employment in the private sector. In any case, as was pointed out by Lt.-General (rtd) Talat Masood, Zia used the top positions in the foundations to reward officers for their exceptional obedience to him, or to sideline those who posed a potential threat to him or to his system.[22]

The system of appointments in the foundations, and in other public sector organizations and government departments, especially at senior positions, was subject to the pleasure of the service chiefs. Employment in the foundations was part of the system of reward or punishment that the senior management of the armed forces as principal conferred on their 'clients', almost like a monarch or a feudal lord, to nurture a sense of comradeship and enforce greater obedience. Zia, being a pragmatic man, was driven by his sense of personal survival, and this depended on strengthening the corporate ethos of his institution. Hence, despite his reputation of being religious-minded, the general did not discourage corruption or activities that gave the officer cadre opportunities to gain financial advantage, since this ensured their support. There were no visible checks on serving or retired senior officers.

The horizontal expansion of the military's economy took the form of an increase in business operations. The bigger foundations such as the FF and AWT moved into fertilizer production, which is a consumer-oriented industry with high demand. The Fauji Fertilizer Company Ltd (FFC) was incorporated in May 1978. Its first plant was established in 1982 to manufacture urea, at a cost of Rs.3,300 million (US$56.9 million) with equity of Rs.814 million (US$14 million). This operation was similar to the jute factory opened in what was then East Pakistan. Just as jute was the mainstay of the economy in the country's eastern wing, the western wing's economy was highly dependent on agriculture.

In the mid-1980s, FF also entered strategic sectors such as oil and gas by establishing the Mari Gas Company Ltd (MGCL). The FF purchased 40 per cent of the stakes of the Pak Stanvac Petroleum Project, which made it the biggest stakeholder in the company. The other shareholders are the Government of Pakistan (20 per cent), Oil and Gas Cooperation Ltd (20 per cent) and the general public (20 per cent).[23] The fully paid-up capital is Rs.367.50 million (US$6.34 million). The FF's 40 per cent shareholding gives it both profit and management rights over the company, and it appointed a retired lt.-general as a director. The company claims to have an authorized capital of Rs.2,500 million (US$43.1 million), and contributed to providing jobs in Dharki, Sindh, where it operates the country's second-largest oil field.[24]

The claim regarding jobs for local people is, however, contested by people in Dharki. Reportedly, the local population protested in 1984 that the company showed a bias in not providing jobs to the residents. The tension between the people and the company's management escalated into a conflict, leading to an unfortunate incident in which the protestors were fired on, and one woman lost her life.[25] The people still complain about not getting jobs in the company, which exploits local resources. The story is a reminder of a similar situation which prevailed in Kinshasa, Congo around 1890, where the king's agents established a system of administration that was 'chiefly occupied with the extraction of revenue from the vast territory', especially areas where ivory was found.[26]

The AWT also expanded into other agri-based industries such as the sugar industry. In 1984 the foundation opened a sugar mill in Badin, Sindh, and rice, ginning and oil mills, a fish farm and a bicycle manufacturing plant in Lahore, as well as a hosiery factory in Rawalpindi. According to Lt.-General Rizvi, who was the first head of AWT, the capital for these ventures was found by borrowing from public-sector banks.[27] The intention was to make profits from industries in high-demand sectors.[28] All these projects were eventually closed because they were not found to be profitable. This could be the result of inept management rather than the lack of demand for products produced (see Chapter 9 on the efficiency of the AWT).

Besides its industrial operations, the AWT also acquired land and established five farms in Sindh and Punjab, totalling about 18,000 acres. According to Lt.-General (rtd) Moin-u-Din Haider, the army's welfare foundation was also given 'enemy land' recovered after the 1965 war.[29]

It must be noted that although the AWT was established in 1971, it actually started its operations after 1977. A number of serving officers were posted to it, especially in the early 1980s.[30] From a rehabilitation perspective, the welfare foundation was an opportunity to give extended employment to officers. For example, starting from 1984 Maj.-General Rizvi was posted to the AWT for a period of ten years, along with some other officers.[31] These posts retained their status as serving officers. These officers clearly were those not considered suitable for further promotion in the army, but the postings gave them a chance to draw an income and to retain and perpetuate their formal links with the army.

Rizvi and the other officers were not formally trained for managing businesses, but Lt.-General (rtd) Mohammad Amjad claimed, 'if military officers can run the country, why can't they run business ventures? We are trained in management.'[32] Other senior officers also subscribe to this view. They are of the opinion that senior officers have ample experience of personnel and materials management during their military careers, and that this gives them an advantage in running commercial ventures. Lt.-General Qazi, who became the federal minister for railways, and later education, threw a challenge by saying, 'show me one business run by any serving or retired military officer that has failed. Remember that the only time the railways was out of deficit was when it was run by a general.'[33] He was referring to his own tenure, but he did not point out that the railway came out of deficit mainly because of the sale of its land, which resulted in an injection of capital.[34]

The system for the appointment of retired military personnel was further fine-tuned under Zia. It shifted from a policy where officers at the tail-end of their military career took these postings: the new approach was to appoint them to posts in these foundations or similar organizations for a set period of time immediately after retirement.

The SF and BF followed the example of the two army-controlled foundations in opening their own business ventures. The SF established an advertising agency in 1977, a knitwear factory in 1981 and an airport service company in 1982. The concept behind the knitwear business was to benefit from the PAF's demand for hosiery: it had a large budget for this purpose. So, to accommodate retired senior personnel and the service at the same time, the SF management started that this industrial unit that would basically 'recycle' PAF's resources for the purpose. No assessment was made about the future of the business, and especially what would happen when the PAF's hosiery budget was exhausted. Knitwear production for local consumption was soon terminated, and the business switched to exports, but reportedly with unimpressive results.

This pattern was also followed by Shaheen Aerotraders, established in 1988 to supply hardware and other required material to the PAF.[35] Although the financial details of the company's operations during the 1990s are not known, in 2000 the SF's management claimed an average annual turnover of about Rs.40–50 million (US$690,000–852,000).[36] This venture was completely geared to providing for the PAF's needs for spare parts and components. The business was handy particularly after the imposition of an arms embargo in 1990, when the PAF was forced to acquire spares and components for its US-built F-16s from the arms market. Creating its own company of course minimized the involvement of private contractors in such operations.

Other ventures such as Shaheen Airport Services also benefited from PAF's influence and contacts. The company was set up to provide ground handling at major international airports in the country. The human resources it acquired from the PAF, and its influence in getting things done, proved crucial. Domestic airlines and related business fall under the purview of the MoD, which is controlled at the top by military officers. The service also provides the bulk of pilots to the national carrier, Pakistan International Airlines (PIA).

Meanwhile the BF set up its Falah Trading Company in 1982. The company supplies stationery and office supplies to government offices, particularly to agencies with which the navy interacts, such as the Maritime Security Agency (MSA), Karachi Port Trust (KPT) and the director-general defence procurement (DGDP). The underlying concept was to set up companies that could then do business with all those departments controlled by the MoD. For instance, BF's trading company did business with the KPT (in the financial year 2002/03) worth Rs.60 million (US$1.03 million).[37]

The increase in the military's political and institutional power also strengthened the paramilitary forces, which saw themselves as akin to the armed forces mainly because of their connection with the defence establishment. The Pakistan Rangers, which is a border security force, is controlled by the MoD like the three services of the armed forces. In 1977 the Rangers took control of fishing and other resources in four lakes in Sindh. This activity impinged upon the interests of low-income people from the poor fishing community in that area.[38] In this case, strengthening the monitoring of bordering areas was used as an excuse to exploit opportunities to generate funds. The Rangers, which is headed by an army maj.-general, leased out fishing in these lakes to private contractors at the cost of excluding the local fishing community and depriving them of their livelihood. Because the Rangers monopolized the grant of fishing licences, the catch was sold at lower prices than previously, depriving the community of their rights. This was done in violation of the provincial government's Fisheries Ordinance 1980.[39]

Subsequently the Rangers took control of another 20 lakes in the province, and this too ultimately led to a conflict between the Rangers and the fishing community. The intrusion of the Rangers threatened the livelihood of hundreds of fishermen living in about a dozen big villages and thousands of small settlements on the 18,000 km coastline of Sindh and Baluchistan.[40] The bulk of the expansion, however, took place in the 1990s and after 2000. The expansion was directly linked with the increase in the number of Rangers personnel in Sindh. By 2005 there were 11,000 Rangers in the province.[41] There was hardly any intervention from the provincial government because it did not dare stand up to the military. In fact, the federal government, which was called upon for help by the fishing community, took a position in favour of the Rangers. The political opposition in the National Assembly was denied the right to discuss the matter in parliament.[42]

The Zia regime will also be remembered for granting greater perks and privileges to individual officers. Unlike Ayub Khan's regime, which created institutional mechanisms for granting benefits to the military personnel, Zia was far more generous in arbitrarily providing economic benefits to his officer cadre. The difference can be attributed to the fact that the Ayub regime marked the beginning of the military's entry into the corridors of power, and it was too early for the top generals to think of establishing the military as an independent class. Politically, as was shown in Chapter 3, Zia created legal provisions such as Article 58(2)(b) (an amendment to the 1973 Constitution) to institutionalize the military's power. Similarly, he made provisions in the economic sphere to benefit this, his main constituency. Zia spread the net of benefits to include middle-ranking officers.

The process of institutionalizing benefits to military personnel represents a vertical expansion of the military's economic empire. One of the examples is housing for military officers. A scheme was initiated during this period under which the three services took the responsibility of providing houses to their personnel after they retired. Nominal deductions from the pay of all officers were made during service, in return for a house or an apartment which was handed over before or after retirement. The deduction varies from Rs.200 to Rs.1,000 (US$3–16) per month.[43] In the army, officers could join the scheme after ten years of service, with the deductions being made during the remainder of their service. Later, under General Musharraf, the facility was made mandatory for all officers.

This facility, it was hoped, would help individuals to focus more on professional activities. It was part of the 'social contract' between the top management and the officer cadre. Since military personnel, especially those in the army, are displaced often and have to survive in rigorous conditions, providing housing would ensure that the officers had greater peace of mind. Whether it actually enhanced their professionalism is debatable, but it was definitely a measure by the top management to redefine the extent of the 'rent' owed by the nation to the officer cadre for providing security.

Interestingly, the primary beneficiaries of this 'social contract' are the senior officers, and not the (JCOs and other ranks, and their equivalent in the PAF and PN, as was pointed out by Col. Bakhtiar Khan.[44] None of the 27 housing schemes developed by the military on state land catered for the needs of the non-officer cadre. These housing projects, and the allocation of urban land to the officer cadre for constructing houses, was, claimed Brig. Al Tirmazi, a 'scam started by General Zia, which benefited a lot of officers who used the opportunity to make money, hence, encouraging corruption in the defence services'.[45] I argued in the introduction to this book that the monopolization of benefits by senior officers is a key feature of Milbus, which suited the elitist nature of the Pakistan military's officer cadre. The character of Milbus had much in common with the elitist nature of Pakistan's politics and socioeconomics.

An editorial in a Pakistani English-language newspaper, The Nation, claimed that during Zia's regime some senior officers acquired unexplained resources, which it was rumoured were linked with heroin smuggling during the Afghan war.[46] Although the editorial used the word 'rumour', it is a fact that the officer cadre of the armed forces became more affluent during the Zia years than in the preceding years.

The use of state land for constructing housing schemes also encouraged the military's subsidiaries to branch into real estate development. This refers to the BF's housing scheme, started in 1986. Although this was not a new trend – the army already had its DHA schemes – the BF scheme made it clear that the military establishment would promote land development by the welfare groups. The fundamental concept was simple, and was not restricted to the armed forces: other groups including branches of the civil service and the judiciary also indulged in land development. The groups raised money that was invested in purchasing land and the development of housing. The significant issue is that influence and authority were used to acquire the land cheaply and sell it at a good profit. The military was the greatest beneficiary mainly because of the greater confidence it could command from people investing in the schemes. The benefits given to military personnel also included agricultural land, which was distributed to both officers and soldiers from the three services. However, ordinary soldiers got less land and were not provided with the subsidies that were available for the senior officers (see details in Chapter 7).

Other facilities given to senior officers included permission to import luxury cars without paying any customs duty. From 1977 to 1997 approximately 43 senior-ranking officers benefited from this scheme. This included 27 army, 10 navy and 6 air force officers, all above the rank of brigadier.[47] In addition, 115 military officers were re-employed in the public sector on contract. This included 18 ambassadors, a sizeable proportion of the total of 42 ambassadors posted abroad.[48] Clearly, the institutionalizing of perks was mainly concentrated in the officer cadre. The increase in the military's political power resulted in greater economic predatoriness by the higher echelons of the armed forces. They used political influence to grab greater opportunities for themselves, and this trend increased with time. These perks and privileges can all be seen as a part of Milbus, and signify the military's financial autonomy.

As well as the military's autonomy, the other explanation for these trends is that the members of the military fraternity were natural beneficiaries of Zia's overall economic liberalization policy. Zia wanted economic progress, which he aimed to achieve by reversing Bhutto's business and industrial nationalization policy. While he brought the private sector on board with his privatization agenda, the military-business complex also became a partner in furthering the privatization goals. The situation in Pakistan was similar to that in Turkey during the 1960s. The Turkish armed forces benefited from Prime Minister Suleyman Demirel's efforts to reduce the role of the public sector through encouraging the private sector. In 1961, the regime established the Armed Forces Mutual Assistance Fund, popularly known as OYAK. According to this approach, a 10 per cent deduction was made from the salaries of military personnel and civilian employees of the MoD for investment in profit-making ventures.[49] While in Turkey it was the civilian regime that initiated the economic integration between itself and the army, in Pakistan's case it was the army that provided opportunities to the civilian private sector, and in the process of this integration benefited itself.

CIVILIAN–MILITARY POLITICO-ECONOMIC INTEGRATION, 1988–99

Democracy was restored in Pakistan after Zia's death in August 1988. The years after Zia, however, did not witness a reduction in the military's economic stakes. In fact, the commercial network expanded as a result of the efforts of successive civilian governments to work out a détente with the army. The killing of an elected prime minister by the Zia regime indicated the military's immense power, and provided a warning that the politicians must not question the organization's interests. The twice-elected regimes of Benazir Bhutto (1988–90, 1993–6) and Nawaz Sharif (1990–3, 1997–9) tried to appease the army generals through providing greater economic opportunities. According to Nawaz Sharif's finance minister, Sirtaj Aziz, 'for us [the Sharif government] the main challenge was reducing the military's political strength. Had we begun to curb their financial interests as well, it would have had an immediate reaction from the armed forces.'[50] The perks and privileges of the military were considered as a vital part of the military's corporate interests. Challenging these, it was understood, would be tantamount to questioning the authority of the generals.[51]

Most governments used the economic rewards for the military to buy time, as the former speaker of the National Assembly, Elahi Buksh Soomro, explained. Milbus was an area that no government wanted to touch. Soomro claimed that he tried to draw the attention of President Ishaq Khan to the military's bourgeoning economic empire, but was told that 'the issue was like a "beehive" that shouldn't be touched. The military is too powerful an agency and we [the politicians] will get stuck [if we press the issue].'[52] Although Benazir Bhutto denied that she ever tried to ignore the issue,[53] in a two-hour interview on the subject she tended to evade the question about whether she used economic opportunities as sweeteners for the generals. However, one of the prominent leaders of her party, Shah Mehmood Qureshi, who is also a member of the National Assembly elected in 2002, confessed that 'all civilian governments ignored Milbus or provided economic opportunities to placate the military'.[54]

The fact is that despite transferring power to civilian leadership in 1988, the army continued to be a powerful player in politics, and no government dared to challenge its core interests. The political changes that took place in 1988 were essentially superficial. In November 1988 power was transferred to Benazir Bhutto because, according to the then army chief, General Mirza Aslam Beg, he (Beg) was one of the greatest proponents of democracy. He argued that he had done a great service to the country by not taking over the reins of government and instead transferring power to the civilian regime. He further claimed to be different from his predecessor, Zia, in not wanting to perpetuate the military's control of politics.[55]

The fact, however, is that Beg could not have taken over power soon after Zia's death in 1988. There are three explanations for this. First, by 1988 the international environment did not support a continuation of the military regime in Pakistan. Second, the domestic political conditions did not support its extension either. Third, as was explained by the former naval chief, Fasih Bokhari, Beg did not have 'ownership' of the army despite being the service chief.[56] By this, Bokhari means an army chief's confidence that he can carry the entire service with him, should he for instance carry out a coup. General Beg was certainly no proponent of democracy, since he was involved in destabilizing Benazir Bhutto's first regime. In any case, an unstable democracy was part of Zia's legacy. The Eighth Amendment to the 1973 Constitution had empowered the president to dismiss the parliament. This power was used repeatedly during the 1990s to sack governments. The average time served by each regime was about two years, during which the political leadership tried a number of ways to manipulate and influence the armed forces. Providing incentives for military business was seen as one of the methods for a regime to keep the military on its side.

The private sector appeared equally lax in challenging the military's entry into business, for two reasons. First, the private entrepreneurs were used to the nature of the country's political economy, which was semi-authoritarian and where benefits could be gained through aligning with powerful groups including the armed forces. In fact, the military along with the civilian leaders exacerbated the problem of crony capitalism, in which big private-sector groups benefit as a result of their loyalty to those who control the national resources. Economic progress is achieved not through adhering to democratic principles or the concept of a free-market economy, but through a concentration of wealth and opportunities in the hands of a few. One result is that the value of material assets is not disclosed.

According to a news report published in *The Nation* in 2000, Pakistan's underground or black economy was calculated at three times the size of the official economy. Including income from the black economy would have boosted per capita income from US$480 to US$1,700 (Rs.27,840 to Rs.98,600).[57] This was also admitted by the interior minister, Lt.-General (rtd) Moin-u-Din Haider, according to whom the country was losing Rs.100 billion (US$ 1.72 billion) per year as a result of smuggling.[58] The black economy is part of the overall economic structure, which protects the interests of a select group of people. The military, which has always claimed to curb corruption, ultimately fail to do so because of its efforts to build partnerships with politicians and select civil society groups.

Second, private entrepreneurs have always depended on the government for profit-making opportunities, which discourages them from questioning any source of authority in the country. Given the fact that the military represents one of the most politically powerful elements in the country, and has returned to the seat of power on a regular basis, it is not logical for private entrepreneurs to challenge the organization's interests. In this semi-authoritarian environment, the private sector resorts to a Machiavellian technique for survival: cooperating with those in authority where it is necessary, and deviating from the rules to compensate for the fact that they are not playing on a level field, without overtly complaining about the lack of fairness of the system.

The director of the Crescent Group of Industries, Tariq Shaffee, pointed out that the military considers the private sector to be crooked,[59] but does not seem to appreciate that it does not help by ensuring fairness. For instance, as another prominent entrepreneur, Razzak Tabba, pointed out, the FF fertilizer plants get natural gas at concessional rates. He added that the military foundations get more government support, which helps them get things done faster than the private sector.[60] This is not a random complaint of a hard-done-by businessman, but a fact backed by evidence. For example, the government provided subsidies worth Rs.1.5, 1.2 and 1.1 billion (US$25.86 million, 20.69 million and 18.97 million) to the FF in 2004, 2005 and 2006 respectively.[61] It is noteworthy that no private-sector business group received this kind of support.

As a result of all this, Milbus grew exponentially during the period from 1988 to 1999. However, it grew more horizontally than vertically, because the vertical expansion had already taken place in the preceding period. Benefits were provided for individual members of the armed forces in the form of new housing schemes, and these were expanded to medium-sized towns, such as in Jhelum in Punjab. The civilian regimes also provided greater business opportunities to the military's public-sector organizations such as the NLC and FWO. The Sharif government was known for giving major road construction contracts to both these military companies. According to Sharif's commerce minister, Ishaq Dar, projects were given to the military companies to make use of their idle capacity.[62] Others believe that the Punjab chief minister, Shahbaz Sharif, was taking a pragmatic approach to utilizing an efficient organization to improve the road infrastructure in his province and in the provincial capital.[63] The younger Sharif brother was known as a good manager who wanted to put things in order. The Highways Department was rife with corruption and malpractice, and Sharif did not want to waste resources in his development programme.

Interestingly, Sharif did not try to prop up the civilian institutions to make them perform the task better, but the civilian government did make extra efforts to strengthen the military companies. For instance, in 1999 the NLC was given a contract to carry out toll collection and maintenance on the N-5 or Grand Trunk Road, in an effort to increase the company's revenue, which had decreased because of a cut in its budget by the government. It faced a deficit of Rs.4 billion (US$ 69 million) for the financial year 1999/2000, and this work was given it to enable it to meet its obligations.[64] NLC's sister concern, the FWO, was given the management of one of the main highways from Sukkur (Sindh Province) to Lahore (Punjab Province). The FWO was authorized to raise money by charging private-sector companies for installing billboards along the highway.[65]

As these cases demonstrate, the government was a party to allowing the two military companies to monopolize road transport and construction. As Admiral Fasih Bokhari said, this 'destroyed the construction giants like Macdonald Layton Costain, Gammons and others'.[66] More importantly, the civilian government allowed the military-controlled companies to replace public-sector departments. This is perhaps what made a prominent Pakistani analyst, Hassan-Askari Rizvi, claim that 'in Pakistan the military is the state'.[67]

Shanbaz Sharif's attitude to the NLC and FWO was reflective of a state of surrender by the civilian governments, in viewing the military as an alternative institution better poised to carry out development programmes. This 'passing the buck' from civil to military bodies for development work was done in the belief that the military could perform better than the civilians. It is even more intriguing that the political leadership did not raise any voice against the conduct of Milbus. This was because, as one of the top leaders of the PPP, Nisar Khuhro, explained, military companies competed with others in the private sector and got the contracts on merit.[68] However, it is not clear whether he genuinely believed this, or was simply trying to divert attention from Benazir Bhutto and her alleged involvement with the SF. The prime minister was accused of being involved with the SF's radio and television channel project.[69]

The most noticeable expansion of Milbus was at the level of the subsidiaries, which enhanced their operations to include newer areas of business activity such as banking, finance and insurance, real estate, travel, IT, the energy sector and education. Projects were planned that could benefit individual officers as well as the organization as a whole. The expansion of business activities was partly a result of internal pressure on serving generals from retired officers who wanted greater job opportunities. This interest expressed itself in multiple ways, ranging from a continuation of the facilities and prerogatives introduced by the Zia regime to expansion into newer fields of commercial activity and greater dispersion of control.

Commanders showed greater autonomy in selecting commercial ventures. Senior officers were also given greater opportunity to select and establish projects on which they could work for three to five years after their retirement from active duty. Appointments in the welfare foundations and their related businesses were seen as easing an officer back into civilian life. Although not all personnel consider these foundations as the main opportunity for employment, the senior staff tend to view them as a good opening in the commercial sector. The jobs are much sought after, especially at the senior level, because the environment in these organizations is closer to the military environment than anywhere else in the private sector. The discipline in the organizations is similar to that of the forces, so they might not be extremely successful corporate ventures but they are known for greater order than is typically found in the private sector. Senior generals find it comfortable to work in these organizations, and a three-year job in one of the foundations saves them from the immediate shock of working in the private sector or under a purely civilian administration.[70] These concerns, of course, are taken on board while making the decision whether or not to establish or expand the military's business ventures. For instance, in order to accommodate helicopter pilots from the service, who otherwise would not have got a job in the private sector,[71] the army established Askari Aviation in the early 1990s. The company employs five to six helicopter pilots from the service.[72]

A prominent parliamentarian, M. P. Bhandara, explained the expansion of the military's economy as the armed forces 'moving by stealth' into having their 'ears and eyes in all important sectors of the economy and the state'.[73] This movement, he added, 'made the military into a "corporate state", like Japan'.[74] The Pakistan armed forces had by now mutated into a parent-guardian type that would use its muscle to penetrate all segments of the society and economy. As mentioned earlier, there were no resistance from the civilian governments, which not only continued to support these activities, but also did not attend to the issue of correcting the balance between defence and development. Expenditure on defence and all economic interests were part of the prerogatives on which the armed forces were not willing to negotiate during a period when they were not in the forefront in running the country.

The blatant use of intelligence agencies to manipulate the overthrow and change in governments had left civilian governments too insecure to challenge the military's involvement in business. However, the blatant neglect of the military's increasing financial autonomy can also be explained as part of the détente between the civilian governments and the military. The political leadership, especially the successive ruling parties, represented the dominant elite who had also befitted from the gradual process of liberalization of the economy. Nawaz Sharif, in particular, was a product of Zia's military rule. The prime minister was not averse to the expansion of the military's business complex. Hence, he did not question the financial autonomy of the armed forces, except for taking some measures on the advice of his financial team, such as putting an end to the tax breaks of the three foundations, the AWT, SF and BF.

Although there was variation in the percentage paid by each organization,[75] the fact is that the foundations did not resist the imposition of tax. The tax break was a major distortion that was amicably renegotiated during Nawaz Sharif's regime. However, the abolition of this tax break did not apply to individual benefits. For example, military officers continued to enjoy tax breaks on urban and rural properties. It is only civilians who pay taxes while living in a defence housing scheme or cantonment.

In 1999, the Sharif regime also suggested restructuring the AWT, an idea that was finally ignored by the GHQ.[76] The army was far too powerful and autonomous to need to follow a suggestion to downsize its economic empire. In any case, the change of government in October 1999 did not allow the opportunity to negotiate a restructure.

The expansion of Milbus, especially at the level of the subsidiaries, followed three strands:

- establishing ventures that could draw upon the resources of the armed forces
- setting up major import-substituting industrial units producing items with high consumer demand
- starting ventures that brought greater dividends for individual officers.

This period is also known for military bureaucrats turned businesspeople in the foundations becoming bolder in entering new areas of operation, such as banking, investment and insurance. Key projects are the Askari Commercial Bank, Askari Leasing, Askari General Insurance, Askari Commercial and Shaheen Insurance. The establishment of the AWT's bank in 1992 was certainly a major development. Nawaz Sharif's finance minister, Sirtaj Aziz, said that the bank was General Mirza Aslam Beg's idea. He had come to the minister with the plea that 'the military needed a bank to help the soldiers invest their welfare funds that they would risk wasting otherwise'.[77] The bank grew into a major private-sector bank during the 1990s. Compared with other private-sector banks, its record was impressive. Run fairly conservatively, the bank could boast a good reputation, and fairly stable total assets and numbers of customers. In December 2002, for instance, its declared total assets were approximately Rs.70 billion (US$1,207 million approx.) and it had 250,000 banking customers. In 2004, its non-performing loans (NPL) were about 4 percent of the total NPL of private-sector banks.

This performance cannot necessarily be attributed to good planning. The Askari Bank is a fairly conservative bank, and like other commercial banks in the country, it made money through investing in the stock market rather than innovative investment. The leasing and insurance companies owned by the AWT also boast a good turnover thanks to the support provided by Askari Bank. Other banks could not guarantee such high dividends. However, three key factors ensured that the Askari Bank performed well. First, because of the bank's association with the army, most civilians who sought loans were too afraid to default on them. This was different from other public and private-sector banks. Second, the army provided it with financial cover, and finally, it had the confidence of an impressive clientele in the form of the armed forces.

An important question, however, is that why the army thought of entering the banking sector. Experts like Peter Lock are of the notion that it is natural for militaries to enter the banking sector, especially for money-laundering. This comment is based on the observation of similar practices in Latin America.[78] The timing of the establishment of the bank was certainly critical: the early 1990s was a time when rumours were afloat of a lot of drug and corruption-related money in the financial markets. The ballooning of the black market had, in fact, started under Zia and continued through the 1990s. In his book *Whiteout*, Alexander Cockburn, a columnist for the *New York Times*, accused a senior general of Zia's army, General Fazle Haq, who was also the governor of the NWFP, of being part of the drugs trafficking racket. According to the author, opium trucked from Afghanistan into Pakistan was sold to Fazle Haq for further refinement into heroin.[79] Another story appeared in 1997 about the arrest of a PAF officer in New York on charges of heroin smuggling. The story indicated that the officer and his accomplices had used a PAF transport aircraft.[80] It is not known whether those involved in such activities used institutional sources for moving black funds to and from Pakistan. What is certain, however, is that the Askari Bank signified the army's financial autonomy, as in other countries such as Thailand where a powerful military operates a bank as well.

The Askari Bank has been a source of support for other businesses, especially in the finance sector, including SF's insurance business. This company was founded in 1995 in partnership with a South African insurance company, Hollard Insurance Ltd. A partnership deal was finally worked out in 1997, with Hollard owning 30 per cent of the shares in the operation. The South African company was, however, disappointed by the results. Its management considered corruption a big problem which dampened the prospects of the business. It is believed that financial mismanagement is a big problem in realizing the country's huge potential in the insurance field.[81] It is interesting to note that the deal was brokered by an acting air force officer who later, after retirement, got a job in the company. The South Africans asserted that the deal was negotiated on one-to-one basis with the officer involved.[82]

One of the ventures that benefited retired personnel, especially the lower ranks, was private security. The FF, AWT and Bahria all established private security companies which provided jobs to thousands of retired personnel. Their main competition was a multinational, Brinks, a US-based company which finally sold its business interests and left the country after 9/11. Considering the potential of private security, other retired personnel also got involved in this business through using their armed forces and international contacts. For instance Securities and Management Services (SMS), a company owned and run by an ex-army officer, became a prominent stakeholder in the private security business. The increase in domestic insecurity during the 1990s gave a boost to the private security companies. General Zia's generous policy of providing free access into Pakistan for Afghan refugees had a negative impact on Pakistan's economy and ecology.[83] The rise in crime and proliferation of small arms and light weapons, which is referred to as a rise in the 'gun culture' in the country, was a fallout of the Afghan war.

The welfare foundations were good at using the contacts and resources of their parent services to attract business. These companies also had another advantage: access to trained personnel. However, as the owner of SMS, Ikram Sehgal, claims, these companies lost their advantage because of the problems of over-staffing and poor management.[84]

The AWT started smaller ventures as well, such as the Blue Lagoon restaurant and a marriage hall. Although the two projects were open to the civilians, they mainly catered to the military fraternity. Both the projects were opened on army land, which means state land. However, the income was not deposited in the government treasury but retained by the foundation.[85]

The smaller foundations, BF and SF, are particularly dependent on contracts from their parent services. Most of the BF's ventures, for instance, were established around 1995 and were linked with activities conducted around the port area, starting with ship breaking and dredging and moving on to providing harbour services. These were operations that its personnel could undertake as a direct result of their association with the navy. Moreover, given the links, it was possible for them to get these contracts more conveniently than private-sector firms could.

Similarly, the BF's paint factory was established in 1995 to manufacture paints that could be used on naval ships. It must be noted that this was a period when the PN had signed two major contracts to build submarines and minehunters for France. The four vessels were assembled in Pakistan, and the paint job was subcontracted to the BF. The major investment in this project, however, was by the entrepreneur Malik Riaz and other private investors. Riaz, who is a civilian businessman and a significant real estate developer, has been a major investor in several of the BF's projects including its housing schemes.[86] Since there is little accountability and little information in the public domain, it is difficult to be sure how operations were conducted. The probable beneficiaries were the private investors, who got returns on their financial investment, and senior naval officers who allowed the venture to use the BF's logo, and ensured that it got contracts from the navy and other services as well.

Malik Riaz partnered with the BF for the construction of two housing schemes, in Lahore and Rawalpindi. The contract between Riaz and the BF gave the BF 10 per cent of the shares and 25 per cent of the total plots in the housing schemes without the BF making any financial investment. It was also agreed that should the BF agree, Malik could alternatively pay Rs. 100,000 (US$1,725) per plot to obtain full ownership of the developed land. The value of the land would of course have been higher after the completion of the development work. This was partly because of the use of the BF's logo, which gave added credibility to the scheme and resulted in price escalation.

The involvement of the navy, and especially the use of its logo, was subsequently challenged through a writ in the Supreme Court in 1998 by a public-interest lawyer, Wahabul Khairi. He contended that the terms of the contract indicated corrupt intentions and collusion over the personal interests of the contracting parties. He pleaded with the court to ban all the military's commercial activities, because in his view such tasks diverted the armed forces from their core activity of defending the country's frontiers. He also argued that the military foundations were in contravention of the Companies Ordinance of 1984 and Trade Mark Act of 1940, which forbid any private venture or party to use the name of the state, the armed forces or the founder of the country.[87] In its response, the BF denied the charges, and the use of official connections in any form. Khairi's case was thrown out by the court on technicalities, so unfortunately the points he made were not decided in law.

Later in 2000 the BF transferred its entire shareholding in the housing scheme to Malik Riaz, who was arrested after differences occurred between him and the navy's top management. He was accused of defrauding the BF and of paying kickbacks to naval officers.[88] The BF also asked the court to stop Riaz from continuing to use the name Bahria. However, the court decided in Riaz's favour . His counter-argument was that the name Bahria had become synonymous with his large housing projects, and that his business would be affected if he did not use the name and the logo.[89] Interestingly, the court in its findings did not seem to pay attention to the laws that prohibited the use of official logos by private companies.

In any case, Malik Riaz is an extremely influential man, and has relations with prominent politicians and the DHA. In fact, he formalized his relations with the DHA by signing a memorandum of understanding in October 2006 which aimed at a 'seamless integration' of BF and DHA housing scheme infrastructures.[90] Although this partnership was effectively endorsed by the courts, I believe it can be seen as a case of predatory partnership between the military and other influential players in the real estate business.

The subsidiaries also used the military's influence in getting into other completely new areas of business such as broadcasting and telecasting. The SF opened its radio channel, FM-100, and its SB pay-TV system, using the PAF's position as the authority responsible for allocating radio frequencies to potential radio and television channels. The opening-up of these two ventures demonstrates the military's power in manipulating rules to its own advantage. Governments during the 1990s had not yet provided openings to private investors in radio and television broadcasting, but the SF was able to embark on these businesses because of the PAF's clout.

These ventures are also significant because they were a partnership between the SF and influential civilian players. Reportedly, they were inspired by civilian entrepreneurs who had close links with the prime minister, Benazir Bhutto, and her husband Asif Zardari.[91] It was a dubious deal that resulted in losses to the SF. The SF finally took a case against the major shareholder to the Securities & Exchange Commission under Section 263 of the Companies Act. The shareholder was accused of violating the basic rules of the agreement.[92] The case is still under legal review. Benazir Bhutto, who was interviewed and questioned regarding this alleged connection, denied the charges. She nonetheless failed to give any concrete answer. Her main emphasis during the interview was on her harassment by intelligence agencies.

This was not the only instance of cooperation between military-run businesses and the government. There were two other prominent cases where military-run firms became partners with the government in profit-making ventures, one concerning the sale of sugar to India, and the other road construction in Punjab. In the first instance, the FF and AWT sugar mills along with other sugar manufacturers benefited from the sale of 700,000 tonnes of sugar worth Rs.3.5 billion (US$60 million) to India. This trade took place from 1997 to 1999. The FF's share in the sugar exports was 28,716 tonnes, while the rest was bagged by other sugar manufacturers including those owned by the prime minister, Sharif. Islamabad provided a US$100 (Rs.5,800) subsidy per tonne to all manufacturers. This resulted in the sugar industry getting over Rs.5 billion (US$86 million) in the form of direct rebate and excise duty exemptions from the Central Board of Revenue. The decision came under immense fire after the military takeover in October 1999, but while post-coup investigations focused on the privately run mills, no questions were asked about the role of the military foundations.[93] Presumably this was because of the military's influence and its insistence on not being held accountable for its deeds.

It must be noted that the accountability ordinance passed by the Musharraf regime in 1999 precluded the military and judiciary from being questioned under the new accountability rules, as is admitted on the National Accountability Bureau's (NAB's) official website,. The website claims that this is because the military have their own accountability procedures.[94] Hassan Abbas, a former police official who served in the NAB during the early days of the organization, claims in his book *Pakistan's Drift into Extremism* that the NAB's hands were tied in investigating the alleged corruption of senior military officers, such as Generals Aslam Beg, Hamid Gul, Zahid Ali Akbar, Talat Masood, Saeed Qadir and Farrukh Khan, and Air Marshals Anwar Shamim and Abbas Khattak.[95]

The fact is that the expansion of military's economic power was questionable, especially in certain areas such as real estate development. In fact, this is one area of activity that became most noticeable for graft: that is, the use of influence and official position for self-gratification. During the 1990s the military used its influence to grant land and houses to its members. The subsidiaries were also allowed to develop housing schemes. From 1988 to 1999, the military's real estate development took four forms:

- housing schemes by the military at an institutional level
- real estate development by welfare foundations
- construction of commercial buildings in urban centres
- allocation and distribution of land to retired and serving military personnel.

In addition, the foundations entered the travel industry through opening an airline, an aviation company and several travel agencies. Shaheen Air International (SAI) was opened in the early 1990s by the PAF's foundation, the SF. The airline depended on the PAF's human resources. The SF's management was of the view that because the PAF officers were experienced fliers, they were capable of running an airline as well. This perspective was contested by professionals in this field. One source was of the view that managing airlines is a complex operation that requires professionalism and training.[96] Military personnel do not of course share this view. They generally believe that their training in managing human resources and materials in the armed forces enables them to manage commercial projects and companies.[97] This proficiency, however, could not save SAI from incurring losses and temporarily closing down operations in 1996. It was reopened in 1997, only to be sold to a private investor based in Canada in 2004, with liabilities totalling Rs.1.5 billion (US$25.9 million).

It seems clear that the SF's management could not run the airline efficiently, since it kept incurring losses.[98] During its operations it lost about Rs.60 million (US$1.03 million) from December 1999 to May 2000. This was in addition to Rs.70 million (US$1.21 million) it owed the Civil Aviation Authority.[99] The situation in the initial days of the airline's operations was even worse. Some sources attribute this to the mismanagement of the fare discount facility provided by SAI to retired and serving military officers.[100] The fact that the airline acquired a limited number of aircraft on 'wet' lease added to the cost of operations, because of both the nature of the lease and the limited number of aircraft. A limited number of aircraft tends to increase costs because it leads to more technical problems, flight delays and other related factors.

The AWT also opened an aviation company, Askari Aviation, to provide helicopter services. It hires retired personnel from the Army Aviation branch. The company offers helicopter services for the promotion of tourism in the country, the transportation of critical and sensitive cargo, evacuation of casualties and rescue missions in northern areas of the country, including Azad, Jammu and Kashmir. What is most interesting, however, is that it uses resources of the Army Aviation wing like helicopters and pilots to meet its demand. The company director, Brig. (rtd) Bashir Baaz, boasted of his ability to access the service's resources.[101] Clearly, Brig. Baaz did not realize that using public-sector resources, especially from the armed forces, for commercial purposes is illegal. However, the fact that he did not hide the details symbolizes the confidence of military personnel in the organization's autonomy and impunity to use public resources. The AWT and Askari Aviation were not challenged regarding the misuse of government property for commercial purposes despite the fact that this activity was objected to by the Department of the Auditor General in the annual report for 2001–02 on the defence budget. The report also pointed out that the army was hiring out helicopters to Askari Aviation, and the income was being diverted to a private account without approval from the government.[102]

The foundations also opened travel agencies which looked for business from service personnel. The AWT, BF and SF opened independent travel agencies in major cities such as Lahore, Rawalpindi, Islamabad and Karachi. However, the SF closed down its agencies around 2003. This was possibly because the SF management realized these companies could not survive the tough competition in the market. The additional benefit for the officer cadre was that through these travel agencies, senior officers of the three services could make better travel arrangements with no personal costs. It was usual practice for officers to claim back the cost of a portion of their ticket and get it reimbursed to their personal accounts. Travel agencies facilitated this form of reimbursement through issuing miscellaneous charge orders (MCOs) that had a financial value and could be reclaimed at the end of the journey by officers. Since the money was the government's, this was not even considered corruption. Senior officers would also often force the agencies to upgrade their tickets without charge. Having their own travel agencies allowed officers to behave like this without the risk of this information going public, as it would have been had they used open-market resources.

Besides facing pressure from manipulative senior officers, the travel agencies also had to deal with the problem of inept managers. The retired officers who came to run these companies had no knowledge of the market or the travel agency business. The employees found this extremely frustrating and counterproductive for expanding in a highly competitive and low-profit market.[103]

Starting from the early to the mid 1990s, the foundations also entered the information technology and education sectors, with the objective of benefiting from growing demand in these fields. The FF and AWT established independent companies to claim their share of the IT business, which was mainly related to transcription outsourced from the United States and other developed countries to developing countries. However, reportedly Fauji Soft and Askari Information Services (AIS) did not meet with major success.

The military and its welfare foundations had better luck in establishing a network of schools, colleges and universities. Although the education-related activities did not start up during the period from 1988 to 1999, a substantial increase in the number of military-run educational institutions did take place during these ten years. The burgeoning number of educational institutions under the military's umbrella indicates a trend of earning money from the military's existing educational training facilities. The army, in particular, could always boast that it provided a good educational system to its personnel's families.[104] It is well known that its education and health facilities (which are not available to the rest of the population) receive more

162

resources per head than the general public services. This has to be seen in the context of defence spending taking up a large proportion of the national budget, as is apparent from Table 6.2.

During the 1990s, the military commercialized its education system. The fact that these facilities were run from the defence budget made the process of commercialization questionable. Furthermore, the universities opened by some of the foundations such as the BF and SF were built in cantonments: that is, on state land. Since the Bahria and Air Universities in Islamabad were built in restricted military areas, it was necessary to allow civilians to enter these areas with greater ease than was usually possible. This does not indicate that there was integration between the civilian and military population: the relatively freer flow of civilians to these cantonments did not weaken the

Table 6.2 Pakistan: defence versus development

Fin. year	Health %	Education %	Defence %
1981–82	0.6	1.4	5.7
1982–83	0.6	1.5	6.4
1983–84	0.6	1.6	6.4
1984–85	0.7	1.8	6.7
1985–86	0.7	2.3	6.9
1986–87	0.8	2.4	7.2
1987–88	1.0	2.4	7.0
1988–89	1.0	2.1	6.6
1989–90	0.9	2.2	6.8
1990–91	0.8	2.1	6.3
1991–92	0.7	2.2	6.3
1992–93	0.7	2.4	6.0
1993–94	0.7	2.2	5.9
1994–95	0.7	2.4	5.6
1995–96	0.8	2.4	5.6
1996–97	0.8	2.5	5.2
1997–98	0.7	2.3	5.1
1998–99	0.7	2.2	4.9
1999–00	0.7	2.1	4.0
2000–01	0.7	1.6	3.2
2001–02	0.7	1.9	3.4
2002–03	0.7	1.7	3.3
2003–04	0.6	2.1	3.2
2004–05	0.6	2.1	3.2

Notes

Expenditure on health and education is as a percentage of GNP.

Expenditure on defence is as a percentage of GDP.

Expenditure on defence after 2001 does not include military pensions.

Source: *Economic Survey of Pakistan.*

civil–military divide, but strengthened the distinction even further, because many of the civilians saw for the first time how the two different systems operated.

Over the years military cantonments, especially in larger cities, were opened up for restricted use by civilians. For example, commercial markets were opened in restricted areas and provided access for civilians. The commercial markets in the Naval and Air Complexes in Islamabad are among the many examples.

The commercialization of military-controlled educational institutions was started by the army opening up its elite schools for the children of civilians. The overall environment of these schools was elitist. For instance, the PN's internal school system was highly class-oriented, with children of naval ratings and sailors going to PN model schools, while officers' children used BF schools in bigger towns like Islamabad and Karachi, two stations where the navy was present. Since these schools were for the elite, their opening-up primarily benefited the civilian elite rather than the middle class or the lower-middle class. The military schools charged higher fees to civilians, making it impossible for low-income people to access their facilities. The AWT, FF and BF also had their own schools, undergraduate colleges and universities which charged higher fees to civilians and offered subsidized rates to the children of military personnel. The military-run schools and colleges compete with the best private elite schools. Their reputation for cleanliness and discipline are two factors that attract students to them. They do not necessarily enjoy an advantage in the quality of their teaching.

During this period, Milbus also expanded into areas with high capital investment and returns. This included the oil and gas, electricity supply and cement manufacturing sectors. The FF's Fauji Oil Terminal and Distribution Company Ltd (FOTCO) emerged as the largest petroleum-handling facility in the country, capable of managing 9 million tonnes of oil per annum.[105] FOTCO was interested in acquiring Pakistan State Oil (PSO), which is one of the largest public-sector companies in the country. Earning an annual pre-tax profit of about Rs.4 billion (US$69 million), PSO is a major revenue generator for the government and one of the three major oil marketing companies in the country. The company has a 71 per cent share of the domestic market, which made a number of people argue against its privatization.[106] Reportedly, there was apprehension about the sale of the company to foreign investors, which would mean that they controlled a major segment of the domestic market.[107] Therefore, preferring FOTCO was a way of insuring control over strategic resources and preventing them from falling in foreign hands. While seeming to follow the World Bank and International Monetary Fund (IMF) directions on deregulating public sector industries, the government could keep a sensitive asset secure through its sale to FOTCO.

There are others who view such move as contrary to the principle of privatization. The opposing view is that since FOTCO is an extension of the armed forces, PSO's sale to FOTCO would not help in reducing the burden on the public sector.[108] The controversy around PSO's privatiza-tion, however, highlights the manner in which the armed forces and its subsidiaries have the opportunity to benefit from the government's privatization process.

Others view a possible sale of PSO to the FF as meaning the FF acquires greater financial interests and uses its military background to develop greater profit-making capability.[109] The FF does indeed have the political muscle to get favourable contracts, as had happened in the case of the oil deal it signed with the national Water and Power Development Authority (WAPDA) and PSO for the supply of furnace oil. Allegedly, FOTCO managed to get a share in a deal originally signed between WAPDA and PSO. Under this deal, FOCTO was to import 4 million tonnes of furnace oil every year, which PSO would buy at a fixed charge of Rs.278.40 (US$4.80) per tonne. Interestingly, PSO had to pay the charge even if the fuel import was less than the contracted tonnage. PSO would then sell this fuel to WAPDA. However, WAPDA recently terminated its contract with PSO and entered into a new contract with Shell at better rates. But the FOCTO–PSO deal remains, and PSO finds itself in a bind. However, the situation with FOTCO is by all accounts becoming untenable for PSO.[110]

This allegation has been denied by FOTCO's management. Their explanation is that the company has not imposed any deal on WAPDA or PSO, and that it is just handling the front-end operations of the deal, which in any case is being financed by international aid donors like the Asian Development Bank (ADB) and a few others through the FF.[111]

The AWT's major investment in the cement industry was even more questionable. The managing director of AWT, Lt.-General (rtd) Farrukh Khan, signed a contract with the Chinese company, CBSM to install a cement plant at Nizampur in NWFP. Since this was a high-demand item, the plant was expected to bring good results. The cement factory made a big hole in the AWT's coffers. As a result of problems with feasibility, the prof-its were lower than expected. In fact, the only option that remained was for the AWT to invest in expanding the plant size to claim a bigger quota in the cement market.[112] This expansion was done through first borrowing capital of approximately Rs.8 billion (US$137.9 million) from the GHQ and then floating shares in the market. However, this project disturbed the financial balance of the AWT, forcing it to ask the government for a financial bail-out. Hence Islamabad three times gave financial help to the AWT: in 1995–6, 1999 and 2001.[113]

Interestingly, the Bhutto and Sharif governments did not object to such problematic expansions. Objections were raised later once the AWT went into the red as a result of its faulty investment. Sharif's commerce minister, Ishaq Dar, had told the military to merge the FF and the AWT, and for them to change their team of managers and bring in more competent people to run the two companies. This, according to Dar, was conveyed to the army chief, General Pervez Musharraf, who had taken an interest in arranging the financial bailout.[114] Commenting on the case, Dar was of the notion that the financial help was provided in view of the fact that the money invested belonged to poor soldiers and their dependants. AWT's bankruptcy would have hurt the poor investors very badly.[115]

It must be mentioned that the AWT uses pension funds for investment in its projects with the intention of sharing profits with its investors, who are retired military personnel. The governor of the State Bank of Pakistan, Ishrat Hussain, did not agree with Dar's opinion. Hussain was of the view that the bailout was normal and would have been given to any company. In addition, the loan given by a consortium of local banks to the AWT was after the AWT had pledged fixed assets.[116] Dar in turn challenged this assertion. His comment was that the consortium of banks only loaned the money after receiving a 'letter of comfort' from the government, and this was tantamount to an undertaking to meet the loan should the company default. Dar agreed that the company had pledged its fixed assets, but argued that that was a formality required for securing a loan after the consortium decided in principle to grant it.[117] The government eventually gave the letter of comfort. The military had sufficient political clout to get the its help.

In light of the fact that the political leadership was also accused of corruption, it is noticeable that the civilian governments did not make any visible effort not to give financial guarantees to military foundations. Many members of the ruling party, the parliament and their associates had taken loans from the government which turned into bad debts. The list of loan defaulters released in 2003 included the names of the AWT, former prime minister Nawaz Sharif's Ittefaq group, and many others.[118]

CONSOLIDATING THE ECONOMIC INTERESTS, 1999–2005

The year 1999 proved to be a watershed in redefining the military's relations with the political players. The friction between Prime Minister Nawaz Sharif and the army chief, Pervez Musharraf, finally resulted in the latter taking over power on 12 October 1999. The army decided to move in to protect its interests, which it felt were being threatened by an inept political leadership. Sharif certainly did not enjoy a reputation for a sophisticated intellect, or deep understanding of organizational behaviour and state matters. He was reputed to be a good Punjabi man whose main interest was cuisine. This rather uncharitable view of the prime minister does not take into account that Sharif had tried hard to curtail the power of the armed forces. However he made the mistake of miscalculating the tenacity of the organization, and the ability of the generals to protect themselves at all costs. Arguably he did not understand the link between the military's political and its economic power, or understand that greater economic opportunities would not placate the military, but strengthen its appetite for more power. By 1999, the armed forces had become a dominant player in the economy, and the generals had stakes in maintaining their control over both the economy and the politics of the state.

The period after 1999 saw the military consolidating its political power and control of the state and society. Politically, Musharraf institutionalized the military's role in politics through reinstating the power of the president to sack the parliament and establishing the National Security Council (NSC). Musharraf in fact institutionalized the military's power better than his predecessors by creating the NSC and sharing the presidential power of dismissing governments with it. This move surely helped in co-opting other senior generals who were members of the NSC to his political scheme. Like the Turkish NSC, the Pakistani NSC had a wide jurisdiction over all strategic affairs including national security. The NSC had the power to deliberate on all issues of strategic importance. This was the first time that a number of senior generals had an opportunity to participate, almost at an equal level, in the highest policy-making deliberations. Therefore, the act of establishing the NSC was also about crystallizing the military's stakes in maintaining power.

The NSC represented a natural upward progression of the military's power, which by 2004 had given it sufficient autonomy and confidence to participate and shape not only its own organization, but the political and economic destiny of the nation. Musharraf's regime is known for consolidating the economic stakes of the armed forces as well, especially those of the officer cadre. The economic power of the military was an expression of its political power. Senior officers including retired personnel demanded perks and privileges with greater confidence. For instance, the PN's retired rear admirals demanded personal staff, a facility that until then had only been granted to full admirals and vice-admirals. The rear admirals based their claim on the fact that equivalent ranks in the army had personal staffs. This echoed the inter-services rivalry amongst the services, particularly between the army and the navy.

The PN, it must be mentioned, was aggressively struggling to enhance its image in the country, particularly in the plains of the Punjab, where the people are not seafaring. The service had established a college in Lahore and recruitment centres in smaller towns of South Punjab such as Bahawalpur. The expansion in Bahawalpur can also be explained as a corollary of the senior naval officers' stakes in agricultural and urban real estate in the district. The PN posted a junior officer to Bahawalpur to take care of the landed interests of senior officers, but the position was justified on the basis of the navy's recruitment centre there. This presence also attracted the BF to Bahawalpur, where it opened a private college.

The proliferation of the navy's educational facilities marked a general trend in the expansion of the activities of the military subsidiaries in the education sector. During the period under study, the FF, SF and AWT also increased the number of their schools and colleges. In fact, the AWT sought approval from the government to set up the Askari Education Board (AEB) to introduce its own system of examinations. The board represented an alternative to the inefficient government-run primary and secondary education boards. Since 9/11 in particular, there has been a lot of discussion regarding the poor standards of government-run schools and the education system, which are seen as a cause for the popularity of education in *madrassas* (religious schools). But more than improving standards of education, the private education boards represent the military regime's concept of divesting the government of its responsibility of providing quality education and shifting the burden to the private sector, which charges greater fees for providing education.

Building on the military's image as the most capable institution, the AEB presented itself as an organization that could fill the gap created by the non-performing public-sector educational institutions. The establishment of the board was also a case of the military benefiting from the government's overall theme of encouraging public–private partnerships through creating new and more efficient institutional mechanisms. The AEB was responsible for conducting examinations in all army-controlled schools. Its system of examination was also offered to other private schools. The other group allowed to set up an independent board was the Agha Khan University Board. This was owned by the resource-rich community of the minority Ismaili group, which has also opened a private medical college in Pakistan. These are elite groups providing education to the upcoming middle class. Neither system reached out to the grass-roots where the problem of the lack of quality education actually lies.

Following in the army's footsteps, the BF also consolidated its interests in the education sector by getting the government's approval for setting up a university. The Bahria University Ordinance was passed in February 2000, allowing the BF to establish a university and a number of colleges all over the country.[119] The university's administration was completely in the hands of serving and retired naval personnel. The chairman of the University Board is the chief of naval staff (CNS), and other members comprise the deputy chief of naval staff (Operations), principal staff officers (PSOs) to the CNS, and other naval officers approved by the CNS. The rector of the university is also a retired senior naval officer.

This parallel institution building by the defence establishment fits the military's projected image of itself as a parent-guardian force that will step into every major field of activity to ensure better performance and to provide an alternative to inefficient and corrupt civilian institutions. It needs to be mentioned here that the Sharif government had sought the army's help to weed out ghost schools in Punjab. (These are schools that only exist on paper but have no real presence.) Their existence can be attributed to the corruption and negligence of civilian bureaucrats. The generals view their organization as the only option to fulfil the need for modernizing the state, an agenda that civilians cannot achieve because they 'lack spine.'[120] Thus, it is believed that the larger military fraternity was the natural choice for Musharraf to undertake development in the country.

The appointment of serving and retired mid-ranking or senior military officers to key positions in the government was intended to help carry out Musharraf's modernization plans. Given the years spent in the armed forces, these men could be trusted more and had more of the confidence of the president than most civilians. However, this approach would not strengthen civilian institutions. Some mid-ranking officers even discussed their apprehension regarding the military's ability to solve the problem of institutional decay in the country. These officers, who probably are a rarity in the armed forces, are of the view that the defence establishment's consistent involvement in affairs of the state will further depress the growth of civilian institutions.[121]

The spread of the military fraternity in all important segments of the state, society and economy represents more than just a belief in the greater capacity of the armed forces. The military as a group has visibly graduated to become a class, and its serving and retired members are benefiting from the organization's immense power in relation to other domestic players. Individual members, even retired military personnel, get influential jobs in the government.[122] During Musharraf's regime, senior retired military officers have been appointed to head some of the major public-sector universities. The policy of appointing military personnel has led to a diminution in the overall capability of these institutions, mainly because the appointed personnel are not familiar with the university setting and academic environment. For instance, the appointment of about a dozen retired army officers to key positions at one of the oldest universities, the University of the Punjab, led to accusations that these personnel were engaging in nepotism and corrupt practices. These negative impressions are then detrimental to the growth of the academic institution.

The fact that these retired officers tend to appoint people known to them or related to them, and also push out unrelated but qualified people, damages the existing quality of education. According to one professor, in the long term the loss of institutional independence and integrity would lower standards and make it difficult for Punjab University graduates to compete with others from private universities.[123] Protests were made by the teaching staff of the university, but unfortunately they bore no results. In a General Body meeting of the Punjab University Academic Staff Association, around 200 teachers criticized the university's administration by retired army officers, accusing these officers of irrational policies. The teachers also protested against the vice chancellor's attending the meetings of the Advanced Studies Research Board on grounds that he (Lt.-General (rtd) Arshad Mehmood) had no experience of research and hence asked unnecessary questions of the candidates.[124] This is not a random case that can be ignored. It is symptomatic of the damage inflicted by the military's direct involvement in the corporate sector and intrusion into the public sector.

Retired and serving officers also receive agricultural land and are involved in various real estate development schemes. Most of this agricultural land is in areas such as Cholistan in South Punjab, from where military personnel are not recruited. The transfer of land to non-residents creates sociopolitical tensions with the indigenous population, who accuse the military of 'invading' their land. The land allotment, especially in the Cholistan area, has also led to allegations about vested interests behind the distribution of water in the country. The distribution of agricultural land to military personnel is central to the ethnic tension in the country. Given the influence of the armed forces, whose personnel are predominantly Punjabi, smaller provinces are suspicious of Islamabad's decisions over the provision of water. It is believed that water for agriculture gets diverted to lands where the senior generals have their properties rather than being provided to Sindh and Baluchistan, which are lower-riparian provinces. A prominent landowner from southern Punjab, which is not a recruitment ground for the military, also complained that in areas where land was distributed to military personnel, water was being diverted from the existing quotas of local farmers.[125]

These concerns are not being addressed by the government, because of the strong lobby that has developed in the country, primarily comprising the military fraternity including its important civilian clients who are benefiting from the inequitable distribution of land resources. This particular interest group is popularly referred to in the country as the 'land mafia'. The senior retired and military officers have become more demanding of personal financial gains. The growth of DHAs and similar urban schemes is designed to benefit investors. In a number of cases there is collusion between retired and serving officers to acquire land. In some other cases, especially in major cities such as Lahore, there are rumours of a three-way partnership between the serving and retired military and influential political figures. In both cases, the government has had to backtrack on its key agenda of checking corrupt practices.

A number of senior serving generals are rumoured to have made millions through dabbling in real estate development. A fast buck is made through purchasing land at cheap rates and then selling it off at a higher value. In some instances, the pressure of local military authorities is used to acquire the land cheaply. The increased tendency of people to enter into speculative investment after 9/11, especially in better-managed schemes, gave a boost to property prices.[126] This patron–client relationship has marred Musharraf's agenda to cleanse the country from corruption.

A more serious charge is that far from attacking corruption, the president is found outright protecting special interests. His claim is that it is better management of land assets in defence-run housing schemes rather than any manipulation that has resulted in the appreciation in the land value. He is also of the view that the confidence that people have in military-run schemes has brought high financial dividends. His claim was partially right, especially as far as the value of military-controlled property is concerned. The fact that common buyers or realtors attach greater value to military land can be ascertained from a survey conducted in 1998 to study the link between the value of property and the military presence in an area. The survey conducted in three cities, Multan, Lahore and Sargodha (all in the Punjab), showed the price escalating as a result of the military's presence, especially in cantonments. The realtors were of the view that closing down the cantonments would depreciate the price of property in the area. These areas have better facilities and offer relatively greater security.

The benefits provided to individual members of the military fraternity are not always at an institutional level, as is proven by the case of a private sector transportation venture called Varan. Owned by the daughter of the former head of the main intelligence agency, ISI, Lt.-General (rtd) Hameed

170

Gul, the company is a clear example of how a military-oriented patronage system benefits its clients. Varan was given a monopoly on the Rawalpindi–Islamabad route, which pushed out other small private-sector operators. The company, its management and staff are known for flouting laws, rules and regulations because of their access to the centre of political power in the country.[127] This was a case of preferential treatment to which the Supreme Court put an end by revoking section 69-A of the Motor Vehicles Ordinance 1965. This particular law allowed provincial governments to issue preferential contracts to private companies, including Varan, which hurt smaller competitors.[128] The court decision coincided with General Gul falling out of favour with the regime for his views. The company, however, managed to sell its buses to the FF. Varan had in any case purchased the vehicles with a hefty loan from the Askari Bank.

The power exercised by serving officers is undoubtedly more than that of their retired colleagues. The senior serving generals also have greater opportunities to exploit the state's resources. Therefore, economic predatoriness could be observed both institutionally and at the level of individual commanders. At an institutional level, military organizations monopolize major government contracts for road construction and toll collection on major domestic highways. The FWO and NLC have the clout to influence the top management of the National Highway Authority (NHA), a department responsible for construction and maintenance of roads and highways. Incidentally, it is made easier for military-connected companies to bag major contracts because the NHA is also headed by a retired maj.-general who has more faith in giving business to the two military companies than to private contractors.[129] The NLC also uses its institutional influence to strike international partnerships and acquire assets such as state land in Karachi. The NLC in partnership with a Qatar-based private investor purchased railways land for the construction of a huge commercial plaza.

An important development in the commercial activities of the FWO and NLC involves these companies seeking domestic and foreign partnerships. The FWO, for instance, formed a subsidiary called LAFCO in 2004, with a mandate to form a private-sector partnership for the construction of a 115.5 km Lahore–Sheikhupura–Faisalabad carriageway (all three cities are in central Punjab). Reportedly, the partnership was necessary to facilitate successful bidding for the project. The FWO did not have all the equipment to prove that it could undertake the project on its own, and hence it partnered with a few big domestic construction companies including the Habib Rafique group and Sacchal Construction. This partnership also indicates that by 2004 the military companies had become more confident of their role in the economy and their acceptability by other domestic players in business. The private construction companies, on the other hand, thought it a better option to capitalize on FWO's contacts in the government and share the fruits of the company's influence.

The military–civilian business partnerships extended beyond the national boundaries, as is proven by the NLC's partnership with a Qatari company, and the joint ventures between the various DHAs and construction companies in the Middle East. The military, which by now had evolved into an independent class, forged ahead in forming international partnerships in pursuance of its economic interests. In addition, the partnerships indicated the fact that, as in Turkey, the military regards itself as part of the capitalist elite with whom it has common interests, both nationally and internationally.[130] More importantly, as mentioned earlier, the military used the semi-authoritarian nature of the political system to its own advantage of acquiring economic opportunities for itself and its partners at home and abroad.

The defence establishment's power is also used to bail out foundations when they get in financial difficulties. This especially refers to financial assistance given to the AWT, which has always suffered from financial problems despite the fact that it has a considerable source of funding from the Army's GHQ. The AWT asked the government in 2001 for another financial relief package of about Rs.5.4 billion (US$93 million) to meet its deficit of Rs.15 billion (US$259 million).[131] The matter was presented to the Economic Coordination Council, which asked the AWT management to sell its two commercial plazas in Rawalpindi and Karachi to meet the financial shortfall.[132] This was besides other forms of assistance that the trust receives from Islamabad. Since 1995, this was the third time the AWT has been given a bail-out. While rescuing the AWT in 1999, the Sharif government instructed the foundation to sell its commercial plazas, to justify a Rs.2.5 billion (US$43 million) financial guarantee provided to its banks by the government. However, the sale and the other changes recommended were never carried out.[133] The foundations and the military establishment that provided help were not willing to liquidate their interests, particularly in the presence of a weak political administration. Once the government was toppled in October 1999, there was no compulsion on the army to clean up its financial house.

There has also been an increase in the power of the senior commanders: the nine corps commanders manoeuvre resources and operate in a more autonomous manner, with greater confidence, because of the political power of the military. This freedom of action includes exploiting greater opportunities to improve the living standards of individual officers and the organization in general. The exploitation uses varied methods. For instance, while some units were allowed to open gas stations and construct shops that can be leased out, others opened bakeries or started similar ventures. In one particular case in Bahawalpur, the cantonment extended its territorial jurisdiction to land adjacent to a national highway. This was done so the military could impose tolls on the highway, which was used by all and sundry. The money raised was utilized for the upkeep of the local cantonment, an area with restricted access for civilians. Jurists consider the action illegal. A senior judge was of the opinion that the cantonment board was not authorized to levy tolls on a highway, a rule that has been specified in the law books. The toll on this particular highway continued for years until the High Court finally decided the case against the army in 2006. In this case, some of the important judges of the Lahore High Court, Bahawalpur bench were determined to oppose the illegal imposition of tolls. Interestingly, the GHQ has not taken any move to stop this malpractice or abuse of authority.

The army's lack of reaction to requests to put things right is natural in a political environment where the armed forces do not face a serious challenge to their authority. Although the opposition parties, especially Nawaz Sharif's PML-N and Benazir Bhutto's PPP, pledged to reduce the strength of the military internal economy in their jointly formulated Charter of Democracy, issued in May 2006, Milbus in Pakistan is not easy to root out without concerted efforts by political actors to strengthen democratic institutions. The Charter of Democracy is a small step forward to correct the errors committed by the political players, particularly in ignoring the essential link between the military's political power and its financial autonomy. A document alone cannot strengthen democracy until such pronouncements are matched with a serious effort to desist from secretly negotiating with the army. The civilian governments during the 1990s were equally responsible for strengthening the economic power of the armed forces and bolstering the organization's capacity.

The growth of Milbus that has been discussed in this chapter highlights the manner in which the military developed its economic stakes in maintaining its control over the state and its politics. Although the military's internal economy is not necessarily the main cause of its political ambitions, the various financial advantages sought by the senior officers have a cumulative effect in enhancing their interest in staying at the helm of affairs. The growth of Milbus during this period also coincides with the metamorphosis in the military's character from an arbitrator to a parent-guardian type that is far keener to control the society and economy. The organization views itself as an alternative institution that has to keep a watch over all types of national activities. The reasons for the growth of Milbus, however, are not altruistic. The growth of military's internal economy is a case of institutional self-interests and predatory acquisition by senior officers.

The growth of the military's economic empire during the period studied in this chapter was parallel to the increase in the organization's political power and influence in national decision making. As the military consolidated itself into a class, it gained greater confidence to exploit national resources and acquire greater opportunities, which benefited it as an institution and also filled the pockets of the senior generals. The growth of Milbus highlights the consolidation of economic stakes of the military's echelons in keeping the political system as semi-authoritarian, thus allowing the generals to seek benefits for themselves and their clients. The crystallization of these economic interests is a major determinant to the future of democracy in the country.

7 The new land barons

The estimated worth of the legally acquired assets of Pakistan's generals varies from Rs.150 to 400 million (US$2.59–6.90 million), a figure that is based primarily on the senior commanders' urban and rural properties. The systematic exploitation of national resources, especially urban and rural land, has significantly enriched the officer cadre. The military justifies its acquisitions of agricultural land as part of the inherited colonial tradition of granting land to military personnel. Moreover, the real estate acquisitions including properties in the cities are justified on the grounds that since military personnel move frequently during their service, they need to be provided with housing facilities to ensure commitment to their work.

The grant of urban land, in particular, is couched in terms of the greater logic of the nation paying the price for its military's social security. However, it is argued in this chapter that the land acquisition is not driven by concern for traditions or professionalism. The military has expanded its landed interests as part of the desire of the officer cadre to increase its financial stakes. The land acquisition policy belongs to the paradigm of predatory acquisition.

The major expansion of the landed interests of the armed forces took place mainly under military regimes. Land is acquired not just for capital accumulation, but also to exhibit the military's authority and power in relation to other stakeholders such as the landed-feudal class and the masses. In fact, the military's land acquisition, especially agricultural land, has transformed the military into one of the many land barons or feudal landlords. The behaviour of senior military officers towards landless peasants or ordinary soldiers, who are also given agricultural land, is like that of any big feudal landlord. The military agriculturists who enjoy power and authority use the services of soldiers who are paid by the exchequer.

It is worth pointing out that feudalism here is not used in a normative, but in a Weberian sense. The term denotes a set of economic and political relations and a pattern of social behaviour. The monopolization and control of land is understood to be a symbol of power which adds to the powerful image of the armed forces.

THE MILITARY AND LAND

Currently, Pakistan's military is one of the largest landowners in the country. As a single group, the armed forces own more land than any other institution or group. The military controls about 11.58 million acres, which is approximately 12 per cent of the total 93.67 million acres of state land. Other government departments such as the Pakistan Railways also have landholdings, but there is a major difference between the military and other government departments. Unlike any other state institution, the armed

174

forces have the capacity to convert the usage of state land from official purposes to private ones. In addition, they are the only state organization that has institutionalized the acquisition of state land for distribution amongst the members of its fraternity. This practice was streamlined under the Zia regime through starting a new practice of acquiring land that was initially allocated to the military for operational purposes, for redistribution amongst the officer cadre.

The monopolization of land and related resources is used not just to enhance the financial worth of individuals or groups, but also to increase their sociopolitical value. The military owes its authority to change the usage of land to its phenomenal political clout. The land redistribution policy has an impact on the relationship between the powerful ruling elite in the country, of which the military is a part, and the masses.

Military and rural land

The military is a significant stakeholder in agricultural land. Out of the 11.58 million acres that is controlled by the armed forces, an estimated 6.9 million acres, or about 59 per cent of the total land, is in rural areas. The 6.9 million acres are divided as follows:

- controlled directly by the military organization for operational purposes such as camping grounds, and oat, hay and dairy farms (approximately 70,000 acres)
- controlled by subsidiaries such as the AWT, FF and BF (about 35,000 acres)
- owned by individual members of the armed force (approximately 6.8 million acres).

It must be reiterated that no other government department has the authority to redistribute state land for the benefit of its officials. In the military's case, about 6.8 million acres have been distributed among the officers and non-officer cadre for their personal use.

Agricultural land for operational use

The army controls about 70,000 acres for operational purposes, such as oat and hay farms and camping grounds. Out of this total acreage, approximately 60,000 acres is in the Punjab, comprising 35,508 acres of oat and hay farms (which breed horses, and grow oats and other crops for feeding them), and dairy farms. All this land was acquired before the partition of India in 1947. Even today, the army is a major stakeholder in the provincial government's land in the Punjab since it controls 38 per cent of the 68,000 acres of government farmland.[1]

All the farms in the military's use are designated as 'A-1' class land. This designation is part of the categorization of land laid down by the Military Land Manual. The Department of Military Land and Cantonment (MLC) manages military land in rural areas and urban centres. There are

175

about seven types of land managed by the Department of MLC according to the laws laid down in the Military Land Manual, which are based on the British Cantonment Land Administration Rules 1937. Most of the land is A-1 land, which is defined as land meant purely for military purposes, such as fortifications, barracks, stores, arsenals, airfields and hangars, housing for the military, parade grounds, military recreation grounds, rifle ranges, grass and dairy farms, brick fields, and hospitals and gardens for use by the armed forces. A-2 category land is not actually used or occupied by the military, but is used for non-essential activities such as recreation.

The 'B' type lands are again divided into four sub-categories, B-1, B-2, B-3 and B-4. The B-1 type lands are owned and controlled by the federal government, and used for churches, mosques, cemeteries and other ecclesiastical functions. B-2, on the other hand, is owned by the provincial government and used to generate revenue for the government. The B-3 type is private land but where bazaars, religious buildings, sacred tanks or communal graveyards could also be built. The Military Land Manual stipulates that due compensation must be paid to the owner in the case of acquisition of land by the government. B-4 comprises all such land not falling in any of the above three types.

Finally there is 'C' class land, which includes drains and roadside plots. It is worth mentioning that the cantonments in the Indian Subcontinent were not completely owned by the British, but were private property, some of which was acquired to meet defence needs. The defence establishment's ownership of land was limited to areas where it had barracks. Understandably, the British were an invading force and did not want to establish long-term interests.

The British government, and later the Government of Pakistan, acquired land for the military under the Land Acquisition Act 1894, which stipulates, 'Owner of requisitioned property continues to be its owner till possession thereof be taken by the competent authority. Whereupon, owner is divested of his rights, title and interest in property and it vests absolutely in the Government.'[2] The law further states that 'the land of people may be acquired by the State for a public purpose meaning thereby for the use of the public at large'.[3] The legal position does not, however, explain the politics of land acquisition, redistribution and usage.

The law certainly did not hamper the military from using its authority to subsequently change the usage class from farm land into land for golf courses or residential housing schemes, which was not necessarily sanctioned by the civilian government or the civil bureaucracy. A debate in the parliament in 2003 showed that the army had arbitrarily turned some camping grounds into golf courses, which were meant not for the public good but for the benefit of a select few. Parliamentary questions made it clear the parliamentarians considered this an obvious misuse of state land by the military. In its official response the MoD did not challenge the army's authority, but upheld the army's jurisdiction over land under its control.[4] This was done in other cases as well, such as the conversion of a firing range in Nowshehra in NWFP into a citrus farm.[5]

The army vociferously defends its power over these land assets, and controls information about them. A British Broadcasting Corporation (BBC) report indicates that despite his best efforts its journalist could not obtain information on military land from government departments such as the MLC and the Bureau of Statistics. In fact, the journalist was warned that he would not be given any information.[6]

Given the military's political power, the federal and provincial governments usually keep silent about the fact that the armed forces change the usage of land or use the land for the benefit of a select group of people. For instance, the Auditor-General's Department pointed out in 2006 that the Punjab government had violated the Land Acquisition Act by giving the army 30 acres of land, with a conservative estimated value of Rs.72 million (US$1.24 million), for building a golf course in Jhelum. The report further claimed that the market value of the land was much higher, and that the golf course had been constructed on A-1 land which was only meant for defence purposes.[7]

The army's direct involvement in agriculture and its possession of rural land did not become evident until the eruption of a conflict in Okara in Central Punjab in 2001, between landless peasants and the armed services. The Okara farms are part of a military farms group, Okara and Renala, which comprises 16,627 acres of land, consisting of two dairy farms, seven military (oat and hay) farms and 22 villages. Of the total acreage, 16,627 acres were cultivated by 1,323 farmers residing in Okara and Renala. At one point some of these villages and this land was under the control of the Catholic Church in Pakistan, and the village residents were tenants of the church.[8] However the prime proprietor was evidently the government of Punjab, which leased the land to other people or institutions. It had leased it to the military since before Partition.

The ownership barely bothered the tenants, who cultivated the land on a sharecropping basis, under which they shared both the input and the output with the owner or controller of the land. This contractual basis gave the tenants the additional benefit of recognition by law of their claim over the land, which as was firm as that of the owner. If the land was sold, the tenants' claims over it became primary. This arrangement puts tenants in a much better legal position than a simple rental arrangement, where land is cultivated in exchange for money or a specified rent in kind.

The army decided to arbitrarily change the system of contract under which the peasants tilled the land, from share-cropping to paying rent in cash.[9] This decision caused great resentment among the tenants and their families, who had resided in Okara and the neighbouring Renala for quite some time. The tenants feared the new system of contract would empower the army (which was not the original owner of the land) to throw them out of their homes. When the peasants protested, the military tried to enforce its arbitrary decision by force. The army and paramilitary forces besieged the local village community, producing a situation resembling a civil war.

According to well-documented accounts, the military brutalized the poor tenants, and the ensuing severe agitation and violence claimed eight innocent lives. The paramilitary Rangers besieged the villages twice, imposed a curfew, restrained people's mobility, stopped the supply of medicine, food and vegetables, and used numerous pressure tactics. A Human Rights Watch Report has detailed testimonials of village people victimized by the military authorities, which were generally dismissive of the protest.

Army personnel claimed that, rather than being a human rights issue, this was a local law and order issue incited by some non-government organizations (NGOs).[10] They claimed the *muzarain* or tenants were raising the slogan of '*mulki ya maut*' (ownership or death) out of greed and malice. According to a Pakistani researcher, Ayesha Salma Kariappar, the army was not inclined to negotiate the ownership rights because it was conscious of the value of this A-1 land.[11]

As Kariappar indicates, the conflict shows the military using its power and thrust as a capitalist force.[12] However, the brutality clearly represents a feudal style. Kariappar's definition of the military as a capitalist force is based on its rampant profit-making activities. However it can be argued that had the Pakistani Army taken a capitalist stance, it might not have been obsessed with the idea of controlling the Okara farms at all costs. The civil–military conflict at the farms always looked likely to increase the cost of controlling the land, a proposition that a capitalist force might not have entertained.[13] The army's high-handedness is, however, indicative of the authoritarianism which is reinforced as the norm. The story of the pressure exerted on Okara peasants is a reminder of the traditional Sindhi *wadera* (feudal lord) or serfdom system, in which poor tenants are treated brutally and even put in private prisons by feudal lords.

From a sociopolitical standpoint, the conflict is a significant expression of the military's power and its determination to maintain it. The army's top leadership remained fearful that any concession to the tenants would have a knock-on effect.[14] This apprehension, that yielding to the farmers would weaken the military against other social and political forces, and diminish its overall power, was prevalent within the army. Therefore, the issue was not just about the ownership of the land, but rather the larger matter of maintaining political power and authority. Such behaviour is reminiscent of feudal armies in Europe, for whom occupation and control of territory was a symbol of strength.

Interestingly, in the Okara case the military was trying to change the terms of contract for land that did not belong to it. Hence, the army itself came into violation of the contract it had signed with the Punjab Government, which had originally leased out these villages as part of a total of 35,508 acres to the British Army in 1913. The 20-year lease agreement signed in 1913 and renewed in 1933 for another five years stipulated that the land was to be used as 'oat and hay' farms for raising the army's horses. According to senior officials of the revenue department, the Pakistan army, which inherited the lease from the British, did not bother to renew it when it expired 15 years before these incidents, and also stood in violation of the lease agreement by changing the use of land from oat and hay farms to dairy farms.[15] The lease agreement does not allow the service to use the land for any purpose other than growing fodder.[16]

The only detailed study on the Okara farm issue highlights interesting facts about the management of the farms. First, contrary to claims made by the army authorities that income generated from the farms is given to the government; the military farm authorities actually retain all the earnings.[17] Second, the farm produce was being mismanaged, as a large quantity of milk and meat was used to bribe senior officers. In her study on the Okara farms, Kariappar claims that the Auditor-General's Department accused the military farm authorities of mismanagement, rather than holding the tenants responsible for the loss of revenue.[18]

The military's spokesman, the director-general of inter-services relations (ISPR), Maj.-General Shaukat Sultan, said in defence that:

> The needs of the Army will be decided by the Army itself, and/or the government will decide this. Nobody has the right to say what the Army can do with 5,000 acres or 17,000 acres. The needs of the Army will be determined by the Army itself.[19]

This arbitrary conversion of the usage of land violates the principle of 'eminent domain', a concept defined by Hugo Grotius as the law governing the acquisition of the property of subjects of the state. According to Grotius:

> the property of subjects under the law of eminent domain belongs to the state, so that the state or the person who represents the state, can make use of that property, can even destroy or alienate it ... whenever it is to the public advantage.[20]

The application of this law varies according to the political nature of the state. In the United States, the law of eminent domain has been interpreted according to the liberal philosophy of John Locke, so the Fifth Amendment to the US Constitution advocates the preservation of the right to private property. Locke supported the right of a government to claim from its citizens its costs of ruling, but without excessively threatening individual rights to private property, or all such rights as generate happiness.[21] This right is also upheld in the French Declaration of the Rights of Man and of the Citizen of 1789. The declaration stipulates that 'Property being an inviolable and sacred right, no one can be deprived of it unless the public necessity plainly demands it, and upon condition of a just and previous indemnity.'[22] It is noteworthy that these approaches evolved as a result of years of struggle by the people in France and the United States to establish the primacy of private property or the rights of people. Although Pakistan's Land Acquisition Act of 1894 lays down specific conditions for the acquisition of private land by the government, such as 'public purpose', the rules are implemented in letter and not in spirit because of the authoritarian nature of politics.

The opposite to Locke's philosophy is the Hobbesian or 'brutish' approach, based on a more authoritarian control of society by the state, in which the main authority (which could be an individual or a group of people) has the power to determine the good of the rest of the population. This can be seen reflected in the handling of the Okara farms case This Hobbesian notion is truly reflected in the feudal character of the Pakistani state, where 'public good' is determined by the ruling oligarchy. Being part of the dominant elite, the military has aped the feudal behaviour according to which the authoritarianism of the institution determines the flow of capital and the monopolization of resources. The Pakistan military's land appropriation and subsequent possession and profit making are unrivalled in the United States, France, Israel, India and all societies that have consciously moved towards capitalism.

Military subsidiaries in agriculture

The subsidiary foundations, the FF, AWT and BF, are all beneficiaries of the defence establishment's land grant policy. The FF farm in Nukerji in Sindh covers 2,498 acres.[23] Located close to the foundation-owned sugar mills, the farm is used to experiment in trying to develop new varieties of sugar cane. The AWT's main ownership of agricultural land is in the form of its partnership with the army in controlling the Okara farms. The BF's farms are used mainly as dairy farms to provide milk and other dairy products at subsidized rates to serving naval officers.

Military agriculturists

The most conspicuous case of exploitation of land, however, relates to the transfer of agricultural properties to military personnel. The military, as mentioned above, has acquired about 6.9 million acres of land for further redistribution to individual officers and soldiers. The entire concept of land grants to the military is mired in the larger and redundant colonial tradition of buying allegiance in exchange for land. As part of the policy pursued after 1857, the British rewarded their loyal subjects with land and access to water sources for irrigation.[24] According to an expert on comparative and regional studies, Mustafa Kamal Pasha, the military was given land to encourage professionalism or 'specialization', which represented 'a complex interplay of material forces, ideas, and institutions associated with colonial capitalism'.[25]

Laws such as the Punjab Alienation of Land Act 1900 ensured the use of canal colony land as a means of rewarding those serving British interests. (This was a land made cultivable by the construction of new water canals in the Punjab and other provinces.) According to Imran Ali, who investigated the development of agriculture in the Punjab, land was granted to individuals from indigenous communities under various schemes, such as a grant to raise horses which could then be acquired by the British cavalry. Following the principle of rewarding the 'faithful', the Alienation of Land Act specifically stipulated the allocation of 10 per cent of reclaimed or colonized land to the armed forces. This process of land distribution was incorporated later into another law known as the Colonization of Land Act 1912, which was subsequently updated by the Pakistan Government in 1965.

This law had a feudal underpinning, which involved benefiting from the creation of local social classes that would guarantee the interests of the colonial masters. This system impacted on relations within the society, since individuals, groups, tribes or clans required state patronage to enhance their power and financial worth. Relative power determined interpersonal and institutional relations.

The existence of such laws is also a reminder of land distribution in fourteenth-century Asia, where the Ottoman and Mongol invaders rewarded their soldiers in cash or kind (the payment included land grants) to raise fighting forces or ensure allegiance.[26] In Europe, land reward was central to the creation of the broader extraction–coercion cycle. In eighteenth-century Europe, for instance, Charles Martel (686–741 AD), the founder of the Carolingian Empire and known for being a catalyst for the feudal system in Europe, appropriated one-third of the church's lands for redistribution to raise armoured cavalry.[27] The control of land would motivate the soldiers as well as keep the subordinates in awe of the ruling monarch or feudal lord. The authority over land was central to accumulating wealth and influence.

Although Pakistan's armed forces claim to be modern, the generals have never abandoned the arcane feudal-colonial tradition. The Colonization of Land Act 1912 was upheld and used to grant land to military personnel in all the four provinces of the country, at highly subsidized rates varying from Rs.20–60 (US$0.34–1.03) per acre. According to some disaggregated data available for a few administrative districts in the Punjab and NWFP, an average of 190,000 acres was distributed in each of these districts to military officials from 1965–2003 (see Table 7.1). A rough calculation of the value of this land is given in Box 7.1.

The total estimated amount of land and its worth is much higher than is calculated in Box 7.1. A report in the English-language daily *Dawn* indicates that some lands were given in 1981 at the rate of Rs.50 (US $0.86) per acre. This was increased in 1994 to Rs.60 (US$1.03) per acre.[28] It must also be mentioned that the data given in Table 7.1 do not give the total picture of military land in urban and rural areas in the four provinces of the country. A more concise picture is given in Table 7.2.

The land in the military's control is acquired from the provincial or federal governments. Of course, the military does not present its land acquisition as a case of land grabbing. Rather it talks about land acquisition in a very matter-of-fact way.[29] This attitude is a reminder of the fact that the military uses an institutionalized method to acquire land. Agricultural land is regularly transferred from the provincial governments to the MoD, which is finally responsible for dividing the total land acquired at a given time amongst the three services, which then redistribute it among their individual members. This land allocation system, inherited from the British, was fine-tuned during the Ayub regime. The military dictator gave the military

Table 7.1 Land allotment to military personnel, 1965–2003

District	Province	Acreage
DI Khan	NWFP	185,000
Muzaffargarh	Punjab	173,000.7
DG Khan	Punjab	153,000.5
Rajanpur	Punjab	133,000.3
Vehari	Punjab	170,987
Pakpattan	Punjab	193,676
Multan	Punjab	123,793
Khanewal	Punjab	143,283
Sahiwal	Punjab	173,407
Lahore	Punjab	273,413
Kasur	Punjab	387,283
Sheikhupura	Punjab	193,863
Total		2,303,706.5

Box 7.1 Back-of the-envelope calculation
of the value of military land

Taking a higher than average price paid of Rs.50 (US $0.86) per acre, the total amount collected from the allocation of the total number of acres in the 12 districts given in Table 7.1 and the land in Sindh (2,303,707 acres as shown in Table 7.1) amounts to Rs.135.18 million (US$2.33 million). This is the amount earned by the state from 1965 to 2004. However, applying an average market price of Rs.100,000 (US$1,724), the land is worth approximately Rs.270.37 billion (US$4,661.55 million).

Calculated at the current average market value per acre of Rs.250,000 (US$4,310), the estimated value of this land is about Rs.675.92 billion (US$11,653.79 million). Of course, this is a rough calculation. An exact calculation would first determine the exact number of acres given at a certain time and multiply it with the exact value extant in the specific district at that time. Since the exact data are not available, a back-of-the-envelope calculation can take a mean figure of Rs.100,000 (US$1,724). The price during these 39 years from 1965 to 2004 escalated from Rs.30,000 (US$517) per acre to Rs.300,000 (US $5172) per acre.

---

its share of the 'colonized' land. The term refers to land brought under cultivation by construction of new water sources such as barrages or dams. Under this policy, 10 per cent of the land reclaimed through the

Table 7.2 Division of 11.58 million acres of military-controlled land

	Punjab	**Sindh**	**NWFP/Baluchistan**
Total land	62%	27%	11%
Cities	48%	19%	4%
Agriculture	14%	8%	7%

construction of three dams, Guddu, Kotri and Ghulam Mohammad in the Southern Sindh province, during the period 1955–62 was given to military personnel. These are three out of four dams constructed after 1947, resulting in the reclamation of approximately 9 million acres of land, out of which about 1 million acres was given to military personnel. Some of the senior generals benefited from the scheme, including General Ayub Khan (247 acres), General Muhammad Musa (250 acres) and General Umrao Khan (246 acres).[30] In examining the distribution of land within the army (summarized in Table 7.3), it is evident that the senior officers benefited from the scheme more than the ordinary soldiers.

The land allocation for each officer reduced over the years, however, because of an increase in the number of officers. Currently, maj.-generals and above get 50 acres of land, and more is given on the award of medals of gallantry.[31]

The mass distribution of land through military awards has created a class of military agriculturists. This was done for three reasons. First, the intention was to establish communities in border areas that were familiar with the security discourse, and hence could contribute actively to defence in the event of a break-out of hostilities. Since the military personnel had lands in the border areas, they would have a personal interest in securing the frontiers. There is no evidence to suggest that such friendly communities actually emerged, especially because most of the military who are granted land sell it on. This was certainly the case with soldiers, who did not have access to facilities to develop their land and tended to abandon it or sell it to local landowners.

Table 7.3 Land entitlement for military personnel

Rank	Acreage
Maj. general and above	240 acres
Brigadiers and colonels	150 acres
Lt.-colonels	124 acres
Lieutenants to majors	100 acres
JCOs	64 acres
NCOs	32 acres

Source: Siddiqui (1997).

Second, creating a class of military agriculturists was meant to fill a gap in the social development of a rural middle class. The absence of a strong middle class in the rural areas strengthened the big landowners or the feudal class. The Ayub Khan regime, it must be remembered, also introduced land reforms in 1958–9. The primary objective of these reforms was to challenge the power of the landed-feudal class. The politicians who opposed Ayub Khan were from the landed-feudal class, and the general wanted to teach them a lesson about the state or military's power to take away their lands. Therefore, the land reforms signified the power of the military organization over all other institutions and classes.

These reforms did not actually attain much in terms of breaking the back of the feudal class. This is evident in the report of the Land Reform Commission in 1959. The big landlords only surrendered 871,000 acres, or 2.4 per cent of the total 31 million acres of cultivable land in West Pakistan.[32] The reforms only reduced the ceiling for individual landholdings, and big landowners could evade the law through transferring land to other members of their families. According to an analyst, Ronald Herring, the reforms only aimed at 'a forced sale of marginal land by some landlords to some tenants [rather] than a genuine redistribution of wealth or alteration of agrarian structure'.[33] Moreover, the impact of the reforms was reduced because the bigger landowners were compensated with 4 per cent government bonds, thus providing a principal of Rs.89.2 million (US$1.54 million) and an annual interest of Rs.3.3 million (US$56,000) to 902 individuals (see also Chapter 5).[34]

Third, the military was granted land with the expectation that being hard working, armed forces personnel would ensure the greater development of the agricultural land granted to them, and this would bring about socioeconomic and sociopolitical modernization. However, there is no evidence that military agriculturists changed social backwardness in the country's villages, or brought technological and sociopolitical modernization to rural Pakistan. In fact, until the mid-1990s, military agriculturists tended to cash in on the land by selling it to local landowners. This practice not only strengthened the local landowners but also developed common interests between the military and the landed-feudal class.[35] Thus, the military became an instrument of feudalism and part of the feudal class.

As was mentioned earlier, the largest beneficiaries of the land distribution policy are the senior generals. Their benefits are not limited to the larger landholdings they are granted, but are also in the form of indirect subsidies for the development of the land, such as technical assistance and financial aid, access to water, and the availability of farm-to-market roads. It is claimed that some of the foreign military and economic aid received during the 1950s and the 1960s was diverted to the development of land owned by senior generals. In fact, when the finance minister of the Provincial Government of the Punjab, Nawab Iftikhar Hussain Mamdot, was questioned about this diversion of aid, his response to the assembly was that 'foreign aid was meant for the army'.[36]

This was not the only case of indirect subsidies. Actual visits were made for the purpose of this research to land owned by senior generals including Pervez Musharraf, General Zaidi and former naval chief Admiral Abdul Aziz Mirza. It was found that all these senior officers used serving soldiers to guard and work on their lands. There were about nine or ten Ranger officials on duty at all times at the farms of Generals Musharraf and Zaidi in Bahawalpur. Similarly, there was a serving naval rating stationed at the farm of Admiral Mirza. The soldiers serving on the farms of senior generals are reminiscent of the private armies of' knights and barons in sixteenth and seventeenth-century Europe, or of serfdom in Russia. Soldiers do not join the army to do the menial jobs for senior officers that they are eventually forced to perform.

More importantly, these officers use their influence to get access to water and farm-to-market roads, a facility that is not readily available to the small farmers or landless peasants who are allocated land as part of the government's benevolence. In their access to such facilities, there is actually no difference between the landed-feudal class and the senior military officers. Both use their political influence to get facilities that are not available to ordinary soldiers. Furthermore, senior officers who choose to keep and cultivate their land by proxy also get seeds, fertilizers and other agricultural inputs at subsidized rates, which are transported to their land on military vehicles. The profit earned by an officer through the resale of the developed land is phenomenal. Unlike a poor peasant or soldier, who does not get the huge subsidies for making the land cultivable, an officer can obtain land and then develop it at minimum personal cost.

URBAN LAND ACQUISITION

Nothing could have brought greater attention to the military's burgeoning economic empire than its urban real estate expansion. Today, the military is one of the prominent players in urban real estate. The military housing schemes in most major cities are highly overpriced and attract huge amounts of speculative capital. Considering the growing value of real estate, the military's stakes in the sector amount to billions of dollars, and remain largely undocumented.

The defence establishment has the ability to bring any government land under its control for 'public purpose' by using the Land Acquisition Act 1894. As is pointed out by legal commentators Shaukat Mehmood and Nadeem Shaukat, the term 'public purpose' in this context is not a 'static' definition and is defined at the discretion of the government.[37] The military's political influence is critical in defining 'public purpose' as meaning that it may redistribute the land for personal benefit of its officers. This power is unmatched, and explains one of the fundamental arguments of this book: the military's utilization of its influence to engage in economic predatoriness to accentuate the personal political-economic power of the armed forces. The symbiotic relationship between political and economic predatoriness remains most obvious in urban real estate, because of its high financial rewards.

185

Since 1999, the armed forces as a group have owned the largest share of urban real estate in Pakistan. The military's expansion into urban real estate was in two phases: the first starting in the 1980s and marginally expanding during the 1990s, and the second involving phenomenal growth after 1999. The two periods coincided not only with the gradual consolidation of the military's power but also with the flow of capital into Pakistan. The 1980s, when military urban real estate was formally established, was a time when the value of real estate in the country increased as a result of the inflow of capital, part of which was black money generated from heroin smuggling during the heyday of the Afghan war. In the second phase, Pakistan became a recipient of both legal and illegal money from expatriate Pakistanis or citizens of other Islamic states, who no longer found the United States and the West in general to be safe for unquestioned investment.

Until the end of 2005, Islamabad was struggling to bring transparency into its financial system, curb money laundering and document the economy. However, efforts to stop the flow of illegal or undocumented money into the real estate sector were foiled because of the interests of key stakeholders such as the military. Although it must be a major profit earner, real estate was not taxed in the budget for the financial year 2005–6.[38] Reportedly, the strong lobby that benefited from real estate investment checked any proposal to bring this sector into the tax net or document it.[39]

The military's urban real estate comprises commercial ventures and housing schemes as shown in Figure 7.1. It includes markets and commercial plazas, a sector that proliferated during the 1990s, and multiplied after 1999. Most major cantonments, particularly those that are close to major cities and towns, have built commercial plazas that are then rented out. However, the housing schemes and land given for construction of private houses are a matter of greater concern, because the military uses institutionalized methods to acquire urban land for the benefit of its personnel.

There are three methods used for acquiring and developing housing schemes:

- Houses constructed on state land or A-1 land.
- Private land appropriated with or without appropriate compensation and developed into housing schemes by military subsidiaries. Lt.-General (rtd) Rizvi pointed out that the Askari Housing Scheme of the AWT is directly controlled by the GHQ.[40]
- Private land acquired by the Defence Housing Authorities (DHAs), the management of which falls under the purview of the Army GHQ.

The major difference between the first and the last two categories is that while the military acquires state land to build housing that is then sold to officers, or distributes land to individual officers for the same purpose, the other two schemes (managed by subsidiaries and the DHA) are technically private projects. The controlling authorities negotiate the purchase of land like any other private buyer for constructing housing schemes. However, the controlling authority is the military. For instance, the corps commanders in all major

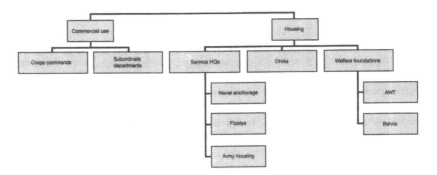

Figure 7.1 Military urban real estate

cities also serve as chairmen of the defence housing schemes. It is important to note that these projects are basically for the military elite. Out of the 46 housing schemes directly built by the armed forces, none is for ordinary soldiers. This fact was admitted by a military spokesman during an interview with a reporter from *Newsline* magazine in July 2006. According to Maj.-General Sultan, a housing scheme for soldiers was approved in principle but has not been constructed.[41] The difference between officers and soldiers is not surprising since such elite schemes, and many others built by major civilian capitalists in the country, do not attempt to meet the severe shortage of lower-income housing in the country. Reports indicate that Pakistan suffers from a deficit of 6.3 million houses. As a result, about 20 per cent of the urban population in the country live in slum areas that are devoid of all basic amenities.[42]

Conversion of state land

The involvement of the military, and especially the army, in constructing houses on state land dates back to the Zia regime, which initiated this policy. Before embarking upon a discussion of this policy, it is vital to trace the origin of urban land transfer to military personnel, a practice that, it is claimed by a senior military land and cantonment executive, can be traced back to the days after the partition of India in 1947. According to Riaz Hashmi, who spent a major part of his career in the MLC Department, a number of officers obtained land on lease in the cantonments after 1947.[43] Evacuee property in the cantonment areas was granted to military officers who had migrated from Muslim minority provinces in India to the new-born state of Pakistan.[44]

Subsequently, a number of non-immigrant officers also obtained land on the basis of their seniority or prominence. For instance, General Azam Khan and several other officers obtained huge chunks of land in the Lahore cantonment. Azam Khan was a Pathan officer whose family had not migrated from the Muslim minority provinces in India. The land was given to the officers on a transferable lease for a period of 99 years. The 99-year lease is extendable, especially in cases where military officers own the

187

property, and there is no bar on the resale of the lease, or any tax charged on profit made through its sale.[45]

The military has continued to pursue this policy. In 2000, the army gave a 1,200 sq yd plot in Lahore Cantonment to its two top generals, Lt.-General Khalid Maqbool and Lt.-General Mohammad Amjad. While Maqbool was subsequently made governor of the Punjab, Amjad got a job as head of the National Accountability Bureau, and later as MD of the FF. According to a report submitted by the MoD to the Senate in 2003, about 78,292 sq yd or 16.3 acres (a total of 130 residential plots) were given to an equal number of officers in different cities in the period from October 1999 to 2003.[46] The locations included the cities of Karachi, Lahore and Rawalpindi, and smaller towns such as Kharian and Jhelum. The officers' ranks varied from full general to captain.

Quantitatively, the distribution was fairly even, with senior, middle-ranking and junior officers getting 46, 36 and 48 plots respectively.[47] However, the plot sizes for senior officers were much bigger than those for junior officers. Generals of all categories received plots of 800 sq yd. Plot sizes for captains, on the other hand, were about 496 sq yd.[48] However, these figures do not show the full extent of the land grab in Lahore. The cantonment area, which up until the early 1980s comprised a large segment of army training grounds and firing ranges, has almost entirely been converted into a residential area. In other words, army exercise and training grounds have been converted from public to private use without the consent of the government or the knowledge of the public for whose safety the land was initially provided.

This was pointed out in the report of the special audit conducted by the Auditor-General's Department in Lahore. The report highlighted the transfer of 400 acres of land to army officers in Lahore. Since the housing schemes that were planned by the Army Housing Directorate (established in 1968) had no constitutional or legal status, the auditors found the construction to be in contravention of existing laws. Furthermore, the government had lost money as the land had been sold for the paltry sum of Rs.17 million (US$293,000). The market value of the land was far more. The auditors also found the army utilizing land that had been given for operational purposes for commercial purposes. Approximately 24 pieces of prime land were being used commercially without money being deposited in the exchequer.[49] In some cases markets had been constructed on B-2 land, which technically does not fall under the ownership of the military. The rent collected from one such commercial market, the Fortress Stadium in Lahore, is retained by the corps headquarters with no accountability.

This exploitative use of state land is done through a process of decision making internal to the organization rather than in consultation with the government. In fact, one of the claims is that decisions on major military housing projects are always made when the parliament is not in session.[50] Such arbitrary redistribution raises concerns about the misuse of state land, especially cantonment land. Major cantonments include Lahore (12,000 acres), Karachi (12,000 acres), Rawalpindi (8,000 acres), Kamra (3,500 acres),

Taxila (2,500 acres), Peshawar (4,000 acres) and Quetta (2,500 acres). A retired senior MLC executive feared that given the fact that there is no check on the military's conversion of land, most of the cantonment land would ultimately be commercialized.[51] In fact, the Lahore, Karachi, Rawalpindi and Peshawar cantonments are no longer restricted army areas. As has been seen in the case of Lahore, officers were given ownership of large residential properties in other old cantonments as well.

A conservative estimate of the worth of the land in Karachi, Lahore, Peshawar and Quetta cantonments is approximately Rs.500 billion (US$8,620.68 million). Although sources blame Ayub Khan for introducing the senior officers to the value of urban property, the actual practice of granting urban land to officers can be attributed to General Zia ul Haq. Zia used such rewards to please his senior officer cadre.[52] He needed the support of the army's senior management, and its officer cadre in general, to consolidate his power. Since then, the three services have followed the practice of allotting urban land to their officers, particularly senior officers. The urban properties enhanced the personal financial value of individual officers. A former army officer who later became one of the country's biggest business magnates, Ikram Sehgal, is of the view that the award of rural and urban properties added to the worth of the senior generals. As a result a typical maj.-general is worth Rs.10 million (US$172,000) and a lt.-general Rs.50 million (US$860,000). However, as a result of the involvement of senior generals in real estate development, such as Lt.-General Zarrar Azeem, who was the corps commander, Lahore later during the Musharraf regime and notorious for his involvement in a DHA land scam, the typical value of a senior general has escalated to Rs.100 million (US$1.72 million).[53] Sehgal's estimation is based on conservative estimates, and if market rates were applied to the properties of the senior generals, their estimated worth would vary from Rs.150–400 million (US$2.58–6.89 million).

It is a fact that a number of senior generals have benefited from the military's land distribution. Some of the prominent beneficiaries include General (rtd) Shamim Alam Khan, chairman, Joint Chiefs of Staff Committee (allotted a 1,066 sq yd plot in the costly F-7 sector on 11 June 1994), former chief of army staff, General (rtd) Abdul Waheed Kakar (allotted a 1,200 sq yd plot, number 6 in sector G-6/4 on 7 September 1996), Air Chief Marshal (rtd) Farooq Feroze Khan (allotted a 1,033 sq yd plot, number 13 in sector F-7/2, on 29 January 1995), former naval chief admiral (rtd) Saeed Muhammad Khan (allotted a plot measuring 1,066 sq yd in sector F-7 on 11 June 1994), former naval chief admiral (rtd) Muhammad Saeed (allotted an 800 sq yd plot, number 19 in sector F-8/1, on 30 August 1987), and former naval chief, Admiral (rtd) Yasturul Haq Malik (allotted a 800 sq yd plot, number 551 in sector F-10/2, on 4 November 1991). The current market value of a single plot of land varies from Rs.70–100 million (US$1.21–1.72 million).[54]

It is also important to note that the allocation of plots to each officer is not necessarily limited to just one piece of property. In certain cases, more than one urban plot was given. For instance, according to a list of land awards to officers, eight plots were allotted in the name of the director general (DG), ISI in 1994. The list placed before the Senate shows that five plots were allotted in the name of the DG, ISI on 15 April 1994 in sector F-11/2. The plots, measuring 666 sq yd in total, included numbers 193, 194, 261, 262 and 263. He was allotted two more plots on 16 November 1994 in sectors F-7/4 and F-7/2, each measuring 1,600 sq yd. Another plot, measuring 1,244 sq yd, was allotted in the same name in sector F-7/1 on 26 October 1994.[55]

Most of the land given directly by the three services is carved out of state land in contravention of the military and land cantonment laws. The Military Land and Cantonment Manual disallows the utilization of the A-1 land for non-military purposes. This type of land is specifically meant for operational purposes. According to Riaz Hashmi, the housing schemes are an anomaly from the standpoint of the military land and cantonment law, which disallows any conversion of this type of land for any purpose other than those stipulated in the law. In Hashmi's view, the precedence for transforming military cantonment land started in the 1950s with Ayub Khan, who rented out his own house built in Rawalpindi cantonment on B-2 land. Other officers followed suit.[56] This was a case of senior officers earning profit from the rental or sale of urban properties that were given to them for their service to the state. Subsequently, state land used by the military for operational purposes was taken by the armed forces and converted for private use. The three services acquired the land for further redistribution amongst its officers.

In response to a question in the Senate regarding the questionable transfer of land, the Army GHQ stated that the service considered itself the sole authority for disposing of land in its use considered surplus by its management.[57] The words of Maj.-General Shaukat Sultan, 'we don't build houses or other projects on state land but on military land', show that the armed forces consider themselves above the law and accountability.[58] The fact that the general drew a distinction between military and state land shows where the army placed itself in reference to the state and its legal provisions. The organization's strength has determined the redistribution of land, resulting in accelerated profits.

The corps commander Mangla, Lt.-General Tauqeer Zia, who was also the chairman of the Pakistan Cricket Control Board (PCCB), during his tenure as the chairman of the PCCB transferred portions of the Karachi National Stadium to Karachi Cantonment Authorities for further transfer to senior officers. The financial returns were superb. A minimum investment of Rs.0.6 million (US$100,000) brought a profit of about Rs.15 million (US$258,000) in a matter of 60–90 days. This minimum investment refers to the development charges taken from each officer for a 600 sq yd residential plot at a prime locality; the second figure is the market price. Therefore, it is not surprising to see senior generals having relatively easy access to capital to multiply their wealth. For instance, General Pervez Musharraf bought farmland in Islamabad worth approximately Rs.40 million (US$690,000), and the former DG ISI made Rs.100 million (US$1.72 million) through the sale of his farmland.[59] The total estimated worth of Musharraf's disclosed land assets is around Rs.600 million (US$10.34 million). Details are given in the later part of the chapter.

This perpetuated nonchalant attitude of the army towards law or government authority has been infectious, and the smaller services are now found to be replicating this behaviour. For instance, the PN used 3,000 sq yd (0.6 acres) of A-1 land to build the Bahria Complex, which is run on commercial lines and generates a profit that is not turned over to the national exchequer.[60] Similarly, the PAF used 735 acres of land on its Risalpur Base for commercial purposes.[61] In both cases, this was the unsanctioned use of military land for non-operational functions.[62]

Senior generals justify the conversion of military training grounds, firing ranges and cantonment land to commercial markets on the basis of welfare for the *jawans*. A case is put up for such actions, and examples of similar activities by the Chinese and Indonesian armed forces are given. However, unlike the Chinese and Indonesian militaries, the needs of the Pakistan's defence establishment are completely catered for by the government. Military expenditure has always received top priority, and this drive to commercialize military areas is a case of economic predatoriness rather than a real necessity.

The stories of the military's economic predatoriness are endless. In Karachi, the largest cosmopolitan centre, the army has set up about eight petrol stations on state land. Advertisements in national papers inviting expressions of interest from private parties for shops and commercial plazas built on A-1 land by different army corps became the fad after the October 1999 military takeover. Moreover, the military and its subsidiaries are also involved in land grabbing. For instance, the National Logistic Cell (NLC), a subsidiary of the army, forcibly occupied land in Malir, Karachi for commercial use. One source claimed that the NLC just extended its boundary and took possession of the land adjacent to its premises.[63] Successive governments have not only ignored these activities but have implicitly approved of this behaviour through providing further incentives. In one case, the government gave Rs.4 billion (US$68.96 million) worth of land in Karachi in 2004 to the AWT.

The army has often forced the provincial governments to grant land for agriculture or other purposes. In most cases, the acquisition is justified in the name of national security or the reason is not given at all. For instance, the service demanded 20,000 acres in 2000 along the superhighway in Karachi, an upcoming area for industrial development.[64] The army also asked for 12,000 acres of agricultural land for transfer to military personnel affected by the establishment of the capital in Islamabad during the 1960s.[65] This particular attitude generates resentment, especially in smaller provinces that see the military as an invading force rather than a national army. The military's acquisition and distribution of land among its personnel is not just about money, but also tells the story of the organization's power and influence.

The resentment increases when people see the military using its authority to forcibly occupy public or private land. For instance Commander Abid Saleem, the commandant of the navy's cadet college, Potaro in Sindh, is accused of forcing the villagers of Mallah in Jamshooro, Sindh to vacate the village so that it could be occupied by the college authorities. These villagers, who had been occupants of the land for the previous 50 years, had finally been given ownership of the land during the tenure of Prime Minister Mohammad Khan Junejo (1985–8). In 2005 the cadet college authorities tried to force the villagers to leave the land, a move protested by the villagers who filed a writ in the Sindh High Court. Although the case was under consideration by the court, the commandant of the cadet college tried coercive methods to harass the village folk, such as building a wall around the village, the access to which was manned by naval police. Although Saleem denied the charges, he admitted that the case was being heard by the High Court. He claimed the villagers were creating media hype to get public attention.[66]

The military authorities levelled similar allegations against the Okara farmers, who were accused of conspiring with some foreign-funded NGOs to take possession of an expensive piece of land. (See page 178.) Similarly, the owners of land in Pattan in NWFP claim that the FWO occupied their land without any compensation. The military's construction company built a temporary camp for its men while it was constructing the Karakoram Highway in 1962–3, and gave the owners the impression that the land would only be occupied for the duration of the road construction. Subsequently, the temporary camp was made permanent, and expanded, without any compensation being paid to the owners.[67]

Similar stories can be heard in Baluchistan, such as the army's occupation of private property in the Chamman district. Reportedly, the villagers of Maarmalang are contesting their claim with the army for ownership of over 129 acres of land. The army, which established itself in Chamman in 1963–4 when the district was being developed, later acquired the ownership of 200 acres of land. In June 2005 the army authorities gave notice to the villagers to leave this further area, on the premise that the land belonged to the army. The villagers claim that the land belongs to the Ashezai tribe, and that its people were farming it even before 1947. They believe the army is interested in the property because it has increased in value. It is no longer farmland but a small town with markets, houses and cinemas.[68] It is possible that the property in Chamman is planned to be used for profit-maximizing activities such as the construction of commercial plazas.

Since the end of the 1970s, the military have become keener to establish profit-making ventures, the returns from which are not transparent or subject to public-sector accountability processes. But even if the intention behind occupying the land in Sindh or Baluchistan is to expand the existing military cantonment in the area, it is at the cost of depriving the local people of their land. A Pakistani political analyst, Kaisar Bengali, views the cantonments in Pakistan as 'the new metropolis and the civilians have been pushed back to the status of the "natives"'.[69] I saw evidence of the mindset described by Bengali during a visit to a restaurant in the Quetta Cantonment in 1996. A sign in the window read 'Civilians not allowed'. It is reminiscent of the colonial regime, when native Indians were not allowed in certain places frequented by the British.

Seeing the military use its authority to control land and its resources, the paramilitary organization, the Rangers, followed suit and exercised its authority over 100 km of the coast in Sindh and Baluchistan. Starting from 1977, the Rangers took control of more than two dozen lakes in the area, with the stated purpose of securing the coastal area from an Indian threat. However, the Rangers then used their authority to stop the local fishermen from fishing in the waters, and sold the fishing permits to big contractors. This had a disastrous effect on the livelihood of local fishermen, whose numbers reduced from 7,000 to about 200.[70] This is clearly a case of the state security apparatus exploiting land resources, endangering the lives and livelihoods of the indigenous people.

To return to military housing schemes, since the early 1980s the three services of the armed forces also began a project to construct housing for officers at subsidized rates.[71] The idea was for every officer to own a house or an apartment by the time he retired from active duty, towards the cost of which a nominal contribution of about Rs.200–1000 (US$3.45–17.24) would be deducted from his pay.[72] The final payment for the construction was then deducted from the officer's commuted pension at the time of retirement.

Interestingly, the cost of the land is heavily subsidized, particularly if the construction is on state land. Therefore, these are private housing projects constructed on subsidized land. Since it is privy to the town expansion plans, the government helps in guiding the cooperative's management over where to purchase the land. Because of its influence the military gets preferential access to resource distribution policy decisions, and this results in what Kaisar Bengali terms 'allocation inefficiency'.[73] According to this concept the military or members of the ruling elite get greater opportunities to invest their capital, particularly ones that are likely to provide handsome returns. A lot of senior military officers seem to have benefited from preferential access to information by buying properties, the value of which is later enhanced. It is partly because of this preferential access to information that the senior generals have turned into a propertied class. For instance, General Musharraf owns about eight properties, which include 2,000 sq yd of land in DHA, Karachi, a 1,200 sq yd plot in Morgah, Rawalpindi, a 900 sq yd plot in Peshawar, 50 acres of agricultural land in Bahawalpur, 600 sq yd in Eastridge in Rawalpindi, 1,200 sq yd in Gwadar, Baluchistan, and a farmhouse in Islamabad.[74]

Housing schemes by the military subsidiaries

Another type of the military's real estate is the private-sector housing schemes. Under this format, cooperatives controlled by the various services of the armed forces purchase privately owned land and develop it for resale. The army-controlled AWT and the Navy's BF take the cake as military-sponsored realtors. The air force has the least share in the housing business. The AWT and Bahria have at least two housing schemes in each of the three major cities of Karachi, Lahore and Rawalpindi/Islamabad. In fact, the navy has a far more extensive presence in real estate development.

While its initial investment was a joint venture with a private investor under the label of Bahria Housing Schemes, later the navy established an independent scheme called 'anchorage'. This was done after relations with the private investor went sour. However the Bahria scheme, which is predominantly run and controlled by the private investor, continues to use the navy's logo and blue emblem. (See page 159.)

The armed forces claim that these projects are private-sector operations run by 'authorities' registered under civilian commercial regulations. The top management of these authorities are retired military officers. The military is also represented on their governing boards by senior serving officers. For instance, the corps commanders head all the DHAs, with serving brigadiers or colonel-level officers serving in the management. In addition, the land is offered for resale only to serving or retired officers or their families. These people are then free to resell their land to whoever can pay the exorbitant price, including civilians. As a result there are more civilians living in cantonments and defence housing schemes. The armed forces still claim, however, that this does not make a strong case for the military's involvement in the real estate business. Defending the DHAs, Musharraf suggested that the argument that the military's real estate is an indication of its commercial interests is evidence of the 'jealousy' of some 'pseudo-intellectuals'. Addressing a congregation during the inauguration of a DHA desalination plant in Karachi in 2004, he claimed that:

> The defence societies everywhere are the top societies of Pakistan ... now, why are we jealous of this? Why are we jealous if somebody gets a piece of land, a *kanal* of land, cheap when it was initially, and because of the good work done by the society, the price rises by 100 times and the man then earns some money. What is the problem? Why are we jealous of this? There's no problem at all.[75]

Partially agreeing with Musharraf, Lt.-General (rtd) Maqbool claimed that the housing schemes show the military's *interest* in developing real estate for the benefit of its members, but not its *involvement*.[76] Such statements are contrary to the fact that the military's political power is crucial in creating 'land entitlements' that benefit its senior officers in particular. The number of officers directly involved in the business is immaterial. What matters is the use of the organization's influence in securing land for the benefit of the military echelons.

The Defence Housing Authorities (DHAs)

One of the important planks of the organization's housing schemes is the Defence Housing Authorities, known by their acronym DHA. The DHAs in major cities such as Karachi, Rawalpindi and Lahore were established through the direct use of the army's political influence. The DHA was created in Lahore in 2002 through taking over the Lahore Cantonment Cooperative Housing Society Ltd, originally established under the Punjab

Cooperative Societies Act 1925.[77] This was the first housing scheme to be taken over and converted into an authority directly controlled by the army. The takeover was done through a Presidential Order, which later became the 17th Amendment to the constitution.[78] From that time, all other private housing schemes in cantonment areas or adjoining military areas were turned into autonomous bodies with their own rules and regulations.

The higher rates of return that are earned by investors in these depend on the influence of the investor or the stakeholder. For instance, the military's influence is crucial in acquiring land at cheaper rates which is then sold at a higher price. This price escalation is what Musharraf refers to above. The secret of high returns lies in ensuring that there is a large difference between the purchase price and the sale price. These profit margins require preferential access to information, which is directly linked to the power of the investor. The ability to control information about town expansion plans, and to influence decision making, is crucial in determining the net value of a town development project. Senior civil and military bureaucrats are well positioned to manipulate such information to their personal advantage.

An expanding town tends to absorb rural land for which the original price is relatively low. It could be argued that the original owners could carry out speculative investment themselves, but the information regarding town expansion is manipulated, and the owners are often subject to subtle coercion as well as the expectation of greater profits if they collaborate. As a result, the land is purchased at lower rates to provide a greater profit margin. The DHA Lahore, for instance, pays original owners in kind and not in cash. The owners are 'advised' to sell their land in return for two 500 sq yd residential plots per acre. The price of these can be expected to escalate after the development of the entire housing project.

There are numerous players that speculate in real estate, but the military remains a major stakeholder. The most benefit in the DHA schemes goes to military officers, who are only liable to pay development charges. There is no payment for land acquisition. Retired and serving military officers are also not liable to pay property taxes and certain other government dues. Most of the money earned by the DHA is through taxes and fees paid by civilians. Although the initial sale is made to military personnel, there is no bar on the subsequent sale of land to civilians. There is not even a time limit for resale, and as a result there is major speculation in real estate. The level of this increased by leaps and bounds, especially after 9/11.

Instead of setting up industries or generating employment, the extraordinary financial flow into Pakistan moved into real estate. This happened during the 1980s as well. The Afghan war fought jointly by the United States and Pakistan brought in a supply of 'greenbacks' to Pakistan, which were invested primarily in real estate. The rows of empty commercial plazas in Islamabad built during the Zia ul Haq regime are evidence of nonproductive and speculative investment.

The DHAs tend to be adjacent to military cantonments, especially in major cities like Lahore, Karachi and Islamabad. Geographically, they are an extension of military-controlled areas and are governed by the same rules as cantonments. The property transfer and taxation laws, for instance, are similar. The similarity of laws means that unlike resident civilians, military personnel do not pay property taxes. Moreover, the management of the areas is almost identical. Leaving aside the technicalities or administrative details, people generally consider DHAs as no different from the cantonments. This linkage actually results in greater private investment in these housing schemes. It is a fact that people have greater faith in investing in military-controlled schemes because there are fewer instances of fraud than in civilian-run schemes. Military personnel attribute this to their indisputable capacity for discipline, and to better management.

The military's internal land redistribution is driven by a hierarchical system in which the senior officers draw maximum dividends. Profit-making opportunities are cautiously trickled down to the mid-ranking and junior officers to ensure a certain level of discipline. A 'free for all' system would eventually result in the extinction of all individual predators. Therefore predatoriness is carefully institutionalized, with an additional concern to keep the share of senior officers larger than that of junior officers. This discipline also guarantees the subservience of junior officers, who remain ever careful of the senior management in the hope of eventually rising to senior positions and thus getting greater perks and privileges.

The perks and privileges provided to senior officers, including land grants, have progressively resulted in increased corruption in the armed forces. This has not remained exclusive to real estate. A number of reports are coming into the fore of officers involved in financial kickbacks related to weapon procurement, and other cases of corruption.[79] This could be as a result of the greater aggressiveness of the media, or it could simply indicate increased corruption amongst the officer cadre. The questionable involvement of senior army officers behind the real estate-related scandal in the DHA, Lahore has raised quite a few eyebrows.

The scandal concerns the DHA entertaining more applications for the sale of plots than the actual number of plots. It must be noted that to apply to buy a plot in a DHA scheme, it is necessary to pay a certain percentage of the total cost of the plot, so there is an obvious financial advantage to the DHA if too many deposits are accepted. Reports indicate that senior generals involved with the development scheme were aware of this scandal.[80] It is fair to say, however, that the military housing schemes generally have a better reputation than some civilian-run operations for the clarity of documentation and transactions. Many private housing schemes launched by influential and moneyed people or companies have proved to be fraudulent, and it is difficult for common people to retrieve their money from problematic or questionable real estate or other investment schemes, because of powerful interests and corruption in the judiciary, which is further weakened through political compulsion. Military-run land development schemes enjoy relative confidence and invoke a greater sense of security.

An ill-founded perception exists that DHAs or military-controlled schemes have better systems of personal security: that is, protection against common theft, robbery and other hazards. They do not, on the whole, but they probably do have fewer robberies and less petty crime than civilian schemes. The fact is that the military's presence and involvement itself results in a better environment and more security. Since a number of senior retired and serving officers have their stakes in these housing schemes or actually reside there, petty criminals are far more wary about targeting these areas. This gives military-run housing projects a better reputation, which is useful for marketing them. The level of cleanliness and quality of infrastructure also tend to be better. This results in relatively good and stable price escalation in military-controlled urban land schemes. Military-controlled schemes have established a clientele even in smaller towns like Bahawalpur, where the Bahria Town scheme resulted in an escalation in the price of land where it was built. Earlier, the original landowner had faced problems in selling his land.[81]

The military's prominent position in the country's power politics is essential for realizing profitability in the real estate projects controlled by the armed forces. Although complete data on the net value of the military's stakes in urban real estate are not available, it is possible to outline some examples to give a sense of the nature of the stakes and profitability. For example, the AWT housing scheme at Sanjiani, Punjab on 750 acres developed at the cost of Rs.720 million (US$12.41 million) earned a profit of Rs.24 billion (US$413.79 million), at a conservative estimate. The profitability of the defence housing scheme (MORGAH-I & II) in Rawalpindi and the Park Town housing scheme in Lahore is equally noticeable. In the first instance, 3,375 acres were acquired at about a total cost of Rs.11 billion (US$189.65 million) and were later sold for approximately Rs.135 billion (US$2,328 million).[82] It is not surprising in the light of these profits that the DHA, with its army management, has gone for an expansion in which it forcibly appropriates private land. The aim was to acquire an additional 4,000 acres through collusion with the local administration and the lower judiciary. The land revenue department was forced to not release any documents pertaining to these 4,000 acres so that the owners could be coerced into selling the land.[83] The villagers lodged a protest against the high-handedness of the DHA authorities. They claimed that they were being forced by the military authorities to move out of their villages and accept Rs.57,000 (US$982.70) per *kanal* (0.125 acre) in compensation.[84]

The second case refers to a new private housing scheme established in the outskirts of the DHA Lahore. Reportedly, the DHA authorities manipulated the law to take control of the scheme.[85] This was a case of a collaboration between the various centres of power which benefited from joint exploitation of land resources, and hence an example of crony capitalism.

Because of its comparatively high value, urban property in particular is much sought after, and has been used to buy loyalty in strategic institutions such as the judiciary. Members of the judiciary are encouraged to acquire residential plots or are offered land as rewards.[86] There have also been instances of more explicit encouragement, in the form of providing opportunities for other social and professional groups to acquire urban land. In 2004–05, the government offered residential plots to journalists. These opportunities are intended to divert essential civil society groups such as the media from criticizing the regime. As the prominent columnist Ayaz Amir points out, the land distribution is done at the risk of destroying the level playing field for everyone to acquire land.[87]

The case of the DHA Karachi, which is in the heart of the main cosmopolitan centre, near the sea and airport, is similar to other such housing schemes. This scheme measures 8,672.051 acres and represents an extension of 35,501.55 acres to the Karachi cantonment.[88] After 1999, another 4,000-unit housing scheme known as Creek City was planned on 90 acres of land adjacent to the DHA. A rough estimate of the worth of Creek City alone is about Rs.400 billion (US$6,896.5 million). Given the volume of profit, it is not surprising that the army authorities pay no heed even to some of their own people who have spoken out against 'institutionalized corruption'. An ex-army officer who is currently a newspaper columnist and businessman, Ikram Sehgal, wrote about the impact of the army's profit-mongering on its professionalism. He was also of the view that housing projects like these were detrimental for the environment of the city of Karachi.[89]

Defence housing schemes in other cities such as Lahore have also undergone substantial expansion. enhancing the total area included in the DHA to 93 sq km. One senior military land and cantonment officer was of the view that the city of Lahore would soon expand to a point where it would touch the border with India. This expansion, he added, was planned solely by the army authorities and with the view of reaping financial benefits.[90]

The negative implications of these elite housing schemes are not limited to the concentration of wealth alone. To begin with, these housing projects do not solve the problem of the general dearth of housing in the country. On the contrary, they lead to a rise in speculative investment. Profits generated through the sale of urban land contribute to the upward social mobility of a certain class. In addition, the elite housing schemes are a sign of problematic town planning. On the one hand, elite, upscale neighbourhoods are created through claiming rural land. On the other, there is an imbalance of town development: some neighbourhoods have better facilities than others, which does not strengthen the overall town ethos or elevate it from a 'ruralopolis' to a metropolis.[91] The disparity between the elite and ordinary urban planning becomes noticeable when the elite schemes are compared with the rest of the city or town structure. It could be argued that such disparities are found across the world, but they become more pronounced where elite structures are combined with disproportional political power.

Coercion for appropriating land

The urban land acquisition raises eyebrows because of the military's use of coercive methods to acquire land. The army has often used its authority to procure private land without due compensation and through arm-twisting the civilian authorities. An example of the illegal use of authority concerns the villages of Niazian, Hummak, Sihala and Dhok Kanial in the administrative district of Islamabad. The villagers filed a writ in the Lahore High

Court (Rawalpindi Bench) against the AWT's grabbing their 4,000 acres of land, an action that was claimed to be justified in the name of 'national interest' and for 'defence purposes', and for which the villagers were not adequately compensated.

These villages are part of the master plan for the expansion of the capital city, Islamabad. The initial no-objection certificate (NoC) given to the GHQ by the Capital Development Authority (CDA) was limited to Hummak village. However, the army extended its control to other villages and forcibly acquired the land without compensating the people. Justifying the acquisition as in the national interest, the AWT's attorney argued that the grant of land for housing army officers was in the interests of the institution. Interestingly, the High Court decided the case in the AWT's favour, upholding the acquisition as being 'in the national and defence interests of the country'.[92] This is an odd judgment considering that the AWT is registered as a welfare foundation and claims to be operating in the private sector. This was a case of the army using its authority to benefit a private venture and a select group of officers at the risk of harming the interests of the general public. The Supreme Court, however, overturned the High Court's decision and asked the AWT to compensate the villagers.

While these villagers had the sense and the will to move the superior court, there are many in cases in the country where the military has not paid any compensation. For instance, in Quetta valley, Baluchistan, the army appears to have forcibly grabbed private property amounting to hundreds of acres. Reportedly, since 1993 the local residents and owners of the land have not been allowed to lay a single brick on their land. The army planned an extension of its garrison, but the GHQ did not have enough funds to compensate people at market rates, or even at the dirt-cheap official rate, so the movement of people was restricted until such time as the service could move the government to pass an order enabling it to acquire the land.[93] A similar situation could be observed in Sindh, where the MoD acquired 210,722 acres during the 1980s and 1990s for the defence services without paying compensation to the provincial government.[94] The military was one of ten departments of the federal government that defaulted in paying the cost of the land to the Sindh Government.

This kind of illegal use of authority in coercing private civilian owners or the government is also obvious in other cases, such as the land acquisition for the construction of the new GHQ in Islamabad. The MoD acquired 1,165 acres of land in 2005 at a throwaway price of Rs.40 (US$0.68) per sq yd, which, as the MoD clarified, was legally considered the right compensation for acquisition of land for official purposes.[95] Later, another 1,085 acres were allotted by the federal government in the same area at the rate of Rs.150 (US$2.58) per square yard. The land will be used not only for construction of the military headquarters, but for residences of officers, schools, markets and other facilities. The army authorities are forcing the government to relocate 3,500 villagers at the government's expense, and to oblige the residents of Chauntra village, who have refused to vacate their land, to move to an alternative location.[96]

THE SOCIOLOGY OF MILITARY LAND

The problems highlighted above are not the only ones created by the military's land acquisition. In fact the whole issue of military land, especially in rural Pakistan, adds to the larger problem of feudalism and unequal social relationships. The military agriculturists are largely absentee farmers who, as mentioned earlier, do not till the land themselves. For instance, during a visit to the farms of General Pervez Musharraf and some other senior generals in Bahawalpur it was learnt that these lands were being tilled by landless peasants who did not get any legal or social protection for their services. Prior to the 1990s, many military agriculturists tended to sell their lands to the local feudal or the new rural capitalists, who purchased the land not to pursue agriculture as a profession, but as a symbol of their influence and wealth.

Sociopolitically, absenteeism perpetrates authoritarianism.[97] The linkage between absentee land ownership and authoritarianism is because it is primarily the large landlords or those with authority who can afford to benefit from the land without actually tilling it themselves. The presence of big or influential agriculturists adds to the problem of inequitable distribution of land resources. According to one estimate, there are 20 million landless peasants in the country. There are also a large number of small landowners who do not match the big landowners in political influence. According to Hamza Alavi, during the 1970s only 5 per cent of landowners controlled over 70 per cent of the landholdings in the country.[98] This situation has not changed substantially, as is obvious from Akbar Zaidi's later analysis in *Issues in Pakistan's Economy*.[99] According to the 1980s census by the government cited by Zaidi, 34 per cent of holdings of farmland in Pakistan fell into the size category of less than 5 acres. This, however, constitutes only 7 per cent of the total farmland. On the other hand, 0.34 per cent of the farms in the country represent ownership of 8.5 per cent of the total agricultural land. Such a division is most pronounced in Sindh and the South Punjab regions, which are the key agricultural areas and are known for large landholdings.[100] Because of limitations on the flow and accumulation of capital, a strong middle class cannot emerge in the rural areas.

The military agriculturists, particularly the senior officers, have adopted feudal norms and seem to compete with local big landowners in areas where they acquire land. For instance, in South Punjab a number of senior army generals-turned-agriculturists have also become *numberdars* (state-appointed local notables who collect water taxes and deal with other land revenue-related issues in the area). Although the government does not pay a *numberdar* for his services, the incumbent has a lot of clout as a result of his position as a representative of the state's interests, with connections to the local police and revenue authorities. This is part of the feudal tradition in Punjab. According to reports, Lt.-General Shahid Pervez, who was once the corps commander, Bahawalpur, and the former interior minister, Lt.-General (rtd) Moin-u-Din Haider, are *numberdars* of the villages of Chak 104 DB and Chak 44 DB respectively. The former chairman JCSC, General Aziz Khan, and secretary establishment, Brig (rtd) Ejaz Shah, also became *numberdars* of their villages, Chak 47 and Chak 143. The appointment as *numberdar* also allows these officers to acquire another 12.5 acres of land. Apparently, General Pervez Musharraf is the *numberdar* for Chak 13 BC.[101] Such appointments flout the spirit of the tradition behind the office of *numberdar*, who is supposed to be a local resident of the area with the ability to perform revenue-collection tasks and strengthen relations with the local community in the process. Since these generals do not reside in the areas where they have become *numberdars*, the task of revenue collection is carried out by their representatives, who are also not local people. The position of *numberdar*, however, is acquired to bolster the political influence of the serving and retired generals in the rural areas and to get them additional land.

The symbiotic relationship between land and authority motivates the upwardly mobile middle class to acquire symbols of power. The symbolism of land, especially agricultural land, was pointed. out by the economist Harris Gazdar in his study on rural land in Pakistan. The author is of the view that the civil and military bureaucracy chose to acquire land because of the peculiar political symbolism of the land.[102] The symbolism is mired in the feudal ethos of the dominant classes, which is followed by most people who want to advance socially and become members of the dominant elite. This is also apparent from the farmhouses built around large cities like Lahore, Karachi and Islamabad. The opulence and lifestyles of the owners mostly display the decadent feudal culture. The show of wealth and blatant imitation of the landed-feudal class in these new neighbourhoods repre-sents a reverse cultural trend of cities aping the cultural norms of feudal villages. Owned mostly by literate, often western trained and educated civil and military bureaucrats and industrialists, who are fully exposed to tech-nological modernization, the farmhouses are a reminder of the traditional feudal-cum-authoritarian lifestyle.

This has been termed the culture of a 'ruralopolis', defined as 'not a homogenous rural region separated from cities. It is the rural part of an extended region comprised of a chain of high-density districts, centred around towns and cities.'[103] This term was coined by Mohammad A. Qadeer, an expert on urban and regional planning. Although Qadeer's explanation is limited to the structure of the city and the infrastructure, the definition could include the cultural dimension as well. A ruralopolis adopts the rural-feudal culture, exhibited through the lifestyle of the 'new feudal lord'. For instance, the wild parties or *mujrahs*[104] held in a lot of these farmhouses are reminiscent of the lives of perverse feudal lords, images of which can be found in Tehmina Durrani's autobiography, *My Feudal Lord*.[105]

The possession of power and authority lies at the heart of the monopo-lization of land by the dominant classes in the country. The poor or the landless peasants on the other hand are deprived of their rights to own land. This is borne out by the case of the village of Nawazabad in Bahawalpur. Hundreds of landless peasants suffered eviction from the state land they had occupied for many years after the land was allotted to mili-tary personnel. In a video interview, these peasants protested against being turned out of the land they had partially developed and reclaimed from the desert without being given any fair hearing. Regardless, the peasants continued to be threatened with dire consequences unless they vacated the land. The peasants understood the court's inability to intervene on their behalf. Furthermore, junior military officers came to threaten these people, ridiculing the law, and advising the peasants that even the courts could not save them from the army's authority. As a result, the affected people of Nawazabad found no difference between the dominant feudal lords and the praetorian military. The traditional feudal lords were as averse to allowing the people to live on their lands as the military, which deprived poor people from their livelihood on state land.

Unable to build their homes on lands owned by powerful landlords, these people often occupied state lands. Their treatment forced one woman in Nawazabad to bitterly demand that 'if there is no place for us here, then they [the authorities] should put us on a truck and drop us in India'.[106] This was an ultimate form of protest to the authorities that had treated these people unkindly. The local civilian administration, for example, supported the military rather than the poor landless peasants. The peasants claimed that the local revenue officers stood aside and let army officials threaten poor peasants with dire consequences if they did not leave.[107]

Equally perturbing was the story of the people of the small fishing village of Mubarik in Sindh. Situated near the Sindh-Balochistan border, their village on the shore was once their territory. For over five years now, they have watched as the land has been slowly pulled from under their feet. Generations of their families have lived there peacefully as fishermen, but no longer. A few years back, the villagers found that they could no longer move freely on their own land. The PN ordered the residents of Mubarik to limit themselves to a small area. But that was not the only restriction: they were also told not to construct houses on the land because the adjoining land fell within the range of the navy's target-practice range. The villagers claim that the PN broke a promise and extended its presence beyond a point that they had previously been assured would be the limit of its expansion. In fact, the PN has continued to expand its presence despite the fact that there is no provision in the existing rules for a naval cantonment. Meanwhile, the uneducated villagers are unable to contest their rights: they neither know the law, nor have the money to take legal action.

However, even those who take recourse to legal action might not necessarily get immediate justice or fair treatment. In Yunisabad near Karachi, the PN took forcible possession of the floating jetty – and the land on which it was built – which belonged to the village and was used to transport locals, especially the sick. For villagers from nearby Shamspir, the jetty was their only access point to land. A writ was filed with the Sindh High Court against the 'illegal act of the navy' and several letters were written to the district administration highlighting human rights abuses by the PN. Despite such action, the people continued to be harassed and occasionally beaten up. The PN failed to honour a court order not to interfere with public traffic.[108] The service had too much at stake. The PN wanted to control the village and the surrounding area, from which it is known to sell sand.

Besides the ill-treatment of poor people, the commercial activity of selling sand is creating environmental hazards. The removal of sand has made the saline sea water come deeper inland. This, however, is not the only case of environmental degradation. Reportedly, a few kilometres of Clifton beach in Karachi are under threat because of the expansion of the DHA Karachi in a scheme worth Rs.1.5 billion (US$25.86 million). The DHA was given public or state property to develop a private housing scheme for which the local people were not consulted regarding their concerns about environmental damage.[109]

The naval authorities appear oblivious of the environmental degradation, and emphasize their authority and profit. Their attitude is no different from the big feudal landlords, who are also only concerned with their personal interests. Obsessed with their personal stakes, the feudal landlords have also been a cause for encouraging the military to acquire land and other essential resources. The big landlords of South Punjab, for instance, where the military has acquired thousands of acres for distribution amongst its personnel, have really not tried to resist the military's land acquisition. For instance, Khursheed Zaman Qureshi, a prominent landowner from Southern Punjab, who also served as the provincial minister for agriculture from 2000–02 in Musharraf's military government, did not object to the armed forces acquiring land in Southern Punjab. Although the common people are anxious about the military getting preferential treatment over the indigenous poor population in the ongoing land distribution in the three districts of South Punjab, Qureshi did not feel obliged to challenge the military's interests. In fact, the former minister appreciated the association between the landowners of Southern Punjab and the military, sharing the view that military agriculturists brought development to the region, which the local landowners could not negotiate with their counterparts from politically significant Central Punjab.

Military agriculturists definitely brought a greater share of water to Cholistan, the desert area of South Punjab, where they were allotted land.[110] A large number of senior military generals benefit from the controversial Greater Thal canal irrigation project, meant to develop agricultural land in the desert of South Punjab. Mushtaq Gaddi, who works on the politics of water distribution in Pakistan, has argued that the Thal canal will primarily irrigate the lands of senior military officers rather than benefit the indigenous Cholistani people.[111] It is worth noting that the local authorities showed more efficiency in distributing the newly reclaimed land to the military than to the landless peasants from the area. This efficiency can also be explained as a result of the organizational structure of the Cholistan Development Authority (CDA). The body responsible for transferring land to various claimants and for development of the area has a number of retired army officers in senior positions.

Meanwhile the land and the related water distribution issue seem to generate a negative social cost, in terms of relations between the centre and the smaller provinces such as Sindh, which face an acute water deficiency. Farmers in Sindh complain of water shortages, which have forced some, such as Basheer Shah, to cut down their mango orchards. Explaining the water crisis in rural Sindh, Basheer Shah claims that 'there is hardly any water in the canals, the lakes are drying up and out tube wells are producing brackish water that forced me to take the brutal action of cutting down trees'.[112]

The development of coastal town of Gwadar in Baluchistan by the federal government is another example of how the state's authoritarian intervention in smaller provinces, for the benefit of the military and other groups with investment capital, can harm the federation. The Baluch leaders and people are unhappy about the fact that Gwadar's ongoing development, which has allowed many influential groups and the military to buy land, is detrimental to the sociopolitical environment of the area and the province at large. The Baluch leader, Ataullah Mengal, was of the view that:

> the construction of Gwadar town and allocation of land to the military, civil bureaucrats and other influential groups from Punjab will result in an influx of outsiders into the province which will unsettle the local culture. It would change politics because the majority will be outsiders.[113]

Such intervention by the state and the resultant opposition to land distribution by the local people is bound to weaken the federal structure of the Pakistani state, a reality that the military generals sitting far away in Rawalpindi do not seem to evaluate out of fear of disrupting their own interests and those of their civilian clients.

The military's political clout is central to its control of real estate in the country. The organization's political power is instrumental in influencing the civil authorities, a fact borne out by a legal dispute between Brig. (rtd) Muhammad Bashir and a landless peasant, Abdul Karim. The provincial government transferred about 33,866 acres of land in Bahawalpur division to the army GHQ in 1993 without checking the title of the land, some of which had previously been leased to landless peasants from the area. About 3 *kanals* (0.375 acres) of the 396 *kanals* (49.5 acres) given to Brig. Bashir was actually the property of Karim. In its eagerness to favour the military authorities, the district government representatives tried to disprove Karim's claim to the land. Karim took action to retain his land, and when Bashir went to court to prevent him, the Lahore High Court supported Karim, overturning the decision by Bahawalpur's local administration to award the land to Bashir.

Bashir then filed an appeal in the Supreme Court of Pakistan. The Supreme Court upheld Karim's ownership of the land, and admonished the district collector for acting capriciously, and arbitrarily transferring land to the army when it had been marked as 'land not available' for allotment. The Court also reproached Bashir for impinging upon the rights of a poor peasant. In the historic Abdul Karim Supreme Court judgment passed in September 2003, the judges repeated the following quotation from John Steinbeck's *The Grapes of Wrath* and cautioned against accumulation of property in the hands of a few:

And the great owners, who must lose their land in an upheaval, the great owners with access to history, with eyes to read history and to know the great fact: when property accumulates in too few hands, it is taken away. And that companion fact: when a majority of people are hungry and cold they will take by force what they need. And the little screaming fact that sounds through all history: repression works only to strengthen and knit the repressed. The great owners ignored the three cries of history. The land fell into fewer hands, the number of the dispossessed increased, and every effort of the great owners was directed at repression. The money was spent for arms, for gas to protect the great holdings, and spies were sent to catch the murmuring of revolt so that it might be stamped out. The changing economy was ignored, plans for the change ignored; and only means to destroy revolt were considered, while the causes of revolt went on.[114]

While Abdul Karim got justice, this decision of the Supreme Court is not being used as a precedent for other cases. Amazingly, Karim received justice not because he had the means to take legal action, but because Brig. Bashir wanted his land and took the case to court. It is unlikely that this historic judgment will help many other poor villagers, though, as the only way for them to benefit from this landmark judgment would be to initiate expensive legal proceedings. It is also unlikely that the senior military officers learnt any lesson from the court judgment: they continue to look at the landless peasants with suspicion and contempt. One naval officer, for example, was of the view that 'Why do landless peasants have greater rights over land? They do not deserve land just because they are poor.'[115] Similar sentiments were expressed by Maj.-General (rtd) Saleem, who believes that 'there is no difference between allotment of land to poor people and the military. The armed forces personnel deserve to be given land as much as the poor landless peasants.'[116]

Over the years, the military elite in Pakistan have joined the club of other dominant classes in the country to exploit resources including land. As I argue in this chapter, the organization has systematically used traditions or created norms to occupy state land for the benefit of the military fraternity. There is a constant threat of alteration in the use of millions of acres of state land that is under the organization's direct control, and for land which is not controlled by it. The military uses its political power to acquire land and to alter the use of state land from operational purposes to private ownership. The change in the use of land from public good to private benefit serves the interests of senior generals and the officer cadre at large, and in this they behave no differently from the big landowners and the landed-feudal class, especially in the treatment meted out to ordinary soldiers and poor indigenous people. The military's authority and linkage with the political and institutional power base is instrumental in turning it into one of the prominent land barons in the country. The exploitation of land makes the generals no different from the top civilian landowners in the country.

205

8 Providing for the men: military welfare

In Pakistan, the military is one of the most attractive professions, especially for the young men from military families and the lower-middle class, who see military service as an opportunity for employment, influence and upward social mobility. The organization's significance in the job market is owing to its political influence and system of welfare, among other reasons. The military has a reputation of taking care of its serving and retired personnel. As well as providing a comparatively sizeable pension, the military provides a variety of compensatory packages to its personnel, including urban and rural land, employment and other facilities. Such schemes are meant to enhance the already existing sense of camaraderie that is central to the ethos of the organization. This chapter analyses the military welfare system, and evaluates its political implications for state–society relations.

MILITARY WELFARE

The military provides post-retirement benefits for its personnel because, as Maj.-General (rtd) Agha Masood Hassan put it, 'the military behaves like a social organization … it is a social organization that looks after its men while the civil and the politicians do not look after their men'.[1] The general's comments show the Pakistan military's efforts to attract and retain relatively good-quality personnel through offering good facilities and an image of an organization that takes care of its people and their needs even after they cease to work. Indeed, there are several methods by which the welfare of military staff is taken care of.

The advantages provided to military personnel can be divided into non-tangible and tangible benefits. The first category relates to the social influence that is gained through working in the armed forces. Over the years, the military class has evolved and become conscious of its power and influence. Since the military jealously guards its superior image, there is a tendency to treat armed forces personnel with kid gloves. This is certainly true of the Punjab and parts of the NWFP, from where military personnel are usually recruited. As a result, military personnel have grown accustomed to being shown respect. Even in smaller towns and villages, an association with the armed forces creates greater opportunities to get problems solved by the district administration. Some of the best clubs, guest houses and other such facilities belong to the armed forces, not to mention the availability of health and educational facilities that are far better than those available for the civilian population.

The tangible benefits include military pensions, the grant of urban and rural properties, and employment provided to retired military personnel. The military caters for the well-being of about 9.1 million people, including retired personnel and their dependants. Every year, the central government spends a hefty amount on military pensions. In order to impress financial aid donors like the IMF and the World Bank with its conservation of resources, the Musharraf government has indulged in cosmetic massaging of the national accounts, such as separating out military pensions from military expenditure and allocating them to the government's overall pay and remuneration account. This change was carried out to reduce the size of the defence budget. However, the fact is that the government pays out a larger sum in military pensions than civilian pensions (see Table 8.1).[2]

This disparity between military and civilian pensions occurs because military personnel get better salaries, allowances and pensions than civil servants. (These figures do not include other forms of compensation provided to armed forces personnel.) The civil bureaucracy suffers from relatively low pay and no additional incentives. The pay scales determine the size of eventual individual pensions. A study by the Pakistan Institute of Development Economics (PIDE) on public-sector wages, which included a comparison of civilian and military pay scales during the period after the 1970s, showed that public-sector wages declined during the 1970s.[3] However, other research for the PIDE by economist Zafar Nasir shows that skilled public-sector workers received better pay than unskilled and less well-educated informal private-sector workers. Civilian government employees, as the study indicates, earn less than formal private-sector workers mainly because of their poor pay structure.[4]

The differential between public-sector pay (especially military pay) and private pay structures is common all over the world. Although US soldiers get better pay than Pakistanis, it still does not bear comparison with private-sector remuneration in the United States. The relatively poor pay of the armed forces also lies at the heart of the system of military welfare all over the world. The armed forces around the world offer additional perks and privileges to their personnel in order to attract good personnel and to be able to retain these people in service. The military welfare or (more

Table 8.1 Comparative sizes of military and civilian pensions

Year	Military pension (Rs. billion)	Civil pension (Rs. billion)
2000–01	28.247	NA
2001–02	26.415	5.393
2002–03	33.494	6.130
2003–04	30.826	6.372
2004–05	30.181	6.156

Source: Office of the Accountant-General Pakistan Revenues (AGPR), Islamabad.

appropriately) retirement system 'is designed to serve as an inducement for enlistment and re-enlistment, to create an orderly career path, and to ensure "youthful and vigorous" military forces'.[5]

The military welfare system includes all post-retirement benefits: financial compensation and other post-retirement facilities such as health care, housing, and re-employment for armed forces personnel. Other militaries, such as the US and British armed forces, also have systems to provide for the welfare of retired military personnel. For instance, in October 1996 the US Congress passed Public Law 104-262, the Veteran's Health Care Eligibility Reform Act of 1996, providing enhanced healthcare benefits to all veterans. In Britain there are specific facilities for war veterans and retired personnel. The Army Benevolent Fund and other charities provide for the welfare of ex-services personnel and their families. The extent of inducements offered varies, however, from military to military.

It is important to note that most armed forces recognize the significance of providing welfare for their personnel and their families. An awareness of the need to take care of soldiers and their families did not come about until the late seventeenth century. Up until the Crimean War (1854–6) there was little recognition of the personal needs of soldiers. In fact, there was little acceptance of soldiers having families.[6] However modern and professional armed forces recognize the need to provide welfare for their personnel, and take care of their personal environment, making pensions the key component of the military welfare system. According to Asch and Warner, researchers at the RAND Corporation, financial compensation is a means for retaining high-quality individuals rather than facilitating the reintegration of military personnel into civilian life.[7] Financial compensations are also an incentive for the least-talented individuals to seek retirement earlier in their careers.[8] Officers are encouraged to leave military service after 20 years of service to allow younger people to replace them, and this makes it possible for the state to maintain a youthful corps. (Officers tend to last a little longer than enlisted or junior commissioned officers (JCOs) and non-commissioned officers (NCOs).) Therefore, a large number of officers and enlisted personnel retire at an early age. The financial compensation provides the necessary cushion for the retirees, especially during the period in which they seek employment in the civilian job market.

The Pakistan military's method for attracting and retaining better-quality personnel is to offer them a far more thorough welfare package than is offered in a number of developed countries. The welfare system is futuristic in providing a financial and social security cushion, which officers and soldiers may need after retirement. For instance, the housing schemes and the provision of agricultural and urban land are meant to relieve the pressure of finding accommodation or alternative means of living after retirement from active duty. Such amenities, it is believed, increase professional efficiency and contribute to the recruitment and retention of better quality officers. However, there is no evidence to prove this hypothesis.

The Pakistani military's welfare system is based on two distinct models, which are explained in the next two subsections.

THE FAUJI FOUNDATION MODEL

The first model is the conservative method of providing health, educational and employment facilities to retired personnel and their dependants. According to this approach, the armed forces raise resources to build facilities for retired personnel. The Fauji Foundation (FF) was built around this concept. The FF uses profit earned from its commercial ventures to build the infrastructure needed to provide health care, education and vocational training for ex-service personnel and their families. The FF runs 276 welfare operations and undertakings, and its primary work includes health care and education. In health care, the organization runs 11 hospitals, 23 medical centres, 31 fixed dispensaries and 41 mobile dispensaries. Of the FF's current Rs.1.6 billion (US$27.58 million) welfare budget, approximately Rs.0.9 billion (US$15.52 million) is spent on health care and Rs.0.7 billion (US$12.07 million) on education. According to the exact figures given by the chairman of the FF, Lt.-General (rtd) Mohammad Amjad, Rs.811 million (US$13.98 million) were spent on health care in the financial year 2002–03. These medical facilities entitle armed forces personnel to health care in areas not catered for by the existing network of the army combined military hospitals (CMH) or the hospitals run by the PAF and PN in larger cities and towns.[9]

The FF has a parallel infrastructure for education. It runs 90 schools and colleges, with an enrolment of about 40,000 students, plus nine technical training centres for males, and 66 vocational centres for females, which provide training in sewing and stitching. The chairman claimed that it has trained about 60,527 women, who receive a monthly stipend of Rs.200 (US$3.45) during their training. Including these stipends took the FF's spending on education to approximately Rs.777 million (US$13.4 million) in the financial year 2002–3.

Since its inception in 1953–4, the FF claims to have provided 3 million stipends to trainees, at a cost of approximately Rs.2.12 billion (US$36.55 million). The FF also provides cash grants to the three service headquarters, supposedly for welfare expenditure. For instance, in the financial year 2002–3 the organization gave cash grants to the army GHQ of Rs.18.6 million (US$321,000), to the navy HQ of Rs.1.4 million (US$24,000), and to the air force HQ of Rs.1.8 million (US$31,000).

The FF's model of post-retirement benefits is categorized in the literature on social welfare as a participatory form of welfare, since it is operated directly by the beneficiaries, often grouped together as a distinct community. The available literature on welfare recognizes the presence of special-interest groups taking responsibility for the welfare of their own members.[10] However, the literature also talks about the representation of the otherwise incommensurable needs of individuals by a relatively small group of people chosen as representatives, or a local elite. The decision-making structure of the FF and other military foundations is highly elitist. Post-retirement benefits are decided exclusively by the military high command, without the participation of the *jawans*. Consequently, there is no system of feedback within the military regarding client satisfaction by the personnel for whom the welfare system is intended, and to whom the various packages are offered. Col. (rtd) Bakhtiar Khan claims that the actual beneficiaries of the welfare system are the officers and not the ordinary soldiers.[11]

The FF is also a source of re-employment for armed forces personnel. The organization has 12,377 employees including about 4,618 ex-service personnel. In most cases, individuals are employed on a three-year contract basis. As in the United States, where financial compensation generates relative lethargy in re-employed military personnel,[12] the retired military personnel in the FF and other military-owned foundations obtain greater leisure mainly by putting in less effort at work. This increases the cost of the foundations' operations substantially. However, the idea behind the foundations is not just to make a profit but to accommodate retired military personnel, in consideration for their welfare.

The FF claims to have 9.1 million beneficiaries, a figure that is likely to increase by another 1 million in the next five years. These figures, it is further claimed, represent approximately 5 per cent of the total population. According to the governor of the State Bank of Pakistan, Dr Ishrat Hussain, this particular figure represents a substantial portion of the population, and the fact that these welfare foundations provide a social security net for these number of people naturally justifies their commercial ventures.[13]

THE AWT MODEL

The Army Welfare Trust (AWT) follows a different model from the FF. Like the Bahria Foundation (BF) and the Shaheen Foundation (SF), it was formed on the principle of generating profit to buy additional welfare for armed forces personnel, and to provide post-retirement employment for retired personnel. As directed by their governing boards, the three foundations directly provide resources to the relevant service headquarters, to be distributed later among individuals or invested in welfare projects. However, in the absence of transparency it is difficult to assess the extent of the three foundations' contribution to welfare. The service headquarters do not provide any data about the finances of their welfare activities. This is because foundations established under the Charitable Endowment Act 1890 are exempt from all public-sector accountability processes. In any case, a glance at Table 8.2 will show the status of the AWT's contribution to the army's Welfare and Rehabilitation Directorate Fund from 1992–2001.

Yet another method of post-retirement compensation is the AWT-controlled Askari Bank's Army Welfare Scheme. Under this scheme, serving and retired officers voluntarily invest money with the bank, which is returned with a dividend after a specified period. There is a minimum investment requirement of Rs.50,000 (US$862) and a maximum of Rs.1.5 million (US$26,000). The AWT's first head, Maj.-General (rtd) Fahim Haider Rizvi, said that an upper limit for investment was introduced to stop individuals from misusing the facility. The Askari Bank provides high rates of return. In 2003, the scheme paid a dividend of about 9 per cent, which was higher than most national banks or saving schemes.[14] In the past, this figure used to be about 16

210

Table 8.2 The AWT's Welfare Fund contribution

Year	Contribution
1993	242,853
1994	407,973
1995	478,201
1996	499,454
1997	2,632,295
1998	707,132
1999	(715,214)
2000	(1,129,988)
2001	971,074

(Figures in brackets represent negative contributions.)

per cent, with no bar on the amount invested. Apparently before the limit was introduced, officers borrowed money from public-sector banks at lower rates and invested it in the Welfare Scheme.[15] The investment scheme and credit facilities are accessible to senior officers rather than ordinary soldiers.

Compared with the FF and the AWT, there is very little information available on the SF and BF. In 2000, the PAF's SF claimed to have spent about 20 per cent of its annual profit on welfare activities. Its financial turnover for that year was about Rs.600 million (US$10.34 million), but that figure gives little indication of the net profit. The SF's other contribution is to provide jobs to approximately 200 PAF officers and airmen. Its reported annual intake of air force personnel is 40, including 4–5 retired officers and 35–40 retired technicians/airmen.[16] Similarly, the AWT provides jobs to approximately 5,000 retired personnel, and the BF to about a hundred naval personnel. The role played by these foundations in providing employment to retired personnel was recognized by President Pervez Musharraf. According to Musharraf:

> there's retired military officers who are the bosses [in the foundations] but, again, they generate employment, not only for retired military officers and men which is essential because military officers retire at a very young age .... A major retires at the age of 40/45. Shouldn't he get some employment? And also, much more than the military, it is the civilians that are employed.[17]

Thus, these foundations are seen as benefiting a larger community than just armed forces personnel, through establishing industries and businesses and generating employment.

WELFARE FOR INDIVIDUALS

The welfare foundations, however, are not the only method of ensuring the long-term well-being of military personnel. As was discussed at length in

Chapters 6 and 7, the military uses various methods to benefit the members of its fraternity. The two critical areas are grants of urban and rural land, and creating employment opportunities for ex-service staff other than through the foundations.

As was mentioned in Chapter 7, the armed forces have acquired millions of acres of agricultural and urban land, which they distribute among their members. While the distribution of urban land is limited to the officer cadre, rural land is provided to officers and soldiers alike at highly subsidized prices. Agricultural land, as mentioned in Chapter 7, is provided at a very cheap rate of Rs.20–60 (US$0.34–1.03) per acre. The distribution of land follows an approach initially instituted by the British, who gave land to those joining military service to secure their loyalty. The colonial power was sensitive to building the local soldiers' stakes in the security of the British Empire. Yong argues that 'it was in the soldier's homes and villages, and not in the regiments, that the "loyalty" of the army was often won or lost'.[18] The process of buying loyalty included keeping the soldiers and their dependants content. This contentment was necessary for insulating these people from external political influences,[19] so welfare was an essential tool for strengthening the professional ethos in the British Indian Army. The British authorities realized that 'when all is said and done, [the men work] for the monthly wage, the other pecuniary wages and the pension'.[20] Pakistan's military continued with this policy to retain the loyalty of its men. In fact, these perks and privileges, especially the land grant, are a major inducement for personnel to join and remain in the armed forces. The higher the rank, the more privileges are received. Promotion in the armed forces, however, is pegged to better performance in staff courses and work in general.

The defence establishment also takes care of its members after they leave service by providing at least some of them with post-retirement employment. Successive military regimes have given retired personnel positions in the civil service. The welfare and rehabilitation directorates in each service headquarters organize employment for retired members. The directorates have the advantage of being able to find opportunities in the civil service.

The military's share of civilian public-sector jobs is specified under the Establishment Code (popularly known as Esta Code) of the federal government. According to Serial nos. 125, 126, 127, 130 and 131 of Chapter II of the Code, 50 per cent of the vacancies in basic pay-scale (BPS) grades 1–3 and in BPS-4 for staff car drivers and despatch riders are to be given to retired military officials. In addition, the military was granted a quota of 10 per cent of civil service positions at grade BPS-17 and above. During Zia ul Haq's regime the government agreed to reserve 10 per cent of all public-sector vacancies for former members of the armed forces.

In an interview in October 2003, the head of the Armed Forces Services Board, Brig. (rtd) Zahid Zaman, strongly objected to complaints that the military was edging out civil bureaucrats from their jobs. According to him, retired military personnel only occupy about 2 per cent of available public-sector jobs, which is far below the specified quota.[21] In any case, finding post-retirement employment is not a huge problem, especially considering the political clout of Pakistan's armed forces. With the strengthening of the armed forces in the country's power politics, defence service is one of the most sought-after careers in Pakistani society, especially for the lower-middle class. Private entrepreneurs are happy to give employment to retired military personnel to boost their business opportunities. According to Kaisar Bengali, private entrepreneurs use these personnel to 'benefit from the military's clout in government'.[22] Even political parties seek out armed forces personnel to develop ties with the military. The opportunities are further enhanced under direct military rule or military-led regimes. For instance, General Musharraf's regime has been accused of increasing the intake of retired and serving military officers in all segments of the government and the public sector. Islamabad inducted over 1,200 armed forces personnel into middle and senior management positions, and about 2,000 NCOs and ORs at lower levels in government departments. In addition, the welfare directorates in the three service headquarters serve as focal points for helping retired personnel to find jobs in the private sector. The Armed Forces Services Board also helps in finding jobs for retired personnel.

THE POLITICAL GEOGRAPHY OF MILITARY WELFARE

The military welfare system, however, creates its own set of problems. The most prominent issue relates to the politics of the distribution of military welfare. Military welfare resources are seen as contributing to the existing imbalance of resources between the various provinces. The smaller provinces complain about the dominance of the Punjab province over other provinces, especially since 75 per cent of the armed forces are from the Punjab. The frustration of the smaller provinces increases because of the Punjab's 50 per cent quota in the civil service, which is the largest share of any single federating unit of the state. Although three out of 22 cabinets have been headed by prime ministers from Sindh and one from Baluchistan, the general perception is that given the influence of the state bureaucracy (both civil and military), the smaller provinces have not received fair treatment and have no share in the distribution of resources or the country's decision making.

The welfare funds are naturally invested in the largest province, as is obvious from Figure 8.1. According to the data given in this chart, the Punjab provides a sizeable majority of JCOs and other ranks (Ors). It is followed by the NWFP, Azad Jammu and Kashmir, Sindh and the Northern Areas (popularly known as tribal areas). Baluchistan, which is politically the most turbulent, has the least share in the armed forces. However, the data given in Figure 8.2 presents a slightly different balance.

The greater share of Sindhi officers shown here does not mean that these are all ethnic Sindhis. It refers to the induction of new Sindhis, or migrants from Muslim minority provinces in India, popularly known as Mohajirs, most of whom settled in Sindh. General Pervez Musharraf, and previously General Mirza Aslam Beg, and other national leaders came from the migrant community.

The Punjab's greater share of military employment also does not mean

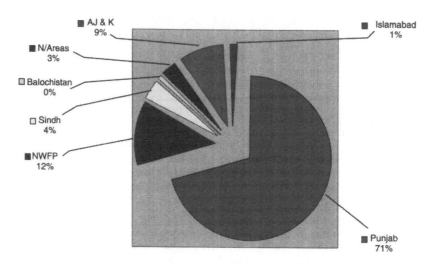

Figure 8.1 Ethnic division of military pensioners: JCOs and other ranks

that the jobs are equally spread across all regions of the province. A glance at Figures 8.3 and 8.4 will show that military recruitment is concentrated in certain parts of the Punjab and the frontier provinces.

The area known as the 'Salt Range' serves as the breeding ground of the present-day armed forces. These figures are endorsed by Stephen Cohen's research. According to the author of *The Idea of Pakistan*, approximately 75

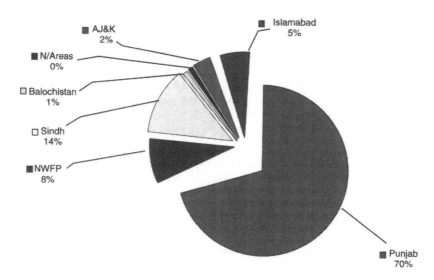

Figure 8.2 Military pensioners: officer cadre

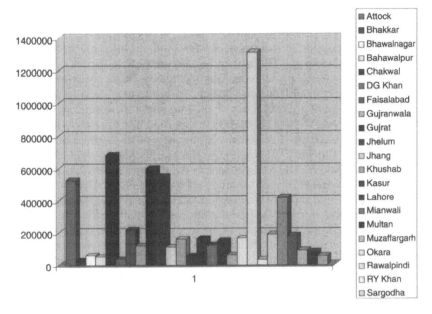

Figure 8.3 Military pensioners data, Punjab

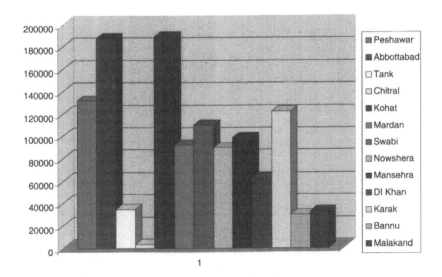

Figure 8.4 Military pensioners data, NWFP

per cent of the army is drawn from three districts of the Punjab and two districts of the NWFP.[23] The military's recruitment pattern follows the British tradition of procuring personnel from certain key areas.

The concentration of ex-servicemen in Sindh, on the other hand, is in two districts, Karachi and Hyderabad (see Figure 8.5).

The share of each province reflects the sociopolitical structure of the state and society. Since Pakistan's society is traditional, social mobility is low and familial ties are strong, hence the majority of personnel are drawn from specific areas. Welfare funds are also invested in areas from where the military is recruited. Approximately 72 per cent of the welfare budget is invested in the Punjab, 13.21 per cent in the NWFP, 2.64 per cent in Sindh, 18 per cent in Baluchistan, 8.92 per cent in Azad Kashmir and 2.87 per cent in the Northern Areas. (This data mainly refers to the FF's welfare budget.[24]) A look at Map 1 will further elaborate the fact that the bulk of the businesses conducted by the four welfare foundations are concentrated in the Punjab. The concentration of the military's business projects in the Punjab is also because of the availability of a relatively better infrastructure. Except for the BF's operations, which are naturally placed in Sindh because it contains the coastal city of Karachi, and some agri-based industries of the FF and AWT, most of the industrial and business projects are located in the largest province of the country.

This naturally increases the bitterness of the smaller provinces. Unfortunately, there is no mechanism available to eradicate the larger problem of the ethnic imbalance of the armed forces, which lies at the heart of the inequitable distribution of welfare resources.

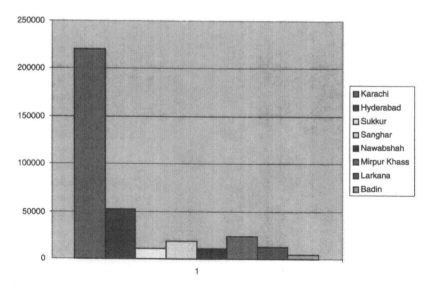

Figure 8.5 Military pensioners data, Sindh

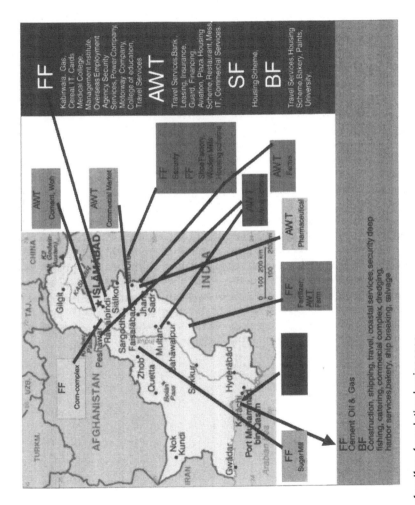

Map 1 Placement of welfare foundation businesses

The military's well-structured welfare system for its serving and retired personnel and their dependants is the envy of most civilians, who do not get similar opportunities. In particular, the re-employment opportunities provide great relief to ex-service personnel in a country that suffers from a high unemployment rate.

The military's welfare system in Pakistan is enviable both inside the country and outside it, especially in most developing states which lack such a robust welfare system for their armed forces personnel or other citizens. Working on the principle of taking care of its personnel 'from cradle to grave', Pakistan's military, unlike most others, provides a number of schemes such as urban housing, rural and agricultural properties, re-employment in the civil service and other public sector institutions, and a system of health and education for the dependants of military personnel. These perks and privileges are in addition to the pension paid to retiring officers and soldiers. The benefits of the welfare system, however, are concentrated on the upper echelon of the armed forces, and this results in the vested interests that were discussed in the previous three chapters.

The system might serve the interests of armed forces personnel and help the organization retain better quality staff, but it has substantial sociopolitical costs, in terms of exacerbating the tension between the Punjab and the smaller provinces. Most of the welfare funds are reinvested in the larger province. However, this discrepancy is part of a larger structural flaw whereby the Punjab is over-represented in the military and civil bureaucracy. Since the state's bureaucracy dominates decision making, this results in greater frustration for the ethnic population of the smaller provinces. Therefore, people who claim that the military's welfare system does a service to the nation by taking good care of a certain segment of the population and being well-run also need to look at its larger cost. The welfare system, or the set of perks and privileges provided to the armed forces, is part of the greater distributive injustice that the country suffers from.

9 The cost of Milbus

Whether the military should be involved in commercial activities and allowed to develop serious economic interests is an important question. The military's direct involvement in money-making activities has significant financial and sociopolitical costs, because the profit-making role is dependent on the armed forces' preferential access to decision making, and this is detrimental for creating a free-market economic environment. The previous five chapters have described and evaluated the structure and growth of the Pakistan military's economic empire and its political might. Since its formal inception in 1954, Milbus has grown exponentially. It is a segment of the military's economy which is largely hidden from the public and not subject to the government's accountability procedures. Moreover, it serves the interests of a select group of people. A combination of these two features of Milbus makes this capital inherently illegal. As has been proved in the case of Pakistan, an increase in the military's economic activities is directly proportional to its political power.

The generals justify Milbus as a contribution to national socioeconomic development and as part of the organization's welfare system for armed forces personnel. However, it will be argued in this chapter that the economic efficiency of the various military-controlled foundations is questionable. The fact is that many of these economic operations pose a burden on the defence budget and the larger national budget, because they use state resources or divert money from the defence budget to finance deficits. Moreover, the military's internal economy has huge opportunity costs, such as encouraging crony capitalism and hampering the growth of a free-market economy.

THE COST OF ECONOMIC INEFFICIENCY

The military's commercial ventures, especially the Army Welfare Trust (AWT), and some operations of the Shaheen Foundation (SF), the Fauji Foundation (FF) and the Frontier Works Organization (FWO), are not cost-efficient. This assessment is based on available financial data for these ventures for the period from 1998 to 2001, and audit reports of the government which have established the fact that resources continuously leak from the government's treasury to these companies, although they are supposed to operate in the private sector.

Given the lack of transparency of the military-controlled companies, it was not possible to access updated financial information. From a technical/legal standpoint, the welfare foundations are not liable to provide information regarding their operations to the public. Since the four foundations were established under the Charitable Endowment Act 1890 or the Societies Registration Act 1860 as private entities, the accounts of these foundations are not audited by the government's prime accounting agency, the Auditor-General of Pakistan. However, some audit objections were raised as a result of the audit of the defence forces, whose financial and other resources were used by the commercial ventures. The available data sought from the AWT HQs does not present a rosy picture.

ARMY WELFARE TRUST: A FINANCIAL ASSESSMENT

The AWT was established in 1971 with an initial investment of Rs.700,000 (US$12,000). Starting with stakes in agriculture and a few other projects, the foundation's operations expanded into almost all significant sectors of the economy, resulting in a balance sheet of Rs.17.45 billion (US$300.86 million) by the end of the financial year 2001. The foundation's 31 projects in agriculture, manufacturing and the service sector, all three major sectors of the economy, are described as fully owned projects and registered companies. AWT also has stakes in the financial and non-financial sectors.

In 1996 the company expanded into the cement and pharmaceuticals sectors, with two fully owned projects, the Nizampur Cement Project (AWNCP) near Rawalpindi and a pharmaceuticals factory near Lahore. Subsequently, in 1997, it acquired another cement unit near Rawalpindi, Askari Cement Ltd (ACL). This cement factory was one of those sold by the government as part of its privatization policy. The AWT raised loans to purchase and set up these industrial units. In 1997, it further invested in a Line II at AWNCP, which until then had been losing money. This additional cement production facility was meant to bolster the overall production capacity of the unit. These investments, amounting to approximately Rs.8 billion (US$137.93 million), were financed through international loans.

As a result, the AWT faced its worst liquidity shortfall in 1996. After it had made these investments, 39 per cent of its cash outflows each year were required to finance its debt repayment.

Actually, the company used two methods for raising additional debt financing. The financing requirements were initially met by term finance certificate (TFC) financing arrangements of US$100 million, which were subsequently converted into a rupee-syndicated debt financing facility by the National Bank of Pakistan (NBP). Under this arrangement, a loan in US dollars was raised from the international market and an arrangement for its return was made through seeking a financial guarantee or raising another loan in rupees through the national bank. Additional financing was obtained from financial institutions to finance these investments. As a result, the AWT's long-term debt rose from Rs.3.12 billion (US$53.79 million) in 1997 to Rs.12.9 billion (US$222.41 million) in 1998.

Despite the fact that the AWT gets financial help from the army GHQ and the government, its financial consultants, KPMG, did not find its performance impressive. By the end of the calendar year 2001, it had accumulated a huge deficit of Rs.15 billion (US$258.62 million). A newspaper report indicates that these dire straits were caused by poor management.[1] By 2001, the state of affairs at the AWT had deteriorated to the extent that it was forced to ask the government for Rs.5.4 billion (US$93.10 million) to ensure its financial survival.

This was not the first time the company had sought the government's help. The AWT asked for a financial bail-out worth Rs.5 billion (US$86.21 million) in 1997, and was given relief worth Rs.2 billion (US$34.48 million) from the national exchequer by the Sharif government on the understanding between the political government and the army's high command that it would change its management and improve its working. Even in 1997, the foundation was a white elephant which, as the then commerce minister, Ishaq Dar, claimed, 'could not pay its old liabilities'.[2] A bail-out was once again requested from the Sharif regime in February 1999. The Ministry of Finance referred the matter to the parliament's Cabinet Committee of Economic Affairs (ECC), with the request that it approve a guarantee of Rs.2.5 billion (US$43.10 million) which would be used to redeem the earlier guarantee of Rs.4 billion (US$68.96 million). The AWT had sought a fresh loan to pay off part of the earlier financial liability. A fresh financial guarantee was sought from the government despite the fact that the AWF was declared to be a private-sector entity which could not get financial aid from the government, which was not responsible for its debt repayment.

Like most private-sector companies or individual loan defaulters, the AWF borrowed from local national and private banks, and the international financial market. Approximately, Rs.6.5 billion (US$112.06 million) out of the total Rs.15 billion (US$258.62 million) deficit was borrowed from the NBP, Allied Bank Ltd (ABL) and ABN-Amro, against official guarantees. In addition, AWT owed Rs.1.5 billion (US$25.86 million) to a foreign financial company, Laith Ltd, which had filed a recovery suit against it in the United Kingdom.[3]

There are two plausible explanations for the civilian government's decision to provide the financial bail-out. First, the financial guarantees were meant to improve relations between the Sharif government and the army. Given the political track record of civilian governments in the 1990s, which only served for an average duration of two years, the Sharif regime wanted to get the military behind it, since it was one of the important pillars of political power in the country. Since 1977, the army had emerged as a political force to be reckoned with. According to Dar, Sharif's commerce minister, General Musharraf, who was then the army chief, called him to seek help for the AWT in 1998.[4] The government was keen not to overly antagonize the military. Second, the case for bailing out AWT was presented to the government as an issue of protecting the investment of thousands of ex-service employees and their dependants. The potential victims of non-action by the government were widows and orphans. This was effective in blackmailing the government into financing the inefficiencies of the AWT.

Despite the AWT's obvious inefficiencies, the Ministry of Finance agreed to provide conditional help to the company. In return it required it to:

- replace ex-service personnel with professional managers
- sell its commercial plazas by the end of 1999 and June 2000

- accept closer monitoring of its activities by the Ministry of Finance
- seek clearance for its future ventures from the Ministry of Finance.

Reports also indicate that the top management of the AWT met officials from the Ministry in 1999 and agreed on the following steps:

- sell its two commercial plazas in Rawalpindi and Karachi
- sell 50 per cent of its stakes in cement manufacturing
- sell 50 per cent of its shares in the pharmaceutical plant
- lease commercial land transferred from the GHQ after undertaking some development work on the land
- enhance GHQ's existing equity of Rs.4 billion (US$68.96 million) through an injection of Rs.500 million (US$8.62 million).[5]

The financial consultants, KPMG, also advised the AWT management to sell some commercial land in Karachi which had been given to it by the army. Interestingly, neither KPMG nor the Ministry of Finance questioned the legal basis for the foundation leasing out or disposing of government land. It must be mentioned that the land controlled by the army is not its property. Rather, the federal government or one of the four provincial governments has ownership of the land, which makes the sale illegal and against the public interest. Furthermore, no private company can sell or lease government property, a misplaced prerogative enjoyed by the AWT because of its association with the army.

Post-1999, the company's financial situation remained the same. The only suggestion by KPMG that was complied with was the sale of the commercial plazas. According to the AWT's accounts closing in June 2001, the cumulative losses resulted in a negative equity of Rs.5.29 billion (US$91.21 million). It had debts of Rs.8.75 billion (US$150.86 million), mainly owed to the NBP and ABL.

In 2001 the accumulated losses of AWT crossed Rs. 8 billion (US$137.9 million), primarily for the reasons identified above. The total revenue of the AWT group of companies was less than its financial charges for 2001, of approximately Rs.2.74 billion (US$46.55 million). So despite carrying a diversified portfolio of investments, the AWT could only earn a profit of 3.84 per cent of total turnover in 2001.

It was also apparent that the second method described above for making the Rs.8 billion (US$137.93 million) investment in the AWNCP for establishing Line II had been highly questionable because the AWT had raised a loan from the financial market and shown it as equity. In this case, debt was turned to equity through a complex and dubious method of treating the funds as a bridge loan. Moreover, the AWT management also raised an equal amount from the army welfare scheme for investment in the cement project.[6] However, the cement projects had failed to become profitable largely because of the poor performance of the entire cement sector. The situation did not improve until the international community announced its plans for reconstructing Afghanistan after 9/11, increasing the international demand for cement.

According to the company's balance sheet, the AWT had invested approximately Rs.14 billion (US$241.37 million) in various projects and associated companies. However, about 93 per cent of the total investments, amounting to Rs.14 billion (US$241.37 million) were 'stuck-up' funds: funds that could not generate returns. The details of AWT's stagnant investments in 2001 are given in Table 9.1.

Because of the high cost of debt repayment, which amounted to approximately Rs.2.74 billion (US$47.24 million) for 2001, the AWT was forced to sell its commercial plaza in Rawalpindi in 2002 for about Rs.650 million (US$11.21 million). Its cement manufacturing and other projects generated around Rs.41.6 million (US$720,000), which was insufficient to meet expenses and repay its debt. By selling the plazas, the management lost a considerable favourable cash flow which they had enjoyed for the previous eight years, approximately Rs.588.5 million (US$10.15 million) on an average annual turnover of Rs.1.811 billion (US$31.22 million).

Return on assets

The three projects mentioned above were also instrumental in wiping off the company's profits. AWT's managers unwisely ventured into operations that were too competitive or demanded different kinds of expertise than the company could offer. Overall, manufacturing has done more poorly than agriculture or the service sector. Table 9.2 shows the percentage return on assets in the three sectors where the foundation has invested resources.[7]

This shows a relatively better and more efficient performance in agriculture, followed by the services sector. The growth trend in both these sectors was consistently positive. The operating efficiency in the manufacturing sector was least impressive, resulting in continuous losses that affected the overall financial condition of the AWT. The losses occurred because of both poor investment decisions and poor management. The data of return on fixed assets present a similar picture: see Table 9.3.[8]

Here, the performance of the agricultural sector is again relatively better than other areas of activity. The return of the manufacturing sector declined drastically from 54 per cent in 1996 to -25 per cent in 2001, in spite of the fact that the fixed assets are reported at their written-down values.

Table 9.1 AWT's stagnant investments, 2001

	Rs.billion	US$ million
Army Welfare Nizampur Cement Project	5.8	100
Army Welfare Pharmaceutical	3.4	58.62
Askari Cement Limited		
(non-project investment)	3.9	67.24
Total	13.1	225.86

Table 9.2 AWT's percentage return on total assets by sector

Year	1992	1993	1994	1995	1996	1997	1998	1999	2000	2001
Agriculture	31	29	30	26	22	47	33	37	56	57
Manufacturing	11	24	12	16	29	-2	-15	-9	-8	-21
Services	1	-5	1	-1	2	12	7	9	5	5

Table 9.3 AWT's percentage return on fixed assets by sector

Year	1992	1993	1994	1995	1996	1997	1998	1999	2000	2001
Agriculture	139	114	115	118	100	194	133	152	292	376
Manufacturing	21	53	34	52	54	-6	-18	-10	-9	-25
Services	4	-7	1	-2	4	18	11	14	8	7

Return on capital employed

The poor performance of the manufacturing sector can also be gauged from the comparison of return on capital employed.[9] This performance raises concerns regarding the company's solvency. The situation did not improve despite the relatively better performance of the agriculture and service sectors (see Table 9.4).

Return on equity

The return on equity[10] for the agricultural sector was also better than the other two sectors. The service sector was trailing behind, but doing better than manufacturing. The cumulative losses of the manufacturing sector absorbed most of the stakeholders' investment capital (see Table 9.5).

A comparison between the manufacturing and financial sectors shows similar results. Table 9.6 indicates a relatively better performance for associate ventures such as the Askari Commercial Bank, Askari General Insurance and Askari Leasing. Projects such as cement, which has been discussed at length, and Mobil-Askari Lubricants indicate poor investment decisions. Askari Leasing's return on equity was equally unimpressive.

Table 9.4 AWT's percentage return on capital employed by sector

Year	1992	1993	1994	1995	1996	1997	1998	1999	2000	2001
Agriculture	34	34	32	28	24	53	35	46	61	60
Manufacturing	20	42	19	22	34	-2	-18	-10	-9	-23
Services	1	-6	1	-1	2	15	9	11	8	7

Table 9.5 AWT's percentage return on equity by sector

Year	1992	1993	1994	1995	1996	1997	1998	1999	2000	2001
Agriculture	36	36	33	29	24	55	57	94	185	174
Manufacturing	20	44	90	23	48	−3	−27	−13	−10	−23
Services	2	−6	1	−2	6	39	30	41	20	16

Keeping in view the poor performance of the manufacturing sector, KPMG advised the company to carry out a major overhaul of this area of activity, with drastic changes in management, infrastructure and financial arrangements. However, there is no evidence of any major changes in the functioning of the poor-performing projects in 2001 (see Table 9.7), which implies that the AWT did not adhere to the advice of its financial consultants.

Table 9.7 lists the comparative performance of AWT's fully owned projects. Besides manufacturing, which is clearly not its strength, the foundation also lost money in ventures such as its travel agency, commercial markets, commercial enterprises and real estate. The maximum profit, on the other hand, was generated in real estate and agriculture. Real estate, in any case, is one of the major profit-earning sectors in the country, especially after 9/11. This is because of the flow of capital from expatriate Pakistanis, and from other Muslim states. It is not even surprising to see smaller ventures like the Blue Lagoon restaurant making money. Located near the GHQ in Rawalpindi, the restaurant gets a lot of business from the army. Similarly, the hosiery and woollen mill projects depend on contracts from the armed forces.

Surprisingly, the AWT was unable to take advantage of its financial backing from the army GHQ and its military connections to improve its commercial position. Although the company's management and members of the military fraternity shirk from admitting that these companies receive any undeserved perks, the reality proves otherwise. As was discussed earlier, the AWT received financial bail-outs from the government to cover its poor investment decisions. This and the other military foundations pose a financial burden on the public sector, a fact that is usually hidden.

Over the years, the line between the public and private-sector spending has grown fuzzy because of the lack of transparency and accountability. There are disturbing reports of the military's commercial subsidiaries using state resources. For instance, AWT's Askari Aviation has used resources of the Army Aviation wing, like helicopters and pilots, to meet demand.[11] This was confirmed by Askari Aviation's director, Brig. (rtd) Bashir Baaz. The director boasted about his ability to deploy the army's helicopters in times of greater demand by clients.[12] The auditor-general's special report for the financial year 2001–02 discussed the manner in which Askari Aviation not only used the service's helicopters, which were public property, but also did not honour its contractual obligation to deposit Rs.21.463 million (US$.37

Table 9.6 Comparison of the performance of AWT subsidiaries and associates

	% of holding Rs.	Investment	Paid-up capital Rs.000	Profit and loss Rs.000	Dividend Rs.000	Return on invest't %	Dividend payout %	Return on equity %
Askari Commercial Bank Ltd								
1999	44	511,015	986,226	282,446	172,590	15	61	29
2000	44	830,829	986,226	315,588	147,934	12	47	32
2001	44	530,829	1,035,537	550,051	207,107	17	38	53
Askari General Insurance Co. Ltd								
1999	25	12,500	57,500	10,172	-	0	0	18
2000	25	12,500	66,125	13,119	-	0	0	20
2001	25	12,500	76,044	13,588	11,407	23	84	18
Askari Leasing Ltd								
1999	54	125,887	240,000	62,401	48,000	21	77	26
2000	54	183,874	324,000	91,454	64,800	19	71	28
2001	54	183,874	324,000	64,483	-	0	0	20
Askari Cement Ltd								
1999	90	3,176,921	1,600,987	(611,149)	-	0	0	-38
2000	90	3,685,710	1,600,987	(153,374)	-	0	0	-10
2001	90	3,982,950	1,600,987	(218,409)	-	0	0	-14
Mobil Askari Lubricants Ltd								
2000	30	137,644	454,830	(52,078)	-	0	0	-11
2001	30	136,449	454,830	(55,271)	-	0	0	-12

Table 9.7 Profit/loss of AWT projects, 2001

Project	Rs. million	US$ million
Army Welfare sugar mills (Badin)	-31.1	-.536
Army Welfare cement (Nizampur)	-582.341	-10.04
Army Welfare shoe project	-1.805	-31.12
Army Welfare woollen mills (Lahore)	1.472	25.38
Army Welfare hosiery project	0.314	.0054
Army Welfare rice mills (Lahore)	0.166	.003
Army stud farm (Probynabad)	22.435	.387
Army stud farm (Boyle Gunj)	26.454	.456
Army farm (Rakhbaikunth)	11.121	.192
Army farm (Khoski)	0.217	.004
Real estate (Lahore)	0.166	.003
Real estate (Rawalpindi)	39.662	.684
Real estate (Karachi)	25.036	.432
Real estate (Peshawar)	-1.178	-.02
AWT plaza (Rawalpindi)	17.219	.296
Blue Lagoon (Rawalpindi)	11.696	.202
Al-Ghazi Travel	1.083	.0186
Services Travel (Rawalpindi)	-1.005	-.017
Liaison Office (Karachi)	-4.783	-.082
Liaison Office (Lahore)	-1.364	-.24
Askari Pharmaceuticals	-529.591	-9.131
AWT Commercial market project	-1.364	-.024
Askari commercial enterprises	-2.921	-.05

million) of sales proceeds, fuel charges and other expenses it owed to the government for using army helicopters for commercial purposes.[13]

The AWT's financial conditions are far more problematic than those of the other military foundations and companies, and these have not improved despite the claim made by some generals that the military-controlled companies are far more efficient than their civilian counterparts. Most of the senior officers do not consider that the fact the businesses are run by military personnel, who have no prior experience of the private sector, is the reason behind the AWT's financial losses. Maj.-General Jamsheed Ayaz Khan, for instance, claimed that the operations cannot go wrong because 'while the companies' top management is military, it is mainly the civilian experts that are responsible for operational planning and control'.[14] This claim, however, is not borne out by the accounts of the AWT – or of the FF, which is evaluated in the next section.

FAUJI FOUNDATION

The FF has been considered a better performer than the AWT or the other two foundations. Although this segment tries to analyse the financial health of the FF, the evaluation is not as detailed as that of the AWT because of a dearth of data. Established in 1953/54 with Rs.18 million (US$310,000) in capital, the FF currently has capital of Rs.43.32 billion (US$746.89 million). However, a profit and loss statement for 12 out of the foundation's total of 24 projects shows mixed results (see Table 9.8).

Clearly, four of these twelve projects were not making money in 2001. All three of the company's sugar manufacturing plants showed a loss, totalling Rs.58.424 million (US$1.007 million). Another newspaper report indicated that the three sugar mills and the sugar-cane experimental and seed multiplication farm were running an annual loss of Rs.1 billion (US$17.24 million).[15] This explains why the management decided to dispose of the sugar mill at Khoski, Sindh.

Two issues are worth attention as far as the performance of FF's sugar production units is concerned. The first relates to the efficiency of the three manufacturing units. The fact that these units were running at a loss in a sugar-cane growing and sugar manufacturing area indicates poor management. The inefficiency of the company's sugar mills was admitted by one of the retired employees of the Fauji Foundation. According to Brig. (rtd) Sher Khan, who had served as director technical (sugar) at the FF headquarters for five years, the units lost money because of poor standards of accountability, which led the management to engage in corruption and thus compromise the company's interests. He further described the behaviour of the mills' top bosses as public sector-like and insensitive to the larger interests of the organization.[16] It must be noted that most public-sector industrial or business organizations in Pakistan are known for inefficiency and corruption. Khan also added that he had occasionally raised the issue with the FF bosses but with no consequences.

Table 9.8 Profit/loss of Fauji Foundation projects, 2001

Project	Rs. million	US$ million
Fauji Sugar Mills (Tando Mohammad Khan)	(Loss)	
Fauji Sugar Mills (Khoski)	(Loss)	
Fauji Sugar Mills (Sangla Hill)	(Loss)	
Net loss	*-58.424*	*-1.007*
Fauji Sugarcane Experimental and Seed Multiplication Farm	10.258	0.177
Fauji Cereals	9.226	0.159
Fauji Corn Complex	22.78	0.393
Fauji Polypropylene Products	-16.273	-0.281
Foundation Gas	143.071	2.467
Fauji Securities Services	7.634	0.132
FF Institute of Management and Computer Sciences	2.645	0.045
NIC Project	11.865	0.205
Foundation Medical College	3.992	0.069

Second, there is the tricky matter of accountability in the sale of the sugar mill at Khoski. In early 2005, this mill was sold for Rs.300 million (US$5.172 million) despite a higher bid having been received of Rs.387 million (US$6.672 million). The Senate's Parliamentary Committee for Defence questioned the sale, as the unit was sold at an undervalued price. The parliamentary secretary for defence, Tanveer Hussain, admitted the sale at a lower price. Despite this confession the head of the FF, Lt.-General (rtd) Syed Mohammad Amjad, refused to appear before the parliamentary committee. Instead, he adopted a confrontational path by putting advertisements in national dailies, dismissing allegations of any financial mismanagement. This was clearly a breach of the privilege of the parliamentary committee. In fact, during an interview, Amjad claimed that 'the foundation has shown a growth of 50 per cent. Show me one more organization that has progressed so much.'[17]

Despite this lack of compliance to the parliament, the MoD refused to compel Amjad to appear before the committee.[18] The serving generals are never keen to hold 'one of their own kind' accountable, especially Amjad, who had thus far enjoyed the reputation among his peers of being a 'clean' general. He and his organization had both been considered above board.

I conducted four interviews with Amjad during the course of this research, and he seemed to me sadly burdened by a sense of self-righteousness, which led him to criticize all institutions except the armed forces. He even challenged the right of Pakistan's political and civil societies to question the military. According to him, 'no one has the moral authority to question the military or run the country. Are the politicians trained for their job?'[19]

The fact is that the elected representatives do not have the power to hold retired military officers accountable, because of the weakness of political institutions and the ineptness of the political leadership. Despite Amjad's over-confidence, it is impossible to ignore the blatant fact that the FF's manufacturing unit was under-sold and that there were issues of governance regarding the management of this and other FF sugar mills. A former FF employee, Sher Khan, for instance claimed that one of the other FF sugar mills at Tando Mohammad Khan, which was also losing money, had been upgraded by increasing its production capacity to 4,000 tonnes in the early 1990s at huge expense. However, the venture had large costs, was troublesome, and did not reap the desired financial benefits.[20]

Other FF projects, such as the Fauji Kabirwala power company in the Punjab, also encountered problems, as are obvious from its debt to equity ratio for five years (see Table 9.9).[21]

In 1998 the debt-to-equity ratio was 2.96, which is an alarming situation and indicates unsatisfactory performance. This ratio became worse in the following three years, but improved slightly in 2002 when it reached 2.21. Similarly, the net profit to total assets ratio given in Table 9.10 indicates a low return on investment. The situation deteriorated in the three years from 2000 to 2002. A calculation of the 2002 ratio of the project shows that it was not generating sufficient profit to even pay off its short-term liabilities.[22]

As a result, the current liabilities of the FF during the period from 1998 to 2000, as given in Table 9.11, were higher than its current assets. This also had a negative impact on its profit and loss statement. Although the situation seems to have improved slightly since 2001, the FF's assets-to-liabilities ratio did not improve substantially. In 2002, it had the capacity to pay Rs.1.45 (US$.025) for every rupee of liability.

In 2001, the cement factory was also reported to be running at an annual loss of Rs.200 million (US$3.45 million).[23] The financial position of the cement factory could be attributed to the general slump in the cement market, which has led to losses for other manufacturers as well. The reason for reporting this particular loss is basically to highlight the fact that contrary to the general impression given by the FF's management that the foundation is a high performer, it faces financial problems as a result of poor decisions and, at times, market conditions.

The Fauji Foundation's mainstay, however, is its fertilizer manufacturing plants. Since the FF was one of the first companies to enter the fertilizer

Table 9.9 Debt-to-equity ratio, Fauji Kabirwala power company

Year	Total debts Rs.	Total equity Rs.	Ratio
1998	4,630,339,647	1,566,744,540	2.96
1999	6,152,471,538	1,788,950,150	3.44
2000	6,721,437,644	1,818,108,451	3.70
2001	8,186,516,809	2,635,409,004	3.11
2002	6,962,321,872	3,146,791,902	2.21

Table 9.10 Net profit as a percentage of total assets for FF projects

Year	Net profit Rs.	Total assets Rs.	Percentage profit/assets
2000	29,158,301	8,539,546,095	0.34
2001	81,730,053	10,821,925,813	0.76
2002	95,682,043	10,556,351,312	0.91

Table 9.11 Current ratio of liabilities to assets for FF projects

Year	Current assets Rs.	Current liabilities Rs.	Ratio
1998	280,760,097	1,130,271,414	0.2484006
1999	146,549,978	1,180,486,900	0.124143672
2000	926,543,679	1,154,255,411	0.802719805
2001	2,344,497,260	1,813,138,195	1.293060433
2002	2,797,939,792	1,923,531,921	1.454584539

market and has sufficient clout to manipulate the market, it has emerged as the biggest player in the field, with a share of 60 per cent of the Pakistani fertilizer market.[24] This huge market share allows the FF to manipulate fertilizer supply and prices. Its management, however, has been unable to capitalize on this advantage because of poor investment decisions. For instance, the diversion of Rs.1 billion of the Fauji Fertilizer Company's (FFC's) equity to finance the troublesome Fauji-Jordan Fertilizer Company (FJFC) wiped out the FF's overall profits. The FFC, it must be noted, is the key profit-earner for the company.

Considering the poor performance of FJFC, financial analyst Farrukh Saleem considers it was not a good decision to use the FFC equity to heavily subsidize this problematic operation.[25] The FJFC, which is a joint venture of FFC (30 per cent), the FF (10 per cent), Jordan Phosphate Mines Co. (10.36 per cent), Pak-Kuwait Investment Co. (6.33 per cent), foreign private placement (24.72 per cent), local private placement (4.92 per cent), General Public & National Investment Trust (8.58 per cent) and Commonwealth Development Corp. (5.09 per cent), secured four foreign currency loans. This comprised US$30 million from the Canadian Export Development Corp., US$53 million from Kreditanstalt fur Wiederaufabau of Germany, US$57 million from a consortium of French banks and a US$40 million facility from the Export-Import Bank of the United States.[26] The money was used to purchase a second-hand ammonia plant from the United States, worth US$370 million. This did not turn out to be a wise investment. In 2001, FJFC's stock fell by 21.1 per cent within 13 weeks.[27] Table 9.12 shows the poor operating profit margin of the unit for the financial year 2001–02. The upward trend in the profit margin for 2002 can not be considered a major improvement.

Given this performance, the army chief, Pervez Musharraf, asked FF to improve the profitability of several projects and units which were operating below par.[28] This advice was given along with financial help from the government. The government's economic survey shows that since 2003 the FF was consistently subsidized to the tune of over Rs.1 billion (US$17.24 million) annually. No other private-sector organization has been provided with help in the form of loans and financial guarantees like the FF.[29]

The FF's top boss did not confess to any mismanagement or poor

Table 9.12 Fauji-Jordan Fertilizer Company operating profit margin

Year	Net operating income Rs. 000	Net sales Rs.000	Operating profit margin
2000	-970,632	6,068,778	-0.159939
2001	-661,985	6,246,229	-0.105982
2002	450,997	3,964,326	0.1137639

Source: FJFC Annual Accounts, 2000, 2001 and 2002.

performance of the company's projects despite the clear evidence of the financial record. General Amjad in fact defended the military's decision to establish the business ventures, which in his opinion were doing better than most public-sector ventures and even some private-sector businesses. He also ruled out the possibility of the foundations using their connection with the military to gain business opportunities, or imposing a financial burden on the government. During several discussions on the issue of military's internal economy, the chairman of the FF was not inclined to consider the FJFC issue, or the performance of the AWT. Despite that the AWT is generally known as a bad performer, the general tried to defend FF's sister concern in the same breath as his own organization. Amjad, like other beneficiaries of military's commercialism, is not willing to consider the possibility that these commercial ventures have a negative outcome, since he views them from the prism of the armed forces' contribution to development.

SHAHEEN FOUNDATION

There is very little information available on the smaller companies such as those of the SF and the BF. The lack of information is mainly because most of the business operations of the SF and the BF are not listed on the stock exchange. Therefore this analysis is restricted to SF's airline venture, the only project about which some information is available in the public domain.

According to the airline's balance sheet, Shaheen Air International (SAI) lost about Rs.60 million (US$1.034 million) from December 1999 to May 2000. This was in addition to Rs.70 million (US$1.207 million) it owed the Civil Aviation Authority for services provided during this period. The situation in the initial days of the airline's operations during the early 1990s was even worse. An airline industry expert, Saleem Altaf, was of the view that SAI was losing money because it provided such highly discounted fares to retired and serving military officers. The discounted fares added to the high operational costs of the airline, which also had to pay for the 'wet lease' of its three aircraft. (This involves hiring the aircraft along with its crew.) Such a limited number of aircraft does not allow an airline to recover its sunk costs, invested in fixed assets and operations in general. In SAI's case, it ran into the problem of increased cost and limited revenue. The discount facility mentioned above ate into its revenue-generation capacity.

The airline lost out because of its poor business sense. Its operational costs had increased for the reasons mentioned earlier. The management continued to undertake capital investment without a proportional increase in revenue. The airline had acquired six aircraft by the time it stopped operations in 2004. Despite the perception that airforce officers could run an airline, the SF's management could not sustain the venture. SAI was sold to private entrepreneurs Khalid Sehbai and Pervez Ali Khan, along with the airline's financial liabilities of Rs.1.5 billion (US$25.86 million). Reportedly, they paid Rs.30 million (US$517,000) on 8 April 2004 as part of the agreed price of Rs.600 million (US$10.34 million).[30]

The airline had to be sold because it was in dire straits despite the fact that it constantly used public resources without compensating the government. The special audit report of the PAF bases at Peshawar, Kohat, Mianwali and Rafiqui (Karachi) for the financial year 2001/02 mentions that the airline was unable to pay Rs.8.114 million (US$.139 million) for the period 2001/02 in parking charges. The payment was deferred since SAI pleaded that being an infant airline it could not afford these charges.[31] The auditors expressed astonishment that the airline was incurring losses despite the indirect and unauthorized input by the PAF. Similarly, Shaheen Airport Services (which is considered a lucrative venture) did not pay rent amounting to Rs.5.928 million (US$102,000) for official buildings it occupied for its business operations.[32]

RESOURCE PILFERAGE

The SAI's misuse of official resources is not the only financial burden. Over many years past the state seems to have lost money as a result of the military's appropriation of urban and rural land for distribution amongst military personnel. As was argued in Chapter 7, the senior generals justified their real estate appropriation on the basis of colonial traditions and the welfare of military personnel. While agricultural land was distributed among ordinary soldiers as well, urban property was reserved for the officer cadre. This redistribution of land has turned the military into one of the dominant players in the real estate business. The land acquisition provides the senior officers, in particular, with the ability to capitalize on their authority to generate money for personal affluence. The generals use the power of the armed forces to acquire land at little or no personal cost.

The trend in land acquisition seems to have increased proportionately to the political influence of the armed forces, their intervention in governance (during both direct military and civilian rule), and the weakness of the government. The military's stake in real estate is worth billions of dollars. The defence establishment's interests in land derive from two kinds of operation: appropriation of land for individual members, and conversion of state land from defence to commercial purposes, with the military retaining the rent proceeds without any accountability. As was explained in Chapter 7, because it has flouted legal procedures, rules and regulations in order to distribute privileges for personnel on the basis of influence, the entire concept of the land distribution is highly kleptocratic. The state could have sold or leased out the land itself, to generate funds for its own use or for the larger benefit of the public.

The conversion of state land from defence to commercial purposes has in fact increased during the Musharraf regime. The mushrooming of commercial markets and shopping plazas on military land is noticeable. Cantonment boards increasingly advertise calls for expression of interest by potential businessmen to build or establish markets. This misuse of state land has been pointed out in several audit reports. For instance, Audit Report 182 pointed out the loss of Rs.15.094 million (US$260,000) as a result of the non-payment of rent of government buildings and shops directly into the government's treasury. These shops were constructed on A-1 land that under the specific CLAR 1937 Rules is primarily meant for military's operational use, and cannot legally be converted for use for any other purpose.[33]

The special Audit Report 187 on the accounts of the cantonment boards of Clifton (Karachi), Walton (Lahore), Sialkot and Gujranwala pointed out a loss of Rs.1,006.083 million (US$17.35 million) as a result of the illegal conversion of military residential land for commercial use, and another Rs.129.700 million (US$2.24 million) because of the commercialization of land originally meant for the army's operational use.[34] The Military Land Manual forbids the use of military land for any purpose other than the defence force's operations.

The values in the audit reports of land lost to commercialization by the military are conservative estimates, and not necessarily the market value of the land or buildings. There is no available record of the money received as rent by the army corps or the air force bases, because of the lack of accountability and transparency. Although it is claimed that the money is spent on welfare, there is hardly any information regarding the expenditure. It is also worth mentioning that it is difficult to calculate the pilferage of resources from the lease of government land or buildings. Since the military is spread all over the country, it is extremely hard to ascertain the extent of the loss of revenue to the state through such forced appropriation.

FRONTIER WORKS ORGANIZATION

There is also evidence of inefficiency in the FWO. According to Audit Report 179, the accounts of the organization for the financial year 1999/2000 showed a deficit of Rs.4076.868 million (US$70.29 million). The organization's receipts for the financial year were Rs.4191.365 million (US$72.26 million) and the expenditure Rs.5171.391 million (US$89.16 million). The difference of Rs.980.026 million (US$16.897 million) represents deficit expenditure that was borne by the state. The audit report further commented that the deficit expenditure demonstrated that the organization's operations were not financially viable, or that the FWO had not managed to receive payments from its clients: that is, government departments.[35]

The details of FWO's deficit spending challenge the claim made by military officers regarding the efficiency of organizations run by the armed forces. Moreover, the fact that the government was responsible for financing the organization's deficit expenditure negates the claim made by the former army chief, General (rtd) Mirza Aslam Beg, that 'NLC and FWO are not military organizations'.[36] Beg's claim, however, was motivated more by the sense that professional militaries do not engage in commercial ventures or perform non-military roles. In fact, most of the senior officers interviewed for this book showed their discomfort in recognizing the army's links with the FWO, NLC and the welfare foundations. These people were also uncomfortable in conceding the fact that these organizations were inefficient, a fact borne out by the data presented in this chapter.

ECONOMIC OPPORTUNITY COST

The data regarding the performance of some of the welfare foundations is largely hidden from public. The lack of availability of information in the public realm helps the military echelons comfortably insist on the efficiency of the armed forces and the military fraternity. Moreover, hiding facts helps present the argument that the armed forces play a major role in economic development. Since the country's birth in 1947, the military and its clients have argued in favour of the defence establishment as an agent of development.[37] Authors such as Raymond Moore have referred to the welfare foundations in Pakistan as a contribution to socioeconomic development. This argument conforms to the thesis presented by western writers such as Huntington and Stepan regarding the military's development role. Huntington in particular emphasizes the development perspective. While eulogizing military general-rulers such as Kemal Ataturk, Gemal Abdul Nasser and Ayub Khan, Huntington was of the opinion that 'The military reformer ... is, for instance, notably more successful at promoting social-economic changes than at organizing the participation of new groups in the political system.'[38] Authors such as Janowitz see the military officer in these rather traditional societies in developing countries as more western in outlook, and a socioeconomic reformer.[39] Therefore, military expenditure or any form of defence spending is not a bane, but a boon for economic progress. Greater defence spending, as part of an increase in government expenditure, is considered to bolster the economy in the short to medium term.

Some Pakistani analysts, especially those categorized as propagandists and those who have partnered with the establishment, build on this notion and present a case for the military's control of politics and society in preference to civilian rule. For instance Ishrat Hussain, who served as governor of the State Bank during the Musharraf regime, talked about military regimes contributing more to economic progress than unstable political regimes in Pakistan. According to Hussain, military governments brought macroeconomic stability to the country as opposed to civilian governments that could not bring economic stability.[40]

Intriguingly, Hussain's perception of the military seems to have undergone a dramatic shift since he wrote his book, *Pakistan: The economy of an elitist state*, in which he admonished military regimes for colluding with other elite groups to monopolize the state's resources. Talking about the macroeconomic stability brought by the two military regimes of Ayub Khan and Zia ul Haq, he pointed out the inequitable distribution of wealth and resources as a problem that lay at the heart of Pakistan's economic instability. Hussain appears to have completely abandoned his earlier standpoint, and criticism of the policies of military dictators like Ayub Khan whom he found extremely monopolistic and opposed to liberalizing the economy.[41] He claimed that this shift in thinking occurred after he had a chance to closely observe Musharraf's military regime, which he joined in 2000. An insight into the military's financial affairs dispossessed him of the notions that the armed forces were hurting the economy, or that the military-business complex had negative costs.[42]

Hussain corroborated his argument with a table prepared from figures provided by the Karachi Stock Exchange (reproduced here as Table 9.13). According to this, the combined assets of all military-owned and related companies are only 3.60 per cent of the total assets of listed non-financial companies.[43]

There are, however, four observations regarding the data given in this table. First, the data presented in the table is based on the available figures of military companies registered with the stock exchange and the Securities and Exchange Commission of Pakistan (SECP). It is important to point out that there are only nine military-owned companies registered with these two organizations. Therefore, the data is not complete and does not give details of many military-owned projects. Second, the 3.60 per cent figure does not include the investment of military foundation capital in other businesses, a majority of which are not even listed. According to one senior source in the SECP, the foundations have investments in around 718 companies. A true picture would be based on adding up of the assets of all these companies. Third, Hussain's assessment does not mention the defence establishment's investment in real estate, which is one of the main profit earners for the institution and its subsidiaries. Adding up all components of military's financial stakes would bloat the figure to around 10 per cent control of private-sector assets, as was claimed by one source. A recalculation would be based on the assets of the small and medium-sized enterprises, the subsidiaries and individual members' stakes. This figure makes the armed forces a serious contender in the market and the economy at large. In any case, Hussain did not mention the opportunity cost of Milbus,

Table 9.13 Assets of military-owned and related companies, 2002

Non-financial	
Total assets of non-financial listed companies (Rs. billion)	1,069.97
Assets of military-owned and related companies (Rs. billion)	59.19
Share of military companies in total assets	5.53%
Financial	
Total assets of financial listed companies (Rs. billion)	2,907.16
Assets of military-owned and related companies (Rs. billion)	84.06
Share of military companies in total assets	3%
All sectors	
Total assets of financial listed companies (Rs. billion)	3,977.13
Assets of military-owned and related companies (Rs. billion)	143.25
Share of military companies in total assets	3.60%

Source: Hussain, 2004.

an issue that will be discussed at length in this section. Fourth, the value assessment done by Hussain is based on a formula whereby liabilities are deducted to calculate the existing net worth of the few companies regis- tered with the Karachi Stock Exchange. Since the liabilities of some these ventures are high, it does not give an accurate picture of the net worth of Milbus.

Ishrat Hussain's *volte face* perhaps demonstrates the comfort tech- nocrats feel towards military regimes and vice versa. Non-political players find the ability of bureaucratic-authoritarian governments to implement unpopular agendas impressive. Talking about the linkages between civil and military bureaucrats and technocrats, O'Donnell asserts that:

> Whatever the social sector in which they operate, the incumbents of technocratic roles share many important characteristics. Their role-models, and through them their basic expectations about the 'proper' state of the social context, originate in the same societies. Their training stresses a 'technical' problem-solving approach. Emotional issues are nonsense; the ambiguities of bargaining and politics are hindrances to 'rational' solutions; and conflict is by definition 'dysfunctional.' Their underlying 'maps' of social reality are similar. That which is 'efficient' is good, and efficient outcomes are those that can be straightforwardly measured.[46]

The military bureaucracy is, indeed, an efficient short-term troubleshooter. Once in power, military bureaucracies anywhere in the world tend to bring a superficial cohesion, which is often more than political regimes do in such fragmented societies. In fact, this observation has been made about other regions and military regimes as well. For example, Alfred Stepan's study of the Brazilian military highlights the institution's outward image as an inte- grator.[47] This nationalism is directed towards reducing sources of internal and external threat. Since the military sees economic and social instability as threatening a nation, it is less scrupulous in implementing polices to attain progress in both these areas. However, better financial or macroeco- nomic performance is not the only criterion for judging the involvement of the military in politics or in economic management.

The fact is that the military's direct involvement in economic develop- ment through its business complex has an opportunity cost, and creates market distortions. Milbus exacerbates cartelization in the corporate sector. The distortion is created by the military's ability to pump funds into its poorly performing ventures and to obtain disproportionate opportunities for its businesses and those of its individual members.

This behaviour has led to the creation of monopoly-like situations in a number of areas. Certain activities such as cargo transportation, road construction, and fertilizer and cereal manufacture are dominated by the military. Those sympathetic to the military and its financial autonomy view the fact that the military does not monopolize all areas of commercial activ- ity as evidence of fair competition. It is believed that the military-controlled companies get contracts as a result of their better discipline and 'cleaner' operations. However, the military does not have to create a monopoly in all sectors. The organization's involvement in entrepreneurial activities gives it a certain advantage over others, especially in areas involving huge capital expenditure which private business groups cannot afford. The military's presence as a commercial player results in creating a monopoly in specific areas, as can be seen in the case of the NLC and FWO, which have a greater capacity to muster human, financial and other resources, enabling them to dominate the cargo transportation and road construction industries.

The NLC even took business from Pakistan Railways (PR), which was once the major cargo transporter in the country. The PR officials are bitter about the situation because the railway was deprived of its monopoly of cargo transport, which is considered the main earner for any railway company. In this case, the business was moved away from one public sector concern to another (the NLC and FWO are part of the defence establishment but are given the task of selling services to the government just like any private sector firm). More importantly, instead of improving PR's management and overall conditions the army raised a parallel public sector organization.

In addition, the military's monopoly over specific activities encourages monopoly control by other players as well. The military, as one of the dominant classes in the country, manipulates national resources and encourages crony capitalism. This makes the military's behaviour similar to other dominant classes in the country which also serve their own interests of power and capital accumulation. Prominent political and private-sector players are encouraged to monopolize resources as long as they side with those in power, including the armed forces. As a result, there is a lack of concerted effort by the entrepreneurial class to resist the military's entry into business.

There have always been some key private-sector entrepreneurs who benefited from partnering with the armed forces. Given the military's clout in governance, it made sense for big businesses, in particular, to seek an alliance with the GHQ. Understandably, the representatives of the Mansha group, which owns one of the most important private-sector banks in the country, did not object to the military's involvement in the corporate sector. According to Aftab Manzoor, president of the MCB Bank, the military's involvement in business, especially in the banking sector, did not pose any competition for his bank.[44] Similarly, Abbas Habib, president of the Bank-Al-Habib, another old and significant private bank, did not object to Milbus.[45] These two groups are among the business houses that have benefited from their association with the military or the ruling civilian regimes. The lack of objection is mainly because authoritarian regimes, including the armed forces, also bring opportunities to other dominant players.

However, others have been critical of both cronyism and military capital. Zahid Zaheer of the International Stock Exchange Karachi, and Tariq Shafee of the Crescent group of Industries, for example, are extremely critical of the military's presence in the corporate sector. Their objection is primarily that military capital constitutes a hidden cost of security, which, if included in the budget, would show a substantial increase in the defence burden. Moreover, Milbus tends to 'crowd out' private-sector investment and is unfair in terms of getting preferential access to strategic business information.

Thus, the military is tolerated as a dominant commercial player in Pakistan (and other countries as well) because this allows certain people to benefit from the same rules or lack of rules as allow the military to enter the commercial sector. The other prominent cases include Turkey and Indonesia. In Turkey, for instance, the military is one of the significant players but not the most important one. Reportedly, OYAK controls only 5 per cent of private-sector assets, which makes the military a significant actor in the market but not one with an absolute monopoly. Similarly, in Indonesia, resource exploitation is done with the help of other influential members of the political society. The Indonesian presidents Sukarno and Suharto were instrumental in institutionalizing crony capitalism, which became one of the hallmarks of their country's economy and contributed tremendously to the financial crash in 1997.

The military, it must be noted, does not intend a complete takeover of the economy. Concerned with economic progress and recognizing the fact that economic functioning is not its core role, the armed forces do not bar other players from playing a more significant role in the corporate sector or in socioeconomic development. The military presents its financial stakes as a benign contribution to its own welfare and the country's socioeconomic development. Military capital, however, creates cronyism in the absence of rules and regulations. The defence establishment becomes central to the system of patronage encouraged both by the armed forces and civilian-authoritarian regimes to perpetuate a kleptocratic redistribution of resources and opportunities. Contrary to its claim that the military supports meritocracy, senior generals in Pakistan support their clients in both business and politics.

In a military government there is greater dependence on technocrats, especially experts in commerce and economics, and on the entrepreneurial class, to earn the bulk of financial resources channelled for military modernization that can be fulfilled from national budgets. The generals prefer to create a model of controlled corporate growth. The role played by the various military regimes in Pakistan in building and rebuilding the corporate sector or bringing the commercial sector under its control bears witness to the fact that the armed forces believe in macroeconomic growth which can help buy weapons. Control is exercised through two mechanisms.

First, control over private entrepreneurs was assured by creating legal mechanisms. For instance, the activities of modern business associations, which had been largely free of government control, were regulated during Ayub's regime. The 'reorganization' scheme adopted in 1958 and given legal effect in 1961 provided the government with the authority to regulate all associations.[48] Second, government's control was further emphasized through indirect means of regulating the resource allocation and distributive process. However, successful entrepreneurs, according to Stanley Kochanek, understood how to use the allocation system to secure benefits.[49]

The Ayub regime initiated a highly kleptocratic redistributive process through using government machinery such as the Pakistan Industrial Development Cooperation (PIDC). This state institution was used for infra-structure development in the private sector. The PIDC helped build 25 industrial projects in West Pakistan from 1962–9, most of which were then transferred to financial-industrial groups.[50] Similarly, the Zia regime rein-carnated a number of business groups which were inducted into the regime-sponsored political structure. Since the 1980s, other business groups too have owed their good fortune to military and civilian government patronage. Given the absence of strong political institutions and the feudal-authoritarian character of the state and society, large private entrepreneurs have benefited from authoritarian regimes. Thus, the rise of a number of large business groups in Pakistan like Mansha and Hashwanee and can be attributed to blatant state intervention.

The authoritarian civilian governments and military regimes supported both large business and the landed-feudal class. For a civil-mili-tary-bureaucratic regime, in particular, players with larger stakes are more manageable. Allowing market forces to naturally chart the development of business and economy could result in a greater number of players, and this option is perhaps not preferred by the military or its clients. As a result, large groups tend to dominate a larger segment of resources. In 1968, for example, the top four business families of Dawood, Saigol, Adamjee and Awan controlled 70 per cent of the total assets. As was explained by Rashid Amjad in his 1974 study of the Karachi Stock Exchange, 41 industrial houses controlled 80 per cent of the private-sector assets.[51]

This situation did not change in the subsequent years despite Bhutto's nationalization policy, which aimed at disintegrating the system of elitist control of the corporate sector. In reversing Bhutto's economic policies, Zia revived the corporate culture by unravelling the industrial and business nationalization policy. Reviving the private sector through bringing back large business was seen as key to economic development. The Nawaz Sharif family, which was one of the beneficiaries of Zia's policies, took the revival of business policy further by using official mechanisms to revive the corpo-rate sector. The Privatization Commission was constituted in January 1991 under Nawaz Sharif's government to denationalize sick public-sector industrial and business units. The mechanism was used to favour key business figures.

Shahid-Ur-Rehman's book of May 1998, *Who Owns Pakistan?* talks about the government's support to the Mansha Group in assisting in its purchase of one of the larger public-sector banks, the Muslim Commercial Bank.[52] The privatization policy aimed at passing on:

the liabilities of the privatized units to the people of Pakistan and assets to the new owners. Zia, it appears in hindsight, and those who designed it [the policy], were not interested in fetching a fair price of the privatized units, but to facilitate their sale to favorites at throwaway prices'.[53]

Therefore, the privatization policy restored the situation prevalent under Ayub of big business monopolizing business resources. The committee reviewing privatization, headed by the former finance secretary, H. U. Baig, in 1993 found that 38 business houses controlled over 60 per cent (Rs.380 billion – US$6,551.72 million) of business assets. The number of prominent business families remained almost constant. While there were 42 prominent families in 1970, the figure only increased to 44 in 1997.[54]

By 2004/05, the military was added to the list of companies dominating the corporate sector. In addition, it had developed stakes in urban and rural real estate. The military's land acquisition, popularly referred to as the organization's land grab, had started during the mid-1950s. Although the distribution of agricultural land was justified on the basis of inherited British traditions, in effect the policy allowed the military fraternity to penetrate a socioeconomic activity that had belonged to the landed-feudal class. The distribution of land to military personnel was meant to neutralize the influence of major civilian land owners and to impress upon the big feudal lords the fact that the armed forces had greater influence and political clout to redistribute the land resources. However, as was discussed in Chapter 7, such an approach gradually led to the building of common interests between the military fraternity and the landed-feudal class. These shared interests then stood in the way of any revolutionary changes in land ownership in the country. Currently the senior generals use their influence, like the big landowners, to draw benefits from their agricultural property which symbolize power more than a mere source of generating capital. The relationship is driven as much by cronyism as is the relationship between the military and big business.

The concept of crony capitalism is a reminder of Fredric Lane's thesis regarding rent and tribute. As was discussed in the introduction, Lane talked about the concept of rent that entrepreneurs in Europe paid to the militaries to seek economic opportunities. In the case of the modern Milbus discussed in this book, the linkage between rent and tribute is quite intense. The armed forces are allowed to engage in profit-making because of to the economic opportunities they create for other influential groups or individuals. This argument applies to all those countries placed in the first two categories of civil–military relations discussed in Chapter 1. However, cases of Milbus that are found in states like Pakistan are qualitatively different. In such cases, the exploitation is not carried out outside the country, but within the country by its armed forces.

The majority of military personnel talk about the exceptional efficiency of military-controlled commercial ventures. The supposed effectiveness and financial viability of these organizations is propagated as a sign of the military's superior capacity to govern the state and the society. This notion, as demonstrated in this chapter, is questionable at best, and arguably only a myth. The financial track record of some of these organizations such as the

AWT and FF is not satisfactory. Given the military's influence and its ability to keep its records under cover, the public are led to believe that the military fraternity is more efficient in running commercial ventures, but this is not borne out by the facts available.

The financial inefficiency of these business ventures places a financial cost on the state. Some of the financial burden, as proven in this chapter, is borne by the state by providing financial guarantees or providing loans to the military-controlled companies. The financial aid given to these foundations is detrimental to the growth of a free-market economy. Private-sector firms do not get such generous assistance from the state as the AWT, the FF and the FWO. The linkage between the state and these companies, and its impact on the overall business environment, is not the only opportunity cost. The presence of the military in the private sector or in profit-making activities results in encouraging crony capitalism in the country. This creates a situation where the dominant classes collude with the military to benefit from the state and its resources at the risk of ignoring all those who are not part of the 'elite consensus'.

10 Milbus and the future of Pakistan

Now that we have evaluated Milbus in Pakistan, it is time to revert to the fundamental research questions with which we began. When the military echelons indulge in profit making and use the armed forces as a tool for institutional and personal economic influence, do they have an interest in withdrawing to the barracks and allowing democratic institutions to flourish? What does Milbus mean for the professional ethos of the officer cadre, which has morphed into an independent class through its domination of the state and its resources? Last but not least, how do the economic interests of the military's upper echelons impact on Pakistan's society and the country's relations with its neighbours and the rest of the world?

RECAPPING MILBUS

Milbus, as was stated in the introduction, is the name used here for a particular kind of military capital used for the personal benefit of the military fraternity, especially the officer cadre, which is neither a part of, nor recorded as part of, the defence budget. The lack of accountability, in particular, makes this type of capital illegal and questionable. Milbus is the military's internal economy, which is hidden from public view. This type of capital is found in most countries of the world. However, it is more pervasive and its consequences much more hurtful in authoritarian countries, especially those controlled by the armed forces. When militaries are not controlled by a civilian government, they tend to extend their tentacles into all segments and levels of the society and its economy.

The simple principle of electoral democracy allows other stakeholders to dominate the armed forces. In countries where electoral democracy is an established norm, the military might engage in profit making through partnerships, or in political coercion of the civil society, but political players can control the military and force it to withdraw from the economy. This was demonstrated in China, where the Communist Party ordered the military to dispose of its financial interests in the service sector. However, this control is difficult to achieve in semi-authoritarian, military-dominated political systems, where the armed forces emerge as the key player in control of the state and society. The military's power allows it to define its economic interests and exploit public and private-sector resources, a behaviour that increases the organization's appetite for power. Pakistan was selected here as a case study for understanding the intriguing linkage between the military's political clout and its economic interests.

243

MILBUS IN PAKISTAN

The Pakistan military's economic interests are a result of the defence establishment's political clout, which allowed it to push for complete autonomy from all civilian stakeholders. Its numerous commercial ventures, undertaken directly by the organization or through its four subsidiaries and individual members of the military fraternity, are an expression of the power of the armed forces compared with the civil society and democratic institutions. However, it is important to point out that these economic interests, which over the years have consolidated into an economic empire, did not precede the military's entry into politics.

Starting from the early 1950s, the military gradually encroached into politics and governance because of the relatively weak democratic institutions, and mainly because of the prominence of military security, which became the national security agenda of the state. Given the threat posed by neighbouring India, the political leadership, which did not have sufficient capacity to manage the defence sector, conceded the management of the armed forces and national security to the military. The political leadership tried to use national security as a tool to build a national consensus, which diverted greater resources and attention to the armed forces. The overemphasis on defence rather than development also complicated the relations between the centre and the four federating units. However, military security was viewed as the panacea for the country's internal and external insecurity. The politicians, who were predominantly from the ruling classes, used national security to strengthen their control over the military and to use the defence establishment to their political advantage. The problematic nature of politics created the space for the armed forces to start building and institutionalizing their economic interests, which were justified in the name of 'welfare of personnel'. Furthermore, the massive industrial projects established during the 1950s and the 1960s were presented as the military's contribution to national development.

A prominent Pakistani columnist, Khaled Ahmed, believes that the military's economic interests in Pakistan are a corollary of the country's peculiar nationalist agenda. In an answer to a question why military personnel get more perks and privileges, he said, 'we should pay the price for what we believe in. There is a paradox triggered by our nationalism which allows the military to monopolize the state's resources.'[1] The strategic-national saviour paradigm invoked by the military to justify its expanding role in the state, society and economy allows it to dominate the polity and acquire financial and other resources as it considers fit.

MILBUS AND MILITARY PROFESSIONALISM

The military's financial autonomy is rooted in its core function of providing security against external threats. The military's primary task, as defined by the constitution, relates to external security and assistance to civilian authorities at their request. However, using the strategic-national security prism, the military expanded its interests to all facets of the state and society, and established a certain ethos that helped the armed forces protect their own interests. This was obvious from a statement the air chief, Air Marshal Tanveer Mehmood Ahmed, made in August 2006, in which he emphasized the significance of the armed forces and strong national security. Speaking in the aftermath of Israel's attack on Lebanon, he said:

> The Lebanese Prime Minister was forced to cry before media because of weak defense capability of his country and no such thing would be allowed to happen to Pakistan ... living nations used to sacrifice their resources for keeping their armed forces combat ready in peace time. This sacrifice was necessary and was aimed at ensuring capability to meet any external threat in future.[2]

Should this statement be interpreted as an indication of the air marshal's inept diplomatic skills, or a warning to those who challenge the military's monopolization of the state's resources? The military justifies Milbus as part of the indirect or larger cost borne by the society for buying national security. The various commercial ventures mentioned in Chapters 5 and 6, and the massive urban and rural land acquisitions, are presented as a cost for keeping well-trained and capable armed forces. However, there is more that can be read into the air chief's public statement. According to Lt.-General (rtd) Talat Masood, 'the statement should be interpreted as a message that since the country cannot survive without its armed forces or cannot stand up to the Indian threat, it must bear all costs for keeping a strong military defence'.[3] A natural corollary of this interpretation is that the military, or those that benefit from the India-centred national security agenda, will not allow national security to be defined in any other way than as an external threat. This possibility means that the state's imagination of itself and the region around it remains captured by a sense of insecurity from India, which in turn signifies the dominance of defence over development. The prominent Pakistani historian Ayesha Jalal terms this the 'state of martial rule', in which the military plays a major role in ensuring the dominance of defence over development.

From a strategic standpoint, this imbalance has an impact on the professionalism of the officer cadre, which does not let itself explore the issue of Revolution in Military Affairs (RMA), a concept that would force them to restructure the armed forces, carry out downsizing or rightsizing, and review the military doctrine to produce a more efficient but effective military force. There are far too many interests involved for the military to be allowed to divest itself of its institutional and non-institutional economic stakes.

The impact of Milbus on the character of the military institution cannot be denied. In fact, the years of involvement of senior generals in profit-making activities had two consequences. First, the military's echelons turned into a powerful group of capitalists who had the financial prowess to exploit the financial and other resources of the state. The senior generals, as was demonstrated in Chapters 5, 6 and 7, used the organization's influence to obtain opportunities to further their financial and political power. Second, given these economic interests backed with political power, the military institution along with its serving and retired members transformed itself into a fraternity which was gradually consolidated into an independent class. There are well-defined rules and control over entry into the class, and developed institutional mechanisms to protect its political and economic interests.

The legal and constitutional changes that were introduced by the Zia regime after the second military takeover in July 1977 were meant to strengthen the military's political power and give it maximum autonomy, which would empower the military over all political stakeholders. The incorporation of Article 58(2)(b) in the 1973 Constitution served as a 'fire break' to discipline errant regimes and to protect the military core interests. The establishment of the NSC in April 2004, which is the core decision-making body, was the culmination of the drive to establish the military as an independent class that could protect its interests and negotiate political terms and conditions with other political players. The four top generals of the armed forces are members of the NSC along with nine civilians. The NSC has the power to decide on all strategic matters including the distribution of national resources.

The gradual enhancement of the military's power has had an impact on the character of military personnel. Although senior generals like to claim that the military is not involved in politics or the economy, the fact is that the organization's political intervention has given the officer cadre the sense of being beyond questioning, a perception which over the years has permeated to the lower rungs of the officer cadre as well. This has resulted in a situation where the acquisition of perks and privileges is taken for granted. The housing schemes and the agricultural land, and other facilities such as subsidized electricity, water and natural gas supply to armed forces personnel, are not taken for granted. These perks are justified as part of the necessary benefits which ensure military personnel's greater commitment to their work. Here, it is essential to narrate the story of one mid-ranking naval officer who thanked his seniors for being provided with a house on his premature retirement. The response of his senior officer was that he shouldn't feel grateful because it was his right as a naval officer.[4]

As far as professionalism in the armed forces is concerned, Milbus serves as a double-edged sword. The financial and other perks have increased competition in the armed forces, especially at the junior and mid-level ranks. These officers understand that the bulk of the rewards await them if they manage to perform well and get promoted to higher ranks. The door to greater opportunities opens once the officer reaches the rank of a brigadier (one-star), and completely opens up with promotion to the rank of a maj.-general (two-star). However, the competition does not always follow rules. In the military's system, which is completely controlled by the upper echelons, the will of the service chiefs and the senior officers is extremely important. In this environment, professionalism does not just depend on the acumen of an individual, but also on his ability to appease his seniors. This increases the risk of questionable decisions and is detrimental to the overall professional ethos. According to the PN's Captain (rtd) Irfan Shehryar:

> Majors and colonels and below are far more into professionalism and training. As long as they are not married there are lesser pressures. Once they get married reality hits. Also, when they interact with the outside world their eyes open and they begin to notice the rewards. So, brigadiers and above are at risk. They interact with higher ranks and see possible economic gains. Two-star generals and above are the ones tasting power since they are part of an elite group with access to power and greater rewards.[5]

This is not to suggest that professionalism has been completely eroded. There is still a corps of officers who only keep to professional duties. Such officers are not even spared for duties in public-sector organizations. The size of this corps of officers, however, is not known. Furthermore, the economic stakes are the highest at the senior level, which is generally responsible for providing direction to the rest of the defence establishment and to the country. A number of senior generals allegedly have used their authority to engage in financial corruption. For instance, Lt.-General (rtd) Zahid Ali Akbar is accused by the National Accountability Bureau (NAB) of indulging in corrupt practices during his stint as chairman of the national Water and Power Development Authority (WAPDA) from 1987 to 1992. Although the extent of his corruption is not known, he is accused of remitting Rs.32.4 million (US $560,000) to his foreign accounts from 1993 to 1998.[6] The naval chief, Mansoor-ul-Haq, was accused of taking bribes in the French Agosta submarines procurement deal. However, these two stories are the tip of the iceberg. There is a lot which remains unearthed because of the lack of transparency of the defence sector.

Moreover, the system of perks and privileges highlighted in this book as part of Milbus allows the military leadership to get the support of the officer cadre, especially in undertaking an action against a civilian regime. The officers, especially brigadiers and above, tend to comply with the will of the service chief out of a fear of losing financial opportunities and possibly jobs. Commenting on the power of Milbus to enforce discipline in the military, the defence analyst and businessman Ikram Shegal is of the view that 'the jump from a major-general is a major financial jump and so a brigadier who has a good chance for promotion does not want to disturb his future'.[7] While the consequent discipline serves the interests of the military leadership, it adds to the imbalance between political forces, the fragmented civil society and the armed forces, which emerge much more cohesive and stronger than the other players.

The political and financial autonomy of the military has negative implications for professionalism in strategic terms. The absolute power and authority of the military, underscored with its financial autonomy, undermines accountability in the organization. Although the organization claims

247

to have stringent accountability mechanisms, these stand in contradiction to the overall political and administrative system which does not hold the military accountable for its actions or question its expenditure. Senior generals challenge the perception that the commercial ventures have any impact on their work. For instance, the former chief of the general staff (CGS) of the Pakistan Army, Lt.-General (rtd) Farrukh Khan, was of the view that 'the military foundations are not affecting our professionalism. As CGS, I never went to the meetings of AWT or FF.'[8] However, the issue under discussion is not really time, but conflicts of interest impinging upon the military's professionalism. In the words of a retired army colonel, who was commenting on the Pakistan military's stakes in real estate, 'officers become property dealers and turned into millionaires overnight and scandals hit this section of the armed forces'.[9]

THE POLITICS OF PAKISTAN

The most serious consequence of the military's involvement in economic ventures relates to their sense of judgement regarding political control of the state. The financial autonomy of the armed forces, which is reflected through the burgeoning economic empire discussed in this book, establishes the officer cadre's interest in retaining political control of the state. Since political power nurtures greater financial benefits, the military fraternity see it as beneficial to perpetuate it. In this respect, economic and political interests are linked in a cyclic process: political power guarantees economic benefits which, in turn, motivate the officer cadre to remain powerful and to play an influential role in governance.

In the initial years after the country's independence, the military's economic stakes were limited to drawing resources from the national budget as part of the annual defence allocation. It could also be argued that the primacy of national security, and the task given to the armed forces of securing the state and its ideology, helped the military build the logic for its initial penetration into the economy and politics. The earlier governments were generous in allocating funds to the armed forces without introducing any proper control over the organization. The military perceived itself as a protector and benefactor that could ensure greater control of the state and its resources. With the passage of time, the defence establishment gradually extended its tentacles into all major segments of the economy and society.

Every military regime created greater openings for its fraternity for benefiting from the state's resources. Using the cover of its image as the state's guardian and the only capable national institution, the armed forces sought greater avenues and opportunities for profit making. Since the military takeover in October 1999, it has employed a greater number of serving and retired personnel in the government and public-sector corporations and other organizations than at any other time in the history of Pakistan. Moreover, larger contracts are awarded to the various military companies, and more opportunities provided to the military-controlled subsidiaries and individual members of the military fraternity. The increase in military employment was explained by Lt.-General Asad Durrani as a natural phenomenon linked with the army's top leadership selecting its trusted people to perform jobs. Since the emphasis was to improve conditions and make progress, Musharraf was inclined to give the jobs to people he trusted the most.

However, this approach weakened civilian institutions further and created stakes in the system that benefited armed forces personnel. In fact, as was argued in Chapter 6, the financial stakes allowed the military fraternity to evolve into an independent class which guarded its own interests along with those of its clients from other dominant classes, and institutionalized its control of the state. Therefore, the financial cost for the army of withdrawing from politics is very high. Under these circumstances, it is almost impossible for the military to totally withdraw to the barracks and allow democratic institutions to flourish.

Senior generals deny any linkage between their political and financial autonomy, and that the military's takeover of the state was driven by their economic interests. Instead, they argue that this was a result of the incapacity of civilian institutions and the political leadership. So, they claim, democracy is impossible because of the incompetent political leadership. According to Lt.-General (rtd) Syed Mohammad Amjad, 'I have asked myself the question, are we ready for democracy? Is the Muslim world ready for democracy?'[10] The general's despondency about the political situation did not appreciate the problematic structure of Pakistan's sociopolitics, which perhaps can only produce a leadership that is not qualified to push the army back into the barracks. While pointing out the flaws of the political system, Amjad did not take into account the fact that the military is a protagonist in a semi-authoritarian system in which the dominant classes are absorbed in pursuing their own interests. The issue, thus, is not about the military being a better performer than the political governments, but about all the dominant classes contributing to creating a predatory cycle of politics.

This predatory cycle creates a situation where the military and civilian leadership reinforce authoritarian rule for their own interests. As was shown in Chapters 2 and 3, successive political regimes have strengthened the army, and the logic for the military's existence, to enhance their own political clout over their political opponents. The military, unfortunately, is no different. The senior generals tend to engage in favouritism and in promoting parties and factions which strengthen the military's control. In addition, the military leaders indulge in monopolizing resources in the same fashion as politicians. The only difference, as was highlighted by the editor of the *Daily Times*, Najam Sethi, is that 'the military bends the rules and make their own rules so that no one can call it corruption'.[11]

The driving force here is not loyalty or ideology but vested interests. Therefore, it is not possible to get the military out of politics, or for the military to strengthen democratic institutions, even if some do claim to bolster democratic institutions.

To reiterate the significance of Milbus, the network of ventures and opportunities created by the military for the benefit of its senior members also reinforces the predatory cycle. These benefits are gained through exploiting the state's resources in partnership with the military's civilian clients. These people have stakes in an authoritarian system which provides them with great financial rewards. The civilian clients aid and abet the military's exploitation of public and private resources in order to gain benefits for themselves. This attitude, however, has a negative impact on the political future of the country. It feeds into the chasm between the centre and the federating units, and the various ethnic communities which remain divided because of the biased policies of the state, which is dominated by military and authoritarian political forces.

Today, the military's hegemony in Pakistan is a reality. It is important to note that this hegemony is three-dimensional: the military has penetrated the society, politics and the economy. Also, it has grabbed the intellectual discourse and the imagination of the people through promoting its own people or luring others to conform to a classical realist paradigm in analysing domestic or external issues. Unlike previous military dictatorships, Pervez Musharraf's military government is far more effective at controlling civil society institutions with minimum cost to its image. Its subtle control of the media is based on a system of rewards and selective punishment, tools used with other civil society institutions as well. Furthermore, the national security paradigm has been marketed so effectively that there is hardly any cogent element in the country that could challenge the basis for the military's existence or its dominance of the state and its society.

In 2006 the top leaders of two prominent opposition parties, Benazir Bhutto and Nawaz Sharif, announced the Charter of Democracy (CoD). However, their joint agenda to protest against the military's domination did not exhibit any clearly defined principle that might push the armed forces out of politics. The CoD emphasized the significance of the Kashmir dispute, an issue that in the long term is bound to keep the military's importance intact. Hence, it appears more a protest against an individual – Musharraf – than a solution to push the military back permanently. Therefore, the governor of the Punjab, Lt.-General (rtd) Khaled Maqbool, is right when he says, 'I don't think there will be any government that wants to weaken the military. The army will never be threatened.'[12]

Hence, the political conditions are not likely to change unless the democratic forces bridge their internal divisions and put an end to the discord that seems to fragment the civil society and the political forces. The political forces would have to strengthen themselves much more than ever before, since their economic stakes have also changed the character of the military. The structure of the political parties needs to be revamped with an emphasis on democratization of the political party system. A continuation of authoritarian principles by the politicians will hardly aid in fighting back against the armed forces.

Alternatively, a possible change in circumstances might occur through the special interest of external forces such as Pakistan's foreign ally, the

United States, on which Islamabad has a strategic dependence. Moral and political assistance from the United States aimed at strengthening societal forces might help the political players to push the army out of politics. Even in this option, the strengthening of domestic political players is almost a precondition. Pakistan's external allies have to realize that superficial steps such as holding elections while manipulating democratic institutions and conducting pre-poll rigging, or localization of politics through local body systems, will hardly serve the purpose of strengthening democracy in Pakistan.

An authoritarian system in which the military has a dominant position is hardly the panacea for Pakistan's political problems, nor does it help the long-term interests of the country's strategic external allies. A politically strong Pakistan will also be a stable Pakistan, which will not be detrimental to the South Asian region or the world at large. It is worth recognizing that Milbus and the military's financial autonomy hampers the growth of democracy in a country. This is borne out by other cases such as Turkey and Indonesia as well. In Turkey's case, the military has established a niche in the economy and the country's polity. International capital also seems to contribute to the military's financial empire. However, such cooperation strengthens the armed forces, which ultimately works against strengthening democracy in Turkey. The lack of a democratic environment, it must be noted, is one of the barriers for Ankara's entry into the European Union.

THE IMPACT OF MILBUS IN THE FUTURE

While it is difficult to quantify the military's internal economy, it is equally difficult to list all the opportunity costs of Milbus. Nevertheless, for those readers who might be interested in shedding greater light on the subject, it is apt to conclude this study with a new hypothesis. It will be advantageous for all to study the linkage between Milbus, the military's transformation into an independent class and a part of the dominant elite in the country, and the rise in religious extremism in societies where this has happened.

The rise in religious extremism is a common factor in all the three countries that have been put here into the category of parent-guardian military dominance: that is, Pakistan, Indonesia and Turkey. The military's transformation into a class and a part of the dominant elite negates the institution's role as an arbiter to which the society looks for providing the necessary social and political balance. The military's evolution reduces the options available to the general public, who then seek alternative ideologies. It is an interesting coincidence that in the absence of any other political ideology after the end of the cold war, religion or religious ideology has emerged as an alternative agenda which the people in these countries seem to have sought in their search of justice and better governance.

In Pakistan, the military has been central in nourishing the religious right without necessarily realizing the strength of religious ideology as an alternative to itself. The military, in fact, also supported and built various militant organizations to serve its national security objectives. The religious parties, the militant groups and the armed forces are bound in a process of reinforcing each other's strength. The greatest beneficiary, however, is the religious right, which seems to have captured the imagination of the common people. The increase in religious conservatism and the attraction of the religious right for the common people also bolster the military's significance as a possible tool for enforcing an alternative fundamentalist sociopolitical system in the country and the world.

Although Pakistan's generals claim that they want to curb religious extremism and militancy, the published reports indicate otherwise. A report published in the English-language magazine *Herald* exposes in detail the government's two-faced attitude to the militants.[13] Such reports raise questions regarding the efficacy of US policy, and that of other Western countries, in dealing with the issue of militancy or democracy in Pakistan, and other states that are partners in Washington's 'war against terror'. The armed forces in Pakistan, Turkey and Indonesia have in fact systematically used religion to further their control over the society. The strengthening of the religious right served the purpose of consolidating the control of the military over the state and society. Is there an essential link between the military institution's evolution as a class and the rise of religious extremism? How does Milbus contribute to restructuring social relationships in a society? Should the rise in religious extremism and xenophobia be seen as one of the costs of Milbus? These are some crucial questions that I leave for readers and future researchers to answer.

Notes

INTRODUCTION

1   The term 'military fraternity' used here refers to both serving and retired military personnel, and a limited number of civilians who are directly dependent on the military business complex.
2   Tilly, 1985.
3   Lane, 1979, pp. 12–65.
4   Nandy, 2003, pp. 7–8.
5   Hobsbawm, 2000, p. 99.
6   Brommelhorster and Paes, 2003, p. 4.
7   Ibid., p. 2.
8   As noted above, this concept comprises both serving and retired military personnel, and a limited number of civilians who are directly dependent on the military business complex.
9   'Ministry refuses to explain Fauji Foundation issue', *Daily Times*, 5 June 2005.
10 Feit, 1973, p. 6.
11 Singer, 2004; see also Davis, 2002, Mulvenon, 2001, Brommelhorster and Paes, 2003 and Holmqvist, 2005.
12 Discussion with Peter Lock via email. See also Lock, 2000.
13 Redlich, Fritz, *The German Military Enterpriser and His Work Force: A Study in European Social and Economic History*, 2 Vols. (Wiesbaden, (1964).
14 Van Crefeld, 1977.
15 Tilly, 1992, p. 87.
16 Ibid.
17 Brommelhorster and Paes, 2003, pp. 2–3.
18 Mulvenon, 2001, pp. 25, 27–8.
19 Huntington, 1996, p. 203; Stepan, 1971, pp. 9–20; Mares, 1998, pp. 3–5.
20 Halpern, 1963.
21 Jalal, 1991, pp. 63–4. See also Robinson, 1996.
22 Callahan, 2003.
23 Huntington, 1996, p. 203.
24 Holmqvist, 2005, p. 39.
25 Wintrobe, 2000, pp. 31–9.
26 Address given at the inauguration of the DHA water desalination plant in Karachi, 2004.
27 Nasr, 2001, pp. 9–12.
28 McCulloch, 2005, pp. 6, 12–19.
29 Lock, 2000, p. 9.
30 Brommelhorster and Paes, 2003, p. 63.
31 Mulvenon, 2001, p. 61. A number of retired military officers interviewed for the study in Pakistan expressed similar views.
32 Ibid., p. 11.
33 For instance, India's first prime minister, Jawaharlal Nehru, encouraged the MoD to initiate a 'double file' system. This concept allowed the civil bureaucracy to override the military. According to this approach, a file containing notes by an official from the service headquarters was not passed on to the top

political leadership. Instead, the MoD would initiate a second file with its comments. As a result, the civil bureaucracy gained greater influence and control over the military (interview with Rear Admiral (rtd) Raja Menon and former federal secretary N. N. Vohra, New Delhi, 2006).

34   Jalal, 1991.
35   Rizvi, 2003.
36   Olson, 2000.
37   For reference see John Lancaster, 'Pakistanis question perks of power', *Washington Post*, 22 November 2002.

CHAPTER 1 MILBUS: A THEORETICAL CONCEPT

1   Dauvergne, 1998, p. 137. See also Migdal's definition: 1988, p. 19.
2   Levi, 2002, p. 40.
3   Tilly, 1992, pp. 96–7.
4   Grindle, 1996, p. 79.
5   For the debate on the tension between the two approaches see Poggi, 1978 and Lasswell, 1958.
6   Krasner, 1984, p. 225.
7   Migdal, 1988; see also Migdal, 2001, pp. 58–94.
8   Grindle, 1996, p. 79.
9   Nordlinger, 1981. See also Greetz, 1981, Skowronek, 1982, Dahl, 1961 and Migdal, 1988.
10   Migdal, 1988, pp. 181–205.
11   For literature on bureaucratic authoritarianism see O'Donnell, 1973. See also Linz, 1978.
12   Schmitter, 1974; see also Schmitter, 1978.
13   Malloy, 1977.
14   Malloy et al., 1996.
15   Although non-state actors challenge the state's monopoly over violence, it is the nation-state's armed forces whose authority to use coercive tools is recognized by the government. I have deliberately not engaged in a tedious debate of how this monopoly is granted and the legality of the ruling regime to recognize a military.
16   Although police can use coercive methods, the capacity of police and paramilitary forces is far less than that of most armed forces. The possession of major weapon systems and greater firepower makes the military's capability far more deadly.
17   Malloy, 1977, p. 4.
18   Perlmutter, 1974, p. 12. According to Perlmutter, India fits the description of a state bordering on praetorianism. This view is subscribed to by Ayesha Jalal in her work: see Jalal, 1995.
19   Interviews with N. N. Vohra and Rear Admiral (rtd) K. R Menon (New Delhi, 13 December 2005 and 12 January 2006). This was done primarily through introducing a 'double file' system. All files from the service headquarters with memos or notes from military officials terminated at the MoD. It is the file with the comments of the ministry regarding a particular case that is then sent up to the political masters for a decision.
20   Peri, 2002.
21   Larry Makinson, 'Outsourcing the Pentagon: who benefits from the politics and economics of national security?' (www.icij.org/pns/report.aspx?aid=385).

22 Ibid.
23 Ibid.
24 Werve, 2004.
25 http://coursesa.matrix.msu.edu/~hst306/documents/indust.html
26 Perlmutter, 1981, p. 59.
27 Migdal, 1988, p. 187.
28 Perlmutter, 1981, pp. 53–4.
29 Ibid., p. 55.
30 Interview with human rights activist Shiral Lakthilaka (Colombo, 9 February 2006).
31 Mulvenon, 2001.
32 Mora, 2002.
33 Joffe, 1997, p. 179.
34 Comments made by James Mulvenon on a research paper presented by the author at the Woodrow Wilson International Center for Scholars (Washington, D.C., 2005).
35 Wintrobe, 1998, p. 138.
36 Klebnikov, 2003.
37 Mora, 2002.
38 Perlmutter, 1981, pp. 10–16.
39 Ibid., p. 39.
40 Ibid., p. 41.
41 Ibid. pp. 41–2.
42 Holsti, 1996, p. 61.
43 Perlmutter, 1981, pp. 42–3, 50–1.
44 Ibid., p. 125.
45 Olson, 2000, p. 11.
46 Callahan, 2003, pp. 205–6.
47 Perlmutter, 1981, pp. 131–2.
48 Halpren, 1963.
49 Weaver, 1973, pp. 78–94.
50 Perlmutter, 1977, p. 111.
51 Feit, 1973, p. 3.
52 Perlmutter and Bennett, 1980, pp. 206–7.
53 Perlmutter, 1977, p. 111.
54 Stepan, 1988, p. 15. See also Stepan, 1971, pp. 60–6.
55 Perlmutter, 1977, p. 106.
56 Crouch, 1978. See also McCulloch, 2003, pp. 96–7.
57 Ibid.
58 Interview with former army chief, Lt.-General (rtd) Mahbubur Rehman (Dhaka, 7 February 2006).
59 Feaver, 2003, pp. 54–95.
60 Resolution No. XX1V/MPRS/1966 of the People's Congress, Article 3, Paragraph 7.
61 McCulloch, 2005, pp. 6–9.
62 Kinzer, 2001, p. 16.
63 Ibid., p. 9.
64 Narli, 2000, pp. 109–12.
65 Roulleau, 2000, p. 5.
66 Monopolizing could take several forms. First, it could involve greater resources: for instance, the Turkish military officers get more perks than the

civil bureaucracy. This is clearly a case of monopolizing resources. Second, it involves establish monopolies, like Pakistan Army's monopoly over the large construction and transportation business.

67   Van de Walle, 2001, pp. 113–51.
68   Ibid., p. 185.
69   Holmqvist, 2005, p. 25.

CHAPTER 2 THE PAKISTAN MILITARY: THE DEVELOPMENT OF PRAETORIANISM, 1947–77

1   Perlmutter, 1977, p. 93.
2   Cohen, 2004, pp. 223–4.
3   Tan Tai Yong, 2005, pp. 62–9.
4   Ibid., p. 65.
5   Ibid., p. 71.
6   Pasha, 1998, p. 135.
7   Interview with Sardar Ataullah Mengal (Karachi, 31 July 2004).
8   Nordlinger, 1977, pp. 35–42.
9   Janowitz, 1971, p. 317.
10   Nordlinger, 1977, pp. 35–42.
11   Discussion with an officer serving in the Military Secretary's branch. This branch is responsible for postings, transfers and promotions of all army personnel.
12   Discussion with PN psychologist (Islamabad, April 1999).
13   Siddiqa-Agha, 2001, pp. 60–3.
14   Interview with General Shamim Alam Khan (Rawalpindi, 21 March 1994).
15   Interview with General (rtd) Jahangir Karamat (Lahore, 12 January 2004).
16   Huser, 2002, pp. 20–2.
17   Cohen, 2004, p. 105.
18   Siddiqi, 1996, p. 70.
19   Haqqani, 2005, p. 15.
20   Jalal, 1991, p. 44.
21   Cohen, 2004, p. 102.
22   Interview with Brig. (rtd) A. R. Siddiqui (Karachi, 20 July 2004).
23   General Pervez Musharraf, television address, 12 January 2002.
24   Haqqani, 2005, pp. 131–97, 261–309. See also Abbas, 2005, pp. 201–16.
25   Khan, 1963, pp. 67–199.
26   Ibid., pp. 239–40.
27   Cheema, 2000, pp. 135–6.
28   Cloughly, 1999, pp. 239–97.
29   During the mid-1990s, the Punjab government run by Prime Minister Nawaz Sharif's brother, Shahbaz Sharif, asked the army to detect and close down ghost schools (schools that only existed on paper), which could then be formally closed down in government documents as well. The education department of the provincial government was unable to verify the number of schools that were actually functional.
30   It must be noted that the term 'counter-plotist literature' is not intended to carry a negative connotation, but merely describes the fundamental drift of the varying arguments.
31   Jalal, 1991, pp. 63–4.
32   Shafqat, 1997.

33   Kux, 2001.
34   Cohen, 2004, p. 102.
35   Shafqat, 1997, p. 21.
36   Waseem, 1994, p. 123.
37   Hamza Alavi, in Waseem, 1994, p. 133.
38   Ibid., pp. 51–131.
39   Ibid., p. 115.
40   Feit, 1973, p. 2.
41   Ibid., pp. 4–5; Banfield, 1958, p. 85.
42   Feit, 1973, pp. 2–5.
43   Alavi, 1983, pp. 42–3.
44   Alavi, 1982a, pp. 172–91.
45   Alavi, 1982b, pp. 296–99.
46   Saeed Shafqat lists personality or personality traits as an independent variable.
47   Alavi, 1983.
48   Haqqani, 2005.
49   Alavi, 1983, p. 66.
50   Ibid., p. 71.
51   Ibid., pp. 66–70.
52   Khuhro, 1998, p. 373.
53   Waseem, 1994, p. 117.
54   Rizvi, 2003, p. 80.
55   Khuhro, 1998, p. 375.
56   Abbas, 2005, p. 28.
57   Rizvi, 2003, p. 80.
58   Interview with Lt.-General (rtd) Faiz Ali Chishti (Rawalpindi, 6 November 2003).
59   Shafqat, 1997, p. 9.
60   Abbas, 2005, p. 35.
61   Ayub Khan was considered after the sudden death of Maj.-General Iftikhar, who was designated as the commander-in-chief. See Abbas, 2005, pp. 27, 51–2.
62   Interview with Lt.-General (rtd) Faiz Ali Chishti (Rawalpindi, 6 November 2003).
63   Interview with Riaz Hashmi (Karachi, 2 August 2004).
64   Khuhro, 1998, pp. 439–40.
65   Jalal, 1991, p. 94.
66   Minutes of Cabinet meeting, 9 September 1947, 67/CF/47, National Documentation Center, Cabinet Division, Islamabad.
67   Haqqani, 2005, p. 32.
68   Shafqat, 1997, p. 31.
69   Cohen, 2004, p. 102.
70   Cheema, 2002, p. 182.
71   Sir Alexander Symon's letter to Sir Gilbert Laithwaite Lintott. In Khan, 2002, p. 12.
72   Edward Feit, 1973, pp. 73–4.
73   Waseem, 1994, p. 145.
74   Rizvi, 2003, p. 9.
75   Feit, 1973, p. 6.
76   McCulloch, 2003, pp. 96–7.
77   Rizvi, 2003, p. 103.

78   Ibid., pp. 104–5.
79   Shafqat, 1997, pp. 45–57.
80   Alavi, 1983, pp. 54–61.
81   Jalal, 1991, pp. 306–7.
82   Haqqani, 2005, p. 67.
83   Ziring, 1994, p. 57.
84   Ibid., p. 29.
85   Salik, 1979, p. 29.
86   Rizvi, 2003, p. 134.
87   Ziring, 1994, pp. 69–70. See also Haqqani, 2005, pp. 72–4.
88   US Consulate (Dacca) cable, 'Selective genocide', 28 March 1971. See also US
      Embassy (New Delhi) cable, 'Selective genocide', 29 March 1971 and US
      Consulate (Dacca) cable, 'Killings at university', 30 March 1971.
89   'Dissent from US policy toward East Pakistan', telegram to the State
      Department, April 1971. See http://www.gwu.edu/~nsarchiv/NSAEBB/
      NSAEBB79/BEBB8.pdf
90   'Policy options towards Pakistan', Henry Kissinger's 'Memorandum
      for the President', 28 April 1971. http://www.gwu.edu/~nsarchiv/NSAEBB/
      NSAEBB79/BEBB9.pdf
91   US Department of State cable, 'USG Expression of Concern on East Pakistan',
      6 April 1971.
92   Henry Tanner, 'Bhutto denounces council and walks out in tears', New York
      Times, 16 December 1971.
93   Kux, 2001, p. 203. Bhutto was sent to China in early November 1971.
94   Shafqat, 1997, p. 79.
95   Haqqani, 2005, pp. 65–7.
96   James, 1993, p. 75.
97   Jalal, 1991, p. 318.
98   Shafqat, 1997, p. 118; Jalal, 1991, pp. 314–16.
99   Alavi, 1983, p. 52.
100   Patrick Keatley, 'The brown bomb', Guardian (Manchester), 11 March 1965.
101   Khan, 1993, p. 407.
102   Ibid., p. 412.
103   Ibid., p. 417.
104   Jalal, 1991, p. 316.
105   Interview with Abdul Hafeez Pirzada (Islamabad, July 2004).

CHAPTER 3 EVOLUTION OF THE MILITARY CLASS, 1977–2005

1   Arif, 1995, p. 72.
2   The News, Lahore, 23 April 1994.
3   Kux, 2001, p. 238.
4   Hussain, 1990, p. 15.
5   Ibid., p. 22.
6   Ibid., p. 32.
7   Ibid.
8   Nasr, 2001, p. 7. The nazim-e-salaat was deputed in every neighborhood to
      ensure that all males attended prayer congregation. Those who did not were
      harassed through propaganda and use of force.
9   Nasr, 2001, p. 144.
10   Ibid.
11   Jacoby, 2004, p. 178.

12   Dad Khan, 1999, p. 158.
13   Jones, 2003, p. 7.
14   Hasnain, 2005, p. 26.
15   Rizvi, 2003, p. 186.
16   Abbas, 2005, p. 120.
17   Interview with Hameed Gul (Islamabad, 15 May 1994). See also Haqqani, 2005, p. 201.
18   Arif, 1995, p. 143. Arif cites Major General Sher Ali Khan advising General Yahya Khan in 1969 about the art and impact of creating a myth about the military as a saviour. This advice was followed by all military dictators.
19   Verkaaik, 2005, pp. 61–87, 111–17.
20   Siddiqa-Agha, 2001, p. 145.
21   Nasr, 2001, pp. 135–7.
22   Shah, 2002, pp. 90–1.
23   Benazir Bhutto (1988–90, 1993–6), Ghulam Mustafa Jatoi, caretaker prime minister (1990), Nawaz Sharif (1990–3, 1997–9), Balakh Sher Mazari, caretaker prime minister (1993), Moeen Qureshi, caretaker prime minister (1993) and Meraj Khalid, caretaker prime minister (1996–7).
24   Rizvi, 2003, p. 209.
25   Ibid., pp. 205–10.
26   Bray, 1997, p. 324. Lt. General Asad Durrani confessed to the operation in an affidavit submitted to the Supreme Court.
27   Shah, 2002, pp. 83–109.
28   Interview with Lt. General (rtd) Talat Masood (Islamabad, 6 August 2004).
29   Hussain, 'Pakistan's political forces and the army', The Nation, 20 May 1990.
30   http://www.pildat.org/eventsdel.asp?detid=70. Comments by Lt.-General (rtd) Tanveer Naqvi at the round-table discussion on 'Parliamentary Oversight of Security Sector' organized by Pakistan Institute of Legislative Democracy and Transparency (PILDAT), Islamabad, 25 February 2005.
31   Interview with Maj.-General Rashid Qureshi (Rawalpindi, 2002).
32   Interview with Donya Aziz (Islamabad, 24 July 2004).
33   Interview with Razzak Tabba (Karachi, 3 August 2004).
34   Interview with Brig. (rtd) Shaukat Qadir (Rawalpindi, 31 October 2003).
35   Discussion with Praveen Swami (New Delhi, January 2006).
36   Jawad Ahmed, 'Political women?' letter to the editor, The News, 18 August 2005. The letter referred to a television interview with the adviser to the minister for women's development, Ms Niloufar Bakhtiar, in which she announced the opening of such an institution.
37   Interview with Asiya Azeem (Islamabad, 28 July 2004).
38   Interview with Justice Majoda Rizvi (Islamabad, 10 August 2004).
39   Interview with Ashley Tellis (Washington, D.C., 11 August 2005).
40   Haqqani, 2005, pp. 205, 220
41   Rizvi, 2003, pp. 210–19.
42   Interview with the resident editor of Dawn, Zia-u-Din (Islamabad, 28 November 2003).
43   Rizvi, 2003, pp 224–5.
44   Haqqani, 2005, p. 237.
45   Ibid., pp. 221–43.
46   Rizvi, 2003, pp. 192–4.
47   Warraich, 2006, p. 136.
48   Interview with Admiral Fasih Bokhari (Islamabad, 6 October 2003).

49   Mohammed Shehzad, 'Musharraf had decided to topple Nawaz much before Oct 12', *South Asia Tribune*, no. 12, 7–13 October 2002.
50   Discussion with bureau chief, *Daily Times*, Rana Qaisar, and editor, *Dawn*, Zia-u-Din (Islamabad, June 2006).
51   'Opposition seeks debate in senate', *Dawn*, 1 August 2006, p. 19.
52   'Pakistan urged to probe 7 reporters' deaths', *Reuters*, 27 July 2006.
53   Waseem, 2006, p. 71.
54   http://news.bbc.co.uk/1/hi/world/south_asia/1958219.stm
55   Abbas, 2005, p. 227.
56   http://news.bbc.co.uk/1/hi/world/south_asia/1958219.stm
57   Ibid.
58   Waseem, 2006, p. 28.
59   Interview with Zafarullah Khan (Islamabad, 21 July 2004).
60   Waseem, 2006, p. 57.
61   Ibid.
62   See *Dawn*, 21 December 2002.
63   'PPP, PML gulf can't be bridged', *The News*, 3 July 2006.
64   'PML will re-elect Musharraf', *Dawn*, 8 May 2006.
65   Interview with member of the National Assembly and PML-Q, Asiya Azeem (Islamabad, 28 July 2004).
66   Maryam Hussain, '56 govt. MNA's protest to Aziz', *Daily Times*, 22 June 2006.
67   Waseem, 2006, pp. 31–2.
68   'Musharraf seeks vote for his supporters', *Dawn*, 1 August 2006, p. 3.
69   'Minister's son beats passenger at airport', *The News*, 11 August 2005.
70   'Law minister takes law into his hands, again', *Peninsula*, 9 May 2005.
71   Hamayun Gauhar, 'The minister, the waiter and the donkey', *The Nation*, 25 September 2005.
72   'PML activists ransack Peshawar Press Club', *The News*, 30 June 2006, p. 12.
73   Mann, 1993, p. 438.
74   Cohen, 2004, p. 69.
75   LaPorte, 1997, p. 121.
76   Interview with Moeen Qureshi (Washington, D.C., 18 August 2005).
77   Abbas, 2005, pp. 160–1.
78   Ibid., p. 227.
79   Banfield, 1958, p. 85.
80   Ibid., pp. 178–9.
81   Shakir Hussain, 'Running scared', *The News*, 3 August 2005.
82   Kux, 2001, pp. 324–5.
83   Interview with Moeen Quresh (Washington, D.C., 18 August 2005).
84   Rehman, 1998.
85   Ibid., p. 26.
86   Feit, 1973, p. 4.
87   Since the president is currently the army chief as well, he has not been included in this count.
88   Mushahid Hussain, 'All parties flirt with Pak army', *Times of India*, 28 September 1990.
89   Jacoby, 2004, pp. 145–8.
90   Hussain, see note 88.
91   Interview with Qazi Hussain Ahmed (Lahore, 2002).
92   Interview with Maulana Fazl-ur-Rehman (Islamabad, 9 March 2004).
93   Jacoby, 2004, p. 137.

CHAPTER 4 THE STRUCTURE OF MILBUS

1   Ref. CMLA letter no. 57/1/CMLA dated 20 July 1978.
2   Interview with Lt.-General (rtd) Saeed Qadir (Rawalpindi, 2005).
3   http://www.fwo.com.pk/intro.php
4   http://www.sco.gov.pk
5   See the *Daily Awaz* (an Urdu paper), 24 July 2004.
6   Ref: Supreme Court of Pakistan, Case No. CP1593/98.
7   Moore, 1979, p. 210.
8   Rizvi, 2003, p. 237.
9   http://www.pakmart.com/fauji/intro.htm
10 Moore, 1979, p. 230.
11 Shafqat, 1997, p. 37.
12 http://fauji.org.pk/Industrial&Commercial/industrial%20and%20 commercial%20operations.htm
13 http://www.fauji.org.pk/investment.htm
14 In 2004 Lt.-General (rtd) Mohammad Amjad was the managing director, Fauji Foundation and Lt.-General (rtd) Mehmood the director-general of Fauji Fertilizer.
15 Interview with Lt.-General (rtd) Mohammad Amjad (Rawalpindi, 2004).
16 http://fauji.org.pk/
17 Email interview with Dr Mubashir Hassan, 18 October 2004. 22:39:52. Dr Hassan was Zulfiqar Ali Bhutto's finance minister.
18 Interview with director of the Shaheen Foundation, Air Marshal (rtd) Shahid Zulfiqar (Islamabad, 12 May 2000).
19 http://shaheenfoundation.com/corporate_profile.htm
20 Siddiqa-Agha, 2003, p. 127.
21 SF sold SAI in 2004.
22 Mora, 2003.
23 Ibid.

CHAPTER 5 MILBUS: THE FORMATIVE YEARS, 1954–77

1   Moore, 1979.
2   Interview with Brig. (rtd) Arshad Tariq (Rawalpindi, 4 November 2003). Such views were expressed by other officers as well.
3   Lock, 2000, p. 4.
4   Interview with Brig. (rtd) Zahid Zaman (Rawalpindi, 7 October 2003).
5   Interviews with Lt.-General (rtd) Syed Mohammad Amjad (Rawalpindi, 12 October 2003), and Maj.-General (rtd) Jamsheed Ayaz Khan (Islamabad, 10 October 2003).
6   Moore, 1979, p. 229.
7   Ibid., pp. 232–3.
8   Alavi, 1979, p. 45.
10 Ibid., pp. 45–9.
11 Jacoby, 2005, pp. 4–5.
12 Ibid.
13 Hale, 1994, p. 174. http://www.oyakbank.com.tr/english/the_oyak_ group.asp
14 Jacoby, 2005, p. 19.
15 Waseem, 1994, p. 93.
16 Khan, 1967, pp. 49–50, 51–66.

17   Alavi, 1979, p. 56.
18   Interview with Lt.-General (rtd) Asad Durrani (Rawalpindi, 3 November 2003).
19   http://www.fwo.com.pk/intro.php
20   Rizvi, 2003, pp. 104–5.
21   Zaheer, 1998.
22   Khan, 1967, p. 32.
23   Rizvi, 2003, pp. 104–5.
24   Sirajul Haque Memon, 'Genesis of separatist sentiment in Sindh', *Dawn*, 23 March 2001 (Pakistan Day Special Issue).
25   Rizvi, 2003, p. 105.
26   Feldman, 1972, pp. 305–6.
27   Interview with Maj.-General (rtd) Fahim Haider Rizvi (Rawalpindi, 9 November 2003).
28   Jones, 2003, p. 55.
29   Ziring, 1994, p. 49.
30   Rizvi, 2003, p. 105.

CHAPTER 6 EXPANSION OF MILBUS, 1977–2005

1   Castro and Zamora, 2003, p. 43.
2   Hale, 1994, p 329.
3   Interview with Lt.-General (rtd) Khalid Maqbool (Lahore, 22 March 2004).
4   Interview with former chief of naval staff, Admiral (rtd) Saeed Mohammad Khan (Islamabad, 3 November 2003).
5   Interview with Col. (rtd) Bakhtiar Khan (Karachi, 5 May 2004).
6   O'Donnell, 1973, p. 87.
7   Interview with Najam Sethi (Lahore, 17 August 2004).
8   Interview with Maj.-General (rtd) Jamsheed Ayaz Khan (Islamabad, 10 October 2003).
9   Interview with the joint secretary (Establishment Division), Zahid Saeed (Islamabad, 9 October 2003).
10   Interview with Lt.-General (rtd) Faiz Ali Chishti (Rawalpindi, 6 November 2003).
11   National Assembly of Pakistan Debates, Monday 29 December 2003 (Official Report: 11th Session, Vol. XI contains No. 1–4), p. 664.
12   Rehman, 2004, pp. 42–72.
13   Interview with Maj.-General Shaukat Sultan (Rawalpindi, 19 September 2003).
14   Ref CMLA letter No. 57/1/CMLA dated 20 July 1978.
15   Interview with financial adviser and chief accounts officer, Pakistan Railways, Mohammad Ali (Lahore, 2 October 2003).
16   *NLC at a Glance. Brief for the OIC NLC* (Rawalpindi: National Logistic Cell Report, 2000, p.16).
17   Interview with General (rtd) Mirza Aslam Beg (Rawalpindi, 29 October 2003).
18   *Shaheen* means eagle, which is part of the PAF's insignia.
19   *Bahria* means force of the sea.
20   Interview with Admiral (rtd) Fasih Bokhari (Islamabad, August 2004); Siddiqa-Agha, 2001, pp. 64–6.
21   Interview with Admiral (rtd) Tariq Kamal Khan (Islamabad, 1 November 2003).
22   Interview with Lt.-General (rtd) Talat Masood (London, January 2000).
23   http://www.marigas.com.pk

24   Ibid.
25   Sohail Sangi, *Maadni Daulat, Fauji Control* (Natural resources and the military's control), Urdu report on BBC Urdu.com, Monday 20 June 2005, 16:25 GMT, 21:25 PST.
26   Paes and Shaw, 2003, pp. 146–7.
27   Interview with Maj.-General (rtd) Fahim Haider Rizvi (Rawalpindi, 9 November 2003).
28   Interview with Brig. (rtd) Ali Jawahar (Rawalpindi, 10 November 2003). He was one of the first officers to work at the AWT.
29   Interview with Lt.-General (rtd) Moin-u-Din Haider (Karachi, 4 August 2004).
30   Interview with Maj.-General (rtd) Fahim Haider Rizvi (Rawalpindi, 9 November 2003).
31   Ibid.
32   Interview with Lt.-General (rtd) Mohammad Amjad (Rawalpindi, 12 October 2003). General Amjad was made the chairman of the FF after his retirement.
33   Interview with Lt.-General (rtd) Javed Ashraf Qazi (Rawalpindi, 5 November 2003).
34   Interview with Mohammad Ali (Lahore, 2 October 2003).
35   http://www.shaheenfoundation.com/shaheen_aero_traders.htm
36   Interview with Air Marshal (rtd) Shahid Zulfiqar (Islamabad, 12 May 2000).
37   http://www.bahria.com.pk/page8.html
38   See *Dawn*, 26 October 2004.
39   Ibid.
40   Syed Mohammad Ali, 'Plight of the fisher folk in Pakistan', *Daily Times*, 14 June 2005.
41   Interview with Zulfiqar Ali Shah, reporter for *The News* (Karachi, 31 July 2004).
42   'Resolution on fishermen issue disallowed', *Dawn*, 26 November 2004.
43   Naveed Ahmed, 'There is no plot that is free of cost no matter what the person's rank', interview of Major General Shaukat Sultan, DG, ISPR, *Newsline*, Vol. 19, no. 01, July 2006, p. 32.
44   Interview with Col. (rtd) Bakhtiar Khan (Karachi: 05/05/04).
45   Interview with Brig. (rtd) AI Tirmazi (Lahore, 23 March 2004).
46   'PAF and heroin smuggling', *The Nation* (editorial), 16 April 1997.
47   Rizvi, 2003, p. 236.
48   Ibid, p. 182.
49   Hale, 1994, p. 174.
50   Interview with Sirtaj Aziz (Islamabad, 8 October 2003).
51   Ibid.
52   Interview with Elahi Buksh Soomro (Islamabad, 26 January 2004).
53   Interview with Benazir Bhutto (London, February 2000).
54   Interview with Shah Mehmood Qureshi (Bhurban, 13 April 2004).
55   Interview with former army chief Mirza Aslam Beg (Rawalpindi, 29 October 2003).
56   Interview with Fasih Bokhari (Islamabad, October 2005).
57   '$1,700 Pak per capita income in real terms', *The Nation*, 25 February 2000.
58   'Smuggling costs govt Rs 100 billion every year', *Dawn*, 25 February 2000.
59   Interview with Tariq Shaffee (Karachi, 31 July 2004).
60   Interview with Razzak Tabba (Karachi, 3 August 2004).
61   Government of Pakistan, 2006, p. 252.
62   Interview with Ishaq Dar (New York, February 2004).

63 Interview with Maj.-General (rtd) Agha Masood Hassan (Islamabad, 26 August 2004).

64 Faheem Basar, 'Army subsidiaries to collect toll on GT road', *The News*, 22 December 1999.

65 Ibid.

66 E-mail interview with Admiral Fasih Bokhari (7 December 1999).

67 Discussion with Prof. Hassan-Askari Rizvi (New Delhi, January 2006).

68 Interview with Nisar Khuro (Washington, D.C., 2004).

69 'Zardari Group controls 4 radio, TV channels', *Takbeer* (Urdu), 11 July 1996.

70 Interview with Brig. (rtd) Bashir Baaz (Rawalpindi, 23 December 1999). The tenure in these foundations for retired officers is usually three years.

71 There is no private helicopter services industry in the country because it is prohibited.

72 Interview with the director of Askari Aviation, Brig. (rtd) Bashir Baz (Rawalpindi, 3 December 1999).

73 Interview with Senator M. P. Bhandara (Rawalpindi, 20 July 2004).

74 Ibid.

75 The FF and AWT are taxed at 20 per cent. The BF and SF, on the other hand, pay around 33 per cent.

76 Interview with Ishaq Dar (New York, 2004). See also Ahmed Murad, 'Army Welfare Trust: vested khaki interests and double standards of business accountability', *The Friday Times*, 14–20 December 2001.

77 Interview with Sirtaj Aziz (Islamabad, 8 October 2003).

78 Email discussion with Peter Lock (Bonn, March 2000).

79 Cockburn and St Clair, 1998, p. 257.

80 'PAF and heroin smuggling' *The Nation*, 16 April 1997.

81 Interview with Miles Jasphet, director, Hollard Insurance (Pretoria, 9 February 2000).

82 Ibid.

83 Dupree, 1991, p. 59.

84 Interview with Ikram Sehgal (Karachi, 2 August 2004).

85 Interview with Maj.-General (rtd) Fahim Haider Rizvi (Rawalpindi, 9 November 2003).

86 Rizwan Qureshi, 'Malik Riaz talks tough', *Blue Chip*, Issue 23, Vol. 2, April 2006, pp. 21–2.

87 Ref: Supreme Court of Pakistan Case No. CP1593/98.

88 http://paknews.com/pk/main1jun-21.html

89 Rizwan Qureshi, 'Malik Riaz talks tough', *Blue Chip*, Issue 23, Vol. 2, April 2006, p. 22.

90 'DHA and Bahria Town to integrate infrastructure', *Daily Times*, 8 October 2006.

91 http://fedworld.gov/cgi-bin/re...5c36&CID=C23168945312500014 3436640

92 http://www.dawn.com/2000/07/12/ebr8.htm

93 Ayesha Siddiqa, 'Military needs to reconsider its functioning', *The Friday Times*, Vol. XIII, No. 49, 1–7 February 2002.

94 http://www.nab.gov.pk/Public_info_material.asp#IMP_doc

95 Abbas, 2005, p. 187.

96 Interview with Saleem Altaf (Frankfurt, April 2000).

97 Interview with Lt.-General (rtd) Asad Durrani (Rawalpindi, 3 November 2003).

98 Capt. Aamir Shah, 'Airline industry on the move', *Dawn*, 10 May 2004.

99   Interview with Air Marshal (retd.) Shahid Zulfiqar (Islamabad,12 May 2000).
100 The airline gives a 50 per cent discount to retired and serving military officers.
101 Interview with Brig. Bashir Baaz (Rawalpindi, December 1999).
102 Auditor-General of Pakistan, 2003a, pp. 5–6.
103 Discussion with employees of Bahria Foundation and Al-Ghazi Travel Agency, Islamabad, 2003.
104 Jalal, 1995, p. 143.
104 http://fauji.org.pk/Industrial&Commercial/Subsidaries&Associated Co/FAUJI%20OIL.htm
106 Jawaid Bokhari, 'Strategic issues in privatization', *Dawn*, 6 October 2003.
107 Ibid.
108 Interview with financial expert Haroon Sharif (Islamabad, February 2004).
109 Interview with Zia-u-Din, editor of *Dawn* (Islamabad, 28 November 2003).
110 Ayesha Siddiqa, 'Military needs to reconsider its functioning', *The Friday Times*, Vol. XIII, No. 49, 1–7 February 2002.
111 Letter to the editor, 15 February 2002.
112 The marketing quota is dependent on the production quota.
113 Ahmed Murad, 'Army Welfare Trust, vest khaki interests and double standards of business accountability', *The Friday Times*, 14–20 December 2001.
114 Interview with Ishaq Dar (New York, 2004).
115 Ibid.
116 Interview with Isharat Hussain (Washington, D.C., 6 October 2004).
117 Interview with Ishaq Dar (New York, 2004).
118 *Dawn*, 2 September 2003.
119 'Bahria Varsity ordinance promulgated', *Dawn*, 8 February 2000.
120 Interview with the former army chief, General (rtd) Jahangir Karamat (Lahore, 12 January 2004). The general was appointed ambassador to the United States in 2004. He was of the view that most civilian institutions, particularly the judiciary, lacked spine.
121 Discussion with two army officers (Islamabad, 8 July 2006).
122 '1,027 civilian posts occupied by servicemen', *Dawn*, 3 October 2003.
123 Discussion with Prof. Farooq Hasnat (Lahore, 26 November 2004).
124 Waqar Gillani, 'Army administration devastating academics, say PU teachers', *Daily Times*, 1 October 2004.
125 Interview with Makhdoom Khursheed Zaman Qureshi (Bahawalpur, 2004). This was certainly the case in Bahawalpur where a large number of senior officers got their land.
126 Interview with Dr Asad Saeed (Islamabad, March 2004).
127 'Is Varan a legal authority?' *The News*, 5 October 2004.
128 See *Daily Times*, 30 October 2004.
129 Interview with Maj.-General (rtd) Agha Masood Hasan (Islamabad, 2004).
130 Karaosmanoglu, 1993, p. 33.
131 Ahmed Murad, 'Army Welfare Trust' (see note 113).
132 Rauf Klasra, 'Army Trust in bad financial shape', *The News*, 29 August 2001.
133 Ahmed Murad, 'Army Welfare Trust' (see note 113).

CHAPTER 7 THE NEW LAND BARONS

1   Kariappar, 2003.
2   Mehmood and Shaukat, 1998, p. 123.
3   Ibid., p. 30.

4   NAP-XI (4)/2003, Monday 29 December 2003.

5   'Improper use of defence lands', *The News*, 11 October 2004.

6   Haroon Rashid, *'Boolon ke naan Boolon'* (should I speak or should I not), Urdu report, BBC Urdu.com, Monday 20 June 2005, 16:05 GMT, 21:05 PST.

7   Zulfiqar Ghuman, 'Army allotted land for golf course against rules', *Daily Times*, 6 August 2006.

8   Kariappar, 2003, p. 18.

9   In share-cropping, the input and output is divided between the owner or controller of the land and the tenants. The two parties distribute the harvested crops rather than money. The tenant's main contribution is labour. Rent-in-cash on the other hand is like any rental agreement, according to which the tenants pay an agreed amount to the owner.

10   Kariappar, 2003, p. 40.

11   Ibid., p. 41.

12   Ibid., p. 2.

13   The cost of the ongoing conflict includes the money spent on deployment of a paramilitary force. Once this expenditure is added to the total cost of managing the farms, the net cost will increase substantially, and is higher than the dividends.

14   'Soiled hands: Pakistan Army's repression of the Punjab farmers' movement', *Human Rights Watch Report*, Vol. 16, No. 10, July 2004, p. 17.

15   Each provincial government has a revenue department that maintains land records and is responsible for collecting taxes. The highest appellate authority in the department is the Board of Revenue.

16   Kariappar, 2003, p. 9. Kariappar quotes Javed Aslam, member colonies, Board of Revenue, Punjab.

17   Ibid., p. 15.

18   Ibid., pp. 24–5.

19   The army's perspective was given by the head of ISPR, Maj.-General Shaukat Sultan, in *Capital Talk* (a television talk show aired on Geo Television), through August 2003.

20   See Bauer, 2003, p. 269.

21   Epstein, 1985, pp. 3–18.

22   See Bauer, 2003, p. 269.

23   http://fauji.org.pk/exp_seed.htm

24   Ali, 1988.

25   Pasha, 1998, p. 5.

26   Finer, 1975.

27   Ibid., p. 103.

28   See 'Land allotment to army officers', *Dawn*, 25 June 2003.

29   Ahmed, 2006. p. 32.

30   Hussain, 2002, p. 61. See also Siddiqa, 2006. p. 21.

31   Rizvi, 1988, p. 132.

32   Government of West Pakistan, 1959, pp. 12–13.

33   Herring 1983, p. 99.

34   Jones, 2003, p. 33.

35   Hamza Alavi, 'Authoritarianism and legitimation of state power in Pakistan', http://ourworld.compuserve.com/homepages/sangat/Power.htm

36   Hussain, 2002, p. 62.

37   Mahmood and Shaukat, 1998, p. 16.

38   'NA passes budget amid criticism', *Dawn*, 18 June 2005.

39 Hoti Ikram, 'Real estate lobby nips proposal for real story', *The News*, 26 May 2005.

40 Interview with Lt.-General (rtd) Fahim Haider Rizvi (Rawalpindi, 9 November 2003).

41 Ahmed, 2006, p. 34.

42 Farooqi, 2005. See also Rao, 2006.

43 Military cantonments in pre-partition days comprised four kinds of land: defence, provincial government, federal government and private. The first three categories were divided into A, B and C types, with certain subdivisions as well. These categories indicate the nature of ownership of the land and the specific purpose for which it could be used. For instance, A-1 land is specifically for defence purposes.

44 According to senior officers of the MLC Department, most property in the cantonments was private land that had been leased by the Royal British Army. This land could have been given to the migrants but was transferred to the officers instead.

45 It must be noted that most of the lease agreements expire around 2020 and there is no government policy regarding the titles. Part of the complication is because the land was sold to civilians.

46 Senate Secretariat, 2003b, pp. 1-8.

47 Senior refers to officers from full general to maj.-general, middle-ranking from brigadier to colonel, and junior from lt.-colonel to captain.

48 Senate Secretariat, 2003b, pp. 1–8.

49 Office of Director Audit, 1998.

50 Farhatullah Babur, 'Another DHA through military fiat', letter to the editor, *The News*, 27 February 2005.

51 Interview with Riaz Hashmi (Karachi, 2 August 2004).

52 Interview with Ikram Sehgal (Karachi, 2 August 2004).

53 Ibid.

54 Siddiqa, 2006a.

55 Ibid.

56 Interview with Riaz Hashmi (Karachi, 2 August 2004).

57 Senate Secretariat, 2003a, p. 12.

58 Interview with DG ISPR, Maj.-General Shaukat Sultan (Rawalpindi, 2004).

59 Zulfiqar Ghumman, 'NA questions land deals by Musharraf and ISI DG', *Daily Times*, 24 July 2004.

60 See Audit Report No. De/R/2001-2002/01 (Islamabad: Department of the Auditor-General of Pakistan, 2001/02).

61 Ibid.

62 From a legal standpoint, sanction is obtained post facto.

63 Interview with a prominent Karachi-based entrepreneur and activist, Nazim Haji (Karachi, 1 August 2004). This story was also confirmed by the former editor of the *Herald*, Amir Ahmed Khan.

64 'Army demands 20,000 acres along super h'way', *Star*, 27 September 2000.

65 'Army tells Sindh govt. to give 12,000 acres', *Star*, 15 April 2003.

66 Sohail Sangi, '*Jamshooro mein Shurish*' (chaos in Jamshooro), Urdu report on BBC Urdu.com, Monday 20 June 2005, 15:15 GMT, 20:15 PST.

67 Tariq Mehmood, '*Karakoram key nijat dahinda*' (the saviours of Karakoram), Urdu report on BBC Urdu.com, Monday 20 June 2005, 16:27 GMT, 21:27 PST.

68 Azizullah Khan, '*Maarmallang peh Zindagi Tung*' (life made difficult in Maarmallang), Urdu report on BBC Urdu.com, Monday 20 June 2005, 16:03 GMT, 21:03 PST.

69   Kaisar Bengali, 'Perils of militarized politics', *Dawn*, 3 August 2006.
70   Sohail Sangi, *'Barrey Mian tu Barrey Mian'* (like the big master), Urdu report on BBC Urdu.com, Monday 20 June 2005, 16:26 GMT, 21:26 PST.
71   The subsidy included the cost of land and covered part of the cost of construction as well.
72   Subsidized construction should not be mistaken for subsidized housing, which is provided to the homeless in a number of developed countries.
73   Kaisar Bengali, 'Perils of militarized politics', *Dawn*, 3 August 2006.
74   Siddiqa, 2006a, p. 29.
75   *The News*, August 2004.
76   Interview with Lt.-General (rtd) Khaled Maqbool (Lahore, 22 March 2004).
77   Farhatullah Babar, 'A DHA in Islamabad now', *The News*, 18 February 2005.
78   Ibid.
79   Following the sacking of the naval chief in 1997/98 on corruption charges, there has been a spate of stories regarding alleged kickbacks in various procurement deals. Some of the stories were published in the *South Asia Tribune*. For instance, see M. T. Butt, 'Army's budding Mansurl Haq pays extra $21 million in hush-hush French deal', *South Asia Tribune*, 30 June 2005. The government did not deny the story.
80   M. T. Butt, 'How a cook unraveled a multi-billion dollar army scam in Lahore', *South Asia Tribune*, 31 May 2005.
81   Interview with realtors/estate agents and architects (Bahawalpur, 2004/2005).
82   The DHA authorities bought 1,250 acres for Rs.2.5 billion (US$43.1 million) and 2,125 acres for Rs.8.5 billion (US$146.6 million).
83   Interview with revenue officials.
84   'Rawalpindi: residents threaten to block G.T road', *Dawn*, 3 February 2003.
85   Interview with realtors/estate agents (Lahore, 10 August 2004).
86   Interview with Justice (rtd) Mian Allah Nawaz Khan (Lahore, August 2004).
87   Ayaz Amir, 'Realtor's paradise', *Dawn*, 10 December 2004.
88   Karachi has multiple cantonment areas. The figure given earlier did not include naval cantonments.
89   Ikram Sehgal, 'Creek City, bleak city', *The Nation*, 2 August 2003.
90   Interview with the chief military executive officer, Lahore Cantonment (Lahore, December 2004).
91   Qadeer, 2000.
92   2004 YLR 629, Basharat Hussain versus CDA (in the court of Justice Tanveer Bashir Ansari), writ petition No. 2524 of 2002 decided on 23 July 2003.
93   Discussion with a senior official in the Baluchistan government (15 July 2006).
94   Government of Sindh, 2003.
95   Rauf Klasra, 'CDA explains cheap land allotment for GHQ', *The News*, 2 February 2005.
96   Ahmed, 2006, pp. 36–8.
97   Herring, 1983.
98   Alavi, 1976, p. 337.
99   Zaidi, 1999.
100 Zaidi, 1999, p. 38.
101 Nadeem Saeed, *'Wardi Walley Numberdar'* (uniformed *numberdars*), Urdu report on BBC Urdu.com, Monday 20 June 2005, 16:06 GMT, 21:06 PST.
102 Gazdar, 2003, p. 3.
103 The term 'ruraloplis' was first used by Dr Mohammad A. Qadeer, an urban planning expert. See Qadeer, 2000, p. 3.

104   This is a dance by lower-class women or prostitutes done in front of men only. It is a symbol of decadence.

105   Durrani, 1996.

106   Video interview with a landless peasant from Nawazabad village (11 July 2004).

108   Interview with Haji Yunis, head of the community in Yunisabad village (Karachi, 1 August 2004).

109   V.A. Jaffrey, 'Allotment of Clifton Beach', letter to the editor, *Dawn*, 17 March 2005.

110   Interview with Makhdoom Khursheed Zaman Qureshi (Bahawalpur, 24 July 2004).

111   Interview with Mushtaq Gaadi (Islamabad, 30 July 2004).

112   Interview with Bashher Shah (Karachi, 5 August 2004).

113   Interview with Sardar Ataullah Mengal (Karachi, 31 July 2004).

114   Civil Appeal No. 30 of 1999, dated 24 September 2003.

115   Discussion with a PN commander (Islamabad, March 2003).

116   Interview with Maj.-General (rtd) Mohammad Saleem (Bahawalpur, 12 August 2004).

CHAPTER 8 PROVIDING FOR THE MEN: MILITARY WELFARE

1   Interview with Maj.-General (rtd) Agha Masood Hassan (Islamabad, 26 August 2004).

2   The figures for the financial year 2004/05 are provisional. The average for military pensions would amount to approximately Rs.30–31 billion (US$517 million–534 million). The provisional figures indicate expenditure incurred up to June and not to the end of the financial year.

3   Bilquees, 1994, pp. 229–51.

4   Nasir, 2000, pp. 111–20.

5   http://usfspa-lawsuit.info/mccarty-mccarty.htm

6   Wilders, nd, pp.1–3.

7   Asch and Warner, 1994.

8   Ibid.

9   Interview with Lt.-General (rtd) Mohammad Amjad (Rawalpindi, 12 October 2003).

10   Kerans, Drover and Williams, 1988, pp. 32, 36.

11   Interview with Col. (rtd) Bakhtiar Khan (Karachi, 5 May 2004).

12   Kerans et al., 1988, pp. 27–36.

13   Interview with Dr Ishrat Hussain (Washington, D.C., 6 October 2004).

14   Interview with Maj.-General (rtd) Fahim Haider Rizvi (Rawalpindi, 9 November 2004).

15   Ibid.

16   Interview with the managing director, Shaheen Foundation (Islamabad, 11 May 2000).

17   Address of President Pervez Musharraf at the ground-breaking ceremony for the DHA desalination plant at Karachi.

18   Yong, 2005, p. 26.

19   Ibid.

20   Ibid., p. 79.

21   Interview with Brig. (rtd) Zahid Zaman (Rawalpindi, 7 October 2003).

22   Kaisar Bengali, 'Perils of militarized politics', *Dawn*, 3 August 2006.

23   Cohen, 2004, pp. 223–4.

24   Interview with Lt.-General (rtd) Mohammad Amjad (Rawalpindi, 12 October 2003).

CHAPTER 9 THE COST OF MILBUS

1   Ahmad Murad, 'Army Welfare Trust: vest khaki interests and double standards of business accountability', *The Friday Times*, 14–20 December 2001.
2   Telephone interview with Ishaq Dar (New York, 2005).
3   Murad: see note 1.
4   Ishaq Dar, 2005.
5   Murad: see note 1.
6   Interview with a source from KPMG (Islamabad, 2004).
7   This profitability ratio is calculated as the relationship between net profits and assets, to show the operating efficiency of the AWT investments in various sectors. The return on total assets is only a measure of profitability of the total funds, without identifying any relationship for specific sources of the funds.
8   The return on fixed assets is based on the relationship between net profits and fixed assets. This measures efficiency in managing and utilizing fixed assets. A low return on fixed assets is indicative of under-utilization, inefficient management and idle capacity of available resources.
9   Return on capital employed is the most accepted measure to assess the operating solvency of any organization, which is calculated as a relationship between profitability and capital employed, including both equity and long-term debt. Return on capital employed is also an indication of the efficiency with which long-term funds of owners and other stakeholders have been utilized.
10   This profitability ratio considers the relationship between profit and exclusively shareholder equity. It reveals how profitably the owner's funds have been utilized.
11   Auditor-General of Pakistan, 2003a, pp. 5–6.
12   Interview (Rawalpindi, December 1999).
13   Auditor-General of Pakistan, 2003a, pp. 5–6.
14   Interview with Maj.-General (rtd) Jamsheed Ayaz Khan (Islamabad, 10 October 2003).
15   Farrukh Saleem, 'Is Fauji Foundation in trouble?' *Dawn*, 14 May 2001.
16   Sher Khan, 'When selling sugar mills isn't so sweet', *The News*, 16 May 2005.
17   Interview with Lt.-General (rtd) Syed Mohammad Amjad (Rawalpindi, 12 October 2003).
18   Farhatullah Babur, 'When foundations are shaken', *The News*, 23 May 2005.
19   Interview with Lt.-General (rtd) Syed Mohammad Amjad (Rawalpindi, 12 October 2003).
20   Khan: see note 16.
21   The debt–equity ratio determines the entity's long-term debt repayment capability. This ratio also determines how well creditors are protected in case of insolvency. From the perspective of long-term debt repayment, the lower this ratio, the better the company's debt position.
22   The current ratio shows the organization's short-term debt repayment ability.
23   Saleem: see note 15.
24   Interview with Ishrat Hussain (Washington, D.C., 6 October 2004).
25   Saleem: see note 15. See also Sultan Ahmed, 'Military's sprawling business enterprises', *Dawn*, 6 October 2003.
26   Saleem: see note 15.
27   Ibid.

28 'CE calls for improving profitability of Fauji Foundation's units', *The News*, 2 February 2000.
29 Government of Pakistan, 2006, p. 252.
30 Interview with a senior source in the SF (Rawalpindi, 2004).
31 Auditor-General of Pakistan, 2003b, pp. 3–4.
32 Ibid., p. 5.
33 Ibid., pp. 5–6.
34 Auditor-General of Pakistan, 2003c, pp. 4–5.
35 Auditor-General of Pakistan, 2003a, p. 4.
36 Interview with General (rtd) Mirza Aslam Beg (Rawalpindi, 29 October 2003).
37 Khan, 1963, pp. 161–77.
38 Huntington, 1996, p. 346.
39 Janowitz, 1964, p. 48.
40 Hussain, 2004.
41 Hussain, 1999, pp. 15–16, 378.
42 Interview with Ishrat Hussain (Washington, D.C., 6 October 2004).
43 Hussain, 2004, pp. 6–7.
44 Interview with Aftab Manzoor (Karachi, 29 July 2004).
45 Interview with Abbas Habib (Karachi, 4 August 2004).
46 O'Donnell, 1973, p. 84.
47 Stepan, 1971, p. 12.
48 Kochanek, 1983, p. 70.
49 Ibid., p. 77.
50 Shafqat, 1997, p. 45-9.
51 Kochanek, 1983, pp. 94, 96.
52 Rehman, 1998, pp. 26–7.
53 Ibid., p. 30.
54 Ibid., pp. 56–62.

CHAPTER 10 MILBUS AND THE FUTURE OF PAKISTAN

1 Interview with Khaled Ahmed (Lahore, 17 August 2004).
2 'Air chief meets governor', *Dawn*, 9 August 2006.
3 Discussion with Lt.-General (rtd) Talat Masood (Islamabad, 9 August 2006).
4 Story narrated by Captain (rtd) Irfan Shehryar (Islamabad, February 2004).
5 Interview with Captain (rtd) Irfan Shehryar (Islamabad, 6 November 2003).
6 http://www.nab.gov.pk/PRESS/NEW.ASP?389
7 Interview with Ikram Sehgal (Karachi, 2 August 2004).
8 Interview with Lt.-General (rtd) Farrukh Khan (Rawalpindi, 15 October 2003).
9 Lt.-Colonel (rtd) Mahmood L. Malik, 'Scheming away', letter to the editor, *Newsline*, Vol. 19, no. 02, August 2006, p. 15.
10 Interview with Lt.-General (rtd) Syed Mohammad Amjad (Rawalpindi, 12 October 2003).
11 Interview with Najam Sethi (Lahore, 17 August 2004).
12 Interview with Lt.-General (rtd) Khaled Maqbool (Lahore, 22 March 2004).
13 Shahzada Zulfiqar, 'Changing loyalties', *Herald*, Vol. 37, no. 8, August 2006, pp. 46–7.

References

INTERVIEWS

Khaled Ahmed (Lahore, 17 August 2004). Prominent journalist and editor of weekly, *The Friday Times*.

Lt.-General (rtd) Syed Mohammad Amjad (Rawalpindi, 20 September 2003 and 12 October 2003). Former MD, Fauji Foundation.

Sardar Asef Ahmed Ali (Bhurban, 13 April 2004). Former foreign minister.

Mohammad Ali (Lahore, 2 October 2003). Financial advisor and chief accounts officer, Pakistan Railways.

Makhdoom Alam Anwar (Bhurban, 13 April 2004). Member PML-Q and National Assembly.

Asiya Azeem (Islamabad, 28 July 2004). Member of PML-Q and National Assembly.

Donya Aziz (Islamabad, 24 July 2004). Member of PML-Q and National Assembly.

Sirtaj Aziz (Islamabad, 8 October 2003). Former foreign and finance minister in Nawaz Sharif's cabinet.

Farhatullah Babur (Islamabad, 21 July 2004). Senator and member of the PPPP.

Sanaullah Baluch (Islamabad, 26 July 2004). Baluch leader and Senator.

General (rtd) Mirza Aslam Beg (Rawalpindi, 29 October 2003). Former army chief.

M. P. Bhandara (Rawalpindi, 20 July 2004). Member PML-Q and National Assembly.

Admiral (rtd) Fasih Bokhari (Islamabad, 6 October 2003). Former naval chief.

Javed Burki (Islamabad, 23 July 2004). Former civil servant.

Lt.-General (rtd) Faiz Ali Chishti (Rawalpindi, 6 November 2003). A prominent member of Zia ul Haq's government.

Lt.-General (rtd) Asad Durrani (Rawalpindi, 3 November 2003). Former head of the ISI and Pakistan's ambassador to Saudi Arabia during the Musharraf regime.

Maj.-General (rtd) Mehmood Durrani (Rawalpindi, 31 October 2003). Former chairman Pakistan Ordnance Factories, Wah. Currently Pakistan's ambassador to the United States.

Azra Fazal (Islamabad, 3 November 2003). Member PPPP and National Assembly.

Abbas Habib (Karachi, 4 August 2004). President Bank Al-Habib.

Iqbal Haider (Karachi, 2 August 2004). Legal expert.

Lt.-General (rtd) Moin-u-Din Haider (Karachi, 9 August 2004). Served as cabinet minister under Musharraf.

Nazim Haji (Karachi, 29 July 2004). Business entrepreneur and social worker.

Col. (rtd) Aziz-ul-Haq (Islamabad, 4 November 2003). Director administration, Institute of Regional Studies, Islamabad.

Hamid Haroon (Karachi, 29 July 2004) Owner of Dawn group of newspapers.

Maimoona Hashmi (Islamabad, 24 July 2004). Member PML-N and National Assembly. Her father was jailed by the Musharraf regime on the allegation of provoking conspiracy in the armed forces.

Riaz Hashmi (Karachi, 2 August 2004). Former officer of the ML&C Department.

Maj.-General (rtd) Agha Masood Hassan (Islamabad, 26 August 2004). Appointed as DG *Pakistan Post* during the Musharraf regime.

Dr Mubashir Hassan (Islamabad, 20 September 2005). Finance minister in Zulfiqar Ali Bhutto's cabinet.

Fakhru-Din G. Ibraheem (Karachi, 30 July 2004). Former justice and currently a legal expert.

Ahsan Iqbal (Islamabad, 1 November 2003). Member PML-N and National Assembly.

Khurram Javed (Islamabad, 6 August 2004). Entrepreneur.

Air Marshal (rtd) Qazi Javed (Islamabad, 14 October 2003). Director Air University.

Brig. (rtd) Ali Jawahar (Rawalpindi, 10 November 2003). Served in the AWT.

General (rtd) Jahangir Karamat (Lahore, 12 January 2004). Former army chief.

Ishaq Khan Khakwani (Bhurban, 14 April 2004) Member PML-Q and National Assembly.

Ahmed Ali Khan (Karachi, 29 July 2004). Former editor of *Dawn*.

Col. (rtd) Bakhtiar Khan (Karachi, 5 August 2004). Manages the Defense club in Karachi.

Lt.-General (rtd) Farrukh Khan (Rawalpindi, 15 October 2003). Former CGS and chairman, AWT after his retirement.

Imran Khan (Islamabad, 9 October 2003). Member National Assembly and leader *Tehreek-e-Insaf* (Justice Party).

Maj.-General (rtd) Jamsheed Ayaz Khan (Islamabad, 10 October 2003). Head of Institute of Regional Studies, Islamabad.

Omar Ayub Khan (Bhurban, 14 April 2004). Member of National Assembly and minister of state for finance.

Admiral Saeed Mohammad Khan (Islamabad, 3 November 2003) Former naval chief.

Admiral Tariq Kamal Khan (Islamabad, 1 November 2003). Former naval chief (1983–6).

Zafarullah Khan (Islamabad, 21 July 2004). Peace and human rights activist.

Kamal Majeed-ud-Din (Karachi, 2 August 2004). Editor of *Daily Star*.

Aftab Manzoor (Karachi, 29 July 2004). President MCB Bank.

Lt.-General (rtd) Khalid Maqbool (Lahore, 23 March 2004). Governor of the Punjab from 2001 through to the time of the interview.

Lt.-General (rtd) Talat Masood (Islamabad, 6 August 2004).

Lt.-General (rtd) Kemal Matinuddin (Rawalpindi, 21 November 2003).

Sardar Ataullah Khan Mengal (Karachi, 31 July 2004). Baluch leader.

Lateef Mughal (Karachi, 4 August 2004). General secretary, People's Worker's Union.

Justice (rtd) Mina Allah Nawaz (Lahore, 18 August 2004). Former chief justice Lahore High Court.

Majeed Nizami (Lahore, 18 August 2004). Owner of English-language daily *The Nation*.

Farid Paracha (Bhurban, 14 April 2004). Member of Jamaat-I-Islami and National Assembly.

Brig. (rtd) Bashir Pawar (Bahawalpur, 12 August 2004).

Abdul Hafeez Pirzada (Islamabad, 1 May 2004). Information minister in the cabinet of Zulfiqar Ali Bhutto.

Lt.-General (rtd) Saeed Qadir (Rawalpindi, 15 October 2003). Former QMG and first head of the NLC.

Brig. (rtd) Shaukat Qadir (Rawalpindi, 31 October 2003). Former president of the Institute of Policy Research, Islamabad (IPRI).

Naveed Qamar (Bhurban, 14 April 2004). Member of the PPPP.

Feroz Qasim (Karachi, 31 July 2004). Prominent entrepreneur.

Lt.-General (rtd) Mohammad Qayyum (Rawalpindi, 14 October 2003).

Lt.-General (rtd) Javed Ashraf Qazi (Rawalpindi, 05 November 2003) Former DG ISI and federal minister for railways, and later education, under the Musharraf regime.

Raheel Qazi (Bhurban, 14 April 2004). Member of National Assembly and daughter of the head of Jamaat-I-Islami, Qazi Hussain Ahmed. Provincial minister for agriculture in Punjab after Musharraf's takeover in 1999.

Moeen Qureshi (Washington, D.C., 18 August 2005). Former caretaker prime minister.

Shah Mehmood Qureshi (Bhurban, 13 April 2004). Member of the PPPP.

Maulana Fazl-u-Rehman (Islamabad, 21 July 2004). Member National Assembly and leader of the religious alliance, the MMA.

Sherry Rehman (Islamabad, 9 October 2003). Member PPPP and National Assembly.

Maqbool Rehmatullah (Karachi, 1 August 2004). Prominent entrepreneur.

Syed Haider Abbas Rizvi (Bhurban, 14 April 2004). Member of MQM and National Assembly.

Maj.-General (rtd) Fahim Haider Rizvi (Rawalpindi, 9 November 2003). Appointed as a senior officer in the AWT in 1984.

Justice Majida Rizvi (Islamabad, 10 August 2004).

Zahid Saeed (Islamabad, 8 October 2003). Joint secretary Establishment Division (ED). This division is responsible for the transfer and posting of all civil servants or those entering the civil service.

Maj.-General (rtd) Mohammad Saleem (Bahawalpur, 12 August 2004).

Abdul Sattar (Bhurban, 13 April 2004). Former foreign minister.

Ikram Sehgal (Karachi, 2 August 2004) Former army officer and currently a prominent entrepreneur.

Najam Sethi (Lahore, 17 August 2004). Editor of English-language newspaper *Daily Times*.

Tariq Shafee (Karachi, 31 July 2004). President of the Crescent Group of Industries.

Basheer Shah (Karachi, 5 August 2004). Agriculturist from Sindh.

Justice (rtd) Naseem Hassan Shah (Lahore, 17 August 2004). Former chief justice Lahore High Court.

Zulfiqar Ali Shah (Karachi, 31 July 2004). Journalist with English-language newspaper *The News*.

Captain (rtd) Irfan Shehryar (Islamabad, 6 November 2003).

Brig. (rtd) A. R. Siddiqui (Karachi, 30 July 2004).

Admiral (rtd) Iftikhar Hussain Sirohey (Islamabad, 3 November 2003) Former naval chief.

Elahi Bukhsh Soomor (Islamabad, 26 January 2004). Former speaker, National Assembly.

Maj.-General Shaukat Sultan (Rawalpindi, 7 October 2003). DG, ISPR.

Brig. Tayyab Sultan (Islamabad, 13 October 2003). Director of National Accountability Bureau (NAB).

Razzak Tabba (Karachi, 3 August 2004). Prominent entrepreneur.

Brig (rtd) Arshad Tariq (Rawalpindi, 4 November 2003).

Brig. (rtd) AI Tirmazi (Lahore, 23 March 2004). Former officer of the ISI.

Fauzia Wahab (Islamabad, 30 May 2003). Member of PPPP and National Assembly.

Mohammad Waseem (Islamabad, 7 August 2004).

Kunwar Khalid Yunis (Islamabad, 21 July 2004). Member of MQM and National Assembly.

Haji Yunus (Karachi, 1 August 2004). Local representative and leader of Yunisabad.

Zahid Zaheer (Karachi, 29 July 2003). President of the Overseas Investors & Chambers of Commerce in Pakistan.

Brig. (rtd) Zahid Zaman (Rawalpindi, 7 October 2003). Head of the Armed Forces Welfare Board.

Zia-u-Din (Islamabad, 28 November 2003). Resident editor, *Dawn*.

PRIMARY SOURCE DOCUMENTS

Government of Pakistan (2006) *Economic Survey, 2005–06*. Islamabad: Government of Pakistan.

Government of West Pakistan (1959) *Report of the Land Reforms Commission of West Pakistan*, Lahore: West Pakistan Government Press.

KPMG Report of the Accounts of the Army Welfare Trust and its Companies, 2000–01.

CMLA letter No. 57/1/CMLA dated 20 July 1978.

NLC at a Glance. Brief for the OIC NLC. Rawalpindi: National Logistic Cell Report, 2000.

National Assembly of Pakistan Debates, Monday, 29 December 2003. (*Official Report: 11th Session, Vol. XI* contains No. 1–4). NAP-XI (4)/2003.

'Un-starred questions and their replies', Islamabad: Senate Secretariat, Friday 26 December 2003.

'Questions for oral answers and their replies', Islamabad: Senate Secretariat, Wednesday 10 December 2003.

Special Audit Report on the Accounts of Controller of Military Accounts, 2001–02. Islamabad: Special Audit Report no. 179, Auditor-General of Pakistan, June 2003 (2003a).

Special Audit Report on the Accounts of PAF Bases Peshawar, Kohat, Mianwali, and Rafiqui, 2001–02. Islamabad: Special Audit Report no. 182, Auditor-General of Pakistan, June 2003 (2003b).

Special Audit Report on the Accounts of Cantonment Boards Clifton, Walton, Sialkot and Gujranwala, 2001–02. Islamabad: Special Audit Report no. 187, Auditor-General of Pakistan, June 2003 (2003c).

Special Study of the Issue of Military Land. Report no. A-Admn-192/SSR/97-98 by the Office of Director Audit, Defense Services, Lahore, 1998.

Audit Report no. De/R/2001-2002/01. Islamabad: Department of the Auditor-General of Pakistan, 2001/02.

2004 YLR 629. Basharat Hussain versus CDA (in the court of Justice Tanveer Bashir Ansari), writ petition No. 2524 of 2002 decided on 23 July 2003.

Civil Appeal No. 30 of 1999 dated 24 September 2003. Ref: Supreme Court of Pakistan. *Case No. CP1593/98.*

US Consulate (Dacca) cable, 'Selective genocide', 28 March 1971.

US Embassy (New Delhi) cable, 'Selective genocide', 29 March 1971 and US Consulate (Dacca) cable, 'Killings at university', 30 March 1971.

'Dissent from US policy toward East Pakistan', telegram to the State Department, April 1971. See http://www.gwu.edu/~nsarchiv/NSAEBB/NSAEBB79/BEBB8.pdf.

'Policy options towards Pakistan', Henry Kissinger's Memorandum for the President, 28 April 1971: http://www.gwu.edu/~nsarchiv/NSAEBB/NSAEBB79/BEBB9.pdf

US Department of State cable, 'USG Expression of Concern on East Pakistan', 6 April 1971.

'Case pending with the various departments of federal government ministries', working paper, Karachi: Government of Sindh, 2003.

SECONDARY SOURCES

Electronic sources

Alavi, Hamza 'Authoritarianism and legitimation of state power in Pakistan,' http://ourworld.compuserve.com/homepages/sangat/Power.htm

Khan, Azizullah *'Maarmallang peh Zindagi Tung'* (life made difficult in Maarmallang). Urdu report on BBC Urdu.com, Monday 20 June 2005, 16:03 GMT, 21:03 PST.

Makinson, Larry 'Outsourcing the Pentagon: who benefits from the politics and economics of national security?' http://www.icij.org/pns/report.aspx?aid=385

Mehmood, Tariq *'Karakoram key nijat dahinda'* (the saviours of Karakoram). Urdu report on BBC Urdu.com, Monday 20 June 2005, 16:27 GMT, 21:27 PST.

Rashid, Haroon *'Boolon ke naan Boolon?'* (should I speak or should I not?). Urdu report on BBC Urdu.com, Monday 20 June 2005, 16:05 GMT, 21:05 PST.

Saeed, Nadeem *'Wardi Walley Numberdar'* (uniformed *numberdars*). Urdu report on BBC Urdu.com, Monday 20 June 2005, 16:06 GMT, 21:06 PST.

Sangi, Sohail *'Maadni Daulat, Fauji Control'* (natural resources and military's control). Urdu report on BBC Urdu.com, Monday 20 June 2005, 16:25 GMT, 21:25 PST.

Sangi, Sohail *'Jamshooro mein Shurish'* (chaos in Jamshooro). Urdu report on BBC Urdu. com, Monday 20 June 2005, 15:15 GMT, 20:15 PST.

Sangi, Sohail *'Barrey Mian tu Barrey Mian'* (like the big master). Urdu report on BBC Urdu.com, Monday 20 June 2005, 16:26 GMT, 21:26 PST.

http://www.shaheenfoundation.com/shaheen_aero_traders.htm

http://www.bahria.com.pk/page8.html

http://wnc.fedworld.gov/cgi-bin/re...7ej5&CID=C74224653515625015000 7556

http://paknews.com/pk/main1jun-21.html

http://fedworld.gov/cgi-bin/re...5c36&CID=C23168945312500014343 6640

http://www.dawn.com/2000/07/12/ebr8.htm

http://www.nab.gov.pk/Public_info_material.asp#IMP_doc

http://fauji.org.pk/Industrial&Commercial/Subsidaries&Associated Co/FAUJI%20OIL.htm

http://fauji.org.pk/exp_seed.htm

http://usfspa-lawsuit.info/mccarty-mccarty.htm

Newspaper articles

Ahmed, Naveed 'The mother of all complexes', *Newsline*, Vol. 19, no. 01, July 2006.

Ali, Syed Mohammad 'Plight of the fisher folk in Pakistan', *Daily Times*, 14 June 2005.

Amir, Ayaz 'Realtor's paradise', *Dawn*, 10 December 2004.

Babur, Farhatullah 'Another DHA through military fiat', letter to the editor, *The News*, 27 February 2005.

Babur, Farhatullah 'A DHA in Islamabad now', *The News*, 18 February 2005.

Babur, Farhatullah ' When foundations are shaken', *The News*, 23 May 2005.

Basar, Faheem 'Army subsidiaries to collect toll on GT road', *The News*, 22 December 1999.

Bengali, Kaisar 'Perils of militarized politics', *Dawn*, 3 August 2006.

Bokhari, Jawaid 'Strategic issues in privatization', *Dawn*, 6 October 2003.

Farooqi, Monem 'Housing needs turning into serious problem', *The Nation*, 18 March 2005.

Gauhar, Hamayun 'The minister, the waiter and the donkey', *The Nation*, 25 October 2005.

Ghuman, Zulfiqar 'Army allotted land for golf course against rules', *Daily Times*, 6 August 2006.

Ghuman, Zulfiqar 'NA questions land deals by Musharraf and ISI DG', *Daily Times*, 24 July 2004.

Gillani, Waqar 'Army administration devastating academics, say PU teachers', *Daily Times*, 1 October 2004.

Hoti, Ikram 'Real estate lobby nips proposal for real story", *The News*, 26 May 2005.

Hussain, Maryam '56 govt. MNA's protest to Aziz', *Daily Times*, 22 June 2006.

Hussain, Mushahid 'All parties flirt with Pak army', *Times of India*, 28 September 1990.

Hussain, Mushahid 'Pakistan's political forces and the army', *The Nation*, 20 May 1990.

Hussain, Shakir 'Running scared', *The News*, 3 August 2005.

Keatley, Patrick 'The brown bomb', *Guardian* (Manchester), 11 March 1965.

Khan, Sher 'When selling sugar mills isn't so sweet', *The News*, 16 May 2005.

Klasra, Rauf 'Army trust in bad financial shape', *The News*, 29 August 2001.

Klasra, Rauf 'CDA explains cheap land allotment for GHQ', *The News*, 2 February 2005.

Lancaster, John 'Pakistanis question perks of power', *Washington Post*, 22 November 2002.

Malik, Lt.-Colonel (rtd) Mahmood L. 'Scheming away', *Newsline*, letter to the editor, Vol. 19, no. 2, August 2006.

Memon, Sirajul Haque 'Genesis of separatist sentiment in Sindh', *Dawn*, 23 March 2001 (Pakistan Day Special Issue).

Murad, Ahmed 'Army welfare trust: vest khaki interests and double standards of business accountability', *The Friday Times*, 14–20 December 2001.

Rao, Ishtiaq 'Pakistan lacks need oriented housing policy', *Pakistan Observer*, 8 July 2006.

Saleem, Farrukh 'Is Fauji Foundation in trouble?', *Dawn*, 14 May 2001.

Sehgal, Ikram 'Creek city, bleak city', *The Nation*, 2 August 2003.

Shah, Capt. Aamir 'Airline industry on the move', *Dawn*, 10 May 2004.

Shehzad, Mohammed 'Musharraf had decided to topple Nawaz much before Oct 12', *South Asia Tribune*, no. 12, 7–13 October 2002.

Siddiqa, Ayesha 'Military needs to reconsider its functioning', *The Friday Times*, Vol. 13, no. 49, 1–7 February 2002.

Tanner, Henry 'Bhutto denounces council and walks out in tears', *New York Times*, 16 December 1971.

Zulfiqar, Shahzada 'Changing loyalties', *Herald,* Vol. 37, no. 8, August 2006.

The News, Lahore, 23 April 1994.

'Zardari Group controls 4 radio, TV channels', *Takbeer* (Urdu), 11 July 1996.

'PAF and heroin smuggling', *The Nation*, editorial, 16 April 1997.

'CE calls for improving profitability of Fauji Foundation's units', *The News*, 2 February 2000.

'Bahria Varsity ordinance promulgated', *Dawn*, 8 February 2000.

'$1,700 Pak per capita income in real terms', *The Nation*, 25 February 2000.

'Smuggling costs govt Rs 100 billion every year', *Dawn*, 25 February 2000.
'Army demands 20,000 acres along super h'way', *Star*, 27 October 2000.
Dawn, 21 December 2002.
'Army tells Sindh govt. to give 12,000 acres', *Star*, 15 April 2003.
'Land allotment to army officers', *Dawn*, 25 June 2003.
'1,027 civilian posts occupied by servicemen', *Dawn*, 3 October 2003.
Daily Awaz (Urdu paper), 24 July 2004.
Dawn, 26 October 2004.
'Is Varan a legal authority?', *The News*, 5 October 2004.
'Improper use of defence lands', *The News*, 11 October 2004.
'Resolution on fishermen issue disallowed', *Dawn*, 26 November 2004.
'Law minister takes law into his hands, again', *The Peninsula*, 9 May 2005.
'NA passes budget amid criticism', *Dawn*, 18 June 2005.
'Minister's son beats passenger at airport', *The News*, 11 August 2005.
'PPP, PML gulf can't be bridged', *The News*, 3 July 2006.
'Pakistan urged to probe 7 reporters' deaths', Reuters, 27 July 2006.
'PML will re-elect Musharraf', *Dawn*, 8 May 2006.
'Opposition seeks debate in senate', *Dawn*, 1 August 2006.
'Musharraf seeks vote for his supporters', *Dawn*, 1 August 2006.
'PML activists ransack Peshawar Press Club', *The News*, 30 June 2006.

Journal articles

Ahmed, Naveed (2006) 'There is no plot that is free of cost no matter what the person's rank: interview of Major General Shaukat Sultan, DG, ISPR', *Newsline*, Vol. 19, no. 1, July.

Bauer, Christopher A. (2003) 'Government takings and constitutional guarantees: when date of valuation statutes deny just compensation', *Brigham Young University Law Review 2003*, no. 1.

Bilquees, Faiz (1994) 'Real wages of the federal government employees: trends from 1977–78 to 1991–92', *Pakistan Development Review*, Vol. 33, no. 3, Autumn.

Bray, John (1997) 'Pakistan at 50: a state in decline', *International Affairs*, Vol. 73, no. 2, April.

Krasner, Stephen D. (1984) 'Approaches to the state: alternative conceptions and historical dynamics' (review article), *Comparative Politics*, January.

LaPorte, Robert Jr. (1997) 'Pakistan in 1996: starting over again', *Asian Survey*, Vol. 37, no. 2, February.

Mora, Frank O. (2003) 'Economic reform and the military: China, Cuba and Syria in comparative perspective', *International Journal of Comparative Sociology*, Vol. 44, no. 2.

Nasir, Zafar Mueen (2000) 'Earnings differential between public and private sectors in Pakistan', *Pakistan Development Review*, Vol. 39, no. 2, Summer.

Qadeer, Mohammad A. (2000) 'Ruralopolises: the spatial organization and residential land economy of high-density rural regions in South Asia', *Urban Studies*, Vol. 37, no. 9, pp. 1583–1603.

Qureshi, Rizwan (2006) 'Malik Riaz talks tough', *Blue Chip*, Vol. 23, no. 2, April.

Redlich, Fritz 'The German military enterpriser and his work force: a study in European economic and social history', *Vierteljahreschrift fur Sozial-und Wirtschaftsgeschichte*, II.

Schmitter, Philippe C. (1974) 'Still the century of corporatism?', *Review of Politics*, Vol. 36, no. 1, pp. 85–131.

Siddiqa, Ayesha (2006a) 'General figures: how much is a General worth in real estate terms?', *Newsline*, Vol. 19, no. 1, July.

Siddiqa, Ayesha (2006b) 'The new land barons', *Newsline*, Vol. 19, no. 01, July, p. 21.

Werve, Jonathan (2004) 'Contractors write the rules', *Public I*, Vol 10, no. 3, July. http://www.icij.org/wow/docs/contractorsbattlefield.pdf

Papers and reports

Asch, Beth J. and Warner, John T. (1994) 'A policy analysis of alternative military retirement systems', RAND report MR-465-OSD, Santa Monica: RAND Corporation.

Gadzar, Harris (2003) 'The land question', paper written for Department for International Development (DFID), UK, 4 December.

Hasnain, Zahid (2005) 'The politics of service delivery in Pakistan: political parties and the incentives for patronage, 1988–1999.' World Bank Report No. SASPR-6, May.

Holmqvist, Caroline (2005) 'Private security companies the case for regulation', Stockholm: SIPRI Policy Paper no. 9, January.

Human Rights Watch (2004) 'Soiled hands: Pakistan Army's repression of the Punjab Farmer's Movement', *Human Rights Watch Report*, Vol. 16, no. 10, July.

Hussain, Hamid (2002) 'Armed forces and land policy', paper presented at a conference on 'Sindh, the water crisis and the future of Pakistan', organized by the World Sindhi Institute in Washington, D.C., 9 November.

Hussain, Ishrat (2004) 'Pakistan's economic progress since 2000: false dawn or promising start?' paper presented at a seminar at SAIS, Johns Hopkins University, 6 October.

Jacoby, Tim (2005) 'For the people, of the people and by the military: the regime structure of modern Turkey', paper written for the Institute of Development Policy and Management, University of Manchester.

Kariappar, Ayesha Salma (2003) 'The tenant's movement on the Okara military farm', paper submitted at the Lahore University of Management Sciences, Lahore.

Klebnikov, Paul (2003) 'Millionaire mullahs', *Forbes*, Vol. 172, no. 2, 21 July 2003.

Lock, Peter (2000) 'Exploring the changing role of the military in the economy', paper presented in Jakarta at a conference on 'Soldiers in Business: The Military as an Economic Player', 16–19 October.

McCulloch, Lesley (2005) 'Aceh: then and now', report, Minority Rights Group International, April.

Mora, Frank O. (2002) 'A comparative study of civil–military relations in

Cuba and China: the effects of Bingshang', *Armed Force and Society*, Vol. 28, no. 2, Winter.

Narli, N. (2000) 'Civil–military relations in Turkey', *Turkish Studies*, no. 1.

Peri, Yorum (2002) 'The Israeli military and Israel's Palestinian policy: from Oslo to the Al Aqsa intifada', Washington, D.C., USIP report. *Peaceworks* no. 47, November.

Roulleau, Eric (2000) 'Turkey's dream of democracy', *Foreign Affairs*, Vol. 79, no. 6, November/December.

Wilders, Malcolm 'Army welfare', report of the Office of Population Census and Surveys, Social Survey Division, UK.

Books

Abbas, Hassan (1979) 'The state in postcolonial societies: Pakistan and Bangladesh', in Harry Goulbourne (ed.), *Politics and State in the Third World*, Hong Kong: Macmillan.

Abbas, Hassan (2005) *Pakistan's Drift into Extremism*, New York. M. E. Sharpe.

Alavi, Hamza (1976) 'Rural elite and agricultural development in Pakistan', in R. D. Stevens, Hamza Alavi and Peter Bertocci (eds), *Rural Development in Pakistan and Bangladesh*, Hawaii: University of Hawaii Press.

Alavi, Hamza (1982a) 'The structure of peripheral capitalism', in Hamza Alavi and Teaedor Shanin (eds), *Sociology of Developing Societies*, New York: Monthly Review Press, pp. 172–91.

Alavi, Hamza (1982b) 'State and class under peripheral capitalism', in Hamza Alavi and Teaedor Shanin (eds) *Sociology of Developing Societies*, New York: Monthly Review Press, pp. 296–99.

Alavi, Hamza (1983) 'Class and state', in Hassan Gardezi and Jamil Rashid (eds) *Pakistan the roots of dictatorship*, London: Zed Press.

Ali, Imran (1988) *Punjab Under Imperialism, 1885–1947*, New Jersey: Princeton University Press.

Arif, Khalid, Mahmud (1995) *Working with Zia*, Karachi: Oxford University Press.

Banfield, Edward C. (1958) *The Moral Basis of a Backward Society*, New York: Free Press.

Brommelhorster, Jorn and Paes, Wolf-Christian (eds) (2003) *The Military as an Economic Actor: Soldiers in business*, Basingstoke: Palgrave.

Callahan, Mary P. (2003) *Making Enemies: War and state building in Burma*, Ithaca: Cornell University Press.

Castro, Arnoldo Brenes and Zamora, Kevin Casas (2003) 'Soldiers as businessmen: the economic activities of Central America's militaries', in Jorn Brommelhorster and Wolf-Christian Paes, *The Military as an Economic Actor: Soldiers in business*, Basingstoke: Palgrave.

Cheema, Pervez Iqbal (2002) *The Armed Forces of Pakistan*, Karachi: Oxford University Press.

Cloughly, B. (1999). *The History of Pakistan Army*, Karachi: Oxford University Press.

Cockburn, Alexander and St. Clair, Jeffrey (1998) *Whiteout: The CIA, drugs and the press*, London: Verso.

Cohen, Stephen P. (2004) *The Idea of Pakistan*, Washington, D.C.: Brookings Institution.

Crefeld, M. van (1977) *Supplying War: Logistics from Wallenstein to Patton*, Cambridge: Cambridge University Press.

Crouch, Harold (1978) *The Army and Politics in Indonesia*, Ithaca.

Dahl, R. (1961) *Who Governs? Democracy and power in an American city*, New Haven, Conn. Yale University Press.

Dauvergne, Peter (1998) 'Weak states and the environment in Indonesia and the Solomon Islands', in Peter Dauvergne (ed.), *Weak and Strong States in Asia–Pacific Societies*, Australia: Allen and Unwin.

Davis, James R. (2002) *Fortune's Warriors: Private armies and the new world order*, Canada: Douglas & McIntyre.

Dupree, Louis (1991) 'Pakistan and the Afghan problem', in Craig Baxter and Syed Raza Wasti, *Pakistan Authoritarianism in the 1980s*, Lahore: Vanguard.

Durrani, Tehmina (1996) *My Feudal Lord*, London: Corgi Adult.

Epstein, Richard A. (1985) *Takings*, Boston, Mass.: Harvard University Press.

Feaver, Peter D. (2003) *Armed Servants Agency, Oversight, and Civil–Military Relations*, Boston, Mass.: Harvard University Press.

Feit, Edward (1973) *The Armed Bureaucrats*, Boston: Houghton Mifflin.

Feldman, Herbert (1972) *From Crisis to Crisis: Pakistan 1962–69*, Karachi: Oxford University Press.

Finer, Samuel E. (1975). 'State and nation-building in Europe: the role of the army,' in Charles Tilly (ed.), *The Formation of National States in Western Europe*, New Jersey: Princeton University Press.

Government of Pakistan (2006) *Pakistan Economic Survey, 2005–06*, Islamabad: Government of Pakistan.

Greetz, Clifford (1981) *Negara: The theatre state in nineteenth century Bali*, Princeton, N.J.: Princeton University Press.

Grindle, Merilee S. (1996) *Challenging the State: Crisis and innovation in Latin America and Africa*, Cambridge: Cambridge University Press.

Hale, William (1944) *Turkish Politics and the Military*, London: Routledge.

Halpern, Manfred (1963) *The Politics of Social Change in the Middle East and North Africa*, Princeton, N.J.: Princeton University Press.

Haqqani, Hussain (2005) *Pakistan Between Mosque and Military*, Washington, D.C.: Carnegie Endowment for International Peace.

Herring, Ronald J. (1983) *Land to the Tiller*, New Haven: Yale University Press.

Hobsbawm, Eric (2000) *Bandits*, New York: New Press.

Holsti, Kalevi J. (1996) *The State, War, and the State of War*, Cambridge: Cambridge University Press.

Huntington, Samuel P. (1996) *Political Order in Changing Societies*, New Haven, Conn.: Yale University Press.

Huser, Herbert C. (2002) *Argentine Civil-Military Relations From Alfonsin to Menem*, Washington, D.C.: National Defense University Press.

Hussain, Mushahid (1990) *Pakistan's Politics: The Zia years*, Lahore: Progressive Publishers.

Jacoby, Tim (2004) *Social Power and the Turkish State*, London: Frank Cass.

Jalal, Ayesha (1991) *State of Martial Rule*, Lahore: Vanguard Books, Pakistan edition.

Jalal, Ayesha (1995) *Democracy and Authoritarianism in South Asia: A comparative historical perspective*, Cambridge: Cambridge University Press.

James, Sir Morrice (1993) *Pakistan Chronicle*, Karachi: Oxford University Press.

Janowitz, Morris (1964) *The Military in the Political Development of New Nations*, Chicago: University of Chicago Press.

Janowitz, Morris (1971) 'The comparative analysis of Middle Eastern military institutions', in Morris Janowitz and J. Van Doorn (eds), *On Military Intervention*, Rotterdam: Rotterdam University Press.

Joffe, Ellis (1997) 'Party–army relations in China: retrospect and prospect' in David Shambaugh and Richard H. Yang, *China's Military in Transition*, New York: Oxford University Press.

Jones, Philip E. (2003) *The Pakistan People's Party Rise to Power*, Karachi: Oxford University Press.

Karaosmanoglu, A. (1993) 'Officers: westernization and democracy', in M. Heper, A. Oncu and H. Kramer (eds), *Turkey and the West*, London: IB Taurus.

Kerans, Patrick, Drover, Glenn and Williams, David (1988) *Welfare and Worker Participation*, New York: St. Martin's Press.

Khan, Ayub (1967) *Friends not Masters*, Karachi: Oxford University Press.

Khan, Major General (rtd) Fazal Muqeem (1963) *The Story of the Pakistan Army*, Karachi: Oxford University Press.

Khan, Gul Hassan (1993) *Memoirs of Lt. Gen. Gul Hassan Khan*, Karachi: Oxford University Press.

Khan, Lt.-General Jahan Dad (1999) *Pakistan Leadership Challenges*, Karachi: Oxford University Press.

Khan, Roedad (ed.) (2002) *The British Papers: Secret and confidential India, Pakistan, Bangladesh documents 1958–69*, Karachi: Oxford University Press.

Khuhro, Hamida (1998) *Mohammad Ayub Khuhro: A life of courage in politics*, Lahore: Ferozesons.

Kinzer, Stephen (2001) *Crescent & Star: Turkey between two worlds*, New York: Farrar, Straus and Giroux.

Kochanek, Stanley A. (1983) *Interest Groups and Development: Business and politics in Pakistan*, Delhi: Oxford University Press.

Kux, Dennis (2001) *The United States and Pakistan 1947–2000: Disenchanted allies*, Baltimore, Md.: Johns Hopkins University Press.

Lane, Frederic C. (1979) *Profits from Power*, Albany, N.Y.: State University of New York Press.

Lasswell, Harold (1958) *Politics: Who gets what, when, how*, Cleveland: World Publishing.

Levi, Margaret (2002) 'The state of the study of the state', in Ira Katznelson and Helen V. Milner (eds), *Political Science: State of the discipline*, New York: W.W. Norton.

Linz, Juan (1978) *Breakdown of Democratic Regimes: Latin America*, Baltimore, Md.: Johns Hopkins University Press.

Malloy, James (ed.) (1977) *Authoritarianism and Corporatism in Latin America*, Pittsburgh: University of Pittsburgh Press.

Malloy, James, Chalmers, Douglas, Newton, Ronald, Schmitter, Philippe, Stepan, Alfred and Grindle, Merilee S. (1996) *Challenging the State. Crisis and innovation in Latin America and Africa*, Cambridge: Cambridge University Press.

Mann, Michael (1993) *Sources of Social Power, Vol. 2*, Cambridge: Cambridge University Press.

Mares, David R. (1998) 'Civil–military relations, democracy, and the regional neighborhood', in David R. Mares (ed.), *Civil–Military Relations*, Boulder, Colo.: Westview Press.

McCulloch, Lesley (2003) 'Trifungsi: the role of Indonesian military in politics', in Jorn Brommelhorster and Wolf-Christian Paes (eds), *The Military as an Economic Actor: Soldiers in business*, Basingstoke: Palgrave.

Mehmood, Shaukat and Nadeem, Shaukat (1998) *Land Acquisition Laws* (fourth revised and enlarged edition), Lahore: Legal Research Center.

Migdal, Joel S. (1988) *Strong Societies and Weak States*, Princeton, N.J.: Princeton University Press.

Migdal, Joel S. (2001) *State in Society*, Cambridge: Cambridge University Press.

Moore, Raymond A. Jr. (1979) *Nation Building and the Pakistan Army, 1947–1969*, Lahore: Aziz.

Mulvenon, James (2001) *Soldiers of Fortune*, New York: M. E. Sharpe.

Nandy, Ashis (2003) *The Romance of the State and the Fate of Dissent in the Tropics*, New Delhi: Oxford University Press.

Nasr, Seyyed Vali Reza (2001) *Islamic Leviathan: Islam and the making of state power*, New York: Oxford University Press.

Nordlinger, Eric (1977) *Soldiers in Politics: Military coups and governments*, N. J.: Prentice-Hall.

Nordlinger, Eric (1981) *On the Autonomy of the Democratic State*, Boston, Mass.: Harvard University Press.

O'Donnell, Guillermo A. (1973) *Modernization and Bureaucratic Authoritarianism: Studies in South American politics*, Berkeley: University of California Press.

Olson, Mancur (2000) *Power and Prosperity*, New York: Basic Books.

Paes, Wolf-Christian and Shaw, Timothy M. (2003) 'Role of entrepreneurial armed forces in Congo–Kinshasa', in Jorn Brommelhorster and Wolf-Christian Paes (eds), *The Military as an Economic Actor: Soldiers in business*, Basingstoke, Palgrave.

Pasha, Mustafa Kamal (1988) *Colonial Political Economy*, Karachi: Oxford University Press.

Perlmutter, Amos (1974) *Egypt: The praetorian state*, New Brunswick: Transaction Books.

Perlmutter, Amos (1977) *The Military in Politics in Modern Times*, New Haven, Conn.: Yale University Press.

Perlmutter, Amos (1981) *Modern Authoritarianism*, New Haven, Conn.: Yale University Press.

Perlmutter, Amos and Bennett, Valerie Plave (eds) (1980) *The Political Influence of the Military*, New Haven, Conn.: Yale University Press.

Poggi, Gianfranco (1978) *The Development of the Modern State*, Stanford, Calif.: Stanford University Press.

Redlich, Fritz (1964) *The German Military Enterpriser and His Work Force: A study in European social and economic history*, 2 vols, Wiesbaden.

Rehman, Shahid ur (1998) *Who Owns Pakistan?* privately published, May.

Rehman, Tariq (2004) *Denizens of Alien World: A Study of education, inequality and polarization in Pakistan*, Karachi: Oxford University Press.

Rizvi, Hasan-Askari (2003) *Military, State and Society in Pakistan*, Lahore, Sang-e-Meel Publication.

Robinson, William I. (1996) *Promoting Polyarchy: Globalization, US intervention and hegemony*, Cambridge: Cambridge University Press.

Salik, Sadiq (1979) *Witness to Surrender*, Karachi: Oxford University Press.

Schmitter, Philippe C. (1978) 'Reflections on Mihail Manoilescu and the political consequence of delayed-dependent development on the periphery of Western Europe', in Kenneth Jowitt (ed.), *Social Change in Romania, 1860–1940: A debate on development in a European nation*, Berkeley, Calif.: University of California Press.

Shafqat, Saeed (1997) *Civil–Military Relations*, Boulder, Colo.: Westview Press.

Shah, Dr Justice Nasim Hassan (2002) *Memoirs and Reflections*, Islamabad: Alhamra.

Siddiqa-Agha, Ayesha (2001) *Pakistan's Arms Procurement and Military Buildup, 1979–99: In search of a policy*, Basingstoke: Palgrave.

Siddiqa-Agha, Ayesha (2003) 'Power, perks, prestige and privileges: military's economic activities in Pakistan', in Jorn Brommelhorster and Wolf-Christian Paes (eds), *The Military as an Economic Actor: Soldiers in business*, Basingstoke: Palgrave.

Siddiqi, Abdurrahman (1996) *The Military in Pakistan, Image and reality*, Lahore: Vanguard.

Singer, P. W. (2004) *Corporate Warriors: The rise of the privatized military industry*, Cornell: Cornell University Press.

Skowronek, Stephen (1982) *Building a New American State: The expansion of national administrative capacities*, New York: Cambridge University Press.

Stepan, Alfred (1971) *The Military in Politics: Changing patterns in Brazil*, Princeton, N.J.: Princeton University Press.

Stepan, Alfred (1988) *Rethinking Military Politics*, Princeton, N.J.: Princeton University Press.

Tilly, Charles (1985) 'War making and state making as organized crime', in Peter Evans, Dietrich Rueschemeyer and Theda Skocpol, *Bringing the State Back In*, Cambridge: Cambridge University Press.

Tilly, Charles (1992) *Coercion, Capital and European States*, Oxford: Blackwell.

Van de Walle, Nicolas (2001) *African Economies and the Politics of Permanent Crisis, 1979–99,* Cambridge: Cambridge University Press.

Verkaaik, Oskar (2005) *Migrants and Militants: Fun and urban violence in Pakistan,* New Delhi: Manas.

Warraich, Sohail (2006) *Ghaddar Kaun Nawaz Sharif Ki Kahani Un Ke Apni Zabani (Who's the Traitor? The Story of Nawaz Sharif in his Own Words),* Lahore: Sagar.

Waseem, Mohammad (1994) *Politics and the State in Pakistan,* Islamabad:

Waseem, Mohammad (2006) *Democratization in Pakistan: A study of the 2002 elections,* Karachi: Oxford University Press.

Weaver, Jerry L. (1973) 'Assessing the impact of military rule: alternative approaches', in Philippe C. Schmitter (ed.), *Military Rule in Latin America: Functions, consequences and perspectives,* California: Sage.

Wintrobe, Ronald (2000) *The Political Economy of Dictatorship,* Cambridge: Cambridge University Press.

Yong, Tan Tai (2005) *The Garrison State,* Lahore: Vanguard.

Zaheer, Hassan (1998) *The Times and Trials of the Rawalpindi Conspiracy, 1951: The first coup attempt in Pakistan,* Karachi: Oxford University Press.

Zaidi, S. Akbar (1999) *Issues in Pakistan's Economy,* Karachi: Oxford University Press.

Ziring, Lawrence (1994) *Bangladesh from Mujib to Ershad An interpretive study,* Dhaka: University Press, reprint.

286

Index

Contents   Page

Author's Note

These notes are structured around central themes of the novel and a synopsis of each chapter. I have both 'made points,' based upon my own reading of the novel, and posed questions of the reader in order to encourage a subjective engagement with the novel. The students awarded the highest marks are those who offer original, independent readings of the novel. Direct quotations have been written using the italic font to distinguish them from authorial quotations.

A complete essay has been included in these notes, which is similar to an 'A' level essay question. I have also shown how an essay should be structured: the introduction being an exploration and 'interrogation' of the question. A typical 'A' level question will invite the student to offer a discursive engagement with the question; for example it might ask the extent to which he or she agrees or disagrees with a specified point of view, thus demanding a discursive 'tension' in the response. The 'body' of the essay is an exploration of the 'tensions,' using discourse markers: however, whereas, on the other hand, never the less and so on, which should be substantiated with textual evidence. The summary 'pulls together' the central 'argument' and makes a conclusion.

Foreword

Graham Greene objected to being described as a Catholic writer, rather than a writer who happened to be a Catholic, and yet many of his novels engage with spiritual dilemmas which challenge his characters. Catholic theology underpins many of the ideas explored, as the realistic human beings that he portrays grapple with life experiences and their own weaknesses.

The four novels which predominately concern issues of faith in the world are *Brighton Rock (1938); The Power and the Glory (1940); The Heart of the Matter (1948)* and *The End of the Affair (1951).*

Greene converted to Catholicism in 1926 and described his experience of accepting "the supreme, omnipotent and omniscient power" of God in his autobiographical '*A Sort Of Life.*' He did not embrace his faith with enthusiasm, rather he "fought and fought hard." He described himself as a "dogmatic atheist," saying that the fight against belief in God "was like a fight for personal survival". His encounter with the priest, Fr. Trollope to whom he went for instruction at Nottingham Cathedral, at first reinforced his antagonism toward the Church. Soon, however, he was forced to realise that his initial impression had been false, and that he was "faced with an inexplicable goodness."

When Greene was asked in an interview whether faith gave an extra dimension to his writing he answered: "Human beings are more important to believers than they are to atheists." He criticised modernist writers such as Virginia Woolf and E.M. Forster for having no religious sense, and consequently producing characters in their writing with no real depth, who "wandered about like cardboard symbols through a world that is paper thin." For Greene the dramatic power of the novel resides in an understanding of the truth of the spiritual warfare which exists between the power of goodness, God, and the power of evil, the Devil. This fundamental duality underwrites his 'Catholic novels,' and his characters wrestle with knowledge in the light of this truth, which is revealed through the gift of faith,

6

against the weakness of his or her own nature, which inclines like a tropism toward the 'darkness' of sin.

In Brighton Rock Greene presents the character Pinkie who has an absolute belief in the personified power of evil, and who believes that the 'wages' for un-repented evil to be the fires of hell: everlasting torment. The abiding mystery of what has been described as the 'banality of evil' presented in this novel, is the hold that it appears to have upon the individual who, whilst acknowledging his peril, continues his miserable descent upon the 'slippery slope.'

Greene finds human behaviour fascinating because he is aware within himself of the dissonance of his internal life: man was made to love God and yet he persists in choosing to follow the ways of the world. Greene shows penetrating understanding of the wickedness in the world and the inclination of all human beings to sin rather than to embrace righteousness.

In Brighton Rock he makes a distinction between the secular sinfulness of Ida, which she calls human nature, and the proud renunciation of goodness and allegiance to evil epitomised by Pinkie; yet Ida, because she is unable, through her unbelief, to access the grace of God, is further from the kingdom of heaven than Pinkie, who might, by turning from evil, be forgiven. This is the enigma at the heart of his novel: what the elderly tired priest calls 'the ...appalling... strangeness of the mercy of God.' Pinkie has 'knowledge,' the truth which might have set him free, had he turned and sought redemption through the gift of faith.

The priest to whom Rose goes, not to confess her sins, but rather to proclaim her rebellion and allegiance to 'love,' does not refute her claim for the transcendence of love, rather he reinforces it.

Greene was criticised for placing the inclination to sin, i.e. failure, at the centre of his novels. In spite of 'knowledge,' his characters are doomed to fall from grace: sinful conduct is inevitable. The theologian Hans Urs Balthazar accused him of giving sin a mystique. Greene responded by asserting that the creation of pure faith and goodness in a novel was beyond his talents.

The Authorial Voice in Brighton Rock

'One sees absolutely no one here of one's own class. In the street, in the cafes, anywhere. It destroys democratic feelings at birth.'

The quotation above was taken from a letter written by Graham Greene to his future wife. He was writing about Nottingham where he lived and worked in 1926. During the General Strike Greene enrolled as a special constable and wrote about the fun he was having breaking the strike, likening the atmosphere to a 'rugger match played against a team from rather a rough council school.' There is evidence in the novel that Greene did feel contempt for what John Carey terms 'the masses,' which Carey declares is a 'linguistic device…to eliminate the human status of the majority of people'. In his book 'The Intellectuals and The Masses', Carey describes 'Brighton Rock' as 'a contemptuous indictment of England in the 1930s'. Certainly there is evidence in the novel of Greene's distaste for the crowds of working class day trippers to Brighton: the hairdressers with *'bleached and perfumed hair'*, the clerks and the gamblers who came in *'bewildered multitudes'* on day trips to Brighton did not represent the class into which Greene was born.

Greene's dislike of the populist culture of modern life, which has been criticised by Carey, also excited contempt from other writers and intellectuals of the time who made disdainful reference to the rise of populist culture in their work, which they believed was fed by newspapers and advertising, and promoted by the weakening of class barriers.

In this novel the breakdown of class barriers is exemplified by the criminal Colleoni's easy acceptance into the opulent world of the Cosmopolitan Hotel. He is ostentatiously wealthy; however the trappings of wealth do not redeem his vulgarity. He tells Pinkie that he *'likes things good'* when Pinkie comments upon his gold lighter. However, it is clear that he is not a gentleman in spite of his expensive clothing and jewellery and his desire to distance himself from the criminal origins of his wealth.

The name of the hotel might suggest that the value system of the modern age is becoming progressively more 'worldly:' more orientated toward money, less inclined to discriminate between wealth acquired through nefarious practice, and inherited wealth, or 'old money.' The allusion to a bygone age which was *'faded like peace'* suggests nostalgia for a world which was ordered by class distinction, which was not egalitarian: a more 'gentle' age: *'Three old ladies went driving by in an open horse drawn carriage: the gentle clatter faded like peace. That was how some people still lived.'* Yet in Greene's depiction of Brighton in the 30's there is too the paradox that *'the world never moved: it lay there always, the ravaged and disputed territory between the two eternities'* (Part five, Chapter two).

There is a distinction between the 'world' and the 'spirit,' or things which are eternal, rather than temporal or secular. The 'two eternities' are heaven and hell: the 'disputed and ravaged territory' being a reference to creation in general, and human beings in particular. In this quotation Greene implies that human nature does not change and the war between good and evil, or heaven and hell, remains the same. As a Catholic, Greene believed for most of his adult life in the truth of this 'war' between good and evil: God and the Devil.

Many contemporary readers warm to Greene's depiction of Ida, the fun loving, warm, generous spirited character that, at some personal risk, pursues Pinkie, the vicious killer without a conscience. However Greene's attitude toward his crusader for justice is undeniably ambivalent: she certainly shows courage, and she is indisputably fighting on the side of the law; nevertheless the portrayal remains irrefutably derogatory: *Her 'cow-like eyes', 'vulgar summer dress' 'big blown charms', 'rich Guinness voice,'* and fondness for sentimental music-hall ballads depict the *'accommodating'* Ida as cheap, vulgar and sexually 'accommodating' to her numerous men friends. It might be argued that Greene's regular references to her breasts and mouth communicate at least ambivalence in his attitude toward her: is she depicted as admirable or even sexually desirable? Or does he present a character whose motives are selfish rather than righteous, self gratifying rather than sacrificial? Is her '*soft gluey mouth affixed in taxis,*' frequently described eating, drinking, and bawdily singing, a representation which communicates warm sexuality or a voracious, rather repellent appetite demanding consummation?

For the modern reader there may be much to admire in Greene's portrayal of Ida. She is '*a sticker*' and she is '*optimistic*' in her determination to enjoy life. However the narrator comments '*there was something dangerous and remorseless in her optimism.*' Her definition of life is one which might be argued is a modern one: life is to be enjoyed, and could be summed up: 'eat drink and be merry, for tomorrow we die.' Certainly she could have decided to pocket her winnings on the horse that Hale tipped to win, forget him and continue to enjoy all the consumerist delights on offer in Brighton; for which she possessed a considerable appetite.

The narrator comments '*Man*' (and presumably woman too) '*is made by the places in which he lives.*' Ida's mind, works we are told, '*with the simplicity*' of '*a sky sign,*' or neon light. These signs are used in adverts for products of the modern age in which the novel is set. Adverts were regarded by some 'thinkers' of the time, along with populist newspapers, as catering for the growing consumerist appetite of the masses. It is the crowd of working class trippers who are entertained and 'fed' by the popular newspapers and seaside pleasure industry. All harmless fun the modern reader is likely to claim; however is this how Greene presents Brighton and Ida? Is her philosophy presented as an admirable one? Or is it a dangerous one?

Ida is described as '*life' itself:*' '*Life was here beside him, he wasn't going to play around with death.*' So thinks Fred Hale, as he sits with the generous spirited and rather inebriated Ida in the bar. Hale asks for her company and she tells him '*I warn you – I like to spend.*' Ida, with her '*immense store of masculine experiences,*' likes to drink, eat, have sex and spend money. Many contemporary readers might similarly summarise their philosophy of life. Ida believes life can be summed up as '*sunlight on bedposts, Ruby port, the leap of the heart when the*'
10

outsider you have backed passes the post.'
Ida has no religion, but she is superstitious and enjoys the thrill
of the occult. Ida's belief could be read as being in justice: *'a
determination grew...somebody had made Fred unhappy, and
somebody was going to be made unhappy in return. An eye for
an eye.'* Ida is quoting the Bible, and yet she is not religious:
'vengeance was Ida's, (rather than God's) *just as much as reward
was Ida's.'* Yet it is clear that her motivation is the gratification of
self, rather than justice for Hale. Her 'reward' is, as she asserts,
the thrill of the chase: *'It's exciting, it's fun, it's living'.'* Life
and its meaning for Ida is defined in terms of entertainment and
consumption: Guinness or ruby port; the cream éclair 'oozing'
between her teeth; sex in hotel rooms with men with whom she
has no depth of relationship, and the pursuit of excitement through
confronting the criminal underworld define Ida's philosophy of
life, and was for her *'the only reward there was.'*
Modern values are represented in the novel as entirely temporal;
Ida's flirtation with the occult via the Ouija board exemplifies
religion's decay.
Cremation was a modern way of disposing with the dead, and
was one disliked by the author. The address given at Hale's
cremation was modelled on the one given at Greene's mother-
in-law's cremation in 1933. He commented upon its 'air of
irreligion posing as undogmatic Christianity,' describing the
officiating cleric as 'an emaciated vulture.' The 'consolations'
offered to the bereaved are vague and meaningless, they could
not be ascribed to any orthodox belief system, other than what we
might term today 'New Age.' Its effects are anodyne: superficial
platitude rather than offering the bereaved either comfort or
challenge. The dead Hale is described as having *'attained unity'*
with *'the One.'* A belief is expressed, *'with certainty,'* that Hale
has been *'reabsorbed into the eternal spirit.'* There is no mention
of God, heaven, Christian salvation, indeed anything pertaining
to mainstream theological belief. Reference is made by the
(protestant) clergyman to a *'Truth loving generation:'* this has
to be Greene's ironic voice. Following the mass destruction of
humankind as a consequence of The Great War, most modernist

writers and intellectuals such as T.S.Eliot, D.H.Lawrence, H.G. Wells, Virginia Woolf and James Joyce, expressed loss of certainty in any kind of absolute values through their writing. Auden summed up his view of the thirties as 'A low dishonest decade.'

Greene's depiction of modern life is a negative one, represented by the self-indulgent Ida, the dilution of religious belief, shown at Hale's cremation and the crumbling of class boundaries shown by the acceptance of Colleoni by the worldly elite. The novel is, as Carey claimed, 'a contemptuous indictment' of thirties Britain. But what moral values, if any in the novel, receive authorial approbation?

Ida confronts the evil Pinkie and defeats him. Pinkie, like the fallen angel Lucifer, who was once God's servant, sang in a church choir and swore he would be a priest. Pinkie describes Ida as *'just nothing.'* *'She doesn't even know what a mortal sin is'* scoffs Rose, and Greene, as narrator seems in agreement: *'she was as far from either of them as she was from Hell—or Heaven.'* From the point of view of the atheist reader, Ida has the ultimate victory: she has avenged Hale and saved Rose. And yet, from the point of view of the Catholic believer, the victory in this novel, in spite of Pinkie's death, belongs to the World.

Graham Greene declared at a dinner party that only Roman Catholics were capable of real sin 'because the rest of us were invincibly ignorant.' These words are strikingly similar to the words given to the priest: *'A Catholic is more capable of evil than anyone.'*

The real victory, from a spiritual and arguably narrative viewpoint, comes through grace (the freely offered gift of God's love and forgiveness) and is demonstrated through the words of the Catholic priest. Rose, the rebellious sinner, declares that Ida *'ought to be damned'* because she *'doesn't know about love.'* Rose chooses to reject absolution because of her unrepentant love for Pinkie. The priest, unlike either Pinkie or Rose, sees love rather than judgement at the centre of his religion. He declares that *'The Church does not demand that we believe any soul is cut off from mercy.'* The priest's exhortation that she should *'hope*

12

and pray' is delivered *'mechanically,'* because, as he tells Rose, *'if he* (pinkie) *loved her'* it shows that he had *'some good'* in him, however the priest, unlike the clergyman in the crematorium, is unable to claim 'certainty' about the state of anyone's soul, or the sincerity or otherwise of their relationship with God. *'The worst horror of all,'* as Rose would discover when she played the record, is that far from loving her, Pinkie declares his hatred. Rose, given hope of the triumph of love over evil, experiences *'a sudden feeling of immense gratitude...as if she had been given the sight a long way off of life going on again.'* It is the Catholic priest, who in a world dominated by human desire for gratification of the self, violence and hatred, offers Rose hope in *'the appalling...strangeness of the mercy of God.'* If there is hope and approbation in the narrative voice, it comes through the old weary priest who offers hope for the despairing sinner, rather than condemnation. And yet, the novel ends with the inevitability that Rose will discover the terrible truth: she will replay the record and hear his message to her: the declaration of his hatred.

The novel can certainly be read as a thriller, a depiction of the criminal underworld juxtaposed with 'real life' in Brighton between two world wars.

It can also be read as Greene's representation of a deeper spiritual truth about modern life, as experienced by the common man, or in Ida's case, the common woman: an exposition of 'The World' (symbolised by the Cosmopolitan Hotel and the value system of the unreligious); The Flesh (epitomised by Ida's demand for self gratification—the ever open mouth); and The Devil (a determined and deliberate renunciation of goodness and mercy, personified by Pinkie).

In the film of the book, the needle miraculously sticks on 'I love you, I love you,' giving Rose hope of Pinkie's redemption through love. Pinkie had started his speech to Rose saying *'you want me to say I love you, but God damn you, you little bitch...'* and so on. Finally the camera focuses on a crucifix upon the wall. Greene declared his liking for this ending.

He also said of his novel 'perhaps it is the best I ever wrote.'

Men and Masculinity in Brighton Rock

Graham Greene was inspired to base his novel about Catholicism and mob culture in Britain in the 1930's upon newspaper accounts of an attack upon a bookmaker at the Brighton Races in July 1936. A gang of sixteen men with hammers, iron bars and hatchets attacked the bookmaker and his clerk. The gang leader, called Spinks, was nicknamed Spinky. Graham Greene remarked 'the Brighton race gangs were to all intents and purposes quashed forever as a serious menace.' All those involved were given prison sentences. When Graham Greene read the report he wrote to his brother inviting him to a day of 'low sport' at the races. 'I warn you that I will want to spend my time in the lowest enclosure.' The press reported 'unusually large crowds' at Brighton. Greene spent some time in conversation with a man 'who could have belonged to Pinkie's gang…a man whose face had been carved, because he was suspected of grassing to the bogies after a killing at the stadium.

Other than the victim Hale, the solicitor Prewitt and Ida's two male friends, Phil Corkery with whom she spent the night at the Cosmopolitan Hotel, and her friend Clarence, the men delineated in the novel are violent gang members. The mob use intimidation to extract 'protection money' from their victims. Pinkie's gang extort money from the racecourse bookies, who are the victims of the protection racket. Colleoni, although sounding Italian, is Jewish in earlier editions of the novel. The origins of his wealth have been, as far as the world was concerned, sanitized. He claims *'I haven't been near a racecourse in years.'* He describes himself as *'just a business man,'* and his interests, rather than criminal, are suggested to be 'of the world.' He tells Pinkie: *'The World needs young people with energy.'* He looks 'at home' in the opulent hotel, he brushes shoulders with the aristocracy, comments that he *'likes things good.'* He talks to Pinkie *'like a father'* telling him *'I like you, you're a promising youngster.'* However, his vulgar backstreet gangster origins are revealed when Pinkie asks, following his brag that Napoleon and Eugenie had slept in his room at the Cosmopolitan, *'who was she?'* and he responds *'one of those foreign polonies.'* Colleoni's gangster wealth is presented as acceptable currency in the 'cosmopolitan,' worldly value system of the exclusive hotel. His image, as a 'man of the world,' has been air brushed with the aid of material props: fine clothing, expensive cologne and valuable jewellery, his underworld characteristics swept beneath a gilded veneer, and the violent extortionist merges almost seamlessly with the rich and famous 1930's elite.

The theme of material and moral values is explored through the way in which the world has apparently embraced the successful criminal.

Misogyny, or at least an ingrained disrespect for women, is a characteristic of all of the 'men of violence.' Colleoni's ignorant dismissal of the empress Eugenie as *'a foreign polony'* reveals the attitude of the men toward women, irrespective of class. Women in general are referred to as 'polony', women believed to be whores are referred to as *'buers.'* Pinkie's hatred of women is clear and consistent. Even the doll that he chooses for his prize on the rifle range, described as possessing *'glassy innocence'* and reminding Pinkie of a church statue of Mary is *'held by her hair.'*

Phil Corkery is initially described by Ida as *'Too quiet. Not what she called a man.'* Although this man sleeps with Ida in the Cosmopolitan Hotel, his manner toward her is diffident, if not fearful. Before Ida's powerful certainty that she is Right, he *'was shaken by a sense of terrific force, she is a woman of fiercely held convictions, and he feels it was astonishing that he ever had the nerve to send her...postcards from seaside resorts.'* He speaks *'nervously,'* suggesting that confrontation with Pinkie should be *'a matter for the police'* and she 'gently' but resolutely *'set him right.'* She is firm in her judgments and *'rebellion bobbed weakly up'* in him only to be firmly quashed. His hands are described as *'too sensitive'* and when he tells Ida *'a man can't help feeling,'* she *'was shaken by immense glee:'* Men who are sensitive, who 'feel,' are presented in the novel as, if not

15

weak, then certainly vulnerable.

Prewitt, Pinkie's corrupt solicitor, has sold out to *'sickly despair'*: although appalled by his level of collusion with the gang, he has neither the physical or moral strength to extricate himself. He describes himself as *'ruined'* as a consequence of being married to *'the spouse.'* Interestingly, although apparently not religious, he sees his suffering as interminable. He tells Pinkie *'Has it ever occurred to you that you're lucky? The worst that can happen to you is you'll hang. But I can rot.'* He is desperate 'to unburden' himself, and chooses the entirely unempathic Pinkie to hear his *'confession...of uncontrollable passion,'* which led to his marriage to the woman he describes as *'the old mole.'* Quoting Mephistopheles from Marlowe's play *Dr Faustus*, he comments of his life: *'Why, this is Hell, nor are we out of it.'* Pinkie watches Prewitt in horrified fascination as *'the nerves set to work in the agonized flesh, thought bloom in the transparent brain.'* Prewitt carries *'the secrets of the sewer'* and his mental anguish is physically manifest in *'his tormented stomach.'* The parallel between this character and Dr Faustus, who sells his soul to Mephistopheles for temporal power, is clear.

The violent gang members might be described as 'real men' in that they are men of conviction. Their creed is that violence is power. The 'weak' member of the gang, Spicer, is dispatched without qualm by Pinkie. His dream of owning a pub in Nottingham and retiring from criminal activity is portrayed as rather pathetic. He'd been *'a loyal old geezer'* to Pinkie, yet his desire to get out of the gang is presented as weak and deserving of a death sentence.

Dallow is depicted as a man with limited imagination and therefore he suffers little from guilt. His identity is defined by his moral abdication to Pinkie. He is valuable because he does not think or feel. Pinkie *'could trust Dallow – receiving from the ugly and broken face a sense of triumph and superiority. He felt as physically weak but cunning schoolboy feels who has attached himself in an indiscriminating fidelity the strongest boy in school.'* It is the physical strength of Dallow which communicates a powerful masculinity, and his 'indiscriminating' faithfulness to

Pinkie which ensures both his safety and his peace of mind. The men of religion in the novel are the protestant clergyman at Hale's cremation and the Roman Catholic priest to whom Rose goes to assert her defiance of the Catholoc religion and alliance to the memory of the dead Pinkie.

The minister at the cremation speaks words without real comfort or meaning. Rather than referring to God, he speaks of *'the One,'* his words are described as like *'little pats of butter:'* neatly packaged, unctuous and having no authority other than *'his personal mark.'* He speaks of *'a truth loving generation'* yet does not articulate an allegiance to a recognisable version of truth to which he subscribes. His message to the bereaved has been emptied of any meaning, and the vagueness of his *'certainty that our brother is reabsorbed in the universal spirit'* is delivered with all the easy aplomb of *'a conjurer who has produced his nine hundred and fortieth rabbit without a hitch.'* This presentation of a modern clergyman is obvious in its intention to derogate a religious belief that has been purged of real meaning: without mention of God, Heaven or Hell. This is not a 'manly' religious faith, it is impotent and sterile.

The old Catholic priest on the other hand is presented as wise; he offers no specious certainty to the tortured and rebellious Rose, yet he gives her comfort and hope: *'you can't conceive, my child, nor can I or anyone the ...appalling...strangeness of the mercy of God...we must hope and pray.'* These words, offered to the suffering but unrepentant sinner are not specious, neither are they weak. They are delivered with a tired conviction and compassion which seems to represent the best in mankind: with humility rather than pride. He asks the unrepentant sinner to pray for him, and she responds *'yes, oh yes.'*

Synopsis of Structure

Part One

Chapter One

The novel opens with an introduction to the *'nervous'* outsider in the sea-side resort. We are told that before he had been in Brighton for three hours, Fred Hale *'knew'* that *'they meant to murder him.'* Hale is in Brighton as 'Kolley Kibber' to promote his newspaper to the Whitson holiday crowd. The crowd is described as progressing, animal like, *'two by two...with sober and determined gaiety.'* The day trippers' experience is familiar to most: *'sun...music...sticks of rock...sailors' caps...ghost train'*, as is the description of the *'weary walk home'* and the *'immense patience'* required to extract the *'grain of pleasure'* from the day.

Hale's attitude toward the holiday makers is described as 'cynical,' yet the atmosphere *'pulled at his heart.'* The first description of Ida is of a woman in *'the late thirties or early forties...of big blown charms and rich Guinness voice.'* Her manner toward the group of men who surround her is described as *'accommodating.'* She is not referred to by her name; the men call her 'Lily,' suggesting a 'type of female' rather than a person. The lonely Hale watches her *'covetously.'* At this point Pinkie, a seventeen year old boy with a face of *'hideous and unnatural pride,'* calls him by name. Hale denies his identity, clearly afraid of the boy. Pinkie's focus upon Hale is described in terms of prey and predator. Pinkie's intense regard of Hale is distracted by the woman, whom he watches with an expression of *'furious distaste.'* Hale feels as though the hatred directed at him had, *'like handcuffs'* been *'loosened'*, *'to be fastened around another's wrists.'*

• The description of Pinkie is almost oxymoronic in the opposition of ideas: the 'fair, smooth skin' of youth is juxtaposed with the description of eyes with an *'effect of heartlessness like an old man's in which human feeling has died.'*

• The intensity of hatred is switched with startling ease from Hale to the woman who is referred to as *'that buer'* by Pinkie, suggesting that the boy has a ready reservoir of hatred which is affixed, almost arbitrarily, upon people who excite his 'distaste.'

• Hale gazes at the woman in the *'vulgar'* summer dress as though he *'were gazing at life itself'*... *'the big tipsy mouth, the magnificent breasts.'* The narrator comments upon her name, Ida: *'the old and vulgarised Grecian name.'*

• Consider the language used to describe Ida: *'cowlike eye'*, *'vulgar summer dress'*, *'warm port-winey laugh' 'rich Guinness voice.'*

• Consider the description of other women: *'bright brass hair and ermine coats, heads close like parrots exchanging metallic confidences...they flashed their painted nails at each other and cackled.'*

• Hale believes that his safety depends upon finding a companion. One of the *'clerks, shop girls, hairdressers '* with *'new and daring perms' 'bleached and perfumed hair.'*

• Hale sees a *'fat spotty creature in pink'* with a friend, a *'pale bloodless creature.'*

• How would you summarize the tone used to describe the female visitors to the resort?

• What do you infer from Hale's perception that Ida is like *'life itself.'*

• Ida leaves Hale alone while she visits the washroom and upon her return she finds him vanished, leaving her with ten shillings and a 'tip to win' for the races.

Chapter Two

Pinkie searches the holiday crowd for Hale. He wins a doll on a shooting stall which is described as possessing eyes with '*glassy innocence, like virgins in a church repository.*' He takes the doll '*by the hair...his fingers pulled absentmindedly at the doll's hair detaching the brown wool.*'

• The doll is likened in its 'innocence' to the Virgin Mary. Pinkie refers to all other females as either polonies or buers; both are derogatory expressions.

• Pinkie's eyes are again described as possessing an '*annihilating eternity from which he had come and to which he went; 'his ageless eyes.*' These descriptions refer to the personification of evil, which Greene, as a practising Catholic, would have believed entered the world as a consequence of Adam's choice: he obeyed the voice of temptation, rather than God's explicit commands. He ate from the tree of knowledge of evil, allowing Satan to enter the world. This event is referred to as 'the fall of man'; the descriptions of Pinkie suggest that he is the embodiment of this ancient evil.

• Pinkie's thoughts alternate between violent thoughts and lines and phrases from the Catholic liturgy.

Spicer has left one of Hale's cards in the teashop; the gang realise that this might cause one of the waitresses to remember that the man who left the card was not Hale, thus linking Spicer, and ultimately Pinkie, to Hale's murder. Pinkie decides to go to Snows the tea shop to retrieve the evidence against them: '*you couldn't tell if he was scared his young ancient poker face told nothing.*'

Greene uses the motif of the mouth throughout the novel. In this reference it is directly linked with 'the world': '*a great vox humana trembled across the crumby stained desert of used cloths; the world's wet mouth lamenting over life.'* The waitress who is assigned the table is Rose. Pinkie realises that she is in possession of the card and she will be able to identify Spicer as the person who left it.

Pinkie makes a mild effort of ingratiation with the girl, who is responsive and attentive, although he *'despised her quiet, her pallor, her desire to please.'* She gave the appearance of being *'afraid of her own footsteps.'* Pinkie looks at her with *'dangerous and unfeeling eyes.'* He tells her that they will meet again because *'you and I have things in common.'*

Chapter Three

Ida meets Clarence, a male friend in a pub who makes it clear that he would like to resume their (sexual) relationship. The nature of their relationship is implied when she comments about her husband Tom, and he replies *'there's been more than one Tom in your life'*; Ida responds *'you should know.'*

The newspaper reports the death of Hale, and Ida remembers the short time she spent with Hale. The narrator comments: *'the cheap drama and pathos of the thought weakened her heart towards him.'*

Clarence had been a married man during Ida's relationship with him. At this point his wife is dead and he wants to resume their relationship, however Ida comments *'I like to start something fresh.'* Her warmth is described by the narrator as *'Guinness kindness'* which *'winked up at her, a bit sly, a bit earthy.'*
Ida's feeling for Hale and her determination to avenge his murder is motivated by her *'friendly and popular heart.'*

• What do the narrator's descriptions of Ida's manner toward men imply?

- Ida attends Fred's cremation in *'a bare cold secular chapel which could be adapted quietly and conveniently to any creed.'*

- What is the narrative tone/attitude toward cremation suggested by these words?

The address given by the clergyman is closely based upon the address given at the cremation of the author's mother-in-law. It was the first cremation that Greene attended and he wrote disparagingly of this method of 'disposal' of the 'last remains' of people, which like Fred Hale's body, enter the furnace to be *'dropped in indistinguishable grey ash on the pink blossoms: he became part of the smoke nuisance over London.'* Only in the last fifty years has cremation become acceptable to Roman Catholics.

Ida's life philosophy is delineated; she defines life in terms of sex: *'Sunlight on bedposts;'* drinking: *'ruby port'* and the thrill occasioned by backing a winner at the races: *'the leap of the heart when the outsider you have backed passes the post.'* Ida is decidedly irreligious. She consults spirits through séances; she is described as feeling *'an enjoyable distress'* over Hale's death; her optimistic outlook on life contained something *'dangerous and remorseless.'* The narrative voice may be ironic when it says that *'she took life with a deadly seriousness.'* Can you think of any other way in which this, rather ambiguous comment might be read?

Ida's character is anatomised further. The narrator comments that *'man is made by the places in which he lives'* and goes on to describe the neon signs which illuminate much of London's west End, advertising products to persuade people into making a purchase. Britain was becoming, in the late 1930's, an increasingly consumerist society. Ida's mind, comments the narrator, *'worked with the simplicity and regularity of a sky-sign: the ever tipping glass, the ever–revolving wheel, the plain question flashing on and off: 'do you use Forhams for the gums?'*

What is the significance of this comment, both in respect of the characterisation of Ida and the social context in which the novel is set?

- Ida is not religious, yet a Biblical quotation is used to communicate her tenacious will: *'Vengeance was Ida's, just as much as reward was Ida's'* suggesting that Ida's will had replaced God as the ultimate instrument of justice, demanding the gratification of 'reward': *'the only reward there was. Fun.'*

- Ida decides that she wants to know 'the truth': *'it always costs money if you want to know the truth,'* she asserts. Clearly 'the truth' for Ida lies in what the world has to offer, rather than any theological or philosophical answers to 'big questions.'

- Ida describes the seedy 'old fashioned' con man Charlie Moyne, as a *'sporting gentleman'*...and goes on to outline her definition of the word generally: *gentlemen, freehanded gentlemen, real gentlemen.'* The narrator seems to be making a point here about Ida's judgement, the criteria that she uses to make value judgements, about worthiness or moral value. The original definition of a gentleman was a person of 'independent means,' belonging to the upper class and possessing wealth, which was likely to have been inherited, rather than acquired. The meaning of the word has changed, making this word associated with value judgement, rather than defining class. Consequently some lexicologists would argue that the word itself has become worthless as a meaningful term.

- Ida has a copy of J.B. Priestley's *'The Good Companions'* on her book shelf. Graham Greene was taken to court by this author because he made what was considered libellous comments about the writer's literary talent and his populist readership.

- When Ida has consulted the spirits with the help of old Crowe, she declares her intention to *'make those people sorry.'* She has pointed on the Ouija board to *'that eye'* assumed it to mean that she should demand 'an eye for an eye' (Exodus 21), She *'drew in her breath luxuriously'* saying *'it's going to be fun, it's going to be a bit of life...giving the highest praise she could to anything.'*

Do you think that this is a moral crusade? Is Ida standing up for Justice; Right over Wrong? Is she avenging the murder of a man for whom she felt genuine respect or affection? Why do you think that Graham Greene has given this character a Biblical reference: 'Vengeance is mine sayeth the Lord': 'an eye for an eye and a tooth for a tooth,' as her moral signposts? How would you summarise her belief system?

Part Two

Chapter One

Pinkie meditates upon murder, reflecting that '*when people do one murder they sometimes have to do another—to tidy up.*' The narrator comments that Pinkie's 'strength' lay in his lack of imagination: 'He couldn't see through people's eyes, or feel with their nerves.' This lack of empathy and consequent lack of conscience is symptomatic of psychopathology. A modern psychologist would define Pinkie as having a personality disorder. A recent British study suggests that 26% of the prison population are psychopaths.

Pinkie has arranged a date with Rose, the waitress from Snows teashop. Spicer asks Pinkie whether he has a gun in his pocket. Pinkie replies that he doesn't carry a gun and doesn't '*need a razor with a polony.*' He asserts that he carries vitriol because '*Vitriol...scares a polony more than a knife.*' The narrator comments that Pinkie derived a '*sensual pleasure*' from touching the vitriol in his pocket.

Rose tells Pinkie that the man who placed the card wasn't Fred Hale; she also comments '*I've got a memory for faces*' thus sealing her fate. He warns her of the danger of mixing with the mob telling her an anecdote of a female who incurred their wrath and '*they spoilt her looks. She lost one eye.*' Rose is terrified feeling a mixture of '*horror and admiration*' for the boy's knowledge.

• The word knowledge is used frequently in association with Pinkie. Consider the significance of this scriptural allusion to evil, sin or loss of innocence.

• Rose is interestingly described as avoiding living in the present: '*when she wasn't living in the future she was living in the past....running away from things, running toward things.'* To what extent would you say that many people experience life in this way? What is the problem with this habit?

• Rose is juxtaposed with Pinkie: *'the eyes which had never been young stared with grey contempt into the eyes which had only just begun to learn a thing or two.'* Eyes and mouths are motifs in the novel. Pinkie's eyes are described in numerous places. References to Ida's mouth are frequently made, and there are three metaphors linking the world to a mouth. What significance do these motifs have to your reading of character and theme in the novel?

• The narrator interestingly presents Pinkie as a multidimensional character. He is a misogynistic and emotionless killer; yet there are references to a Pinkie who had 'feelings,' who enjoyed music, who had religious beliefs, who indeed vowed to be a priest: *'The boy stared at the spotlight: music, love, nightingale, postmen: the words stirred in his brain like poetry.'* Pinkie experiences the temptation to do evil as he touches the bottle of vitriol in his pocket. Evil is presented as a force within Pinkie that is too hard to resist: *'you can't always help it. It sort of comes that way.'*

• Pinkie asks Rose whether she had been in love. When she replies in the affirmative he tells her *'with sudden venom, "you would have been. You're green. You don't know what people do...you don't know anything" he tells her.'* Again there is the reference to evil as knowledge or loss of innocence.

• Pinkie digs his nails into Rose's flesh in a *'sensual rage.'* Rose is delighted by what she perceives is his passion for her and tells him that he could carry on hurting her if he *'liked that.'*

• Pinkie experiences a curious mixture of anger and pleasure when he inflicts pain: *'anger like a live coal in his belly.'* Whilst simultaneously he asks himself: *'what would be the fun if people didn't squeal?'*

- Pinkie catches sight of Rose's rosary beads and realises that she, like him is a Roman Catholic. He remembers Latin from the mass that he had sung as a choir boy: '*in his voice a lost world moved.*' In Pinkie the narrator seems to personify the pathos of fallen man; the sense of loss is suggested, as is the sense that evil is a force which may reside within a person, almost, but not entirely, annihilating the 'original' personality. How else coule the phrase 'a lost world' be read.

- The narrator presents the loss of Pinkie's childhood faith as part of the symptoms of his evil state: as a deficit of goodness rather than the presence of evil. Pinkie's remembrance of his '*lost world*' generates compassion for this character. He seems to be a victim of a force which is now out of his control, luring him toward greater acts of hatred and violence and yet bringing no peace. He has no doubt of the truth of his religion: he tells Rose '*of course it's true...it's the only thing that fits.*' The thing '*that fits*' for Pinkie is not the presence of God, rather it is the truth that evil exists. He goes on: '*these atheists they don't know nothing. Of course there's Hell. Flames and damnation.*' Rose responds: '*And Heaven too.*' Yet this concept is too nebulous for Pinkie to grasp. He answers '*Maybe.*'

- Spicer jokingly suggests that Pinkie would have to marry Rose in order to 'make her safe.' He responds '*I don't need to marry a squirt to make her safe.*' He goes on to describe Rose as '*that cheap polony.*'

- The absence of peace is strong in the narrative comments about Pinkie. All expressions of joy or human animation seem to have been excised leaving symptoms of his sickness. When Dallow endeavours to exchange banter with him the narrator describes '*the ague wringing his face.*'

- Pinkie and his henchman Dallow visit one of their victims of the protection racket who has reneged on his payments. He explains that he is now giving protection money to Colleoni.

• Dallow shows his loyalty to Pinkie, and Pinkie reflects that he could trust him: '*He felt as a physically weak but cunning schoolboy feels who has attached to himself in an indiscriminating fidelity the strongest boy in the school.*' Although Dallow is physically strong, he offers unthinking allegiance to Pinkie, whom he believes to be the 'brains of the outfit.'

The chapter ends with a conversation between Pinkie and Spicer, who hearing Rose's voice on the telephone, is nervous; he recognises it as belonging to the waitress who served him in Snows. Pinkie reassures him, telling him not to be '*milky.*'

Chapter Two

The chapter opens with Pinkie writing a 'business letter' to a 'customer'. The reality is that he is an extortionist who demands money with menaces from his victims. The narrator comments that Pinkie's sleep is '*functional. He had no dreams.*' This further delineates his character as sub-human, or reinforces the idea that he exists rather than lives.

• Colleoni, the successful criminal, has written to Pinkie inviting him to call to see him at the Cosmopolitan Hotel. A dictionary definition of the word cosmopolitan is one who 'knows the world.'

• E. Cobham Brewer 1810-1897; Dictionary of Phrase and Fable gives a definition of 'The World' as it is used in scripture and liturgical writings: The World, the Flesh and the Devil: 'The world, i.e. the things of the world, in contradistinction to religious matters; the flesh, i.e. the love of pleasure and sensual enjoyments; the devil, i.e. all temptations to evil of every kind, as theft, murder, lying, blasphemy and so on.'

• Pinkie surveys his reflection in the mirror prior to his meeting with Colleoni. Again there is the juxtaposition of images suggestive of innocence, the '*smooth, never shaven cheek, soft hair,*' with eyes which suggest a primeval force, the *'old eyes'*. This inference that the wickedness in Pinkie's character is a manifestation of an ancient, spiritual malaise of man is reinforced by the many references to his pride and knowledge (of sin). Both of these are recognised by theologians as spiritual errors which separate man from God. It was knowledge of sin (or the fall from innocence) that was represented by the apple partaken by Adam. It was pride that caused Satan to seek equality with God, and the reason that he was cast out of heaven. Knowledge and Pride are motifs that are repeated throughout the novel.

• The Hotel Cosmopolitan is described in some detail - as are the residents. The women accompanying the wealthy patrons of the hotel are described as *'small tinted creatures, who rang like expensive glass when they were touched but who conveyed an impression of being as sharp and tough as tin.'* This is the narrative voice describing a 'type' of female. How do you read this description? What impression have you been given of their characters from the imagery used?

• Pinkie's reaction to these expensive females is revealed: *'a little bitch sniffed at him and then talked him over with another little bitch on a settee.'* Does this description of their attitude toward Pinkie and Pinkie's response suggest that he is intimidated by them, or embarrassed by his clothes or class?

• The patrons of the hotel seem to be from different classes of society: *'Sir Joseph Montague…a woman in mauve with an untimely tiara'* rubs shoulders with the gangster Colleoni, who is *trying to convey that his place in elevated society has been long held.'* He tells Pinkie, *'The service here is not what it used to be.'*

• The narrator has created a setting of worldly values, money buys a place in this world and no one cares about the origins of wealth. Colleoni, the violent extortionist, and Pinkie the murderer feel at ease in this setting, and yet the narrator's image of them hints that they are discontented individuals. As they enter the lift the narrator comments that they *'rose angelically towards peace'.* Clearly *'angelically'* is an ironic reference to them, as symbols of vice; yet a possible progress *'towards peace'* suggests that their lives, dedicated as they are to vice and what many would term evil acts, does not bring them peace or contentment; on the other hand we might infer that peace and comfort *is* literally obtainable: that money can buy anything. Even the ill-gotten gains of the criminal are acceptable currency, indeed they are 'laundered' by their acceptance in the Cosmopolitan world.

• As Pinkie examines Colleoni's gold lighter, Colleoni declares *'I like things good.'* There is detailed description of the ornate furnishings, *'stamped with crowns in gold and silver thread.'* Pinkie comments that Colleoni *'won't want to hear the details'* of Kite's murder. Pinkie can see that Colleoni has been 'sanitized' by the respectability of wealth. He has become a *'business man,'* far removed from the brutal origins of his fortune.

• Pinkie is not awed by Colleoni's wealth or power. He warns him *'trespassing's not healthy.'*

• Colleoni beams his approval on Pinkie, referring to him as *'my child.'* Although he tells him that Pinkie can do him no harm, he says *'I like push...The World needs young people with energy.'* What is the significance of using the words as proper nouns (with capital letters?) Consider the use of the euphemisms *'energy'* and *'push'* what are more honest descriptions of Pinkie's modus operandi, and why do you think Colleoni substitutes these euphemisms?

• Colleoni has referred, patron-like, to Pinkie as 'my child,' yet he comments *'nothing you might try to do to my men could affect me. I've got two in hospital now.'*

• Colleoni, the criminal businessman, *'looked as a man might look who owned the whole world, the whole visible world that is, the cash registers and policemen and prostitutes, parliament and the laws which say this is Right and this is Wrong.'*

- Consider the significance of (i) *'the whole visible world'* (ii) *'the laws which say this is Right and this is Wrong'* (iii) the reason for the capital letters (which make the words proper nouns).

- The narrator repeats his assertion *'The visible world was all Mr Colleoni's'*. Why has the repetition device been used? What is the recurring theme in the novel suggested by the narrator's distinction between the visible and invisible worlds?

- The police inspector who comes ostensibly to investigate Brewer's assault invites Pinkie to *'have a friendly chat with the inspector,'* but reassures him that he *'needn't get fussed'* about it, he should simply have an alibi ready.

- The inspector is described as looking tired. He finds the fight against evil exhausting, therefore is ready to make compromises telling Pinkie *'I don't mind you carving each other up in a quiet way...but when two mobs start scraping people who matter may get hurt.'* The policeman advises Pinkie to *'Clear out of Brighton'* because he is no match against Colleoni. Why do you think that the law's acceptance of criminal activity in the world is made explicit? What point is being made about the link between Evil and The World?

- Pinkie leaves the police station telling the inspector *'I'm too young to retire.'* He congratulates himself on his cleverness in getting away with murder, pulling the wool over the 'bogies' eyes.

- The narrator ends the chapter with paraphrase from the poem 'Intimations of Immortality' By William Wordsworth: *'He trailed the clouds of his own glory after him: hell lay about him in his infancy.'* Whereas Wordsworth's poem says that the infant comes from God to earth, trailing clouds of glory from heaven. The poem goes on to say that 'shades of the prison house begin to close around the growing boy.' Wordsworth believes in the immortality of the soul and that birth involves a separation from God: the older the child becomes the more his memories of heaven are replaced by The World i.e. 'the prison house'. Where does the narrator believe is Pinkie's 'origin?' How has the narrator linked the scriptural origin of evil in the world with Pinkie?

Part Three

Chapter One

Ida has booked into a Brighton boarding house. She plans to meet a man friend at Snows tea shop. Ida reflects that her investigation of Hale's murder is likely to be expensive and she decides to follow Hale's tip and back Black Boy to win. The bookie gives her information about the mob: that Colleoni is now. *'taking over from Kite.'* It seems to be common knowledge that Kite's murder was unplanned: *'a razor slipped'* and that 'the boy' is presently leading the mob, although Colleoni's *'out for a monopoly.'*

As Ida surveys the Brighton scene and enjoys the last dregs of her *'cheap port,'* Ida reflects that it *'was a good life.'* Interestingly the narrator comments that *'the darkness in which the boy walked... was alien to her; she had no pity for something she did not understand.'*

• Does this comment imply that the narrator believes that Pinkie is deserving of pity? Or is it rather implying something about Ida?

• At Snows Ida orders a stout and questions Rose, who is, she discovers, the waitress who found the card under the tablecloth. Rose lets slip that the fellow who left the card *'wasn't so little,'* then, realising that she might have said too much tries to cover her tracks by telling Ida that she hadn't a *'memory for faces.'*

• Ida, seeing that Rose was *'pale and determined and out of breath and guilty,'* knows that she has something to hide. When Phil Corkery joins her she tells him: *'I always had a feeling it was fishy.'* Phil warns her that her curiosity *'Could be dangerous'* and that she shouldn't *'get mixed up in anything.'* Ida replies *'an eye for an eye Phil.'* Phil, placing his hand on Ida's knee tells her *'I'd do anything for you.'*

• Ida and Phil go to the police with their suspicions. The police inform her that Fred's post-mortem indicated that he died of natural causes, and that the case was closed.

• The narrator gives a detailed summary of Ida: 'the tart with a heart.' She was an 'ordinary sinner' who enjoys drink and sex, yet who wouldn't *'tell tales to your wife.'* Ida was *'the cheery soul...who wouldn't remind you the next morning of what you wanted to forget, she was honest she was kindly, she belonged to the great law abiding class, her amusements were their amusements, her superstitions their superstitions.'*

• The narrator's comments characterize Ida as a modern, harmless female out for a bit of fun; she enjoys her life of drinking and casual fornication, she is irreligious and she dabbles in the occult. Is there any hint that Ida's attitudes and life style might be somehow 'missing the point' from the narrator's point of view? That, typical as she is of the average modern individual, that *'their amusements and superstitions'* are being disparaged?

• Ida keeps Phil on side by hinting at sexual favours to come: *'be a good boy and you don't know what mayn't happen.'*

• The chapter closes as Ida reflects that *'the horse has got to win'* to provide funds for 'the investigation.'

Chapter Two

The chapter opens with a delineation of Spicer, one of Pinkie's men. Spicer, who left the card in Snows Tea shop, has been called *'milky'* by Pinkie and his state of mind has been further upset by the mysterious verdict brought by the coroner of Hale's death. He wanted to *'be satisfied that the cops were doing nothing.'*

The consequences for Spicer of his involvement with the mob are physical ill health. Although he believes that his ailments are *'all nerves'* and that he will be better when the races start, the narrator comments that he was *'like a man with a poisoned body who believes that all will be well when a single tooth is drawn.'*

• Spicer's misery is graphically drawn: *'pale with bloodshot eyes...fear upset his bowels and the spots came...he sweated.'*

• What do you infer is the point made by the narrator by the use of imagery in this delineation: *'The smell of dead fish was in his nostrils, he was a sick man...it was like an abscess jetting its poison through the nerves...he creaked his tortured way up the stairs.'* Part of Spicer's panic is that he knows that he is *'in the mob for life.'*

• Rose calls to speak to Pinkie, Spicer answers the phone and is further terrified that she might recognise his voice. She tells Spicer that Ida has been into the café asking questions about Hale. He ponders, with sick dread, upon his predicament. The chapter ends with a reference to 'Brighton rock'.

• What ideas or images are associated with this cheap candy that is for sale in every sea-side resort?

Chapter Three

• The chapter opens with a metaphor describing Pinkie: *'Poison twisted in the boy's veins.'*

• What is the link between Spicer and Pinkie? What do you infer is the reason for these parallel images? Do you think there might be a link with an earlier narrative comment that Ida was unable to feel pity for Pinkie because she 'did not understand?' What do you infer from this about the 'sickness' that is common to these two criminals?

• Pinkie goes to Snows to find Rose. His first instinct is to intimidate her. He tells her *'I could break your arm.'* Part of his fury is that he is being treated by contempt by the staff who judge him to be poor and of no account because of his youth and shabby clothing. The narrator comments: *'his mind staggered before the extent of his ambitions.'* What is the significance of this comment?

• Rose remarks that she thought that the man who answered the phone at Pinkie's lodgings, was the same man who left the ticket. Pinkie decides that *'she's got to be scared again.'*

• Pinkie tells Rose again *'you're green. You don't know a thing.'* He goes on to criticise her appearance telling her *'you look awful.'* He looks at her with *'distaste.'* He thinks: *'...that was what they'd joked about him marrying. That.'*

• The narrator comments that Pinkie *'watched her with his soured virginity.'* What is the effect of this image upon your perception of Pinkie? What associations does the word 'soured' have? His physical reaction to Rose is extreme. The narrator comments that he would rather die, or cause others to die, than marry Rose. However poor Rose is totally oblivious to his feelings, and remains so throughout the novel. She thinks that it is *'lovely'* to be out in the countryside with Pinkie.

• Rose's comment about Ida is interesting. She sees a clear distinction between Ida and herself and Pinkie. She tells him that *'she wasn't our kind'* the reason given being that her manner implied that *'she hadn't a care.'* What unites Rose and Pinkie other than their shared knowledge that it was Spicer rather than Hale who left the card in Snows, is that both are Roman Catholic. Why does the Catholic religion seem to Rose to confer anxiety upon the believer?

• Pinkie warns Rose: *'you don't seem scared. It's serious what I'm telling you.'* And Rose replies with great sincerity: *'I wouldn't be scared Pinkie- not with you about.'*

• At this point, as Pinkie realises that in the eyes of the world he and Rose are 'walking out,' he reflects upon the *'frightening weekly exercise of his parents that he watched from his single bed...every polony you met had her eye on the bed.'* It becomes clear that Pinkie has a strong disgust and fear of sex.

• Rose picks up Pinkie's deep rooted anxiety about sex and asks him whether he is scared of anything. He replies: *'Me scared? That's funny.'*

• Rose tells Pinkie about her home: *'We're all Romans in Nelson Place. You believe in things. Like Hell'.* She remarks about Ida: *'You can see she don't believe a thing...the world's all dandy with her.'* Pinkie responds *'I don't take any stock in religion. Hell – it's just there. You don't need to think of it – not before you die.'* Rose replies *'you might die sudden.'* And Pinkie quotes *'Between the stirrup and the ground, mercy I asked, I mercy found'* (quoted by Malone in Boswell's Johnson vol. 4). Pinkie is referring to the absolution granted by a Catholic priest to the repentant sinner. Pinkie seems to be relying on avoiding hell-fire and damnation by claiming forgiveness of his sins before death (often referred to as shriving when the priest gives the Last Rites of The Church to a dying penitent.)

• Rose perceives his dislike of her manner and appearance and in a sudden flash of anger she tells him that if she *'doesn't suit him'* he should leave her alone. Pinkie, realising his vulnerability should she be alienated from him, tells her that she was wrong, that she 'suited' him. Rose, *'with a blind willingness to be deceived,'* apologises to him.

• Rose confesses her sexual ignorance and Pinkie thinks of his own *'horrifying ignorance' of sex...he'd never yet kissed a girl.'*

• As Rose and Pinkie walk down the promenade at Brighton beach, Rose sees a photograph of Spicer and tells Pinkie that he was the man who placed Hale's card beneath the cloth in Snows. Pinkie is reminded of his vulnerability unless he ensures Rose's silence.

Chapter Four

Pinkie realises that his safety is bound up with Spicer, who is scared. He returns to their lodgings and tells him '*you're too old for this life...you'll have to disappear.*' Spicer, suspecting the worst, is immediately nervous of Pinkie's intention, but Pinkie reassures him that he means that he should take 'a holiday.' Spicer is eager to be allowed to retire, but Pinkie thinks enviously of Spicer 'getting away with his evil deeds and evading Hell and achieving '*a glassy sea, a golden crown*' as a reward in heaven. Pinkie phones Colleoni telling him about the complication of Spicer, and the solution of Spicer's 'holiday' which Colleoni, seems not to believe, realising the dark violence within Pinkie.

The chapter ends as the tune that Pinkie is singing in his head becomes part of the Latin Mass: '*Agnus Dei qui tollis peccata mundi...dona nobis pacem:*' Lamb of God, who takes away the sin of the world, grant us peace.

Part Four

Chapter One

Ida, Pinkie and Spicer join the crowd at the races. Pinkie thinks of Spicer's 'stupidity' and 'that woman' who was asking questions. He thinks of marrying Rose 'as a last resort,' but 'it wouldn't be for long.' Pinkie promises Spicer that he was going to arrange peace: 'no one's going to break this peace' he tells him. Spicer day dreams about the pub that he would buy in Nottingham. Whilst Pinkie linked his arm through Spicer's his mind dwelt upon 'the finest of all sensations, the infliction of pain.' The boy encourages Spicer to 'have a good time while you can.'

The horse tipped to win by Hale comes in first place and Ida wins £250.

Pinkie bids farewell to Spicer, wishing him well and then they are both attacked. As the blows rain down of him, Pinkie reflects that Colleoni's mob was, 'enjoying themselves, just as he had always enjoyed himself.' Pinkie 'wept and begged.'
Pinkie, wounded by Colleoni's mob reflects that 'this was a temporary defeat.' And that 'one confession' would 'wipe out everything.'

• Pinkie has no compunction about arranging the murder of Spicer. He has no regrets about either the murder of Kite or of Hale. He is not a Christian by any definition, and yet he has faith that confession and absolution will restore him to 'righteousness.' His religion is a facility which he hopes will ensure that he will not have to pay the penalty of a life dedicated to evil. He promises 'I will give a statue.' Pinkie imagines that God is 'in his pocket' and will respond to Pinkie's bribe, as the corrupt policemen responded.

• Pinkie goes to Rose and tells himself that he would '*crack the vitriol*' if she sent him away. However Rose was '*as dumb and devoted as ever she'd been.*'

• Pinkie tells Rose that Spicer is dead. Rose tells Pinkie that Ida had called asking questions. Rose promises that she would never divulge that Hale was not the man who had left the ticket, she assures Pinkie of her loyalty saying '*I don't care what you've done.*' Rose expresses her contempt for Ida, demanding 'what does she know about us? ...she doesn't know what a mortal sin is.' Ida only spoke of Right and Wrong. 'Knowledge' of the Truths of Catholicism is perceived by Rose to make them, as Catholics, superior to Ida and her contemptible moral code: '*oh she won't burn. She couldn't burn if she tried.*' Rose believes that their religion elevates them above the common herd of un-believers. Rose goes on to recount the story of Molly Carhew who killed herself, and in her despair put herself outside the pos-sibility of forgiveness. Is there any evidence that there is sympa-thy for Rose's attitude in the narrative voice?

• Pinkie's solicitor is summoned to give advice about Pinkie's marriage to Rose. Prewitt is described as '*tough as leather*' in spite of his '*deprecating ...sympathetic*' manner. Interestingly the narrator comments that his court room victories were '*more damaging than defeats.*' To whom are they 'damaging?'

• The boy tells Prewitt that he wants to be married to Rose. Pre-witt is under no illusions about the reason for the marriage. When Pinkie asks whether the marriage would make it impossible for the police to use Rose as a witness for the prosecution, Prewitt reassures him.

• Pinkie tells Prewitt that '*it won't be a real marriage*' because they would not be married in church. Prewitt ironically replies '*your religious feelings do you credit.*' Pinkie believes that his religion can be exploited: there are hard and fast rules in being a Catholic, but he thinks that they can be manipulated with a bit of luck. He is expecting to defer obedience to 'the rules' until it is convenient (to him) to obey them. He thinks that confession will ensure absolution and therefore he will escape God's judgement. His 'relationship' with God seems to be like his relationship with secular laws. He bribes law enforcers or finds people who will provide a false alibi for a price; he has found a corrupt lawyer who enables him to interpret the letter of the law whilst totally disregarding the spirit entirely. He seems to think that he can arrange his 'contract' with God similarly. As Rose pointed out, the problem would come if he was to die without having time to find a priest 'to hear' his confession and grant absolution. This too was Hamlet's problem. He delayed seeking vengeance for the murder of his father because he feared dying un-shriven and consequently suffering hell fire and damnation. Everything in the world Pinkie believes has a price and can therefore be bought. These beliefs are reinforced by Prewitt who tells him *'You've only to give the word...we'll fix it together.'* The price of fixing Pinkie's marriage to Rose was to be found under the soap dish.

• Pinkie, on the run from Colleoni's men, hides out in *'a kind of poting shed.'* It is filled with the derritus of family life and Pinkie is filled with hatred for the owner, *'He was nameless, faceless, but the boy hated him.'* Pinkie expect Colleoni's men to hunt him down and kill kim. He tries to *'make his peace'* with God. However, he discovers that he is unable to repent. He was incapable of regretting Spicer's death: ... *"they've got Spicer. It was impossible to repent of something which made him safe."* Pinkie realises the problem with his assumption that he could evade God's judgment by seeking mercy *"at the eleventh hour."* he was unable to feel contrition.

• The chapter ends with the return of Spicer, who Pinkie believed had been dispatched by Colleoni's henchmen. Pinkie's surprise and fear at seeing Spicer gives away his expectation that he was to have been the victim.

Chapter Two

This chapter opens with Ida's declared intention of extracting information from Rose, which she believed would lead to a conviction for Hale's murder. Ida has now 'the funds' to support her investigation from her winnings. The narrator makes a link between the theme of the last chapter: that everything in the world has a price: *'an infinite capacity for corruption: two hundred pounds.'*

• Ida tells Rose that she *'doesn't want the Innocent to suffer.'* Rose's inner voice comments: *'As if you knew ...who was innocent.'* Rose, as a Catholic, believes that she has an understanding or 'knowledge' of sin and guilt. And that Ida, as an unbeliever, is ignorant.

• Ida attempts to persuade Rose to tell the truth about Pinkie's involvement. She thinks that telling Rose that the boy is *'wicked'* will make her turn against him. But Rose tells Ida *'you don't know a thing.'* In other words a non believer is unable to judge what is wicked. Rose makes no distinction between 'sin', in the Christian sense of the word, and wickedness. An argument with which many people would be in agreement: that that which is *'natural'* or part of 'human nature,' such as sex outside marriage, is acceptable because it is 'human.' Ida tells Rose as *'a human... not a Puritan'*: *'I've done a thing or two in my time – that's natural...it's in my hand: the girdle of Venus.'* Ida tells Rose to *'be sensible...he doesn't love you.'* However she replies *'I don't care...I love him.'*

• The chapter ends with an image of Rose as an animal in a hole with the experience of the world in which she, as a child reared in Nelson Place had known: *'murder copulation, extreme poverty, fidelity and the love and fear of God.'* Why is the narrator contrasting Rose's 'world' with the 'outside world?' In part one chapter three the narrator commented that *'man is made by the places in which he lives.'*

Chapter Three

At the opening of this chapter, Pinkie is regarding Spicer's dead body at the bottom of the stairs. Pinkie implies to Prewitt that the 'accident' happened as a consequence of the rotten wood. Prewitt replies *'his legal voice tremulous'*, that the wood which was placed across the body happened *after* the fall.

• What is meant by the comment that his 'legal' voice was tremulous?

• Prewitt is immediately concerned for his own safety, telling Pinkie *'you can't mix me up in this.'* But Pinkie demands that Prewitt stand by him as witness. Prewitt has taken Pinkie's money and is now complicit in all Pinkie's designs. Prewitt declares that he has a splitting headache. Again the narrator makes a connection between physical and moral sickness. At this point Prewitt wants to remain in ignorance of Pinkie's further plans: *'don't tell me,'* he repeated in a low voice, *'what things.'*

• The narrator uses an image of a railway line in his evocation of Pinkie's life journey. *'Every station was one nearer safety, and then one farther away.'* He then goes on to include *'the middle-aged whore on Hove front'* in this metaphor. What point is the narrator making here? He goes on to comment that both Pinkie and the whore *'have the same end in view, if you could talk of an end in connection with that circle.'*

• Pinkie visits Rose at Snows and over hears a snatch of the conversation between Rose and Ida. As he sees the confrontation between the two women through the half-open door he is aware that Rose *'completed him'* *'... what was most evil in him needed her: it couldn't get along without goodness.'* What is meant by this comment do you think?

• When Ida spots Pinkie, she tells him to leave Rose alone *'I know all about you.'* Again Rose tells Ida, *'You don't know a thing.'* The narrator remarks that Ida was like *'the typical*

Englishwoman abroad. She hadn't even got a phrase book. She was as far from either of them as she was from Hell – or Heaven. Good and evil lived in the same country spoke the same language, feeling the same completion.' What is the narrative attitude toward Ida that is revealed in this comment? What point is made about goodness and evil?

• Rose has knowledge of *'her sin.'* When Pinkie tells her *'you'll never be anything but good'* she disagrees saying that she is *'bad'* and that she *'doesn't want 'to be like her'* (Ida). Yet Pinkie sees a sharp distinction between doing bad things' which the Church would define as sin, and being evil, which he claims is innate, within the individual, *'hard wired'*: *'It's not what you do, it's what you think'*. Pinkie tells Rose.

Pinkie has made an important theological point without realising it. The Christian concept of absolution, or being forgiven and 'washed clean' of sin,' only 'works' if the penitent repents of his or her sin; that is has a sincere intention of turning away from the sin from which he or she wishes to be absolved. Pinkie is therefore correct in his distinction between 'goodness and evil' as being rooted in thought. If Pinkie confessed his sin, any absolution granted by a priest would not be valid without the sincere abhorrence of the act for which he claimed absolution. Therefore Pinkie mind-set, fixated as it is upon violence; steeped as it is in pride and hatred, would preclude him from receiving God's forgiveness. Although Pinkie has not realised this, Graham Greene had a thorough understanding of Catholic theology and would have understood: because the author was unable in his private life, to 'turn away from' what the Church would have called adultery; he chose to be excommunicated from the Church. This did not, as he said, mean that he rejected the Church; he knew his own weakness, and also understood that repentance is real only when there is a sincere determination to 'turn from error.' Graham Greene spoke of his Catholic faith in an interview entitled 'The Uneasy Catholicism of Graham Greene' in 1983: "If I went to communion, I would have to confess and make promises. I prefer to excommunicate myself…My faith remains in the background, but it remains."

• Pinkie secures Rose's promise to marry him in a registry office. Pinkie regards Rose's *'unmade-up mouth with faint nausea.'* The narrator describes Pinkie's mouth as *'hard'* and *'puritanical.'* The word puritan means one with censorial views about pleasure or sex. The narrator goes on to comment that he would have preferred that Rose's mouth tasted of *'Coty powder or Kissproof Lipstick or any chemical compound.'* Pinkie experiences an almost visceral reaction to Rose's 'innocent' mouth: as though he is repelled by virtue.

• Pinkie smiles at Rose's *'blind, lost face, uneasily, with obscure shame.'* What are the implications of the description of Rose as 'lost?' Why is the shame experienced by Pinkie described as 'obscure?'

Part Five

Chapter One

It is the day of the inquest into Hale's death. The coroner has recorded a verdict of natural causes. Pinkie should be feeling relief and yet he is paranoid. He asks Dallow whether a woman is following him.

There is a band playing; all of the members of the band are blind. Pinkie pushes them roughly out of the way, not realising that they cannot see. Darrow remonstrates with him, but Pinkie, rather than admit his mistake, tells him *'why should I get out of my way for a beggar.'* Pinkie's descent unto ever more 'inhuman' behaviour is shocking even to him: *'it was as if he were being driven too far down a road he only wanted to travel a certain distance.'* The verb usage here suggests that evil has a momentum of its own: he is no longer in control of the progressively more desperate and 'evil' actions to which he is 'driven' in order to insulate himself from the repercussions of Hale's murder. Darrow continues to be optimistic that they have got away with murder; however, Darrow has previously been described as 'indiscriminating.' He is the only member of the mob that Pinkie can trust because of the combination of his blind devotion and limited imagination.

Darrow persuades Pinkie to have a 'night out' and relax. In the bar they see 'Spicer's girl', she is described as having a *'vacuous brow'* and knowing *'the game.'* 'The game' is sex, and Sylvie, Spicer's girl is impressed by Pinkie's 'power' and willing to transfer her affections in the back of a car.

• The narrator comments that Pinkie was 'fascinated' by her infidelity. Compare his reaction to Sylvie's lack of moral values to his abhorrence of Rose's innocent declarations of loyalty and devotion.

• Pinkie is presented as alienated from people and common experience. He is sexually inexperienced not because of moral scruple, rather because he had a deeply ingrained repugnance of the sex act because of his childhood memories of witnessing his parents' sexual practices. Pinkie also dislikes alcohol. The characterisation of Pinkie is interesting and deliberate. He is a combination of inexperience and depravity: '*this was what people called pleasure – this and the game.*' Pinkie is presented as an emotional cripple. His 'revulsion' toward sex is part of his isolation from humanity.

• Pinkie goes outside with Sylvie, but is unable to have sex with her. The imagery communicates his twisted psyche: '*he was conscious of his enormous ambitions under the shadow of the hideous and commonplace act...fear and curiosity ate at the proud future, he was aware of nausea and retched.*'

Chapter Two

Pinkie is stung by the teasing laughter of Dallow and Cubitt. He asserts that he will not marry. On his return to his lodgings he discovers Rose waiting for him and tells her that their marriage is impossible. Rose has come to see him with a newspaper; on the front page is a photograph of Spicer and she identifies him as the man who left the card. Pinkie tries to convince her of Spicer's 'accident' on the stairs, and he realises that he must marry Rose in order to ensure that she could never testify against him.

• When Pinkie declares that Spicer had met with an accident, Rose stares at him in dumb silence. The narrator contrasts their 'imaginations:' '*His mind, he knew could contemplate any treachery... but she was bounded by her goodness; there were things she couldn't imagine.*' The narrator has made allusions to the imagination on previous occasions. The implication is that evil begins in the mind: in the contemplation of evil acts. Clearly Pinkie's mind has no 'moral boundaries' beyond which it is unimaginable for him to traverse. He has, as a consequence of his ability to 'imagine' evil, an unbounded propensity which inclines toward evil. The narrator makes clear distinctions between 'sinful acts,' to which all humankind including Rose are inclined, and evil; which he seems to imply is rooted in the mind, possibly even innate: 'bred in the bone' or 'hard wired' within the individual.

• Rose's imagination of evil is bound up with her love for Pinkie. The worst that she is able to imagine is Pinkie's death. Pinkie, all too readily, imagines harm coming to Rose by his own hand. He dallies in his imagination with scarring her face with the vitriol in his pocket, and finds his fingers wandering toward the bottle, as though his imagination enjoys flirting with the idea of causing her pain. Evil is as fixated in Pinkie's mind as the temptation to sexual sin is rooted in the minds of many people. This inclination, claims Ida, is 'natural.' Pinkie's inclinations are not.

• The narrator again establishes the theme of the eternal nature of evil. Pinkie tells Rose, in support of his intention to marry without the blessing of the Church, that *'times change.'* Yet the narrator asserts that *'ideas never change.'* This is an allusion to 'the things of the world', a concept rooted in theology that teaches the distinction between religious and worldly matters. E. Cobham Brewer in the Dictionary of Phrase and Fable 1810-1898, offers a definition of the temptations which separate man from God: The World, i.e. vanity, greed and worldly ambition; The Flesh i.e. the love of pleasure and sensual enjoyment; and the Devil, who tempts human beings to evil of every kind, as having jurisdiction over the world. All three are represented in this novel. The narrator comments: *'the world never moved: it lay there always, the ravaged and disputed territory between the two eternities...but like troops at Christmas time they fraternised.'* The narrator has used the metaphor of warfare and the much reported cessation of hostilities that occurred on Christmas Eve in World War One, to communicate the idea of eternal 'dispute' between the forces of Evil (ruled by the Devil) and Goodness (presided over by God).

- Pinkie tells Rose that he will call to see her father to obtain permission for their marriage.

Chapter Three

As Pinkie takes the route on foot to the slums of Brighton from which he and Rose originate, *'extreme poverty took him back.'* Memories of his horrified witnessing of his parents' sexual practices come to haunt him. Pinkie tells Rose's impoverished parents that he's *'come to do business'*; although they reject his implied offer of payment Pinkie saw *'swimming up through the blind vindictive silence incredulity, avarice, suspicion.'* The narrator shows the tussle between *'fidelity'* and *avarice* and they barter a price for their daughter, hiding their appreciation of a cash offer behind concern that Pinkie would *'treat her right.'* They come to an agreement and Rose comments ingenuously *'I've never known a mood go so quick. They must have liked you.'*
The narrator comments that Roses praise of Pinkie's ability to 'handle' her parents was 'poison' to him because it marked her possession of him and reminded him with dread of her coming expectation of intimacy.

Chapter Four

- A graphic description of Ida's consumption of a cream filled éclair opens the chapter as she and Phil Corkery enjoy life at The Cosmopolitan Hotel. The motif of the mouth has been used before in connection with Ida. It suggests sensual pleasures, 'fleshy' enjoyments or self gratification. This close-up of the *'cream spurting between her two front teeth'* is also faintly nauseating. She is relishing the excitement of the chase; she is enjoying the thought that she is 'in the money' as *'a wedge of cream settled on her plump tongue,'* although she admits the danger to Phil Corkery *'no real sense of danger could lodge behind those vivacious eyes.'*

• The narrator again makes implicit reference to the imagination: *'no real sense of danger could... make her believe that one day she too, like Fred, would be where the worms...'* There is the sense that Ida gives no thought either to the physical danger that her involvement in the crime industry could result in her death, or to her soul and the possibility of eternal life. Ida has no religion, she lives for the pleasures offered in life, she could not engage in any philosophy other than the simple one that life was to be enjoyed. When she thought beyond these boundaries of her imagination: *'the points automatically shifted and set her vibrating down the accustomed line, the season ticket line marked by desirable residence and advertisements of cruises and small fenced boskages for rural love.'* (A boscage is a fenced wooded area). Ida's imagination does not allow her to wander from the well-trodden path of pleasure; no 'morbid' thought is allowed to take root in her mind which is finely tuned to sensual gratification.

• The narrative spotlight then turns to Colleoni, whose mind is also on sensual pleasures which he is able to indulge because of the profitability of a life of crime. He gives orders to his secretary to order a range of expensive *'hothouse'* delicacies. Colleoni talks to his wife on the telephone and Ida overhears the word 'passion'; Ida *'watching his mouth,'* tells Corkery *'we could have a fine time here.'* Ida and Colleoni have something in common yet she makes a distinction between pleasures of the flesh: food and sex, and the evil acts that provide the wherewithal for Colleoni's self-gratification. Ida tells Corkery...*'it doesn't do any harm that I know of. It's human nature...it's only fun after all.'*

• The narrator follows Ida's comment on the 'harmlessness' of her inclination to sensual pleasure: *'Fun to be on the right side, fun to be human'* his meaning is ambiguous possibly intending it to be read as a question or challenge.

• Ida is honest about her sexual desires and the pleasure that she derives from sex. She tells Corkery that she will pay for their stay at The Cosmopolitan out of her winnings from 'Black Boy.' She makes reference to his sexual performance, causing him to 'flush' a little; she also comments slyly *'Trust me, I know what a man likes.'* This level of sexual freedom would have been highly unusual for a woman at this time. Her delineation is detailed and contains many characteristics usually associated with men: she likes sex; drinking; ribald laughter; gambling and feels no need to limit her sexual pleasure to one partner. She is more confident and assertive than the men in her life appear to be: she sets the ground rules in her sex life and likes to 'pay her debts:' an allusion to meeting the costs incurred in facilitating sex: usually considered a man's obligation. Ida *'was shaken by a Bacchic and a bawdy mood. In every word either of them uttered she detected the one meaning.'* In contrast 'Corkery *'blushed, plunged deeper in his embarrassment.'* (Bacchic implies riotously or jovially intoxicated; drunken). The delineation of Ida contains many characteristics considered masculine; her extreme sexual confidence seems to have the effect of emasculating, or at least embarrassing men; she is predatory and demanding sexually. Although she allowed herself to be picked up in the pub by Hale, it is clear that she is in control and never passive.

• The narrator sets the scene for Ida's sexual gratification at The Cosmopolitan Hotel in graphic detail. Brighton has a long association with illicit sex, the term 'dirty weekend' was once synonymous with Brighton. We're told that Ida *'made her preparations for carnival...she gazed round the big padded pleasure dome of a bedroom with bloodshot and experienced eyes...and sat planning the evening's campaign.'* Ida admires her naked reflection in the mirror, her imagination full of *'popular phrases... A night of Love, 'You Only Live Once.'*

- While Ida waits for Corkery she '*sucked a chocolate between her* teeth.' Again the motif of the mouth as a symbol of self gratification. Notice that it is she who waits in sexual anticipation for the modest Corkery, who has retired, female-like, presumably to perform his ablutions.

- The chapter ends with an ironic narrative comment: '*It was the time of near-darkness and of the evening mist from the channel and of love.*'

Chapter Five

Pinkie is feeling power slipping away from him. His marriage to Rose has become something of a joke among his men, and as he looks at Dallow and Cubitt he sees '*two hungry faces he hardly knew, hangers on at the fringes of the great racket.*' Throughout the novel Pinkie is presented in a turmoil of turbulent and unpleasant emotions: hatred, envy, disgust, fear, contempt: he is never shown enjoying peace or contentment; he seems incapable of experiencing joy. In some ways he is a prisoner of his own moral depravity, and the turmoil inside which urges him on to greater acts of evil, take him further into the realms of darkness. Yet his pride blinds him to the truth of his predicament. He tells himself that '*he hadn't made a single false step.*'

- Pinkie's pride forces him to pretend, even to his partners in crime, that he has chosen to marry Rose because she '*is lovely... And intelligent*' He tells them '*don't make any mistake...I'm glad*' whilst at the same time he felt '*the secret fear and the humiliation*' at the thought of the sex act, desperately hiding his fear behind the boast: '*she's not one of your dyed totsies she's got class. I'm marrying her for your sake, but I'm laying her for my own.*'

- Pinkie is almost pushed to confessing Spicer's murder to Cubitt by their teasing. He feels '*hatred and revulsion*' for the men with whom he is locked in a contract of violence and fear. He tells Cubitt to '*clear out and starve*' and Cubitt tells him '*there's others in this town...*'

• On the eve of his wedding, as the chapter closes, Pinkie is presented in turmoil of fear, hatred and revulsion. His 'friendship' with Dallow gives him no comfort, there is hostility between himself and Cubitt, and he is marrying because he believes the alternative is to dangle at the end of a noose. His anguish is mental and physical as he '*tried to picture peace...his imagination wilted...a saw a grey darkness going on without end.*' Pinkie has no conscience, and his imagination, which is so fixed upon the possibilities of evil, can no longer recall how it feels to be at peace. And yet he feels no compunction about his actions, telling himself '*it's not my fault they get me angry so I want to do things.*'

• What do you find interesting, or ironic, about the way in which Pinkie's internal life is presented.

Chapter Six

In their room at The Cosmopolitan Hotel, Phil Corkery and Ida wake after a night of passion which is made rather repulsive by the description of Phil in his pants: '*his mouth open a little showing one yellow tooth and a gob of metal filling.*' The narrative voice comments upon disappointment and shame following illicit sex: '*excuses in the sad dissatisfied brain – nothing ever matched the deep excitement of the regular desire.*' Nevertheless Ida rejects self recrimination, telling herself '*it was just human nature... God didn't mind a bit of human nature...her mind turned to seeing that the evil suffered.*'

• The narrator makes an interesting comparison between the net of evil and vice which has closed around Pinkie, and the 'triumph of hope over experience' which seems to characterise the cycle of sexual indulgence of Ida's life: she '*felt excitement stirring again in the disappointed body.*'

- Ida tells Phil, *'what we really need now is one of Pinkie's men. Somebody scared or angry.'*

Part Six

Chapter One

Cubitt has parted company with Pinkie and reflects upon his 'value.' He, like Pinkie, is proud: '*He stared like Narcissus into his pool...*' At the pub he is treated with deference by the grocer who offers to buy him a drink. Cubitt imagines that he is everything that a man should be. He believes himself to be involved in '*high politics...he felt as important as a Prime Minister making treaties.*' When other men in the pub leave him he thinks that it is because '*they couldn't stand the company of a Man.*' He thinks of Pinkie and is not sorry to have left the employ of '*a boy like that..... give me a Man's job and I'll do it.*' Yet his grandiose reflections are short lived and soon he is feeling lonely. Cubitt's vanity belies his sentimental inadequacy. Soon he needs to be absorbed into another 'gang' and decides to offer his services to Colleoni at The Cosmopolitan Hotel where he runs into Crab, an ex-member of Kite's gang who immediately realises that Cubitt is 'looking for a job.'

• The narrator draws attention to class mobility: members of Colleoni's mob are rubbing shoulders with 'ladies and gentlemen' even though one '*old man with a monocle on a black ribbon*' is affronted to be acknowledged as an equal by Crab as the mobster '*bowed slightly*' to his female companion. Crab sees Ida and comments that she is '*a fine woman.*' Clearly Crab feels that he has advanced socially as a consequence of working for a more successful criminal. Although the hotel is tasteful in its decor, and there are signboards which read '*Ladies' Hairdressing*' and '*Gentlemen's Hairdressing:*' not all of its patrons could be described as either ladies or gentlemen. Crab has the accoutrements of wealth however, which he believes are class signifiers, and yet those belonging to the leisured class recognise that

Colleoni, and the minders who surround him, are not of their milieu.

• Crab has studied the mannerisms of the gentry and makes efforts to ape their behaviour: '*he had picked up between Doncaster and London a hundred different mannerisms travelling first class ...he had learnt how Lord Feversham spoke to a porter...*' Cubitt looks at the patrons of the hotel and is able to tell Cubitt 'how much they are worth.' One of the individuals pointed out by the mobster is a '*brewer...worth a hundred thousand nicker.*' The narrator shows that the thirties as a time of social mobility: the low—vulgar classes are storming the previously held bastions of privilege.

• Crab points out to Cubitt that Colleoni runs a superior outfit: '*He likes things done properly. No violence. The police have great confidence in Mr Colleoni.*'

• Ida has found her weak link: she can see that the discontented and maudlin Cubitt might give her the information that she needs to take to the police. Ida finds him ready to talk: *He had an enormous urge to confession.*' However Cubitt realises in time that the temptations indulge in sentimental gossip with this woman, who seems to already know too much, would be dangerous and he vanishes when she went '*to put on a bit of powder.*'

• Ida has learnt from Cubitt that Pinkie and Rose were to be married: '*A kind of righteous mirth moved her to add with excitement, 'we've got to save her Phil.*' What does the narrator imply is Ida's motive for 'saving Rose?'

Chapter Two

Pinkie, Prewitt and Dallow wait at the registry office for Rose. Pinkie dwells with horrified fascination upon their coming wedding night. His memories of sexuality activity that he witnessed as a child haunt him. Pinkie is unable to keep his thoughts to himself; even Dallow is made uncomfortable by his unusual garrulity; he tells him that when he was a kid he 'swore' he'd be a priest. He remembers a girl from school who was so despairing that she *'put her head on the line'* when she discovered that she was pregnant for the second time at the age of fifteen. All the associations with sex are horrifying for Pinkie, and all talk of love or romance provokes bursts of hatred.

• Rose is late because she went to church to find a priest in order to make her confession; however she realises the pointlessness of this because she wouldn't be able to make an act of contrition, showing that she was truly sorry and intended to 'turn from' her error. She knows that she is about to commit a mortal sin; and Pinkie tells her *'with bitter and unhappy relish, "It'll be no good going to confession ever again."'* Pinkie makes no effort to comfort her, or to tell her that is doesn't matter. Their faith in the Church's teaching remains intact.

• The narrator uses a scriptural quotation when commenting upon Pinkie's 'graduation from childhood things' to crime and violence: *'he had put away childish things.'* However rather than feeling despair or any shade of contrition, Pinkie *'was filled with awe at his own powers.'* The narrator regularly alludes to Pinkie's pride, which is said to be the greatest spiritual sin because it separates man from God [and which was Satan's downfall].

• Pinkie's forthcoming marriage to Rose is by far, for him, the most awful thing he has done: he thinks of *'his temporal safety in return for two immortalities of pain.'* The measure of Pinkie's distance from his God and repentance is shown in the narrative comment about the mortal sin that he is about to commit: *'he was filled with a kind of gloomy hilarity and pride.'* His mindset is undoubtedly diabolical.

• Pinkie taunts Rose with lines from the Rite of Marriage; and Rose knows *'that this evening meant nothing at all, that there hadn't been a wedding.'*

• Pinkie's pride takes him to the Cosmopolitan Hotel. He does not try to register at the best hotel in town either because he wants to celebrate in style, or out of a desire to please his bride: he wants to make a statement to the world about his value. He believes that *'It's the right place'* for him because it was the best. He tells his bride: *'you needn't think there's going to be a honeymoon.'* Pinkie and Rose are turned away from the hotel; they tell him that that there is no room free.

• Rose insists that Pinkie make a recording of his feelings for her. He does this because he is made nervous by her outburst of disappointment. This recording, in which he calls Rose a bitch and tells her that he wants her to go back where she came from, is Rose's treasured possession at the end of the novel following Pinkie's death.

• The only feeling that Pinkie has for Rose was an intermittent *'sensuality: the coupling of Good and Evil.'* It could be inferred that Pinkie is stimulated by the thought that he is in possession of, and has power over, something that he defines as good. Or it could be that Evil is only defined in juxtaposition with innocence. And Pinkie is proud of the extent that he has fallen from innocence.

• Pinkie and Rose return to Frank's lodgings where he brutally has sex with Rose and reflects that *'he had graduated in the last human shame.'* He also believes that he would not be afraid of anything again: *'he had been afraid of pain and more afraid of damnation – the sudden and unshriven death. Now it was as if he was damned already and there was nothing to fear ever again.'*

• Rose thinks, that when Cubitt knocks at the door, it is the police come to arrest Pinkie. Pinkie realises that she 'knows' about Fred Hale and he laughingly tells her that *'There's not a pin to choose between us.'*

• Pinkie wakes to the realisation that he is a married man; that the registry office wedding was *'as irrevocable as a sacrament. Only death would set him free.'*

Part Seven

Chapter One

Rose wakes to the realisation that she has joined Pinkie in exile from God's Grace: '*What was the good of praying now? She'd finished with all that: she'd chosen her side: if they damned him they'd have to damn her, too'*.

The narrator delineates the hopeless squalor of the house. Dallow tells Rose that there's no need to cook or light the stove because there were plenty of tins. He tells her that it was '*Liberty Hall… you don't want to work do you?'*

• The narrator makes two references to a sense of pride which is beginning to grow in Rose: '*Pride swelled in her breast…she was sensible of an immense freedom'*. Rose decides to return to Snows to flaunt her new freedom and maturity as a married woman. She reflects that '*she was having her cake in this world, not in the next, and she didn't care.'* What is the significance of this burgeoning pride which is rising in Rose?

• Ida comes to the lodgings to see Rose. When Rose asks what she wants Ida replies '*I want justice.*' Ida tells Rose about Hale and her suspicions about Spicer's death. Rose responds with disbelief, saying, '*You don't kill a man for no reason.'*

• Ida explains to Rose the distinction between 'human nature' and Pinkie's wickedness. She uses the metaphor of rock: '*bite it all the way down you'll still read Brighton.'* Can this innate and inescapable property of 'human nature' apply to the presentation of Evil in this novel? How is 'human nature' represented by the narrative voice?

• Ida tells Rose that Pinkie is dangerous, but she is confident: '*he wouldn't do me any harm.'* Ida argues that she '*knows the difference between Right and Wrong*.' But Rose is adamant: '*the two words meant nothing'* to her because she believes in a higher authority than the temporal one to which Ida offers obeisance.

• Ida tells to *'take precautions'*: *'you don't want a murderer's baby.'* The narrator's comment that Rose *'thought of what she might have let herself in for like a sense of glory'* shows the extent of her devotion to Pinkie and hints that Pinkie's ingrained pride is beginning to be adopted by Rose.

Chapter Two

Pinkie returns in time to see Ida leaving the lodgings. He is surprised to see the good natured Ida giving a penny to a child in the street. Acts of kindness are so alien to Pinkie that he believes she is drunk. Darrow has assumed Ida to be Rose's mother and Pinkie, trying to catch her in deceit, asks whether her mother has visited. Rose tells him that it was her mother, this causes Pinkie to tell Darrow that she is a danger to them and *'It ought to be easy to quiet her.'* Darrow tells him that he *'won't stand for any more killing.*

• Rose changes her mind about keeping the truth of Ida's visit from Pinkie. Pinkie is not reassured of Rose's loyalty: he continues to be in turmoil of paranoia, but he tells Rose *'you can trust me.'* He uses Prewitt, who he ironically describes to Rose as *'the Soul of Honour'* as his alibi, reassuring her that Spicer's death was an accident: he couldn't have killed him because his solicitor was a witness. Although Rose reminds him *'with dread,'* that murder is a mortal sin.

• Pinkie reassures Rose that *'it won't hurt,'* when she asks him *'what won't hurt, Pinkie?* He answers *'the way I'll manage things'* and he *'started agilely away from the dark suggestion.'*

Chapter Three

Pinkie's paranoia continues to grow. He believes that Prewitt is the 'weak link' in his armour. He is oddly fatalistic, knowing that '*all he had to do was let himself easily go.*' Prewitt, like the other members of the vice gang, is characterised as spiritually sick; the symptoms are a mind in a turmoil of dread, physical symptoms of malaise and an utter absence of peace. He is presented as an individual who, like Faustus in Marlow's play has 'sold his soul.' He recognises this parallel himself and quotes Faustus: '*You know what Mephistopheles said to Faustus when he asked where Hell was? He said 'Why this is Hell, nor are we out of it'.* The narrator has presented the practice of evil throughout the novel as ultimately demanding a price from the practitioners: a loss of peace, which is characterised as physical sickness, and finally despair.

Faustus makes his pact with the devil, Mephistopheles and initially is delighted by the temporal rewards that he receives as a reward for his soul eternally. However the pleasures become dimmer each time they are indulged and he experiences a relentless hunger for more, which is never satisfied. Faustus, like Pinkie who the narrator declares: '*... knew what the end might be – it didn't horrify him: it was easier than life,*' finds that he has sold his peace of mind, as well as his soul. This idea that the practice of evil destroys the peace of those who are caught in its snare is a common theme in classical Literature. Shakespeare shows this too in his play Macbeth. This character perpetrates one act of evil after another: he is unable to free himself from the web of violence and fear in which he is enmeshed; as a consequence he expresses his lack of peace to his wife, telling her: 'Macbeth has killed sleep.'

Prewitt tries to escape from his tortured mind and body by '*watching the typists.*' It was lust which began his descent into despair: he tells Pinkie that his marriage was brought about by '*An affair of uncontrollable passion,*' and it seems that his addiction continues its hold on him as he watches the '*little typists...so neat and trim.*'

• Prewitt says, '*Eat, drink for tomorrow*... The end of this quotation, which is taken from The Bible, where variations of the quotation 'Eat, drink and be merry,' are to be found in Ecclesiastes, Isaiah, and The Gospel of Luke. The quotation in Isaiah ends 'for tomorrow we die.' The irony in Prewitt's case is that he is unable to eat, drink or be merry because he has a tormenting digestive ailment.

• Prewitt is in a state of '*sickly despair.*' His marriage to the woman he refers to as 'the spouse' is a torture to him. The narrator uses interesting imagery, which creates an impression of the 'hell' in which Prewitt exists: '*The smoke came down outside the window like a blind.*' He tells Pinkie '*The worst that can happen to you is you'll hang. But I can rot.*' He experiences physical agony: '*the nerves set to work in the agonised flesh.*' His mind, he tells Pinkie, '*carries the secrets of the sewer.*'

• Pinkie, who is nervous of Prewitt's vulnerability on his own behalf, advises him to '*take a holiday.*' The irony is of course, that Prewitt has no where to run and no where to hide from the 'self' that he has become.

Chapter Four

Pinkie tells Dallow that Prewitt says that 'he *is in Hell.*' Dallow laughs, telling Pinkie, '*I don't believe in what my eyes don't see.*' Pinkie replies: '*You don't see much then.*' Rose senses Pinkie's troubled mood. He tells her '*We could go out into the country where no one would hear.*' He seems to enjoy annihilating her peace of mind: '*he measured her terror carefully.*'

• The narrator comments that Pinkie '*discovered in himself an odd nostalgia for the darkest act of all.*' For Catholics, the 'darkest act' is suicide because it cuts the sinner off forever from the possibility of God's forgiveness. The act of suicide is believed to be the ultimate sin by Catholics and for this reason until modern times suicides were not allowed to be buried in consecrated ground.

- Rose hints that pregnancy may be a consequence of their coupling and Pinkie looks at her with renewed *'terror and disgust as if he were watching the ugly birth itself.'* Pinkie experiences an inversion of emotion that people usually experience toward love, sex and the birth of a child. The evil within him has alienated him from the best of human experience.

- The chapter ends with a narrative comment upon Rose's state of mind, which reinforces the theme that evil inevitably devours peace of mind. It seemed that she *'had passed through years of anxiety and knew that the relief never lasted long and that the anxiety always began again.'*

Chapter Five

The focus of Pinkie's anxiety is his marriage to Rose. His turmoil is two fold: he is insecure on account of his paranoia, and doesn't entirely trust her loyalty; his overwhelming nightmare however, is that he is locked into relationship with this girl for whom he feels a mixture of disgust and contempt.

The narrator has shown throughout the novel that the inclination to do evil begins in the mind and Pinkie is preoccupied by thoughts of ridding himself of his burden. His mental turmoil is manifested in symptoms of sickness: *'His eyes were bloodshot. He carried down with him the marks of a fever – the beating pulse and the hot forehead and the restless brain.'* Again the narrator emphasises the extent to which evil infects the mental, spiritual and physical health of the perpetrator. Pinkie has proudly embraced his inclinations to cruelty and violence and he no longer has any moral boundaries. He seems driven to commit greater atrocities and rather than increasing his security, he becomes more deeply enmeshed in the sickness of evil.

• Pinkie tells Dallow '*She's got to go before she...*' But Dallow, who seems to becoming nervous of Pinkie's inclination to murder anyone who he perceives to be a problem to him, tells him '*it's not safe to quarrel.*' Pinkie's paranoia is relentless; he tells his henchman that '*it won't ever be safe again...No divorce. Nothing at all except dying.*'

• Dallow too has experienced the slippery slope of sin. He tells Pinkie that he is feeling trapped by his illicit relationship with Judy: '*I started something there alright...I wish I hadn't. I don't want trouble with poor old Frank an' she's so careless.*' Dallow's relationship with Frank's wife is entirely about sex: he cares nothing for her and tells Pinkie that if she should become pregnant it would be '*her funeral.*'

• Pinkie tells Dallow of his idea for ridding himself of Rose: a suicide pact. Pinkie's thoughts are described as '*like heavy bales.*' The initial idea has grown and has now become something weighty which dominates his consciousness and has to be dealt with. His brain is described as '*poisoned.*' The overwhelming effect of the description of Pinkie's predicament is that it is out of control. He has become inhuman in his compulsion to destroy and his inability to experience any peace of mind. He has long been a stranger to joy and does not experience any emotions other than hatred, contempt, and anxiety: in spite of this his pride remains.

• Colleoni has offered Pinkie three hundred pounds: a 'goodwill offering' he wants pinkie to leave Brighton.

• Prewitt has left Brighton. He has taken Pinkie's 'advice' and gone to France on 'holiday.'

Chapter Six

Ida and Phil are out drinking and they find themselves sharing the venue with Pinkie's diminished gang. Phil Corkery challenges Ida's continuing involvement saying *'you're only doing it because it's fun'* Ida does no deny this asserting that she *'liked doing what's right'*. Phil points out that her ready enjoyment of illicit sex made her unable to claim a moral high ground, yet Ida asserts *'That does no one any harm. That's not like murder.'*

• The authorial voice is somewhat ambiguous in the portrayal of Ida. She believes herself to be a moral crusader, and yet certainly at the time in which the novel is set, her promiscuous enjoyment of sex would be regarded as immoral. Never the less her argument that sexual relationships between adult single people is 'harmless' seems valid to many. It would not have been regarded as such by people with religious inclinations. Illicit sex would have been called a mortal sin by Catholics. Although Ida is presented as well meaning and kindly, the life embracing tart-with a heart, the authorial voice undoubtedly suggests that she is vulgar, common and self-indulgent.

• The chapter ends with Ida's self congratulatory reflections on *'the people she had saved: a man she had once pulled out of the sea when she was a young woman, the money to a blind beggar, and the kind word in season to the despairing schoolgirl in the Strand.'*

Chapter Seven

Dallow's suggestion that they all leave town and take a pub together inadvertently strengthens Pinkie's resolve to be rid of Rose. He thinks with horror of sixty years: *'a horror without end ... the contact and the sensual tremble and the stained sleep and the waking not alone.'* He persuades Rose to come *'for a drive in the country.'* He has Rose's note in his pocket in which she wrote that she would follow him 'anywhere.' Rose felt '*terror.*' His suggestion of a suicide pact fills her with horror: '*it was said to be the worst act of all, the act of despair, the sin without forgiveness.*'

• Pinkie loads his revolver and imagines that '*life would go on. No more human contacts, other people's emotions beating at his brain.*'

• The chapter ends with the mouth motif: '*a huge darkness pressed a wet mouth against the panes.*' This metaphor suggests both oppressiveness and the seamy and repulsive nature of the life of vice which is engulfing these two people. This motif has also been used to describe self indulgence and the sordid aspects of sexuality.

Chapter Eight

Dallow, whose '*brain worked very slowly,*' begins to realise that Pinkie has been gone a long time and is uneasy. He notices Ida's stare and approaches her demanding to know who she is and what she wants. Ida is not intimidated by the gangster and tells him that Prewitt has been apprehended by the police and is giving evidence against them. She advises him to turn against Pinkie.

• The narrator comments that Ida carried '*her air of compassion and comprehension about her like cheap perfume.*' What is your impression of the authorial attitude toward this character and her motives?

• Dallow is tempted by Ida's suggestion that he 'changes sides'. The narrator comments that he is also tempted to ignore the suspicion of Pinkie's intent: '*Better to wash his hands of the whole thing...after all he didn't know...but he knew very well in his heart that* (the car) *would never come, not with both of them.*'

• Ida challenges him shaking his complacency: '*you know what they've gone for.*'

• Dallow goes with Ida in search of Pinkie and Rose and yet his belief in the superior judgement of his leader remains: *'Pinkie thought of everything...he hadn't got the imagination to know what they'd find.* The narrator has shown that the origin of evil is in the mind; his characterisation of Dallow shows the dangers of having a weak mind and a limited imagination. Dallow's defence to Rose and his protestations at Pinkie's plan to dispose of her reveal him to be a less malignant character than Pinkie, and yet his admiration of Pinkie's superior intelligence and his consequent malleability makes him dangerous.

Chapter Nine

• Pinkie and Rose stop for a drink and Pinkie recognises a boy that he had tormented at school. He taunts him, asking whether he still goes to mass. He tells the boy: *'you're afraid of burning...I'm not.'* In spite of his near despair, his pride and defiance remain.

• The narrator seems to suggest that, poised as Pinkie is on the brink of a more terrible outrage, he experiences *'something trying to get in; the pressure of gigantic wings against the glass. Dona nobis pacem. He withstood it...'* Pinkie knows the awfulness of the act that he is about to commit, and it seems that God does not give up trying to resurrect his Christian teaching, offering him the prospect of peace. Yet Pinkie rejects this attempt at 'eleventh hour' redemption.

• Pinkie instructs Rose on the use of the gun and leaves her to her dissonance telling her *'it won't hurt.'*

• Ida, Dallow and a policeman arrive as Rose rejects Pinkie's insistence that she shoot herself; she flings the gun into the undergrowth.

• Pinkie, outraged at what he perceives to be Dallow's betrayal, uncorks the vitriol. The policeman smashes the bottle and the acid burns Pinkie's face which *'steamed'... 'he screamed and screamed ...his hands up to his eyes.'* Pinkie falls to his death.

Chapter Ten

The chapter opens with Ida recounting the details of her triumph to another man friend, who tells her *'you're a terrible woman Ida,'* when she comments that Phil Corkery would be unlikely to send her 'any more postcards' as a consequence of her tenacious pursuit of the criminal gang.
Ida visits old Crowe in order to contact the spirit world about her love life.

Chapter Eleven

The final chapter follows Rose's desperate attempt to come to terms with Pinkie's death. She is angry and rebellious when she visits the priest. She tells him: *'I wish I'd killed myself.'* The priest is old and tired, and yet is able to offer her hope that the 'love' that Pinkie had for her might be sufficient to redeem him in the eyes of an ever merciful God. Yet when Rose tells him that Ida believed that Pinkie *'didn't know about love,'* murmured *'perhaps she was right.'*

• The old priest tells Rose: *'You can't conceive, my child, nor can I or anyone the ...appalling...strangeness of the mercy of God.'* He tells her to *'Hope and pray,'* and should there be a child as a result of their coupling, she should bring him up as a *'saint to pray for his father.'*

• The priest also remarks that 'a *Catholic is more capable of evil than anyone.'*

• The priest's words are a balm to Rose's anguished mind. When he asks her to pray for him she responds *'yes, oh yes.'* Rose has received comfort and hope from this priest.

• The comparison between the words of this priest and the specious words of the clergyman at Hales funeral is stark. The priest's response to Rose's anguish is compassionate; he does not attempt to instil fear neither does he offer specious comfort. There is the sense of 'mysteries' of God's love and inclination to forgive which bring a chink of light into Rose's darkness. The authorial voice is undoubtedly approving of his theology.

• Although Rose has received some comfort of God's unfailing mercy, the novel ends with a reference to *the worst horror of all,* ' which is yet to be experienced. Rose's most treasured possession is the recording that Pinkie made for her. She believes that his hateful words are a declaration of love. The narrator comments of Pinkie: *'He had existed and would always exist.'*

The Presentation of Popular Culture and Ida as the Symbol of the Popular Culture of the Masses in Brighton Rock's 1930's Britain

Graham Greene declared that he enjoyed Brighton, but the question of what he saw to admire in Brighton is not easy to discover in his novel.

The novel opens with Hale, the promoter of a popular newspaper in the style of today's tabloid newspaper, feeling that he *'did not belong'* to the *'holiday crowd,'* which descended in *'bewildered multitudes'* into Brighton. Brighton is presented as well on the way to profitable recovery from post war austerity: *'new silver paint sparkled on the piers ...an aero plane advertising something...'* trails banners in the sky.

The critic John Carey describes the novel as "a contemptuous indictment of England in the 1930's" and the opening scene, depicting the masses at play, reveals the authorial voice, clear in its contempt for the fat spotty girls, ripe for sexual encounter, described as *'creatures;'* the hairdressers with *'bleached and perfumed hair;'* the women who *'flashed their pointed painted nails at each other and cackled,'* form the close-up delineation of the crowd of trippers which *'uncoils endlessly, two by two, each with a determined air of sober and determined gaiety.'* The animal imagery is clear, as is the suggestion that the pursuit of pleasure, although determined, is somehow false, and the reward, *'the grain of pleasure,'* from inane amusements: *'ghost trains... grinning skeletons, sticks of Brighton rock, paper sailors' caps,'* receives the author's amused disdain.

Kolley Kibber is based upon the real life Lobby Lud of the *News Chronicle,* and the stunt to promote increased circulation of his newspaper is based upon a similar incentive to boost sales by a newspaper of the time. The victim Hale is presented as one of the crowd, a plebian by birth and instinct although *'condemned by higher pay to pretend to want other things;'* his 'sneer' and assumed air of superiority a veneer beneath which the popular attractions *'pull at his heart.'* He is presented as manipulating the masses who read the newspaper, whilst pretending contempt for them.

Ida is presented as drunk in an *'accommodating way;'* there are numerous allusions to her large breasts which although 'magnificent' *'great, open and friendly'* had *'never suckled a child of her own'*: there is the suggestion of essential sterility beneath the apparent nurturing and fecund exterior. Descriptions of her *'cow-like eyes' 'vulgar summer dress'* and *'rich Guinness voice'* suggest the author's contempt for her class and blowsy *'big blown charms.'* Hale gazes at Ida in the public bar *'as if he were gazing at life itself.'*

The 'life' that Ida represents is the cheap, secular, consumerist, self indulgent world of the masses, written about disparagingly by many 1930's intellectuals.

A motif for the growing consumerism of the 1930's could be Greene's repeated allusion to the functions of the mouth; its demands and gratification given in graphic and rather disgusting close-up. The depiction of Ida's consumption of the éclair, the cream *'oozing'* between her teeth; Phil's mouth *'half open as he sleeps'* revealing *'one yellow tooth and a gob of metal filling;'* Judy fastens on Rose *'a mouth wet and prehensile like a sea anemone'*; Ida relishes *'the soft gluey mouth affixed in taxis;'* the sea, *'like a wet mouth',* darkness presses *'a wet mouth against the panes.'* The cheap music coming out of the wireless in the café is *'the world's wet mouth lamenting over life.'* The world offers sensual experience: seductive and yet somehow revolting.

Ida, the champion of the Wronged, is the tart with a heart: the detailed and insulting delineation of Ida, who takes up a brave fight against Pinkie because she believes *'in right and wrong,'* is startling in its clear disdain for both her morals and her motives for setting herself in opposition to him.

Although consistently portrayed as proudly evil, Pinkie is simultaneously presented as somehow superior to Ida because of the validity of his *'knowledge'*: he, the violent sadist is spiritually superior because he inhabits the world of Good and Evil, rather than the secular world of Right and Wrong. Despite the success of Rose's rescue and the triumph of justice, Ida's motives are presented as self gratifying in her crusade: ethics as entertainment. Beneath the *'melancholy and resolution...her heart beat faster...with a sigh of happy satiety.'* She declares to old Crowe, *'it's going to be fun, it's going to be a bit of life.'* Ida, whose name is the *'vulgarized Greek original,'* *'believes in ghosts.'* She visits old Crowe and dabbles in the spirit world, she meditates upon men and death: she has no faith or creed except that life is to be enjoyed and her senses gratified. Ida declares to her friend Clarence *'Let Papists treat death with flippancy: life wasn't so important perhaps to them as what came after: but to her death was the end of everything.'*

Ida declares to Clarence: *'I like a funeral.'* In spite of her belief that death *'is the end of everything,'* Ida's stated enjoyment of a funeral reflects her general enjoyment of a celebration; a party - in all likelihood one ending in drink and maudlin sentimental reminiscences.

Greene's depiction of Ida suggests that she is a woman of feeling, and yet when the manifestations of her emotional responses are studied, it is the sentimental enjoyment of tragic ballads, poignant sob-stories and *'the enjoyable distress'* that she experiences when she thinks of Hale's last hours, rather than compassion or empathy. Greene's ironic depiction of her finer feelings is laced with contempt for her hedonistic philosophy of life: *'life was sunlight on bedposts, Ruby port, the leap of the heart when the outsider you have backed passes the post and the colours go bobbing up...poor Fred's mouth pressing down on hers.... She took life with deadly seriousness: she was prepared to cause any amount of unhappiness to anyone in order to find the only thing she believed in.*

The narrator's comment that Ida took life with *'deadly seriousness'* could be ironic in the light of the list of hedonistic pleasures by which she defines the meaning of life. It seems to be the authorial view that, although single minded and brave in her pursuit of justice for Hale, her motivation was selfish. It was the drama, and the powerful feeling of moral righteousness which provokes her confrontation with the adolescent psychopath, rather than either the desire for justice or compassion for

72

Rose. Greene seems to find 'feelings' suspect, luring the self indulgent Ida onto the moral high ground: possibly the modern 'feel good' culture is being starkly contrasted with religious absolutism of 'the Papists.' She defines the meaning of life for her by a list of hedonistic and largely sensual pastimes which she defends with single minded 'seriousness.' From the point of view of the seriously religious however, life, the way in which it is lived and the belief system which underwrites it, *is* literally a matter of life or death. A concept understood and embraced by the author, who declared himself to be 'intellectually convinced' by Catholic doctrine before he was 'emotionally' converted.

Fred Hale's cremation is held in a *'bright new flowery suburb'* which sounds positive, although the detailed delineation of the *'bare cold, secular chapel'* where there are no *'unhygienic burials'* and which could be adapted *'quietly and conveniently to suit any creed,'* seem to be a part of the rise of brash, vulgar secularism epitomized by Brighton. Modernity, like cremation, although *'hygienic'* is presented as a sterile simulation of the religious rite: religious neutrality devoid of real comfort; the clergyman peddling empty words purged of any real meaning. The clergyman, unwilling or unable to declare allegiance to clear doctrine, nevertheless proclaims a *'disbelief in the old medieval hell.'* He does not refer to God, rather he alludes to *'the One'* confidently asserting that *'our brother'* is *'at one'* with it. His words are described as *'stamped'* with his *'personal mark'* rather than his personal belief. The author's contempt is clearly felt for the *'Truth loving generation,'* and its comfortable, unchallenging litany of meaningless 'theology.' The clergyman is described as *'a conjurer who has produced his nine hundred and fortieth rabbit without a hitch.'* Greene attended his first cremation, of his mother-in-law, in 1933 and was disgusted by 'the air of irreligion posing as undogmatic Christianity.' Modern religion is presented by Greene as, to use Marx's expression, the 'opium of the people,' and Ida is the champion of the people. Pinkie describes Ida as *'just nothing'* and the narrator seems to be in agreement: *'she was as far from either of them* (Rose and Pinkie) *as she was from Hell - or Heaven.'* Greene, like Pinkie found

Hell entirely believable. He wrote: 'it gives something hard, non-sentimental and exciting.'

Greene has commented 'the ideas of my Catholic characters, even their Catholic ideas, were not necessarily mine': which makes his likening of Pinkie to Christ possibly less disturbing. When Cubitt denies that he was a friend of Pinkie's, Ida is reminded of '*a vague memory of The Bible...a courtyard, a sewing wench beside the fire, the cock crowing.*' Ida's modern spirituality is presented as spurious, like the clergyman's, whereas Pinkie's beliefs are real. His conviction that he is one of the damned is a part of the old world of religious certainty, whereas Ida's modern creed of sensuality and vague goodwill toward (particularly) men is presented as fatuous pap, without validity or substance.

Ultimately Pinkie, the boy who once dreamed of being a priest and who was once a choirboy, is presented as demonstrating adherence to the sound doctrine of Catholicism, whereas Ida, with her '*friendly and popular heart*' represents the masses: cheap and determinedly cheerful, intellectually weak, self-gratifying and in spiritual error.

The Representation of Evil, Catholicism and Redemption in 'Brighton Rock'

'A Catholic is more capable of evil than anyone.'

Pinkie has a strong concept of sin and the consequence for him of dying in a state of sin for which he has not been absolved through the Catholic act of repentance and confession. He knows that he will be called to account for his wrong doing before God, although he at no time mentions God; it is the concept of hell and damnation which dominates his consciousness. However his sense of sin it is not experienced as a conscience, an innate sense of culpability and consequent shame, rather it is experienced as *'knowledge.'* Rose also has a Catholic imprinting of the concept of sin and accepts *'as a stranger in the country of mortal sin,'* (part7) that she will be called to account for her transgression before God, unless she confesses, repents and receives absolution. This would mean a renunciation of Pinkie and repentance for the marriage, which was not a sacramental union in the eyes of the church. Both of these characters as 'cradle Catholics' would have had the catechism of absolution through confession and repentance deeply instilled into them. Both would have understood that mortal sin (in contrast to venial or minor sin) means 'death' or eternal damnation, for the sinner who does not turn from sin and receive absolution. However, whereas Rose faced the consequences of their flouting of the sacrament of marriage with considerable trepidation, Pinkie, although in no doubt about the seriousness *'that this was a mortal sin...was filled with a kind of gloomy hilarity and pride.'* *(*Part 6 ch.2)

This is the second time in the novel that Pinkie is described as 'proud' explicitly, although there are a number of occasions when his behaviour implicitly suggests pride. The first occasion is at the beginning of the novel, when he is introduced with a startling juxtaposition of imagery as having *'a face of starved intensity, a kind of hideous and unnatural pride.'* He is also described as *'the boy'*, *'his smooth skin with the faintest down'* contrasting sharply with the description of his eyes *'like an old man's'*.

It is interesting that 'hideous pride' was the sin committed by Satan who sought equality with God and was, for his disobedience ,by the 'Almighty Power' 'Hurled headlong flaming from...the sky...to bottomless perdition...there to dwell...in penal fire.' (Paradise Lost)

When Ida, referred to as Lily at the start of the novel, is described as a *'cheery soul'* by Hale, Pinkie *'who looks at her with furious distaste'* says *'you've no cause to talk about souls.'* He, as a Catholic, believes himself to be a member of a religious aristocracy, because he has 'the knowledge' of the gulf between good and evil. This reference to 'knowledge' is made many times in the novel, and is an allusion to the tree of knowledge in the Garden of Eden from which Eve, who succumbed to Satan's temptation, persuaded Adam to eat an apple against God's express command. It is described in the Bible as the tree of knowledge of good and evil. When Rose goes to confession after Pinkie's death (not initially to confess, rather to proclaim her defiance to the priest,) it is clear from the priest's comment that *'a Catholic is more capable of evil than anyone,'* that the author has an understanding of the Catholic catechism, and that the concept of evil as knowledge is a central theme in the novel. The comment reveals that having 'knowledge' of sin and wilfully embracing it, obviates any claim to transgression through ignorance: the sin committed by Pinkie and Rose can only be described as being in the 'deliberate fault' category, therefore magnifying culpability of offence against God.

At the end of the novel, Rose finds comfort in the belief that she might be carrying Pinkie's child. The narrator uses Rose's meditation that her life would continue *'just as if the boy has never existed at all,'* to ambiguously go on to comment that he *'had existed and would always exist':* like evil itself.

The narrator's presentation of evil in the novel is interesting. In part 4, chapter 3, it is implied that evil might be understood as spoilt innocence. Pinkie says of Rose, *'what was most evil in him needed her; it couldn't get along without goodness.'* Suggesting that the 'darkness' within his soul could not be defined as such without a concept of the light of innocence or goodness, within

Rose: evil cannot be understood without an idea that goodness exists. Yet later in the same section, Pinkie goes on to explain to Rose the contrast between them, when she insists that she, like him, is bad:

> 'You'll not be anything but good...it's not what you do, it's what you think...it's in the blood. Perhaps when they christened me the holy water didn't take. I never howled the devil out.'

Evil is understood by Pinkie to be innate, an integral part of who he is, 'bred and nurtured in the mind,' rather than defined by an action or behaviour, if wrong doing is embraced as Pinkie embraces evil, with pride and in full knowledge of the offence against God, then the spiritual rift, Greene seems to imply, becomes more difficult to bridge.

Although there are plenty of descriptions of Pinkie's physical appearance to suggest that he embodies attributes of youthful freshness usually associated with innocence, his knowledge of evil seems to be part of him and is 'ageless' rather than acquired; he is depicted as a personification of evil which is an inescapable part of humanity: *'Good and evil lived in the same country, spoke the same language, came together like old friends, feeling the same completion.'* (Part 4, chapter 3)

The narrator's acceptance of the inevitability and the eternal permanence of evil is felt throughout the novel. Pinkie's eyes are described in several places, possibly as 'mirrors of the soul' which reveal, like a barometer, the ruthless dedication to hatred and violence by which he lives: *'the slatey eyes were touched with the annihilating eternity from which he had come and from which he went.'* Evil is understood by the narrator to be that which destroys or 'annihilates;' the devil too is referred to as the destroyer in The Bible. The suggestion that the evil revealed in Pinkie's eyes is timeless and eternal further reinforces the understanding of Pinkie as a living representation of evil.

The novel has been described as 'a classic study of the banality of evil'; although some aspects of Pinkie's behaviour might be understood as 'banal' or commonplace, his utter disregard for human life is extreme; even other members of his murderous band have a sense of moral boundary which should not be crossed. Interestingly Pinkie's ability to detach emotionally from the suffering of his victims is described as '*his strength... He couldn't see through other people's yes, or feel with their nerves.*' A psychologist today would describe an individual with these characteristics as a psychopath. Even Dallow, Pinkie's admiring henchman, baulks at Pinkie's hint that Rose should be murdered. There is a moment when he is tempted to ignore his growing conviction that Pinkie's drive into the country would end in Rose's death: '*Better to wash his hands of the whole thing... after all he didn't know.*' (Part, Ch.8.) Yet Dallow cannot, ultimately, cross this moral boundary. Ida refuses to allow him to deceive himself. He tries to convince himself that '*they've only gone for a drink.*' Yet Ida challenges his self deceit: '*You know what they've gone for.*' Although he continues to insist '*I don't know a thing*', he goes with Ida to find a policeman to accompany them on their journey to rescue Rose. The narrator interestingly comments that Dallow '*hadn't got the imagination*' to think of what they might discover, suggesting that some acts of evil are committed by ignorance, an inability to see the consequences of an abdication of responsibility, rather taking a determined stance against evil. Dallow refuses to 'imagine' because it is uncomfortable for him to accept that by doing nothing he is colluding in an act which contravenes an internalized sense of what is right.

Later in part 7, chapter 9, as Pinkie prepares to murder Rose he curiously asks her '*You'd love me always, wouldn't you?*' Her affirmation doesn't reassure him that she wouldn't betray him to the law. He '*began wearily the long course of action which one day would let him be free again.*' Pinkie feels that he is 'bound' in his compulsion to murder Rose; he feels that he will not be 'free' unless he annihilates her. She is his wife and he was determined to marry her; he admits that '*he hadn't hated her; he hadn't even hated the act. There had been a kind of pleasure...*' (in the sex act). And yet he cannot allow her to live. Pinkie's twisted psyche is anatomized by the narrator, but not explained:

An enormous emotion beat on him; it was like something trying to get in; the pressure of gigantic wings against the bitter force of the school bench, the cement playground, the St Pancras waiting room, Dallow's and Judy's secret lust, and the cold unhappy moment on the pier. If the glass broke, if the beast—what ever it was—got in, God knows what it would do. He had a huge sense of havoc - the confession, the penance and the sacrament – and awful distraction...

Although it is suggested that Pinkie's decision that Rose must die is motivated by his desire to be 'free' of the bonds of matrimony, the compulsion to murder her seems to be an obsessive drive to commit an evil act; evil is depicted a compulsion within Pinkie, an addiction from which he cannot be free. Pinkie is portrayed as a miserable, lonely individual in bondage to evil from which he cannot escape; he is driven by a compulsion which consumes peace of mind to commit ever more gross acts of violence. He is unable to experience the *'Dona nobis pacem.'* The 'beast' of repentance ending in *'confession, the penance and the sacrament'* is that which terrifies Pinkie: evil then is presented as an inversion of all that is commonly held to be good, moral, and virtuous and Pinkie is depicted as enslaved.

When he looks with disgust at an old woman (part 6 ch. 2) with *'a rotting and discoloured face: It was like the sight of damnation'* to Pinkie, and yet she is whispering the rosary, and his terrible inversion hits him with *'horrified fascination: this was one of the saved.'* The inversion of what is usually regarded as good is also revealed in Pinkie's fear and hatred of anything which reminds him of sex: Ida's blatant sexuality; Rose's blind adoration; even a wedding ring provokes in him not simply distaste, but hatred, which might be explained by his early exposure to parental sexual activity.

His memories of being bullied at school might explain his refuge in violence as a way of life, and an explanation of his renunciation of love and all that affirms life, which has left him: *filled with hatred, disgust, loneliness…completely abandoned: he had no share in their thoughts – like a soul in purgatory watching the shameless act of a beloved person.* ' This revelation of the origin of Pinkie's disgust for women and his fear of sex enables the reader to feel some compassion for Pinkie's extreme alienation from love, beauty all that is experienced with pleasure by human beings.

To what extent would you argue That Graham Greene challenges gender stereotypes in his novel 'Brighton Rock?'

It is important to understand that there have been changes, largely brought about by challenges to the patriarchal system, in what most people would understand to be 'typical' male and female characteristics in the seventy years since the novel was published.

In 1938 the role of women, in the workplace and their standing in the world in general, had changed as a consequence of the First World War: the ratio of males to females had declined dramatically, and women were valued for their labour, showing their ability to take challenging roles outside of the home. There have been even greater changes in the way that women are perceived in the intervening years between 1938 and our current age.

It could be argued that Greene's portrayal of the power obsessed, violent and arrogant mob members, the meekly submissive, fearful Rose and the sexually exploited landlady Judy represent characteristics that would have been considered stereotypical of gender types in the 1930's.

The dictionary defines gender as 'properties belonging to sexual classification i.e. male and female'; and a stereotype is character which conforms to an 'unjustifiably fixed mental picture.' According to this definition, Pinkie, his 'men' and Rose and Judy *do* conform to popularly ideas held of male and female behaviour. However I would argue that his characterisation of Rose, Pinkie and his henchmen are not stereotypes; because they are delineated in depth, their characterisation has subtleties which *challenge* the idea that they are representations of 'fixed gender types' of men and women.

The way in which Greene presents Ida is particularly interesting. Greene wrote to his agent upon completion of his first 30,000 words, saying that his novel represented: "the contrast between the ethical mind (Ida's) and the religious (Pinkie and

Rose's.)" He also worried in retrospect of his delineation of this character saying that she had "obstinately refused to come to life."

Some critics have objected to Greene's characterisation of Ida. John Carey has argued that she is the victim of 'assault', Greene's characterisation of her is so "crude and snobbish," that it "swings (the reader) in her favour". However conversely, he goes on to admit that Greene has "a sneaking sympathy with her and with the sleaziness she flourishes in." She is certainly not presented as a model of right female behaviour morally, and it is arguable that she was selfishly motivated, rather than ethically motivated, in her confrontation of Pinkie and her demand for justice.

Greene presents Ida as sexually voracious with an appetite for life, food and alcohol. She is strongly assertive and tenacious and apparently completely lacking in fear. The men in her life are dwarfed by her large personality; she 'calls the shots' sexually, and decides when their appeal or even their use to her has expired. Clarence, one of her men friends, says at the end of the novel, when she reflects on the end of her relationship with Phil Corkery: '*You're a terrible woman Ida.*' There is a strong possibility that in the time in which the novel was written and set, that a woman who behaved as Ida did would indeed have been regarded as 'terrible' in her refusal to conform to gender expectations.

It can be asserted that Pinkie manipulates and exploits Rose, it can be argued that Dallow exploits Judy, but Ida challenges all female stereotypes of the 1930's, and might be argued to hold common ground with women who embrace the much criticised 'lad' culture, adopted by some young women in our current times: although some would say that this too is a 'gender stereotype.'

Pinkie is referred to throughout the novel as '*the boy*:' his physical characteristics as well as his actual age making him the adolescent, rather than the man. However, in spite of his tender years, he is said to possess a '*hideous and unnatural pride.*' It might be argued that this 'pride' reveals a 'masculine' arrogance and belief in the power he wields because of the boundlessness of his inclination to violence; his lack of any moral regulation. This character is paralleled with descriptions of Satan from Literature, such as Milton's Paradise Lost, who, because of his 'hideous pride', was cast out of heaven. In spite of his air of what many might call 'masculine arrogance,' Pinkie presents many characteristics which belie characteristics of typical 'macho' behaviour: his preference is for milk over alcohol; he is fastidious about the dingy poverty of his 'native streets, when he feels the *dim desire for annihilation*' in him. Pinkie's extreme aversion to bodily functions, sex and childbirth create something more than revulsion in him: his disgust at the sensory experience of sex and poverty is more akin to fear. His terror at the prospect of consummating his marriage to Rose, and his horrified rejection of Sylvie, Spicer's 'bereaved' whore, betray his weakness: '*fear and curiosity ate at the proud future and fear won*': his '*cruel virginity which demanded some satisfaction different from theirs*'...marks Pinkie as essentially untypical as an adolescent male.

Pinkie, the boy gangster,' whom Dallow hero worships as the fearless leader, is psychologically and emotionally crippled. He is unable to function as a man sexually. Although, as he tells Dallow, he 'knows' the rules of sexual behaviour, on the eve of his marriage to Rose, '*his eyes flinched as if he were watching some horror.*' When he remembers his childhood and the horrifying proximity of his parents' copulation, 'his *whole mouth and jaw loosened: he might have been going to weep.*' Pinkie's memories of growing up in poverty, and the deprivations and ignorance associated with extreme poverty, have turned him into a twisted, vulnerable boy-man. He cannot grow up and mature into what Dallow believed him to be: a fearless and emotionally detached leader of men, because he would always be the terrified boy who had witnessed the sordid and brutal expressions of human nature at a young age, and been irreparably damaged by the experience. The maturation process was in him fatally arrested. Pinkie was doomed to remain emotionally stunted, without moral boundaries and devoid of most of the civilising characteristics of a human being: compassion; tenderness an innate belief in the value of justice.

Cubitt and Dallow are superficially presented as the 'hard men' in Pinkie's gang. Spicer is disposed of because he is perceived by Pinkie to be a 'weak link in his armour,' and might, by his 'milky' character, have led the law to him. Dallow however is presented as deficient mentally; his admiration of Pinkie is based upon his inability to 'think for himself:' Pinkie seems to have some kind of affection for this 'mug' who offers unconditional devotion.

Cubitt challenges Pinkie's authority however: he decides that he *'won't work under a boy like that.'* Cubitt is perceived by Ida to be the real chink in Pinkie's armour, because he is *'scared and angry.'* When he is banished by Pinkie he leaves the house in umbrage without his coat: *'he was as angry as a child: he wouldn't go back for it: it would be like admitting he was wrong.'* Pinkie's gang are presented as violent aggressors who demand what they want from victims, whom they perceive to be weaklings. They exploit women without compunction, and are willing to murder in order to pursue their own ends; yet their main and overriding characteristic is their childishness: they are arrested in their moral and emotional development. Cubitt reflects upon his 'value' as a henchman. His vanity and self belief blind him to his real predicament: he is out in the cold without a leader and therefore quite powerless in the vicious and cut-throat world of violence and extortion to which he belongs. However *'He stared like Narcissus into his pool and felt better.'* Yet this comfort is short lived and he finds himself crying into his beer, alone and rudderless. He tells himself *'give me a man's job and I'll do it:'* his definition of masculinity implies a willingness to abdicate any moral sense: he is ready to sell his loyalty and his macho attributes to anyone who will give him orders—which he would obey without question or reason.

Prewitt is also presented as weak. He has 'sold his soul' to Pinkie and lives in terror of his wife ': *'her indoors, the old mole'* who dominates his consciousness and poisons his life. He tells Pinkie *'I can rot:'* he perceives his life to be one of decay and torment, because of the dominating character of '*the old hag.*' His only comfort seems to be his distant and impotent lust for the '*little typists.*' He says '*I'm harmless;*' and yet his corruption has left Pinkie free to murder and intimidate his victims.

Ida alone in the novel has strength of purpose in her opposition of Pinkie, and a determination not to be cowed by his violence; although arguably it is her dislike of boredom, which is stronger than her imagination, which motivates her 'moral stand'. Nevertheless she resists Pinkie and his henchmen knowing them to be ruthless killers. In her relationship with the men in her life she is equally dominant. Although it might be argued that she allows Hale to 'pick her up' in the pub, and is a victim of theft, she remains philosophical about the theft of her purse. She does not give an impression that she is any man's victim. When Hale believes the loss of her purse to be his means of laying claim to her, she says '*I'm not worrying. Some nice feller will lend me tenbob...she began to laugh again...they've pulled my leg properly...*' she tells him; quite lacking in self-pity or 'female vulnerability'. Ida does not allow herself to be exploited or manipulated. When she capitulates sexually it's because of her own desire, rather than because she 'gives in' to a man's demands. Ida describes herself as '*a sticker*' which is a summary of her character: she is decisive and tenacious, even dominant, in her sexual relationship with Phil Corkery. She 'pays her way' in the Hotel Cosmopolitan, paying for the room that she shares with Corkery out of her winnings from the tip given by Hale. She offers to buy the sulking Cubitt a drink: it is she who makes social advances to him, offering a listening ear and alcohol to inflame his grievances against Pinkie. It is Ida who is sexually demanding of Phil: She leaves him exhausted after their night of passion. Although Ida '*smiled at him with enormous and remote tenderness,*' there is no suggestion that she loves him, or wants emotional commitment from him; indeed her manner is one of patronage. She revels in her independence and singleness. She dallies with the notion of returning to '*her Tom*', but she doesn't need him; and her inclination to '*give their relationship another go*' does not limit her sexual appetite for other men.

It is Corkery who seems to have some moral compunction about their fornication. Phil's description of their proclivities as *'wrong,'* is countered by Ida, who declares: *'Oh no. That's not wrong. That does no one any harm.'* Ida is not persuaded to any point of view from her own moral certainty that behaviour which does not do anyone actual 'harm' can be wrong: although she did have a sexual relationship with one of her male friends before the death of his wife.

The narrator comments that Phil was *'shaken by a sense of terrific force...when she wanted a good time nothing would stop her...'* in contrast he is made *'nervous'* by her fearlessness and tenacity.

Rose's willingness to submit to Pinkie's cruelties might seem to represent female vulnerability and submission to male dominance, and as such could be regarded as demonstrating stereotypical behaviour; yet ultimately she *does* stand against Pinkie's attempt to fatally dominate her; she throws away the gun and rejects his determined effort to victimise her by persuading her to shoot herself.

When Rose visits the priest she does not go with an attitude of repentance and submission. She will not return to her childhood subjugation to Catholic doctrine. She is entrenched in her rebellion. When she does seem to submit to the priest's suggestion of redemption through Love and Grace, it is Pinkie's soul, rather than her own that she is hoping will receive salvation. Therefore I would argue that she is brave, but deluded: self sacrificing in her love of Pinkie rather than showing female submissiveness to 'authority.'

In conclusion Greene seems to take an idea of gender stereotypes and by detailed characterisation reveal the underlying truths of the characters in his novel: those initially perceived to be invulnerable and strongly masculine are undermined by a fatal flaw: deeply ingrained weakness. Ida, the stereotypical 'tart with a heart,' is really a woman with a mind of her own and an overriding inclination to *self* gratification, rather than *male* gratification. Rose does go a long way down the road of subjugation to Pinkie's stronger will. Yet ultimately she rebels: and survives.

Sample Essay Question:

"Greene presents a distorted picture of humanity's preoccupations: Of course there is Hell, flames and damnation." Explore this view of Greene's presentation of morality and judgement.

In your response you should focus upon Brighton Rock to establish your argument and you should refer to the second text you have read to support and develop your line of argument.

Introduction

It is true that Greene presents a Catholic view of God's judgement of human sin in the 1930's. It is also true that in his novel Greene presents a modern, secularist view of morality; a concept of Right and Wrong. In Brighton Rock Greene presents characters who are apparently amoral, who have no internalised concept of a higher authority to whom they are answerable; who live their lives without moral constraint and who have no consideration for any law, moral or secular. Although the central character is a Catholic, his behaviour suggests that his prime motivation is fear of temporal rather than eternal law.

Arguably society has become more secular since the novel was published. Today a focus upon God's judgement, hell and damnation might well be considered a 'distortion' of Christian teaching. The Catholic theological emphasis of Christianity tends toward love and forgiveness, and contemporary readers would be likely to regard Rose and Pinkie's 'preoccupation' with hell, fire and damnation as 'distorted.' However, Greene has set these characters in a society which has replaced a preoccupation with eternal life and the possibility of eternal damnation with self gratification and populist culture. Therefore I would argue that his novel is a stark juxtaposition of beliefs: the Catholic, medieval tradition of divine judgement and the individual 'value judgements' held by 'the world', and exemplified by Ida.

Greene's Catholic characters, Pinkie and Rose, whilst frequently articulating their belief in the reality of Heaven and Hell, nevertheless experience dissonance: they know that they should live their lives according to the tenets of their faith, and yet they manifestly fail to do so; through in Pinkie's case, 'deliberate fault, and in Rose's case, weakness. Rather than being a "distortion of humanity's preoccupations", I would argue that the gap between what an individual knows that he should do, and what he or she actually does in his or her life, is an experience common to the majority of people.

The 'argument' outlined in the introduction is presented in the 'body' of the essay supported by textual evidence:

Presentation of 'the world': the rise of populist culture and weakening of class barriers:

• *'The new silver paint sparkled on the piers...a race in miniature motors, a band playing...an aeroplane advertising'*: Post W.W.1 Britain is emerging from austerity and a new culture of entertainment is emerging. Greene presents a society of people who, far from being 'preoccupied' with divine retribution, are determined to enjoy themselves.

• *'Kolly Kibber in Brighton today...'* This fictional character is based upon a real life individual who promoted one of the popular newspapers of the thirties by visiting seaside resorts and offering prizes to the mainly working class readers of the newspaper, who could respond to a simple question. We are told that Hale, the Kolly Kibbber character, *'despised the crowd.'*

• Greene presents a newly emerging world of populist preoccupations: entertainments and consumerism. An older world is presented by Pinkie and Rose's Catholic, arguably medieval view of divine judgement, and a brief glimpse of a rigid class divide represented by *'three old ladies'* who *'went driving by in an open horse drawn carriage.'* The narrator comments: *'that was how some people still lived,'* which implies that some people, those of a higher social class, still held on to the relics of a bygone age. We might infer that the new affluence of the working class, with money to spend on drink and popular entertainment at the seaside, was not embraced or welcomed by every sector of society.

• The aptly named 'Cosmopolitan' Hotel accepts the criminal nouveau riche: Colleoni, the Jewish 'Godfather' character, rubs shoulders with the British aristocracy: *'A page came from the Louis Seize writing room, called 'Sir Joseph Montagu...a woman in mauve with an untimely tiara was writing a letter...'* Far from exclusively focusing upon *"distorted human preoccupations'of sin and divine judgement,"* Greene presents a world where money, however obtained, is a dominating preoccupation: power, which once resided with the Church and the upper classes, is conceded to those who have obtained wealth from corrupt practices. It is interesting that one of the bars in the hotel is named *'the American Bar.'* Might the author be suggesting that worldly values which are taking the place of religious values have come from those held by American society?

Secular morality represented by Ida:

• Although Ida articulates *'scorn'* for 'papists who, she believed treat death with *'flippancy',* she does believe in 'life after death.' However her belief in ghosts and the spirit world, which she connects with using the Ouija board, does not make her take the idea of death lightly, as she (mistakenly) believes Catholics do. Ironically her *'horror'* of death as *'the end of everything'* could be compared to Rose and Pinkie's horror of the fires and torments of hell.

• Ida's morality is based upon her belief in *'Right and Wrong.'* Her concept of right and wrong has not been inscribed by any doctrine however. The origin of her morality is interesting and hinted at in part one chapter 3: *'man is made by the places in which he lives and Ida's mind worked with the simplicity and the regularity of a sky sign: the ever tipping glass, the ever revolving wheel, the plain question flashing on and off: 'do you use Forhams for the gums?'* The 'sky sign' is an allusion to the neon signs used for advertisements in London, and the rhetorical question refers to an advertisement for tooth powder. The 'tipping glass' refers to her fondness for drinking, and possibly the 'revolving wheel alludes to gambling: the 'wheel of fortune.' That she is a regular 'punter' is shown in her knowledge of horse racing and her decision to place a large bet on the horse recommended by Hale. Charlie Moyne recognises that she is ' *a sporting woman.'* She has a deep belief in 'fate' and sees herself as an instrument of justice and retribution. That her moral code is a product of the modern consumerist society is shown in the references to advertisements in Greene's comment about the 'simplicity' of her mind.

• Ida's determination to 'seek justice' for Fred Hale's murder might be read as deriving from a moral imperative, however her pursuit of truth was motivated by a desire for excitement, which she sees as the meaning of life: *'all the time beneath the melancholy and the resolution, her heart beat faster to the refrain: it's exciting, it's fun it's living.'* The earlier link between Ida's mind set and consumerism suggests that the modern rise of atheism leaves a vacuum which demands to be filled. Ida's pursuit of entertainment in the forms of sex, drinking and gambling and the occult has become *a raison d'etre* for her: the determination to discover the truth about Hale is another form of self gratification.

• It is interesting that in Ida's room is a copy of J.B. Priestley's 'The Good Companions'. Graham Greene had to answer a libel case brought by the author for his satirical portrayal of him as a populist (i.e. second rate) writer.

• Greene seems to draw a parallel between Ida's sexuality, her view of life and the moral code by which she lives. She is described as 'accommodating' and her sensuality is emphasised by repeated descriptions of her mouth: eating, drinking and kissing are described graphically. Her thoughts are described with words which suggest self gratification: *'she drew in her breath luxuriously...with a sigh of happy satiety.'* These descriptions are not linked with sex, they are linked with her meditations on 'Right and Wrong;' however at the same moment she thinks of Phil Corkery, a man whom she had earlier dismissed as not *'someone she liked to encourage. Too quiet. Not what she called a man.'* Nevertheless this man, whom she seemed to neither like nor respect, is the man with whom she spends the night at the Cosmopolitan Hotel. When she declares to Corkery that she *'likes doing right,'* he challenges her, alluding to their night of passion, *'and what's wrong too.'* Her definition of what is 'Right and Wrong' is one that many people share: if it causes no harm, then Ida claims, *'That's not wrong.'* Corkery recognises that she's determined to find Hale's killers *'because it's fun,'* which she doesn't deny, admitting that *'she felt quite sorry it was all over.'* Ida declares *'I know the world.'* Her morality is that 'of the world:' she has no concept of spiritual sin and is scornful of what she calls *'Romans,'* who by implication, might lay claim to an understanding of Divine authority , yet, unlike herself do not *'know people.'* The Catholic mistrust of all that is of *'the world'* and *'the flesh'* seem to combine in this character.

In conclusion:

Although Graham Greene depicts the Catholic understanding of sin, divine judgment and *'the fires of hell and damnation,'* this is not a *'distorted view of human preoccupations'* they are the views held by Catholics at this time in history. Although it is important to note that although both Rose and Pinkie are convinced of their eternal fate as unrepentant sinners, they are inclined to follow their human nature and the 'desires of their hearts,' rather than adhere to the Catholic teaching.

Greene has set these characters in a context in which people are more concerned with enjoying themselves or acquiring wealth, than in the state of their souls. The Cosmopolitan Hotel might be read as a microcosm: the guests are a mixture of those born to wealth, those who have acquired wealth through crime and those who are 'living sensually': *'Young men kept on arriving in huge motoring coats accompanied by small tinted creatures...a stout woman in a white fox fur.* Greene comments *'the visible world was all Mr Colleoni's.* Greene juxtaposes the 'visible world' with the unseen' world perceived by the religious characters; for the 'fallen' religious, the prospect of hell, fires and damnation are presented as being as real as the marble floors, gilt chairs and opulent world of the Cosmopolitan Hotel.